India and China in Africa

With their phenomenal growth rates, India and China are surging ahead as world economic powers. Due to increasing instability in the Middle East, they have turned to Africa to procure oil to fuel their industrialisation process. Africa's economy stands to be impacted in various ways due to the increasing interaction with these 'Asian Giants'.

This book analyses the acquisition of oil blocks by Indian and Chinese oil corporations in 11 West African countries. It describes the differences in how India and China mobilise oil externally to meet their respective goals and objectives. The book examines the rate of return on capital, rate of interest on loans and the ease of availability of loans, the difference in the level of technology and ability to acquire technology, project management skills, risk aversion, valuation of the asset and the difference in the economic, political and diplomatic support received by the Chinese and Indian oil companies from their respective governments. It is argued that the difference in the relative economic and political power of India and China accounts for the ability of Chinese oil companies to outbid their Indian competitors and/or be preferred as partners by international oil companies.

Containing interviews from Indian and Chinese oil company executives, government officials, industry officials, former diplomats and scholars and academics from India, China and the UK, this book makes a valuable contribution to existing literature on India, China and the oil industry in West Africa. It will be a valuable resource for academics in the field of International Relations, Foreign Policy Analysis, Asian Business and Economics.

Dr Raj Verma is Assistant Professor in International Relations and Foreign Policy at the School of International and Public Affairs at Jilin University, China. His research is focused on India's and China's foreign policy and comparative political economy, India and China in Africa, India–China–US relations and international relations theory.

Routledge Series on India–China Studies
Edited by Raj Verma, Jilin University, China

India and China have many similarities but also many differences. They are both members of BRICS, G20 and other international organisations and regimes. They are also the two most populated countries in the world, sharing a long and respected history of early civilisations and a colonial past that became independent around the same time: India in 1947 and China in 1949. In the 1950s, they were in the forefront of the Non-Aligned Movement and proposed the five principles of peaceful coexistence or 'Panchsheel'. These five principles are the cornerstone of India's and China's foreign policy.

The two Asian giants with their rapid economic growth are surging ahead as world economic powers. They are emerging powers but are still developing countries. By 2030 both the countries are expected to become superpowers. *Ceteris paribus*, China will be the largest economy in the world in the next decade. India will become the third largest economy in 2025, the second largest by 2040 and the largest economy by 2060. As their economies grow, their concomitant political, economic and military power will also increase.

This series provides a platform for scholars to exhibit their research on the political, diplomatic, economic and strategic relationship between these two emerging superpowers.

India and China in Africa

A comparative perspective of the oil industry

Raj Verma

Routledge
Taylor & Francis Group

LONDON AND NEW YORK

First published 2017
by Routledge
2 Park Square, Milton Park, Abingdon, Oxfordshire OX14 4RN
711 Third Avenue, New York, NY 10017

Routledge is an imprint of the Taylor & Francis Group, an informa business

First issued in paperback 2018

British Library Cataloguing in Publication Data
A catalogue record for this book is available from the British Library

Library of Congress Cataloging in Publication Data
Names: Verma, Rajneesh, author.
Title: India and China in Africa : a comparative perspective of the oil
industry / Raj Verma.
Description: 1 Edition. | New York : Routledge, 2016. | Series: Routledge
Contemporary Asia Series, 59 | Includes bibliographical references and
index.
Identifiers: LCCN 2016028672 | ISBN 9781138121935 (hardback : alk.
paper) | ISBN 9781315650685 (ebook)
Subjects: LCSH: Petroleum industry and trade–Africa, West. | Petroleum
industry and trade–India. | Petroleum industry and trade–China. | Africa,
West–Foreign economic relations–India. | Africa, West–Foreign economic
relations–China. | India–Foreign economic relations–Africa, West. |
China–Foreign economic relations–Africa, West.
Classification: LCC HD9577.A358 V47 2016 | DDC 338.27280966–dc23
LC record available at https://lccn.loc.gov/2016028672

ISBN: 978-1-138-12193-5 (hbk)
ISBN: 978-0-367-02539-7 (pbk)

Typeset in Times New Roman
by Wearset Ltd, Boldon, Tyne and Wear

To my family and friends

Contents

Figures

Tables

Preface

The book is based on my PhD thesis at the London School of Economics and Political Science (LSE). I was enrolled as a PhD candidate in the Department of International Relations (IR) from October 2011 to September 2013. However, the genesis of the book can be traced back to December 2006 when I was pursuing an MSc in Comparative Politics in the Department of Government at LSE. Students in the Department of Government were allowed to attend seminars, lectures and workshops at Royal Institute for International Affairs (Chatham House) in London. I visited Chatham House regularly to attend the events and was fortunate to attend a panel discussion on China–Africa in December 2006. The panel discussion was on 'China in Africa' and if my memory serves me right, the panellists were discussing the latest report on China in Africa published by the Centre for Strategic and International Studies (CSIS). The CSIS report provided the basis for my MA dissertation, which I submitted in August 2007.

While preparing for the dissertation, I wanted to use an IR theory to explain India's and China's engagement in Africa but fell short on numerous occasions. In the end, I used concepts drawing from foreign policy analysis (FPA). I was on the verge of submitting the MA dissertation when an idea clicked which I thought could be used for the dissertation. I was on the verge of giving the print command but stopped. I thought hard and realised that I had an IR theory for my dissertation. The deadline was three hours away. I was cursing myself for not thinking enough, not thinking deep, not applying myself and not coming up with the idea in the last two to three months. I was absolutely dejected. I somehow regained focus and submitted the dissertation.

I always wanted to do a PhD and decided to use the idea for the PhD thesis. I took a break from my academic pursuits and joined the corporate sector. I gained admission to the PhD programme in the Department of IR for the academic year 2010–11 but deferred admission and enrolled on a part-time basis for the academic year 2011–12. I also worked in the Africa programme at LSE IDEAS from February 2012 to January 2013 which helped me in numerous ways with the PhD thesis.

In conducting this study, I undertook four field trips to India: in 2012, 2013, 2014 and 2016. I also undertook a field trip to China in 2013 and have been a resident in China since August 2014. I have drawn on primary and secondary sources to gather data. I also conducted semi-structured elite interviews with executives from Indian oil companies, industry experts, analysts, government officials and an executive from a US international oil company (IOC).[1] Relevant data about Chinese state-owned enterprises (SOEs) was primarily drawn from primary and secondary data available in the public domain and semi-structured elite interviews with an executive from China National Offshore Oil Corporation (CNOOC),[2] industry experts, scholars and analysts.

During the course of gathering data, I realised how difficult it was to interview executives from Chinese NOCs China Development Bank (CDB) and China Export–Import (EXIM) among others. I was told by all my Chinese colleagues and friends that I would be unable to approach the officials and that they would not talk to me. My experience in India was much better than China but it was not an easy task to arrange interviews with officials from Indian oil companies. I wanted to compare and contrast the bids placed by Indian and Chinese oil companies for the individual oil blocks in West African countries. However, due to reasons of commercial confidentiality and national security, the Indian NOCs were not willing to provide detailed documentary information on the bids placed. They were also unwilling to provide sensitive information such as details of the bids placed for oil blocks and/or 'farm in' offers during the interviews. I was asked to refer to the website of the NOCs for details. I was forced to use the Right to Information Act, 2005, Government of India (GoI) to access the detailed documentary bids but was unsuccessful due to commercial confidentiality and national security. However, I was able to get some data from the three Indian SOEs: Oil and Natural Gas (ONGC) Videsh Limited (OVL), Indian Oil Corporation Limited (IOCL) and Oil India Limited (OIL) using Right to Information Act, 2005, GoI.

In 2006–7, I was not familiar with neoclassical realism (NCR). I had never heard of NCR and had not read any literature on it. However, my idea – to use political economy as an intervening variable and the difference in the power capabilities of the two countries as the independent variable to explain the interaction of India and China in Africa – was still deeply ingrained in my mind. In April 2009, while writing my research proposal, I was fortunate to come across NCR. If my memory serves me right, I read an article or a book review on differences in armies of different countries and borrowed NCR from that article or book review for the research proposal. However, I was formally introduced to NCR in January 2012.

The book employs NCR as the theoretical construct to explain the differences and the relative success and failure of India and China to acquire oil blocks in 11 countries in West Africa. The book also be of interest to a wide-ranging set of readers. Chapter 7 has a lot of empirical information but lacks a story. I was contemplating adding case studies on Sudan and Democratic Republic of Congo (DRC) in Chapter 7 and moving Ghana and other countries to Chapter 5 but decided against it. This is because of three reasons. First, I wanted to conform to the theoretical framework. Second, West Africa has been missing from the literature on India and China in the oil industry in Africa. Third, Luke Patey (2014) has done excellent work on India and China in Sudan and there is no need for repetition. India and China in DRC requires more attention which I leave for others.

Notes

1 The executives from the Indian national oil companies (NOCs), Essar Oil and the US IOC requested to remain anonymous.
2 The executive from CNOOC requested to remain anonymous.

Reference

Patey, Luke (2014). *The New Kings of Crude: China, India and the Global Struggle for Oil in Sudan and South Sudan*. London: Hurst & Company.

Acknowledgements

Writing a PhD thesis can be an arduous task, a task made less convoluted and challenging, more exciting and fulfilling by the support of many. Converting the PhD thesis into a book is even more strenuous and writing an acknowledgement is the most taxing. How can one express one's gratitude in words to so many people who have been instrumental in ensuring, in one way or another, that the project is completed? I firmly believe that words cannot do justice to express my gratitude for the support and encouragement I have received from numerous people in the course of this project.

It gives me great pleasure to thank my doctoral supervisor, Chris Alden. It was an honour and privilege to be supervised by Chris. Chris has been instrumental in providing support in every way possible to ensure that the thesis was not only completed, but completed in a record time of less than 18 months. Without Chris' support, I would not have been able to pursue the PhD and the thesis and the book would never have been completed.

A special thanks goes to the Asia Research Centre (ARC) at LSE for awarding me with the Bagri Fellowship and the LSE-TISS-TATA Grant for Research Projects, Travel and Workshops. The Bagri Fellowship provided the indispensable financial support for the PhD. The LSE-TISS travel grant supported and enabled me to undertake field trips to India and China and to conduct extensive research in those countries. I am grateful to the ARC's director, Athar Hussain, Co-Director Ruth Kattumuri, and others at ARC for providing the letters of support which facilitated interviews in India and China. I am extremely grateful to Athar and Ruth for discussions and advice regarding how to approach different publishing houses and on various other aspects of publishing. I remember that Ruth put me in touch with Routledge and one thing led to another. Ruth, thank you very much once again. I am also grateful to Keith Tritton and Kevin Shields at ARC for their administrative help and support during my tenure at the Centre and beyond.

I was helped along the way by a huge number of people. Thomas Sattler, Lauren Phillips, Jeffrey Chwieroth and Andrew Walter in LSE's Department of IR allayed my fears and encouraged me to tread on my chosen path, which provided the necessary platform to write the thesis. Michael Cox, Margot Light, Chris Hughes, Jurgen Haacke, Chris Emery and Luca Tardelli provided insightful comments, analysis, suggestions and criticisms which pushed me to clarify my thinking in important ways. I am grateful to Nicholas Kitchen at LSE IDEAS for highlighting errors and omissions and making additions to the draft. The participants in the LSE's IR Research Design seminar, Foreign Policy workshop and North–South Relations workshop deserve a special mention. This is a group of talented people that I have had the pleasure to argue with. I am extremely grateful to my fellow doctoral students in the Department of IR whose company I enjoyed during my stay at LSE and beyond. A sincere expression of gratitude goes to the Department of IR and the LSE as a whole, whose staff and facilities have been exemplary, especially Martina Langer and Adnan Khan.

I am also grateful to my colleagues at the School of International and Public Affairs (SIPA), Jilin University, in particular Dean Liu Debin and Deputy Dean Wang Qiubin, for their continued support since August 2014. I would also like to express my deep gratitude to Yan Zhen and Zheng Guangchao for their help and guidance on a day-to-day basis. It would have been almost impossible to finish the manuscript in time without their help over the two-year period. I am also thankful to all the other faculty members at SIPA for their help and guidance. The staff at SIPA helped me in my time of need. They are humble, polite and excellent people. Last but not the least; I am indebted to Alex Dueben, my friend and fellow doctoral student in Department of IR, LSE and colleague at SIPA. He has been a pillar of strength through the arduous journey of writing this book. I am also grateful to him for hopefully enjoying my company. Thank you very much Alex for reading numerous drafts of some of the chapters in the book and for your critical analysis and suggestions.

In addition, I am extremely grateful to Srikanth Kondapalli at the Centre for East Asian Studies at Jawaharlal Nehru University (JNU) for his guidance and continuous encouragement. His suggestions and advice were extremely helpful in getting a better perspective of Sino-Indian relations and China. I am also grateful to Madhu Bhalla at Delhi University's Centre for East Asian Studies and Ajay Dubey at JNU's Centre for African Studies for their insightful comments and for sharing their views and thoughts. I am thankful to Institute for Defence Studies and Analaysis' Ruchita Beri and Jagannath Panda and also others for their support and guidance during my Fellowship at the Institute. The exchange of ideas and opinions broadened my horizons. I am also grateful to a host of people at the Observer Research Foundation such as Ambassador H.H.S. Viswanathan, Samir Saran and Lydia Powell, among others whose deep insights helped me in my research. I am especially indebted to Keun Wook Paik at the Oxford Institute for Energy Studies and Chatham House for improving my comprehension of the oil and gas industry in China. He was also helpful in arranging interviews with some key Chinese scholars and experts from Chinese oil companies. Furthermore, I am thankful to Ann Twang at Fudan University for allowing me to be a Visiting Fellow at its Centre for BRICS Studies and for my memorable stay in Shanghai. I am also grateful to Wang Lei and Jiejin Zhu at the Centre for BRICS Studies for their insightful comments on China's political economy and its oil and gas industry. It led to a much better understanding of the subject matter.

Numerous people have read the manuscript and provided insightful comments, suggestions and criticisms, which have improved the quality of the writing. As always, all omissions and errors are my own. I am extremely appreciative of Ambassador Shu Zhan at Zhejiang Normal University's Centre for African Studies, Axel Harnet-Sievers at Heinrich Böll Stiftung India and Ambassador David Shinn for their invaluable feedback. I am also very thankful to Issac Nunoo, Issac Frimpong, Dennis Senam Ambale and Bright Lumor Mensah at SIPA for their constructive feedback. All these people have taken time out of their extremely busy and demanding schedules to help me. I am grateful to the entire team at Routledge, Taylor & Francis, especially Dorothea Schaefter, the Commissioning Editor, Lily Brown, Emma Tyce and Jillian Morrison, for their generous encouragement, extraordinary patience and unstinting support.

There are numerous other individuals who I have encountered on this journey, who have each contributed in their own way, and I do not have words to express my sincere gratitude to them. I am also, of course, deeply indebted to my family. I am in lifelong debt to Mr and Mrs Patel, Jiten and Neel, for treating me as a member of their family and looking after me while I was pursuing my PhD at LSE. It would have been extremely difficult to finish the thesis in time without their support. I am incredibly lucky to have received the support that I did from my family and friends, and I thank them again for comprehending that I could not be with them in all their good and bad times. For this, I sincerely and humbly ask for their forgiveness.

Abbreviations

ADB	Asian Development Bank
AP	Addax Petroleum
APCC	Addax Petroleum Cameroon Company LLC
APRM	African Peer Review Mechanism
AU	African Union
BMI	Business Monitor International
BP	British Petroleum
BPCL	Bharat Petroleum Corporation Limited
bpd	barrels per day
BS	Burmah-Shell
CBM	Coal Bed Methane
CCCPI	China Chamber of Commerce for the Petroleum Industry
CCEA	Cabinet Committee on Economic Affairs
CCECC	China Civil Engineering Construction Corporation
CCP	China's Communist Party
CDB	China Development Bank
CIC	China Investment Corporation
CII	Confederation of Indian Industries
CIIS	China Institute of International Studies
CNOOC	China National Offshore Oil Corporation
CNPC	China National Petroleum Corporation
CPC	China Petroleum Corporation
CPCL	Chennai Petroleum Corporation Limited
CPPCC	Chinese People's Political Consultative Conference
CSIH	China Sonangol International Holding Limited
DAC	Development Assistance Committee
E&P	exploration and production
ECOWAS	Economic Community of West Africa States
EIA	Energy Information Agency
ENDIAMA	Empresa Nacional de Prospecção, Exploração, Lapidação e Comercialização de Diamantes de Angola
ETI	Extractive Transparency International
EXIM	Export–Import

FDI	foreign direct investment
FERA	Foreign Exchange Regulations Act
FID	final investment decision
FIE	Foreign Invested Enterprise
FNLA	Frente Nacional de Libertação de Angola
FOCAC	Forum on China–Africa Cooperation
FPA	foreign policy analysis
GAIL	Gas Authority of India Limited
GDP	Gross Domestic Product
GNI	Gross National Income
GNP	Gross National Product
GNPC	Ghana National Petroleum Corporation
GoI	Government of India
GP	Great Power
GUPC	Great United Petroleum Holding Co., Ltd
HDI	Human Development Index
HPCL	Hindustan Petroleum Corporation Limited
IDRA	Industries Development and Regulation Act
IDSA	Institute for Defence Studies and Analysis
IMF	International Monetary Fund
IMR	Infant Mortality Rate
IOCL	Indian Oil Corporation Limited
IOCs	international oil companies
IOR	Indian Ocean Rim
IPR	Industrial Policy Resolution
IR	international relations
IT	information technology
ITEC	Indian Technical and Economic Cooperation
JDA	Joint Development Authority
JDZ	Joint Development Zone
LoC	line of credit
LPG	Liquefied Petroleum Gas
mbpd	million barrels per day
MEA	Ministry of External Affairs
MEND	Movement for the Emancipation of the Niger Delta
MEL	Mittal Energy Limited
MNC	Multinational Corporation
MoA	method of agreement
MoD	method of difference
MOFA	Minister of Foreign Affairs
MoU	Memorandum of Understanding
MP	Middle Power
MPI	Ministry of Petroleum Industry
MPLA	Movimento Popular de Libertação de Angola
MRTP	Monopolies and Restrictive Trade Practices

NAM	Non-Aligned Movement
NCR	neoclassical realism
NDRC	National Development and Reform Commission
NELP	New Exploration Licensing Policy
NEPAD	New Partnership for Africa's Development
NGO	non-governmental organisation
NI	National Income
NNPC	Nigeria National Petroleum Corporation
NOC	national oil company
NPC	National People's Congress
NPNL	Nexen Petroleum Nigeria Limited
NSG	Nuclear Suppliers Group
NTPC	National Thermal Power Corporation
ODA	Official Development Assistance
OECD	Organisation for Economic Co-operation and Development
OEPNL	OMEL Exploration & Production Nigeria Ltd
OIES	Oxford Institute for Energy Studies
OIL	Oil India Limited
OMEL	ONGC Mittal Energy Limited
ONGC	Oil and Natural Gas Corporation
OPEC	Organization of the Petroleum Exporting Countries
ORF	Observer Research Foundation
OVL	ONGC Videsh Limited
PCC	Pecton Cameroon Company
PCY	per capita income
PDG	Partie Démocratique Gabonais
PIB	Petroleum Industry Bill
PLA	People's Liberation Army
PPP	Purchasing Power Parity
PRC	People's Republic of China
PSA	Production Sharing Agreement
PSC	Production Sharing Contract
RFR	right of first refusal
RIL	Reliance Industries Limited
ROC	Republic of China
R/P	reserves to production ratio
SAARC	South Asian Association for Regional Cooperation
SAIIA	South African Institute of International Affairs
SAPTERO	South Atlantic Petroleum
SASAC	State-owned Assets Supervision and Administration Commission
SCO	Shanghai Cooperation Organisation
SEZ	Special Economic Zone
SIIS	Shanghai Institutes for International Studies

SIPC	Sinopec International Petroleum Exploration and Production Corporation
SIPCL	Santa Isabel Petroleum Company
SME	small and medium scale enterprise
SOE	state-owned enterprise
SP	Small Power
SSI	Sinopec Sonangol International
SWF	sovereign wealth fund
tbpd	thousand barrels per day
TVE	Township and Village Enterprise
UN	United Nations
UNDP	United Nations Development Programme
UNITA	União Nacional para a Independência Total de Angola
UNPKO	UN Peacekeeping Operations
UNSC	United Nations Security Council
WHO	World Health Organization
WI	working interest

Part I

Introduction

Introduction

Oil, or 'black gold', is one of the key sources of energy in the world. There is no perfect substitute for oil. It does have theoretical substitutes, such as coal or solar energy, but they cannot be used to operate the majority of the means of public and private transport. None of these substitutes are promising enough to merit development in the future. Oil has been the lifeblood for the global economic system for more than a century and will remain so in the distant future. Almost all the countries in the world are heavily dependent on oil for it is an engine of growth.[1]

A rise in the price of oil can have an adverse impact not only on an individual country per se but the international system – politically, economically and strategically – as was witnessed by the rise in the price of oil in the two oil shocks in 1973–4 and 1979–80, during the first Gulf War in 1991 and during 1999–2000. However, the economic gain from a fall in the price of oil is substantially less acute than the loss from the rise in the price of oil. There are various factors which affect the price of oil, such as demand and supply side factors, speculation and commodity trading, and geopolitical instability, especially in the Middle East.

The presence or absence of significant oil reserves in a country causes a quandary. Countries that have small oil reserves relative to their consumption, such as India and China,[2] or those that have insignificant oil reserves, such as Japan, suffer from energy insecurity. Such countries have to take extensive measures to ensure and secure their energy security. On the other hand, countries which have significant reserves of oil may also suffer from the resource curse, the 'Dutch Disease'. This is evidenced in countries in Africa, especially West Africa, which have significant but not substantial oil reserves relative to countries in the Persian Gulf. Most of the oil-producing countries in Africa, especially West Africa,[3] suffer from 'Dutch Disease'. Over-reliance on the oil industry and the failure to use the proceeds from the oil revenue to diversify into different sectors has blighted the majority of the oil-producing countries in West Africa.

Background debate

India and China

India and China are emerging market economies and rising powers. China, despite being the second largest economy in the world[4] and a permanent member of the United Nations Security Council (UNSC), and India are still developing countries. Both countries need oil to meet their energy security, to fuel their industrialisation process, improve the living standards and quality of life of their citizens, and catch up with the West and sit on the high table in global affairs. India, and more so China, have both played an important role in the rise in the price of commodities in general and oil in particular since the beginning of the new century.

The rising turmoil and political instability in the Middle East has increased India's and China's energy insecurity. The two countries have turned to Africa, especially West Africa, to diversify their energy sources and alleviate their energy insecurity. Africa, especially West Africa, has regained importance as a significant player in the global oil industry since the beginning of the new millennium. This is due to the quality of its oil and natural gas reserves and commercial advantages that it offers to international oil companies (IOCs). In the process, the African continent as whole and West African countries in particular will be impacted economically, diplomatically and politically. The importance of the oil industry in West Africa is discussed in detail in Chapter 2.

Neoclassical realism

The term neoclassical realism (NCR) was coined by Gideon Rose in a pioneering article in the journal *World Politics* in 1998. It is a theoretical paradigm which explains foreign policy outcomes of states. It provides a theoretically inspired framework which strives to explicate the foreign policies of different states facing similar external restraints over a period of time or the foreign policy of the same state over time. Thus NCR provides a comparative perceptive across time and space. It puts forward a well-defined causal chain comprising of three steps: first, the independent or the exogenous variable or a country's relative material power in the anarchical international system. Second is the intervening or the endogenous variable or the domestic level 'transmission belt' which sieves systemic forces. Third is the foreign policy outcome or the dependent variable. Proponents of NCR argue that a country's relative power, i.e. political, economic and military power or hard power, influences and constrains its position in the anarchical international system. There is disagreement among neoclassical realists whether it is a natural extension of neorealism or whether it explains foreign policy muddles or it is a theory of foreign policy or theories of foreign policy. This is discussed in Chapter 1.

There has been a rapid surge in literature on NCR since the late 1990s across time and space, and it is gaining momentum as a theoretical paradigm. Despite the recent spurt, NCR is still in an embryonic stage. Additionally, there is paucity of literature on the role of political economy as a domestic or intervening variable in NCR. Most of the existing literature explains or seeks to explain a contradiction in neorealism, like over-balancing or under-balancing, or to explain a structural phenomenon like polarity. This is done by exploring internal mobilisation and extraction of resources to achieve foreign policy outcomes. The role of political economy (political economy as employed in this study examines the structure of the economic system and not the foreign policy executive) as an intervening variable in NCR is discussed in detail in Chapter 1.

The argument and contribution to the existing literature

This study aims to answer the following question: 'Can NCR explain the differences and relative success and failure of China and India in their respective efforts to mobilise[5] oil in the oil industry in West Africa?' In the process, the study makes a theoretical contribution to the existing literature on NCR by extending its research design (Chapter 1). The study uses the difference in the relative power of India and China in an anarchical international system as the independent or the exogenous variable and the difference in the political economy of the two countries as the intervening or the endogenous variable in NCR to explain the differences and the relative success and failure of India and China respectively in mobilising oil in the oil industry in West Africa. In the process, the study extends NCR's research design because, in the past, political economy has been used as an intervening variable in NCR to explicate either a contradiction in neorealism like under-balancing or to explain a structural phenomenon like polarity.

The study asserts that there are three differences in the interaction of Indian and Chinese oil companies in the oil industry in West Africa. First, China is represented by state-owned enterprises (SOEs) in the oil industry in West Africa whereas India is represented by SOEs and/or private enterprises. Second, national oil companies (NOCs) from China have operations in more countries in West Africa relative to India, which indulges in niche diplomacy and has a limited presence in the region. Third, Chinese NOCs are able to outbid Indian SOEs and private sector enterprises if and when they directly compete for the same oil blocks and/or are preferred as partners by IOCs and/or have better quality oil blocks.

The study postulates that the differences and relative success and failure in how India and China mobilise oil in the oil industry in West Africa is explained by two factors: first, the independent variable, i.e. the difference in their material power or economic and political power. Since China has greater economic power and political clout than India, its behaviour and role is different vis-à-vis India in the oil industry in West Africa. This elucidates the ability of Chinese oil companies to outbid their Indian competitors and/or be preferred as partners by IOCs and/or have better quality oil blocks. This also explains China's widespread outreach in Africa compared with India's discreetly selective approach. The intervening variable or the difference in the political economy of India and China explains why China is represented by SOEs in the oil industry in West Africa and India is represented by the SOEs and/or private sector enterprises. The study argues that the difference in the political economy of India and China translates into divergence in the composition of the economy, especially the non-agricultural sector. This explains the diversity in reforms introduced in the two countries and why the Chinese economy is dominated by large scale and mostly subsidised SOEs, and why the private sector has been stifled. India, on the other hand, is characterised by a mixed economy constituting SOEs as well as a vibrant private sector with 'global brand names' which acts as the torchbearer. The difference in the political economy explains why the oil industry in China is almost totally dominated by the SOEs whereas the oil industry in India is represented by SOEs and the private sector with the latter playing an important role in the oil industry. This is discussed in detail in Chapters 2, 3 and 4.

The study also makes an empirical contribution to the existing literature on India and China in the oil industry in West Africa by providing a more comprehensive study of Indian and Chinese oil companies in 11 countries in West Africa (Chapter 2). It examines not only the bids that Chinese and Indian oil corporations place for the oil blocks but tries to explain the reason why they are able to place those bids. It examines the rate of return on capital, rate of interest on loans and the ease of availability of loans or finance, the difference in the level of technology and ability to acquire technology, project management skills, risk aversion and the difference in the economic, political and diplomatic support received by the Chinese and Indian oil companies from their respective governments. It also mentions the reasons why the Chinese NOCs are preferred as partners by African oil companies and IOCs. The empirical contribution to the existing literature is illustrated in Chapters 5, 6 and 7.

Analytical framework and research design

The study employs both deductive and inductive approaches. In deductive research, a conceptual and theoretical structure is developed and then tested by empirical observation. In inductive research, theory is developed from the observation of empirical reality. The study combined inductive and deductive methods. The inductive approach was used in the analysis to inform and expand on the theory. The deductive approach was suitable to establish and develop research questions and a theoretical framework which was used sequentially to form the foundation of how to perform the analysis.

I began with the inductive approach. I observed that Chinese NOCs operate in the oil industry in West Africa while India is represented by both NOCs and private sector enterprises. Empirical evidence also highlighted that Chinese NOCs were operating in more countries in West Africa relative to Indian oil companies and the former outbid the latter if and when they directly bid for the same oil block. After studying and analysing the empirical evidence, I decided to formalise a theoretical framework and decided to employ NCR to explain the outcomes. I reached the conclusion that NCR explicates the differences and relative success and failure of China and India in their respective efforts to mobilise oil in the oil industry in West Africa by employing the difference in the political economy of India and China as the domestic or the intervening variable, and the difference in their relative economic and political power as the independent variable.

For the purposes of this analysis, I adopted a two-pronged approach to establish that Chinese oil companies consistently outbid Indian oil companies and Chinese NOCs operate in the oil industry in more countries in West Africa relative to India. This is discussed below:

I Chinese SOEs outbid Indian companies – This is divided into three cases:

Case 1: Oil blocks acquired by Chinese NOCs: An oil block is acquired by Chinese NOCs by bidding more than Indian oil companies.

Case 2: Oil blocks acquired by Indian oil companies: In these cases, if Chinese NOCs did not bid for the blocks in the first place, it is essential to explore why they did not. If Chinese NOCs bid for the block but did not acquire it, it challenges the hypothesis that Chinese oil companies consistently outbid Indian oil companies.

Case 3: Oil blocks not acquired by either Chinese NOCs or Indian oil companies: If Chinese NOCs and Indian companies bid for the block, but the former bid more than the latter, it confirms the hypothesis. If in such cases Indian oil companies bid more than the Chinese NOCs, it contradicts the hypothesis.

II China has more oil blocks in a country in West Africa and West Africa as a region relative to India – This is divided into two cases:

Case 1: If Chinese NOCs bid for a particular oil block in a country in West Africa and Indian oil companies did not bid for the same oil block, it supports the hypothesis that China has greater outreach relative to India.

Case 2: If Chinese NOCs bid for more oil blocks in an individual country in West Africa and for more oil blocks in different countries across West Africa, then this supports the hypothesis.

Where Indian and Chinese oil companies did not enter into direct competitive bidding to acquire oil blocks, two proxies or dummy variables are used to gauge the difference in their relative economic power. First is the preference as a partner by IOCs and African NOCs in the exploration and production (E&P) process in the oil industry in countries in West Africa. Since China is economically and politically more powerful than India, *ceteris paribus*, oil companies, especially African NOCs, should prefer to have Chinese oil companies as partners. This may also explain why China has operations in the oil industry in more countries in West Africa relative to India.

The second proxy or dummy variable is the quality of the oil block. The premise is that if China is economically more powerful than India, then the quality of the oil blocks that China has acquired would on average be better than the oil blocks acquired by India. The assertion is predicated on human consumer behaviour and spending power. Thus, if an individual has more income and/or wealth, or in simple words is richer than another individual, *ceteris paribus*, he or she will on average have a greater propensity and ability to spend and acquire higher quality commodities.

The difference in wealth also affects the propensity to take risk. A rich individual, *ceteris paribus*, is typically less risk averse as compared to an individual with a relatively lower income and wealth. Because a rich individual is less risk averse, he or she is not only able to spend more money, but is also less concerned about the returns on the investment. A richer individual is able to sustain a longer gestation period compared to a poorer individual. Thus, China, being economically more powerful than India, should spend more money, that is, its SOEs would typically place a higher bid for an oil block compared to India and would also bid for more oil blocks. Moreover, unlike India, China should not be concerned about the rate of return on investment in the short term because it has extremely deep pockets.

Research methodology

Adhering to NCR's research methodology, the study employs case study analysis, process tracing and analytical narrative. Two methods have been postulated by John Stuart Mill for selection of cases. The two methods are: 'method of difference' (MoD) and 'method of agreement' (MoA). In MoD, all factors are kept constant except for the one which is of interest to the researcher. In other words, in this method, the two cases are similar in all respects but have one crucial difference (Van Evera, 1997). For instance, Saudi Arabia and Libya are similar in almost all respects but differ in one crucial aspect, which is that Saudi Arabia is a monarchy and Libya is not. This allows the researcher to understand the causes of monarchical stability. In the MoA, one factor of interest to the researcher is held constant and all the other factors are different. In this method, the two cases are different in almost all aspects but have one crucial similarity (Van Evera, 1997). For instance, Sri Lanka and Northern Ireland are different cases but have one crucial similarity, which is separatism, and the cases can be studied to understand separatism.

The study undertakes a comparative study of the oil blocks bid for and acquired by Indian and Chinese oil companies in 11 oil-producing countries in West Africa. The 11 countries are different from each other in almost all aspects: political, economic and social among others. The common factor in the 11 countries is that they have oil reserves and are oil-producing countries. This conforms to the MoA. However, they differ in the extent of the oil reserves and the quantity of oil they produce. Similarly, India and China, which are emerging economies and rising powers, have different economic and political systems, and different economic structures. Nonetheless, they both are heavily dependent on import of oil, which is the crucial similarity. This also conforms to the MoA. For case study analysis, the study uses a pattern-matching logic. According to Trochim (cited in Yin, 2009: 136), "pattern-matching logic compares an empirically based pattern with a recited pattern". For instance, as discussed above, various scholars have stated that India is represented by SOEs and/or private sector oil companies and China by SOEs. Moreover, Chinese NOCs are globally widespread relative to India and the former outbid the latter in direct bidding for oil blocks and/or preferred as partners and/or have better quality oil blocks. The study pattern matches a predicted pattern mentioned above with an empirical one in 11 countries in West Africa. The study also undertakes in-depth case study analysis of Angola, Nigeria and Gabon. This is discussed in detail in Chapters 5, 6 and 7 respectively.

The study uses process tracing to illustrate how the difference in the relative power of India and China and the difference in the political economy of India and China explain the differences and relative success and failure of China and India in their respective efforts to mobilise oil in the oil industry in West Africa. This leads to an analytical narrative of the political economy of India and China and the oil industry in India and China. The narrative begins with the political and economic structure that prevailed in India and China at the time of their independence. It discusses in a chronological and a sequential order the political economy of the two countries since independence, and the different economic and political reforms undertaken which have led to divergent economies and composition of the industrial structure (Chapter 3). It also provides an analytical narrative of the oil industry in India and China. The different political economies of India and China are reflected in the oil sector in the respective countries. In the post-reform period, the oil industry in India is characterised by dominant SOEs, a vibrant and fast emerging private sector and joint ventures between the SOEs, private enterprises and IOCs. China, on the other hand, has an oil industry represented by the SOEs with joint ventures formed with IOCs and the private sector playing an insignificant role (Chapter 4).

Organisation of the book

The book has an introduction, seven chapters and a conclusion. Chapter 1 is the theoretical chapter. The chapter begins by briefly discussing the progression of NCR and asserts that rather than being a theory of foreign policy, "NCR is theories of foreign policy" (Taliaferro *et al.*, 2009). It illustrates the interplay between political economy and NCR, discusses the existing literature with respect to NCR and political economy, and highlights the existing gap in literature. It also illustrates how political economy is incorporated into NCR to explain the research question. It also explains why it is desirable to use NCR rather than foreign policy analysis (FPA) to explain the research question. In the process, it highlights the difference between FPA and NCR and the significance of the independent variable in NCR.

Chapter 2 compares and contrasts India and China and discusses the importance of India and China in the global arena. It also discusses the rationale for India's and China's engagement with Africa and asserts that energy security has been the driving force for India and China turning to Africa, especially West Africa. The chapter examines why West Africa has become an important player in the global oil industry in recent years. It discusses the prevalent literature on India and China in Africa. It outlines the prevalent discourse on China in Africa followed by India in Africa. It also highlights the comparative aspects of India and China in Africa in the existing literature. It then looks at India and China respectively in West Africa, in the oil industry in West Africa and compares and contrasts India and China in the oil industry in West Africa. In the end, it mentions the gap in the existing literature and provides a rationale for undertaking the research.

Chapters 3 and 4 are background chapters. Chapter 3 explains the difference in how India and China mobilise oil in the oil industry in countries in West Africa. The chapter is divided into three parts. The first part discusses in brevity Sino-Indian relations since the end of the Second World War. It provides the context which facilitates the comprehension of the subject matter, especially the role and the significance of the independent variable which characterises the difference in the relative power between the two countries. The second part discusses the difference in the economic, political and military power of India and China. To gauge the difference in the economic power, it uses indicators like Gross Domestic Product (GDP), Gross National Income (GNI) and other development indicators like Infant Mortality Rate (IMR), life expectancy, etc. To measure the difference in political power, it uses the permanent membership of the UNSC as a dummy variable or parameter, and the perception of leaders, government officials and bureaucrats. The third part discusses the difference in the political economy of India and China since their independence, the trajectory of reforms introduced in the two Asian neighbours and how it has transformed their economic and industrial structure.

Chapter 4 highlights that the differences in the relative economic and political power and the difference in the political economy of India and China are mirrored in the oil industry of the two countries. It illustrates that the oil industry in China is almost entirely dominated by SOEs. On the other hand, both SOEs and private enterprises are active in the oil industry in India and the latter are important players in the industry. It also proves that Chinese oil companies have greater economic power relative to Indian oil companies. Additionally, it highlights the fact that the Chinese NOCs receive more diplomatic and political support from the Chinese state which the Government of India (GoI) cannot match.

Chapters 5, 6 and 7 examine the validity of the research question mentioned above. The chapters explore whether the difference in the relative power of India and China and the difference in their political economy are able to explain the differences and relative success and failure of China and India in their respective efforts to mobilise oil in the oil industry in West Africa. Chapter 5 undertakes a case study 'pattern matching' in Angola. The chapter discusses the oil industry in Angola, the oil reserves and production and the oil blocks bid for and acquired by India and China in Angola. The focus is to find out if India and China entered into direct competitive bidding for the oil blocks and if India is represented by SOEs and/or private sector enterprises and China is represented by SOEs.

Chapter 6 carries forward from the previous chapter and undertakes a case study of Nigeria. Both India and China bid for oil blocks in Nigeria and São Tomé and Principe Joint Development Zone (JDZ). Although both Nigeria and São Tomé and Principe have jurisdiction over the JDZ, the study includes the JDZ and discusses it with Nigeria because São Tomé and Principe is an extremely minor player in the oil industry in West Africa.[6] The chapter does a case study 'pattern matching' in Nigeria. The chapter discusses the oil industry in Nigeria, the oil reserves and production, and the oil blocks bid for and acquired by India and China in Nigeria and the JDZ in Nigeria and São Tomé and Principe. The focus is to find out if India and China entered into direct competitive bidding for the oil blocks and if India is represented by SOEs and/or private sector enterprises and China is represented by SOEs.

Chapter 7 examines the relevance of the hypothesis in eight countries – Gabon, Ghana, Chad, Equatorial Guinea, Cameroon, Mauritania, Niger and Liberia – in West Africa by employing case study 'pattern matching'. The chapter examines whether China is represented by SOEs and whether India is represented by SOEs and/or private enterprises in the oil industry in West Africa. It also examines whether Chinese SOEs outbid Indian enterprises and whether China is spread throughout West Africa relative to India's selective approach. It discusses the presence of Indian and Chinese oil companies and the number of oil blocks that each country has in eight countries in West Africa. It also discusses the oil industry in eight countries: oil reserves and production and the oil blocks acquired by Indian and Chinese oil companies in the eight countries respectively.

The concluding chapter reflects on the findings. It provides a short analysis of the competition between Indian and Chinese oil companies in the oil industry in West Africa. It consolidates our understanding of how the difference in the relative economic and political power and the difference in the political economy of India and China explain the differences and relative success and failure of China and India in their respective efforts to mobilise oil in the oil industry in West Africa. It distils some insights and offers some policy implications moving forward. The study concludes by offering some directions for future research.

Notes

1 There is a huge debate regarding using fossil fuels and renewable sources of energy and the impact of the former on environment and climate change. These debates are

outside the scope of this study. Similarly, the debate on fracking and its environmental impact is outside the scope of this study. There is also a huge debate about peak oil. Peak-oil theory states that global oil production will peak in 10–15 years and then oil production will decline because the existing reserves will be start getting depleted and no new reserves will be found which will compensate for the decline in production. The debate on peak oil is also outside the scope of this study.

2 In the study, the People's Republic of China (PRC) and China have been used interchangeably. Similarly, Taiwan and Republic of China (ROC) have been used interchangeably.

3 Geographically, according to the United Nations (UN), West Africa includes 17 countries. The study excludes Saint Helena and includes Angola, Equatorial Guinea and Cameroon in West Africa. The 11 countries examined are Angola, Ghana, Chad, Equatorial Guinea, Cameroon, Liberia, Niger, Mauritania, Nigeria, Gabon and Nigeria–São Tomé and Principe JDZ. Although both Nigeria and São Tomé and Principe have jurisdiction over the JDZ, the study includes and discusses JDZ with Nigeria because São Tomé and Principe is an extremely minor player in the oil industry in West Africa.

4 There is a lack of consensus amongst scholars whether China is an economic superpower. Scholars argue that although China has the second largest economy and the largest economy in Purchasing Power Parity (PPP) terms, GDP or National Income (NI) is not a good indicator of economic power. The debate whether China is an economic superpower or not and whether GDP and NI by themselves are a good measure to superpower status is outside the scope of this study.

5 Mobilisation and extraction can lead to confusion in the context of the oil industry. The two words have different meanings. In the oil industry, the term 'exploration and production (E&P)' is used to explain extraction of oil. Mobilisation used colloquially means to acquire resources. Extraction implies consumption of wealth and formation of power. For a more detailed discussion see Mastanduno *et al.* (1989). The study focuses on mobilisation only.

6 A formal declaration for the joint development of oil and other resources in the areas over lapping their respective maritime boundaries was signed by Nigeria and the Democratic Republic of São Tomé and Principe in 2001. This led to the establishment of the JDZ and the Joint Development Authority (JDA), an administrative body that supervises the enactment of the treaty and underlying licence areas.

References

Mastanduno, Michael, Lake, David A. and Ikenberry, G. John (1989). Towards a Realist Theory of State Action. *International Studies Quarterly*, 33 (4), pp. 457–474.

Rose, Gideon (1998). Neoclassical Realism and Theories of Foreign Policy. *World Politics*, 51 (1), pp. 144–172.

Taliaferro, Jeffrey W., Lobell, Steven E. and Ripsman, Norrin M. (2009). Introduction: Neoclassical Realism, the State, and Foreign Policy. In: Steven E. Lobell, Norrin M. Ripsman and Jeffrey W. Taliaferro, eds. *Neoclassical Realism, the State, and Foreign Policy*. Cambridge: Cambridge University Press, pp. 1–41.

Van Evera, Stephen. (1997). *Guide to Methods for Students of Political Science*. Ithaca and London: Cornell University Press.

Yin, Robert K. (2009). *Case Study Research: Design and Methods*. Applied Social Research Method Series Volume 5, 4th edn. Los Angeles: Sage Publications.

Part II

Conceptual framework and background

1   Neoclassical realism

In 1948, Hans J. Morgenthau wrote *Politics Among Nations: The Struggle for Power and Peace*. The book was primarily responsible for cementing realism as the prevailing theoretical paradigm in the field of international relations (IR). In 1979, Kenneth N. Waltz wrote *Theory of International Politics*, which led to a new structural version of realism – neorealism[1] – becoming the dominant paradigm in IR. However, it was only when Ashley (1986) drew a sharp distinction between the work of earlier realist scholars and Waltz's theory of international politics that the terms neorealism and classical realism became widespread.

In the field of international politics, structural realism or neorealism, the dominant paradigm, has tended to abstract from domestic politics to explain international outcomes such as system stability, economic openness or regime creation as a function of international attributes, principally the distribution of power. The inability of neorealism to explain the peaceful conclusion of the Cold War and the international politics in the post-Cold War period led to great disenchantment with neorealism (Schmidt, 2004). Scholars from other paradigms, especially the liberalists, commented that 'realism was on the decline' or 'the retreat of realism' or neorealism was no longer a dominant paradigm or neorealism was defunct. Consequently, modifications or addition of variables were suggested by various neorealists and liberals that needed to be incorporated in the 1990s to explain and come to terms with the changing global political and economic landscape (Jervis, 1978; Krasner, 1978; Gilpin, 1981; Gaddis, 1987; Walt, 1987; Van Evera, 1990–1; Buzan, 1993; Wohlforth, 1994–5). Thus in 1997, postclassical realism was coined by Stephen G. Brooks.

In the 1990s, books by scholars like Wohlforth (1993), Brown *et al.* (1995), Christensen (1996), Schweller (1998) and Zakaria (1998), and a compendium of articles previously published in *International Security* – a globally renowned journal – incorporated both the systemic or the exogenous variable and the domestic or unit level variable. Subsequently, in 1998, in an article in *World Politics*, Gideon Rose coined the term NCR – a fusion of classical realism and neorealism. Adherents of NCR argue that they are realists because "The scope and ambition of a country's foreign policy is driven first and foremost by its place in the international system and specifically by its relative material power capabilities" (Rose, 1998: 146). It is neo because it still retains the primacy of the systemic variable, i.e. the level of external vulnerability due to the anarchical nature of the international system. It is classical because it incorporates unit level variables like beliefs of leaders, the degree of state autonomy from society, the extractive and mobilisation capacity of political-military institutions, the influence of interest groups, domestic societal actors and others.

The purpose of the chapter is to show that NCR explains foreign policy outcomes of states and how political economy can be incorporated into NCR to explain the research question: 'Can NCR explain the differences and relative success and failure of China and India in their respective efforts to mobilise oil in the oil industry in West Africa?' The chapter is divided into three sections. Section I discusses NCR as a theoretical paradigm and states that while neorealism is a theory of international politics, NCR explicates foreign policy outcomes. Thus, it is a 'theories of foreign policy'. Section II shows the interplay between political economy and NCR. It discusses the existing literature with respect to NCR and political economy, and highlights the existing gap in the literature. It also illustrates how political economy is incorporated into NCR to elucidate the difference in the interaction of India and China in the oil industry in West Africa. Section III discusses the importance and significance of using NCR and states why it is desirable to use NCR rather than FPA to explain the research question.

I

For more than three decades, IR theory has been dominated by the debate between neorealists and their various critics. Much of the debate has occurred over questions about the nature of the international system and its effect on patterns of international outcomes such as war and peace. Scholars have disputed whether a multipolar system is less stable and generates more conflict than a bipolar one or whether international institutions can increase the incidence of international co-operation. Since neorealism is not a theory of foreign policy but of international politics, it neither seeks to expound their actions in all cases nor in great detail. Thus the daily occurrences and events are explained by theories of foreign policy. The dependent variable in these theories is the conduct of individual states rather than the pattern of outcomes of state interactions. Contrary to neorealism, theories of foreign policy strive to expound the aims and objectives of states in the external sphere and how and when they try to achieve those aims and objectives.

NCR, coined by Gideon Rose (1998), is a theoretical paradigm which explains foreign policy outcomes of states. It aims to explicate the foreign policies of a state across different time periods or different states facing comparable external constraints and provides a theoretically inspired framework to do so (Taliaferro *et al.*, 2009). According to Rose (1998: 146):

> Its adherents argue that the scope and ambition of a country's foreign policy is driven first and foremost by its place in the international system and specifically by its relative material power capabilities. This is why they are realist. They argue further, however, that the impact of such power capabilities on

foreign policy is indirect and complex, because systemic pressures must be translated through intervening variables at the unit level. This is why they are neoclassical.

According to Waltz (1959), the first and second images are important and provide knowledge of the factors that determine and influence policy, whereas the third image provides the structure for international politics. However, without the third image, it would be difficult to assess the influence of the first and second image and/or predict the outcome. Fareed Zakaria (1992) avers that a good analysis and comprehension of a foreign policy of a state should incorporate systemic, domestic and other factors, and it should be specified what aspect of a policy can be explained by what factor. Taliaferro *et al.* (2009) aver that NCR incorporates the theoretical perceptions and the scrupulousness of neorealism but it does not sacrifice the practical insights and the convolutedness of state craft that exists in classical realism. According to Rose (1998), NCR puts forward a well-defined causal chain comprising of three steps: first, the independent or the exogenous variable or a country's relative material power in the anarchical international system. Second is the intervening or the endogenous variable or the domestic level 'transmission belt' which sieves systemic forces. Third is the dependent variable or the foreign policy outcome.

In consonance with other schools of realism, neoclassical realists assume that states are unitary actors and systemic forces are the foremost contributing factor of outcomes. According to Schweller (cited in Juneau, 2010: 2), based on this assumption,

> structure encourages certain actions and discourages others, i.e. systemic pressures are directly 'translated' into state actions…. Thus, in the long term, a state's behaviour will most likely converge with predictions based solely or mostly on structural factors. In the short term, however, divergences must be expected, and are accounted for by the integration of domestic-level variables. The intervening domestic-level variables which channel, mediate and (re)direct systemic pressures represent one of the main, and most controversial, innovations of neoclassical realism.

The domestic variables enable an exploration of the internal practices which enables states to formulate policies and act in accordance to the systemic pressures (Sterling-Folker, 1997). Thus NCR incorporates first, second and third image variables. The causal chain of NCR is depicted in Figure 1.1.

Like classical realism, NCR states that there is an explicit distinction between state and society and does not view the state as completely autonomous from society. According to neoclassical realists, states are the principal actors in international politics (Taliaferro *et al.*, 2009). It represents a 'top-down' conception of the state which implies that external behaviour is eventually driven by systemic forces. In other words, it views the states as embodied by the national security executive comprising the head of the

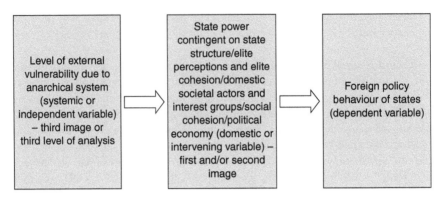

Figure 1.1 Diagrammatic illustration of neoclassical realism.

government, ministers and government officials in charge of making foreign and security policy (Ripsman, 2002).

Although the executive branch is independent from the society, it is frequently compelled by political agreements to bargain with domestic actors like political parties, the legislature, economic sectors and classes or the public to implement policy and extricate resources in order to implement policy choices. Hence contrary to Marxism and liberalism, NCR does not view states as merely accumulating the demands of disparate economic classes or social interest groups. According to neoclassical realists, leaders delineate the 'national interests' and direct foreign policy on the basis of the intentions of other states and relative shift in power, but always subject to domestic constraints. Consequently, policy responses are observed by neoclassical realists as a result (at times) of struggle and of state–society co-ordination (Taliaferro *et al.*, 2009).

In recent years, scholars have debated whether NCR is a "theory of mistakes" (Schweller, 2006: 10) or as a standard foreign policy theory. According to Waltz (2003: 53), states can "do any fool thing they care to, but they are likely to be rewarded for behaviour that is responsive to structural pressures and punished for behaviour that is not". Thus the system guides states in the direction of the paramount foreign policy but states recurrently diverge from the best solution because they are pushed in other directions by 'domestic pathologies' (Snyder, 1991).

According to Rathbun (2008: 319):

> Neoclassical realism should be viewed as a logical and necessary extension of structural realism. It is "a theory of mistakes." It explains how domestic factors distract "from ideal foreign policy as understood by neorealism" which provides a baseline of what an ideal rational unitary state would do.... It begins with the premise that ideal state behaviour is that which conforms with the unitary actor and objectivity premises of neorealism but

shows that when these conditions are not met empirically, domestic politics and ideas are the culprits.

(Rathbun, 2008: 312)

"States that stray too much from ideal behaviour, then, suffer severe consequences" (Rathbun, 2008: 317). This methodology is exemplified by Christopher Layne's (2006) examination of US foreign policy. Layne asserts that the misguided grand strategy of extra-regional hegemony has guided US foreign policy since 1945. He argues that the United States should instead espouse a grand strategy of offshore balancing.

However, this does not bear consonance with all neoclassical realists. Rose contends that NCR is a theory of foreign policy. Norrin Ripsman, Steven Lobell and Jeffrey Taliaferro posit that contingent on (1) clarity of threats and (2) clear information on policy responses, NCR can not only simply explain foreign policy puzzles, but also foreign policy of states (Ripsman *et al.*, 2009). They also contend that there are diverse neoclassical realist 'theories of foreign policy' and not one single neoclassical realist theory. Thus NCR is 'theories of foreign policy'.

Zakaria (1998) does not focus on mistakes and severe consequences. Zakaria identifies incongruence in US foreign policy. The divergence is the imperial under stretch of US foreign policy in the nineteenth century, which contradicts the paradigms of classical and defensive realism. Although Zakaria's state-centred realism offers a better structure to explicate this contradiction, he does not prescribe the course of action the United States should take or has taken. Thus it is conceivable that the different approaches to NCR can be observed as comprising a spectrum. The spectrum ranges from the Rathbun on one end and Taliaferro *et al.* and Rose on the other with Zakaria in the middle (Juneau, 2010). Figure 1.2 depicts the spectrum of NCR. The study adheres to Taliaferro *et al.*'s assertion that NCR is 'theories of foreign policy'.

According to Juneau (2010), unlike Waltz who sought to explicate a small amount of large and significant things, NCR aims to expound numerous amounts

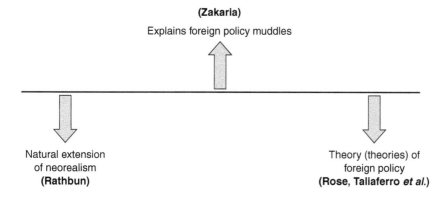

Figure 1.2 Spectrum of neoclassical realism.

(n) of small things (t). More importantly, its objective is to explain these things rather than just describe them. Thus, there is flexibility in achieving a balance between the 'n' and the 't' in NCR and the balance should be struck only in accordance with the research question under consideration. Consequently, the researcher has two options to choose from if the objective is to seek an extremely specific and accurate account of foreign policy: first, to add additional intervening variables and, second, to operationalise them in an increasing number of specific ways.

> A more general account (smaller n, larger t's) could, for example, use one intervening variable, either 'leaders' or state interests (status quo vs. revisionist), while a more specific study (larger n, smaller t's) could not only incorporate both, but increase their individual specificity by changing the first one to factional politics (which incorporates the balance of power among key regime factions) and the second one to either Schweller's (1998) model which further divides state interests into five categories or into the more nuanced variable of 'regime identity'.
>
> (Juneau, 2010: 4)

According to Schweller (2003), NCR presents progress within the realist research tradition. Neoclassical realists emphasize problem-focused research that seeks to clarify and extend the logic of basic classical and structural realist propositions by specifying and further developing the non-structural arguments, causal processes and linkages at the domestic and international levels implied by structural theories of balance of power and hegemonic rivalry. NCR employs the case study method to test general theories, explain cases and generate hypotheses. It incorporates first, second and third image variables. It not only addresses important questions about foreign policy but has also produced a body of cumulative knowledge.

Taliaferro *et al.* (2009) assert that NCR is not a modification of neorealism proposed by Waltz and it is also not an endeavour to put unit level variables in a theory to explicate an aberration. Additionally, it is wrong to typify realism as a strictly constructed research programme as postulated by Lakatos. Moreover, neorealism should not be characterised as the hard core of realism and any departure from neorealism should not be considered as verification of a degenerative problem shift (Vasquez, 1997). Thus, NCR might expound the likely military, diplomatic and economic responses of specific states to systemic constraints, but it does not explicate the systemic outcomes of those responses (Taliaferro *et al.*, 2009).

II

Section II shows the interplay between political economy and NCR. It briefly discusses political economy and provides a working definition of political economy. It also discusses the existing literature on NCR and political economy and highlights the gap in the existing literature. It illustrates how political economy is incorporated as a domestic or intervening variable into NCR to explain the differences and relative success and failure of China and India in their respective efforts to mobilise oil in the oil industry in West Africa.

Political economy and NCR

The phrase 'political economy' has had a long and distinguished history with numerous and diverse elucidations and import. According to Adam Smith, it was a science of management of a country's resources to create wealth. Karl Marx, on the other hand, defined it as the way in which the ownership of the means of production affected historical processes. It has had differing meanings for most of the last century. It was viewed as a methodology or as an interrelationship between politics and economics, i.e. as an area of study. The methodological approach was split into two segments: the economic approach and the sociological approach. The former laid emphasis on rationality and was also coined as public choice, and in the latter, the level of analysis was the institutions (Weingast and Wittman, 2006). According to Weingast and Wittman (2006), "political economy is the methodology of economics applied to the analysis of political behaviour and institutions". Although political economy as a methodological approach is important, it lies outside the scope of this study. Thus the study discusses the political economy as an area of study, i.e. the interrelationship between politics and economics.

The study employs a simple but comprehensive definition of political economy as a

> branch of social science that takes as its principal subject of study the inter-relationships between political and economic institutions and processes. In other words, political economists are interested in analysing and explaining the ways in which various governments affect the allocation of scarce resources in society through their laws and policies as well as the ways in which the nature of the economic system and the behaviour of people acting on their economic interests affects the form of government and the kinds of laws and policies that get made.
>
> (Johnson, 2005)

Thus, political economy of a country is a domestic or an endogenous variable.

Accordingly, different economic and political systems exist in different countries. Different political economies in different countries have a direct bearing on how the state mobilises and extracts resources from the domestic society via the institutions of the state (and other means like nationalism and statist or anti-statist ideology) to achieve foreign policy objectives. Following Marx, capitalism and communism are two systems at the opposite end of the spectrum with a combination of the two in varying degrees and forms lying between the two. For the sake of simplicity, the study mentions three different political and economic systems: capitalist system where the means of production are in the hands of private enterprise, as in the United States; socialism/communism[2] where the ownership of the means of production are in the hands of the state, as in China before the economic reforms in 1979; and a mixed economic system where the state controls the means of production in the key and strategic industries (private enterprise entered these industries at a later stage of development) and the consumer goods industry is in the hands of private enterprise, as in India.

According to Taliaferro *et al.* (2009), NCR might explicate the likely military, diplomatic and economic responses of specific states to systemic constraints. Neoclassical realists have incorporated state power contingent on state structure, elite perceptions and elite cohesion, domestic societal actors and interest groups and social cohesion as domestic variables to explain foreign policy outcomes of states. Similarly, political economy can also be incorporated as a domestic or intervening variable into NCR to explain the foreign policy of a country. Political economy of a country is a domestic variable and the relative power of a country in the international system is the systemic variable, and these two factors influence and impinge the foreign policy of a country. Political economy as a domestic or intervening variable in NCR is depicted in Figure 1.3.

Literature review

NCR: empirical studies

There has been a spurt in literature since the 1990s but NCR is still in an embryonic stage. However, it is gaining momentum as a theoretical paradigm. The genesis of NCR can be traced to work by William Wohlforth, Thomas Christensen, Fareed Zakaria and Randall Schweller, among others, in the 1990s. They aim to explicate the grand strategy of a state at a specific time and/or place. Wohlforth (1993) asserts that the sway of communism on USSR's net assessments and the incongruity between the United States and the USSR regarding the distribution of power in post-Cold War Europe was instrumental for Soviet grand strategy during the Cold War. Schweller (1998) examines Hitler's expansionist grand strategy and asserts that there were two reasons which facilitated Hitler's strategy: the tripolarity in the international system from the late 1930s to the early 1940s and the status quo and revisionist interests among the three poles, i.e. the United States, Germany and the Soviet Union.

Figure 1.3 Political economy as intervening variable in neoclassical realism.

Since Rose's article was published in 1998, scholars have utilised NCR to deal with myriad policy, historical and theoretical debates. Lobell (2003) and Schweller (2006) investigate and explicate the politics of alliance formation and threat assessment in Paraguay, Brazil and Argentina before the 1870 War of the Triple Alliance, and in France and Britain respectively before the two world wars. Davidson (2002, 2006) employs NCR to examine the geneses of Italy's anti status quo grand strategy in the 1920s and 1930s. Taliaferro (2004) examines the interventions of Germany, Japan and the United States in the periphery regions. McAllister (2002) and Barth (2005) investigate the beginning of the development of the US military commitment from the 1940s to the 1960s to Western Europe and containment. Brooks and Wohlforth (2000/1) explore the interaction of the domestic constraints on the Kremlin's response to the deep relative decline in the 1980s, the relative shifts in power and the evolving nature of global production. Sterling-Folker (2002a) explores the beginning of the US monetary policy since the fall of the Bretton Woods system in 1973.

Schweller (1994, 2001) and Edelstein (2002) investigate the quandaries in assessment of the capabilities and intentions of emerging great powers. Byman and Pollack (2001) assess how grand strategy is influenced by ideology and the impact of individual leaders. Ripsman (2001, 2002) employs NCR to address the impact of domestic constraints on the ability of great powers to create long-lasting agreements after major wars. Layne (2006) and Dueck (2006) investigate the 2003 invasion of Iraq and the genesis of the Bush doctrine. Haglund and Onea (2008) use NCR as a theoretical paradigm to understand the making and analysis of Canadian foreign policy. Building on neoclassical realist thought, Weiss (2009) argues that a two-stage analysis of the power context offers a comprehensive explanation of some of the recent changes in German foreign policy, especially the shift in preferences for institution building in the European Security and Defence Policy. Costalli (2009) argues that NCR is relevant in interpreting and explaining phenomena of current global and regional politics such as Euro-Mediterranean relations.

Cha (2001, 2002) examines the strategies of Japan, South Korea and the United States during the North Korean nuclear crisis. An attempt to comprehend the foreign policy decision-making in China from a comparative point of view is undertaken by Hao and Hou (2009). They also highlight the basic tenets of Chinese foreign policy and possible options for the future. Basrur (2009) avers that NCR should be refined. This can be achieved by focusing on the relationship between the role of the structure and degrees of interdependence which will enable India to have an improved basis for understanding the evolving international system and forming a suitable comprehensive strategy towards it. Focusing on Central Asia, Ferguson (2011) uses NCR to assert that Russia and China have espoused a strategy of soft balancing to indirectly balance US hegemony in the region.

NCR: theoretical studies

Scholars have also contributed to theoretical debates using NCR, and about NCR as a research programme and its contribution to IR. Sterling-Folker (2002b, 2004) also makes a theoretical contribution by studying the ontological convergence between NCR and constructivism. Kitchen (2010) utilises a neoclassical realist approach that incorporates the impact of ideas in the formation of a grand strategy. Schweller (1997, 2003), Glaser (2003) and Wohlforth (2003), in their appraisal of the theoretical developments in IR, focus on debates regarding the practicality of employing Lakatos' methodology of scientific research programmes. Ducek (2005) uses a dual case study of US strategic adjustment after the first and second world wars to test a 'neoclassical realist' model. He avers that NCR fares well against cultural and purely structural options. Glenn (2009) avers that great insights can be obtained by different explanations for behaviour of states provided by NCR and strategic culture. He posits four key concepts of strategic culture and investigates the kind of collaboration that the four concepts can have with NCR. By examining regime types and viewing those through the lenses of state power extraction in an anarchic and competitive world, Caverley (2010) avers that neo-conservatism falls in the NCR domain.

NCR and political economy

Tomes of literature have been written on political economy and international political economy. However, there is a paucity of literature on NCR and political economy. In recent years, there has been an increase in literature on NCR and political economy where political economy has been used either directly or indirectly. Zakaria (1998) uses NCR and political economy to explain normal expansion, Christensen (1996) to explain why leaders inflate external threats to sell costly internal mobilisation campaigns, Snyder (1991) to explain reckless over-expansion, Schweller (2004) to explain under-balancing, Taliaferro (2006) to explain that states sometimes do not imitate the successful practices of the system's leading states in an apt and identical way, and Brawley (2009, 2010) provides a political economy interpretation of balancing. All these studies focus on using NCR either to explain a contradiction in neorealism or to explain a structural phenomenon like polarity. Although not postulating NCR, Mastanduno *et al.* (1989) emphasised the role of political economy as a domestic variable to achieve international objectives. In similar vein, they discussed the role of international variables or strategies to achieve domestic goals. The aim of both the strategies is state survival.

According to Mastanduno *et al.* (1989), there are two distinctive domestic strategies that states utilise in the quest of foreign policy objectives: mobilisation and extraction. Mobilisation normally takes two forms: direct mobilisation and indirect mobilisation. Under direct mobilisation, the state can directly influence economic activity and redistribute resources via centralised planning and other measures including the nationalisation of key and strategic industries and other sectors. This strategy is extremely useful if the country (let us say 'X') is in the initial phase of economic growth. A 'Big Push' is required to catch up with other countries that embarked on the process of economic growth before country X (Rosenstein-Rodan, 1943). This was the strategy adopted by both India and China after independence but led to different economic growth trajectories. This is discussed in greater detail in Chapter 3. Direct mobilisation can also be extremely effective when the country is in an extensive growth phase, a strategy adopted by China and India since the beginning of the new century. The state may also interfere indirectly in the economy to enable the accretion of wealth in the society and the concomitant tax revenue that accrues to the state. Mastanduno *et al.* (1989) assert that mobilisation is an investment in international power. By expanding wealth, the state or the executive facilitates the creation of the resources necessary to sustain military expenditures, stimulate technological innovation and expand the political and economic bases of power. Thus, the state increases its material power and also its comprehensive national power or strength. There is an economic and political cost associated with both mobilisation strategies. In direct mobilisation, the state has to incur a cost for the enormous administrative system. On the other hand, in indirect mobilisation, the state may have to provide concessions and subsidies to non-state actors as an incentive to expand output.

The state extracts resources from society for military expenditures, foreign aid, contributions to international organizations and other exercises to increase its power – hard power as well as soft power. Wealth provides the basis for international power, but it is not synonymous with power. The state must convert wealth into power by taxing, requisitioning or expropriating social resources. Extraction like mobilisation does entail costs and diminishes the present and future wealth of the nation-state. Using extracted resources to increase power consumes rather than produces wealth. Thus there exists an inverse relationship between the two strategies of mobilisation and extraction. Mobilisation is synonymous with the creation of wealth and it is an investment in power. Internal extraction implies the consumption of wealth and formation of power. With an increase in extraction, it is possible that the state may enhance its endeavours at mobilisation. However, the effectiveness of the mobilisation may decline due to two reasons: first, the sum of investable wealth has decreased because of extraction. Second, incentives provided to create wealth in the future may be diluted by the introduction of inefficiencies in the economy and dissuading investment. Although these problems are less acute in direct mobilisation, it involves the introduction of greater economic inefficiencies. Extraction is necessary but costly in its long-term effects on the nation-state's capability to compete in the anarchical international system (Mastanduno *et al.*, 1989).

Contribution to existing literature

Although Mastanduno *et al.* (1989) emphasised the role of political economy as a domestic variable to achieve international objectives, they did not emphasise that political economy should be used as an intervening or domestic variable while retaining the primacy of the systemic variable. Moreover, they discuss internal mobilisation of resources by a state to increase its wealth and power. The study uses NCR as a theoretical construct to discuss external mobilisation. The study uses political economy as an intervening variable in NCR to explicate the divergence and relative success and failure of China and India in their respective efforts to mobilise oil in the oil industry in West Africa. In the process, the study extends NCR's research design because in the past, political economy has been used as an intervening variable in NCR to explicate either a contradiction in neorealism, such as under-balancing, or to explain a structural phenomenon, such as polarity. The utilisation of political economy in NCR to explain the differences and relative success and failure of India and China in mobilising oil in the oil industry in West Africa explains a systemic rather than a structural outcome. It is not explaining deviation from neorealism or polarity. With respect to India's and China's interaction in the oil industry in West Africa, the driving force is economic relations, to mobilise oil, a key resource. The rationale is regime survival as well as augmenting both absolute and relative power. Thus the study provides a theoretical contribution to the existing literature on NCR in general and NCR and political economy in particular. The theoretical contribution to the existing literature on NCR and political economy and NCR is illustrated in Figure 1.4.

III

Section III discusses the importance and significance of using NCR to explain the research question. It highlights why it is desirable to use NCR rather than FPA to explain the research question. This is done in two ways: first, by

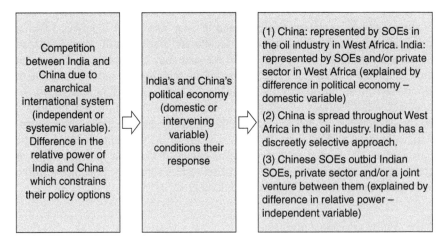

Figure 1.4 Political economy of India and China as the domestic or intervening variable in neoclassical realism.

discussing inherent problems of using FPA. Second by discussing the primacy and significance of the independent variable or the relative distribution of power in an anarchical international system.

Foreign policy analysis

FPA literature categorises countries on the basis of their power into three categories: Great Powers (GP), Middle Powers (MP) and Small Powers (SP). Based on the difference in their power potential, different countries have different goals and different strategies to achieve those goals. Thus they behave differently in the international system. The study does not delve into the different characteristics of GP, MP and SP and the different strategies they adopt to achieve their goals and objectives.

It is arguable that FPA provides an alternative way to illustrate the differences and relative success and failure of China and India in their respective efforts to mobilise oil in the oil industry in West Africa. The difference in the relative power of India and China necessitates that they behave differently. Based on the difference in their power potential, China can be categorised as a GP and India as a MP. This is based on the contention that China is economically, politically and militarily more powerful than India. The difference in the power potential of India and China can explain why Chinese NOCs are able to outbid Indian NOCs and private sector enterprises oil companies and why Chinese NOCs operate in more countries in West Africa relative to India which indulges in niche diplomacy and has a limited presence in the region.

However, the use of FPA to elucidate the differences and relative success and failure of China and India in their respective efforts to mobilise oil in the oil industry in West Africa has myriad problems. This is because, first, there are definitional problems associated with GP and MP. Second, categorising India as a MP and China as a GP is also problematic.

Great powers and middle powers: a definitional dilemma

The term major powers or GP have been used interchangeably in diplomatic parlance since the mid-eighteenth century. However, ambiguity has clouded the term and its definition (Danilovic, 2002; Buzan, 2004). According to Waltz (1979) and Wight (cited in Buzan, 2004: 59), a consensus exists about who the GPs are although the power of the states cannot be reliably measured. However, Buzan (2004) highlights that Wight's comments are inconsistent regarding which countries classify as GP. The definition of GP falls under three dimensions: power, status and spatial. The power dimension encompasses economic, military and political capabilities. Waltz (1979) defines major power on the basis of their material capability and social role and Posen and Ross (1996/7: 17) as "powers that have substantial industrial and military potential". However, the definitions suffer from methodological disagreements. Waltz's definition fails to state how the different material elements are to be weighed against each other.

Moreover, the analysis of political competence is subjective (Buzan, 2004). Posen's and Ross' definition allows China to scrape through for its ability to trade on capabilities that it does not currently possess but is likely to do so in the near future.

Hedley Bull's (1977) definition encompasses the status dimension. Bull states that a GP must be recognised by its leaders and populace and other countries people and leaders to have certain special rights and duties. According to Danilovic (2002), the status dimension is the most subjective since the official or the unofficial status of a GP also requires the willingness of a nation to act as a GP. Buzan (2004) elaborates that the definition does not discuss whether self-conception or acceptance should be given more weight than the other. Wright and Morgenthau (cited in Buzan, 2004: 62) point to the problems that formal recognition may entail when some GP politically promote a state's status. For example, China after the Second World War was co-opted by the United States in the UNSC.

The spatial dimensional definition of a GP emphasises the geographic scope of actions, interests or projected power. The definition is helpful in distinguishing between a regional power and GP. According to Buzan (2004), GP are global system phenomena whereas regional powers are confined to a region. However, the spatial dimension is based on perception rather than reality and thus is subjective (Danilovic, 2002).

The term MP is not bereft of definitional and conceptual ambiguities either. The definition of MP also falls under three dimensions: hierarchical, behavioural and functional. MP in its most basic definition is a state i.e. in the middle – neither a GP nor a SP (Holbraad, 1984). States classified as MP in one fall under SP in the other which obfuscates the notion and makes it difficult to achieve a consistent definition (Chapnick, 1999). According to the hierarchical model, as Keohane (1969: 296) avers, "[A] MP is a state whose leaders consider that it cannot act alone effectively but may be able to have a systematic impact in a small group or through an international institution". However, this definition is politically subjective (Chapnick, 1999). Holbraad (1984: 76) argues that "MP can be distinguished best in terms of strength they possess and the power they command". But this definition is flawed because it fails to explain the term 'power'.

The proponents of the behavioural model, like Holmes (1976) and Cox (1989), state that MP asserts a distinct and identifiable type of statecraft known as "middlepowermanship" or MP diplomacy. Andrew Cooper, quoting Evans and Bruce (1991: 323), develops the argument further by linking this discussion to the concept of niche diplomacy which involves "concentrating resources in specific areas best able to generate returns worth having rather than trying to cover the field". However, the behavioural dimension fails to provide an objective definition of MP as any state big or SP could be or behave like a MP. Additionally, that the behaviour of MPs is described by MP internationalism and that MPs are states that follow MP internationalism is a tautology (Chapnick, 1999). The functional model differentiates MPs by identifying them as states which possess the capability albeit in special instances of influencing global affairs. Because of fluctuations in the power of states across time and space (which is contingent on their economic and political capabilities), the model lacks precision and as soon as a state's capability to contribute to an issue in global affairs declines, an MP loses its middle quality (Chapnick, 1999).

India a middle power? China a great power?

A dilemma exists regarding the power status of India and China in the IR literature. Segal (1999) and Goldstein (1997–8) classify China as a regional power but Buzan (2004) and others classify it as a GP. Similarly, India falls under a category of a GP on the basis of Waltz's (1979) definition but Buzan (2003) classifies it as a regional power and Buzan (2004) classifies it as a regional GP falling between regional powers and GP. Alden and Vieira (2005) on the other hand, associate India and China as rising powers with resource capabilities greater than those possessed by MP, namely Norway, Canada, Sweden, the Netherlands and Australia. Due to the ambiguity in the definitions and power status of India and China, and definitional dilemmas regarding GP and MP, FPA cannot be used to illustrate the difference in the way India and China mobilise resources externally in the oil industry in West Africa.

NCR and the independent variable

The definitional dilemmas associated with GP and MP to gauge the difference in the power potential of countries highlights the salience of the independent or systemic variable. FPA and NCR both aim to explain the foreign policy outcomes of states. However, the difference between FPA and NCR is the independent variable, i.e. the difference in the relative power of states in the international anarchical system. While FPA employs the categorisation of states into GP, MP and SP to highlight the difference in the states behaviour, NCR employs the difference in the relative power of states in the international anarchical system.

Neoclassical realists argue that "the scope and ambition of a country's foreign policy is driven first and foremost by its place in the international system and specifically by its relative material power capabilities i.e. its hard power or economic, political and military power" (Rose, 1998: 146). It is the systemic variable which limits the ambitions or goals and objectives of countries and the means to achieve these. As the relative power increases, states will seek more influence abroad, and as their relative power decreases, their actions and ambitions will be scaled back accordingly. What is important is that one state has more or greater power than the other or vice versa. Thus, categorising countries into GP, MP or SP is not important. This not only removes the definitional dilemmas but also describes the constraints that confine states, and the range of likely outcomes of the actions of states within a given system. The anarchical structure of the international system compels China to follow a different strategy with respect to India. Similarly, India's actions are constrained by the anarchical international system which leads to a different strategy compared to China.

Conclusion

The chapter discusses the progression of realism from classical realism to NCR. Neorealism postulated by Kenneth Waltz is the most dominant paradigm of realism. It is a structural and a systemic theory. It is a theory of international politics and not foreign policy, and seeks to explain important international outcomes. NCR coined by Gideon Rose provides a theoretically inspired framework which seeks to explicate the foreign policies of a state across different time periods or states facing comparable external constraints. There is a debate amongst neoclassical realists whether it is a natural extension of neorealism or it explains foreign policy muddles or is a theory of foreign policy or 'theories of foreign policy'. Following Taliaferro *et al.* (2009), the study contends that NCR is 'theories of foreign policies' and it explains foreign policy outcomes of states.

Although literature on NCR has increased since the 1990s, it is still in its embryonic stage but it is gaining momentum. Despite the increasing use of NCR, there is a paucity of literature on the role of political economy as a domestic or intervening variable in NCR. Most of the existing literature explains or seeks to explain a contradiction in neorealism or to explain a structural phenomenon like polarity. This is done by exploring internal mobilisation and extraction of resources to achieve foreign policy outcomes. The study uses political economy as an intervening variable to discuss external mobilisation of resources by India and China to enhance their industrialisation and economic growth and concomitant absolute and relative power. The chapter then illustrates that political economy can be used as an intervening variable in NCR to explain the research question. In the process, the study seeks to expand the research design of NCR. This is discussed in more detail in the concluding chapter.

Notes

1 Neorealism as postulated by Kenneth Waltz is a structural theory but not the only structural theory. Robert Giplin's Hegemonic Stability theory and Robert Keohane's Modified Structural Realism are also structural theories.
2 There is an inherent difference between communism and socialism but for the ease of comparison the study uses the terms interchangeably.

References

Alden, Chris and Vieira, Marco (2005). The New Diplomacy of the South: South Africa, Brazil, India and Trilateralism. *Third World Quarterly*, 26 (7), pp. 1077–1095.
Ashley, Richard K. (1986). The Poverty of Neorealism. In: Robert O. Keohane, ed. *Neorealism and its Critics*. New York: Columbia University Press, pp. 255–300.
Barth, Aharon (2005). American Military Commitments in Europe: Power, Perceptions and Neoclassical Realism. PhD thesis. Georgetown University.

Basrur, Rajesh M. (2009). Theory for a Strategy: Emerging India in a Changing World. *South Asian Survey*, 16 (1), pp. 5–21.

Brawley, Mark R. (2009). Neoclassical Realism and Strategic Calculations: Explaining Divergent British, French and Soviet Strategies toward Germany between the World Wars (1919–1939). In: Steven E. Lobell, Norrin M. Ripsman and Jeffrey W. Talia-ferro, eds. *Neoclassical Realism, the State, and Foreign Policy*. Cambridge: Cambridge University Press, pp. 75–98.

Brawley, Mark R. (2010). *Political Economy and Grand Strategy: A Neoclassical Realist View*. London: Routledge.

Brooks, Stephen (1997). Duelling Realisms. *International Organization*, 51 (3), pp. 445–477.

Brooks, Stephen and Wohlforth, William C. (2000/1). Power Globalisation and the End of the Cold War: Re-Evaluating a Landmark Case for Ideas. *International Security*, 25 (3), pp. 5–53.

Brown, Michael E., Lynn-Jones, Sean M. and Miller, Steven E. (eds) (1995). *The Perils of Anarchy: Contemporary Realism and International Security*. Cambridge, MA: MIT Press.

Bull, Hedley (1977). *The Anarchical Society*. London: Macmillan.

Buzan, Barry (1993). Rethinking System and Structure. In: Barry Buzan, Charles Jones and Richard Little, eds. *The Logic of Anarchy: Neorealism to Structural Realism*. New York: Columbia University Press, pp. 72–80.

Buzan, Barry (2003). Security Architecture in Asia: The Interplay of Regional and Global Levels. *Pacific Review*, 16 (2), pp. 143–173.

Buzan, Barry (2004). *The United States and the Great Powers: World Politics in the Twenty-First Century*. Oxford: Polity.

Byman, Daniel L. and Pollack, Kenneth M. (2001). Let Us Now Praise Great Men: Bring-ing the Statesman Back In. *International Security*, 25 (4), pp. 107–146.

Caverley, Jonathan D. (2010). Power and Democratic Weakness: Neo-Conservatism and Neoclassical Realism. *Millennium: Journal of International Studies*, 38 (3), pp. 593–614.

Cha, Victor (2001). Abandonment, Entrapment and Neoclassical Realism in Asia: The United States, Japan and Korea. *International Studies Quarterly*, 44 (2), pp. 261–291.

Cha, Victor (2002). Hawk Engagement and Preventive Defence on the Korean Peninsula. *International Security*, 27 (1), pp. 40–78.

Chapnick, Adam (1999). The Middle Power. *Canadian Foreign Policy*, 7 (2), pp. 73–82.

Christensen, Thomas J. (1996). *Useful Adversaries: Grand Strategy, Domestic Mobilisa-tion, and Sino-American Conflict, 1947–1958*. Princeton: Princeton University Press.

Cooper, Andrew F., Higgott, Richard A. and Nossal, Richard Kim (1993). *Relocating Middle Powers: Australia and Canada in a Changing World Order*. Canada: UBC Press.

Costalli, Stefano (2009). Power Over the Sea: The Relevance of Neoclassical Realism to Euro-Mediterranean Relations. *Mediterranean Politics*, 14 (3), pp. 323–342.

Cox, Robert (1989). Middlepowermanship, Japan and Future World Order. *International Journal*, 44 (4), pp. 823–862.

Danilovic, Vesna (2002). *When the Stakes are High: Deterrence and Conflict among Major Powers*. Ann Arbor: University of Michigan Press.

Davidson, Jason W. (2002). The Roots of Revisionism: Fascist Italy, 1992–39. *Security Studies*, 11 (4), pp. 125–159.

Davidson, Jason W. (2006). *The Origin of Revisionist and Status Quo States*. New York: Palgrave Macmillan.

Dueck, Colin (2005). Realism, Culture and Grand Strategy: Explaining America's Peculiar Path to World Power. *Security Studies*, 14 (2), pp. 195–231.

Dueck, Colin (2006). *Reluctant Crusaders: Power, Culture, and Change in American Grand Strategy*. Princeton: Princeton University Press.

Edelstein, David M. (2002). Managing Uncertainty: Beliefs about Intentions and the Rise of Great Powers. *Security Studies*, 12 (1), pp. 1–40.

Evans, Gareth and Grant, Bruce (1991). *Australia's Foreign Relations in the World of the 1990s*. Australia: Melbourne University Press.

Ferguson, Chaka (2011). Soft Power as the New Form: How the Chinese-Russian Strategic Partnership (Soft) Balances American Hegemony in the Era of Unipolarity. PhD thesis. Florida International University.

Gaddis, John L. (1987). *The Long Peace: Inquiries into the History of the Cold War*. New York: Oxford University Press.

Gilpin, Robert (1981). *War and Change in World Politics*. Cambridge: Cambridge University Press.

Glaser, Charles L. (2003). The Necessary and Natural Evolution of Structural Realism. In: John A. Vasquez and Colin Elman, eds. *Realism and the Balancing of Power: A New Debate*. Upper Saddle River: Prentice Hall, pp. 266–279.

Glenn, John (2009). Realism versus Strategic Culture: Competition and Collaboration? *International Studies Review*, 11 (3), pp. 523–551.

Goldstein, Avery (1997–8). Great Expectations: Interpreting China's Arrival. *International Security*, 22 (3), pp. 36–73.

Haglund, David G. and Onea, Tudor (2008). Sympathy for the Devil: Myths of Neoclassical Realism in Canadian Foreign Policy. *Canadian Foreign Policy*, 14 (2), pp. 53–66.

Hao, Yufan and Hou, Ying (2009). Chinese Foreign Policy Making: A Comparative Perspective. *Public Administration Review*, 69, pp. s136–s141.

Holbraad, Carsten (1984). *Middle Powers in International Politics*. UK: Macmillan Press.

Holmes, John (1976). *Canada: A Middle-Aged Power*. Canada: McClelland and Stewart.

Jervis, Robert (1978). Cooperation Under the Security Dilemma. *World Politics*, 30 (2), pp. 183–186.

Johnson, Paul M. (2005). Political Economy. Online. A Glossary of Political Economy terms. Available at: www.auburn.edu/~johnspm/gloss/political_economy (accessed 29 October 2011).

Juneau, Thomas (2010). Neoclassical Realist Strategic Analysis. In: Graduate Student Conference, European Consortium of Political Research. Online. Dublin, Ireland, 30 August–1 September 2010, pp. 1–28. Available at: www.ecprnet.eu/databases/conferences/papers/308.pdf (accessed 29 October 2011).

Keohane, Robert O. (1969). Lilliputians Dilemmas: Small States in International Politics. *International Organization*, 23 (2), pp. 291–310.

Kitchen, Nicholas (2010). Systemic Pressures and Domestic Ideas: A Neoclassical Realist Model of Grand Strategy Formation. *Review of International Studies*, 36 (1), pp. 117–143.

Krasner, Stephen (1978). *Defending the National Interest: Raw Materials Investments and U.S. Foreign Policy*. Princeton: Princeton University Press.

Layne, Christopher (2006). *The Peace of Illusions: American Grand Strategy from 1940 to the Present*. Ithaca: Cornell University Press.

Lobell, Steven E. (2003). *The Challenge of Hegemony: Grand Strategy, Trade and Domestic Politics*. Ann Arbor: University of Michigan Press.

McAllister, James (2002). *No Exit: America and the German Problem, 1943–1954*. Ithaca: Cornell University.

Mastanduno, Michael, Lake, David A. and Ikenberry, John G. (1989). Towards a Realist Theory of State Action. *International Studies Quarterly*, 33 (4), pp. 457–474.

Morgenthau, Hans J. (1948). *Politics Among Nations: The Struggle for Power and Peace*, 1st edn. New York: Alfred A. Knopf.

Posen, Barry R. and Ross, Andrew L. (1996/7). Competing Visions for US Grand Strategy. *International Security*, 21 (3), pp. 5–53.

Rathbun, Brian (2008). A Rose by Any Other Name: Neoclassical Realism as the Logical and Necessary Extension of Structural Realism. *Security Studies*, 17 (2), pp. 294–321.

Ripsman, Norrin M. (2001). The Curious Case of German Rearmament: Democracy and Foreign Security Policy. *Security Studies*, 10 (2), pp. 1–47.

Ripsman, Norrin M. (2002). *Peacemaking by Democracies: The Effect of State Autonomy on the Post-World War Settlements*. University Park: Pennsylvania State University Press.

Ripsman, Norrin M., Taliaferro, Jeffrey W. and Lobell, Steven E. (2009). Conclusion: The State of Neoclassical Realism. In: Steven E. Lobell, Norrin M. Ripsman and Jeffrey W. Taliaferro, eds. *Neoclassical Realism, the State, and Foreign Policy*. Cambridge: Cambridge University Press, pp. 282–287.

Rose, Gideon (1998). Neoclassical Realism and Theories of Foreign Policy. *World Politics*, 51 (1), pp. 144–172.

Rosenstein-Rodan, P. (1943). The Problem of Industrialization of Eastern and South-Eastern Europe. *Economic Journal*, 53 (210/211), pp. 202–211.

Schmidt, Brian C. (2004). Realism as Tragedy. *Review of International Studies*, 30 (3), pp. 427–441.

Schweller, Randall R. (1994). Bandwagoning for Profit: Bringing the Revisionist State Back In. *International Security*, 19 (1), pp. 72–107.

Schweller, Randall R. (1997). New Realist Research on Alliances: Refining, Not Refuting Waltz's Balancing Proposition. *American Political Science Review*, 91 (4), pp. 927–930.

Schweller, Randall R. (1998). *Deadly Imbalances: Tripolarity and Hitler's Strategy of World Conquest*. New York: Columbia University Press.

Schweller, Randall R. (2001). The Twenty Years' Crisis, 1919–39: Why a Concert Didn't Arise. In: Colin Elman and Mirium Fendius Elman, eds. *Bridges and Boundaries: Historians, Political Scientists and the Study of International Relations*. Cambridge, MA: MIT Press, pp. 181–212.

Schweller, Randall L. (2003). The Progressiveness of Neoclassical Realism. In: Colin Elman and Mirium Fendius Elman, eds. *Progress in International Relations Theory: Appraising the Field*. Cambridge, MA: MIT Press, pp. 311–347.

Schweller, Randall L. (2004). Unanswered Threats: A Neoclassical Realist Theory of Underbalancing. *International Security*, 29 (2), pp. 159–201.

Schweller, Randall L. (2006) *Unanswered Threats: Political Constraints on the Balance of Power*. Princeton: Princeton University Press.

Segal, Gerald (1999). Does China Matter. *Foreign Affairs*, 75 (5), pp. 24–36.

Snyder, Jack L. (1991). *Myths of Empire: Domestic Politics and International Ambition*. Ithaca: Cornell University Press.

Sterling-Folker, Jennifer (1997). Realist Environment, Liberal Process, and Domestic-Level Variables. *International Studies Quarterly*, 41 (1), pp. 1–26.

Sterling-Folker, Jennifer (2002a). *Theories of International Cooperation and the Primacy of Anarchy: Explaining US International Monetary Policy Making after Bretton Woods*. New York: State University of New York Press.

Sterling-Folker, Jennifer (2002b). Realism and the Constructivist Challenge: Rejecting, Reconstructing or Rereading. *International Studies Review*, 4 (1), pp. 73–97.

Sterling-Folker, Jennifer (2004). Realist-Constructivism and Morality. *International Studies Review*, 6 (2), pp. 341–343.

Taliaferro, Jeffrey W. (2004). *Balancing Risks: Great Power Intervention in the Periphery*. Ithaca: Cornell University Press.

Taliaferro, Jeffrey W. (2006). State Building for Future Wars: Neoclassical Realism and the Resource Extractive State. *Security Studies*, 15 (3), pp. 464–495.

Taliaferro, Jeffrey W., Lobell, Steven E. and Ripsman, Norrin M. (2009). Introduction: Neoclassical Realism, the State, and Foreign Policy. In Steven E. Lobell, Norrin M. Ripsman and Jeffrey W. Taliaferro, eds. *Neoclassical Realism, the State, and Foreign Policy*. Cambridge: Cambridge University Press, pp. 1–41.

Van Evera, Stephen (1990–1). Primed for Peace: Europe After the Cold War. *International Security*, 15 (3), pp. 14–16.

Vasquez, John (1997). The Realist Paradigm and Degenerative versus Progressive Research Programs. *American Political Science Review*, 91 (4), pp. 899–912.

Walt, Stephen M. (1987). *The Origins of Alliances*. Ithaca: Cornell University Press.

Waltz, Kenneth N. (1959). *Man, the State, and War: A Theoretical Analysis*. New York: Columbia University Press.

Waltz, Kenneth N. (1979). *Theory of International Politics*, 1st edn. Boston: McGraw-Hill.

Waltz, Kenneth N. (2003). Evaluating Theories. In: John A. Vasquez and Colin Elman, eds. *Realism and the Balance of Power: A New Debate*. Upper Saddle River: Prentice Hall, pp. 49–57.

Weingast, Barry R. and Wittman, Donald A. (2006). *The Oxford Handbook of Political Economy*. Oxford: Oxford University Press.

Weiss, Moritz (2009). Power and Signals: Explaining the German Approach to European Security. *Journal of International Relations and Development*, 12 (3), pp. 317–348.

Wohlforth, William C. (1993). *The Elusive Balance: Power and Perceptions during the Cold War*. Ithaca: Cornell University Press.

Wohlforth, William C. (1994–5). Realism and the End of the Cold War. *International Security*, 19 (3), pp. 91–129.

Wohlforth, William C. (2003). Measuring Power—and the Power of Theories. In: John A. Vasquez and Colin Elman, eds. *Realism and the Balancing of Power: A New Debate*. Upper Saddle River: Prentice Hall, pp. 250–279.

Zakaria, Fareed (1992). Realism and Domestic Politics: A Review Essay. *International Security*, 17 (1), pp. 177–198.

Zakaria, Fareed (1998). *From Wealth to Power: The Unusual Origins of America's World Role*. Princeton: Princeton University Press.

2 India and China in Africa and West Africa

The chapter is divided into four sections. Section I compares and contrasts India and China, and discusses the importance of India and China in the global arena. It also discusses the rationale for India's and China's engagement with Africa. Section II discusses the importance of the oil industry in West Africa. It illustrates that despite the fact that West African reserves are Lilliputian relative to reserves in the Persian Gulf states, West Africa has become a significant player in the global oil industry. Section III discusses the prevalent literature on India and China in Africa. It outlines the prevalent discourse on China in Africa followed by India in Africa and highlights the comparative aspects of India and China in Africa in the existing literature. It then looks at India and China respectively in West Africa, in the oil industry in West Africa and compares and contrasts India and China in the oil industry in West Africa. Section IV discusses the gap in the existing literature and provides a rationale for undertaking the research.

I

India and China, with their phenomenal growth rates, are surging ahead as world economic powers. While China has experienced double-digit growth since opening up its economy in 1979 under the leadership of Deng Xiaoping,[1] India has lagged behind. India has been growing at an average of 6 per cent from 1991 to 2000 and approximately 7–8 per cent since 2001. Both India and China are emerging and rising powers in the global arena. Both are members of BRICS – an acronym for emerging economies – coined by Jim O'Neill from prestigious financial house Goldman Sachs. India and China are also members of the G20 – the Group of 20 Finance Ministers and Governors of Central Banks from 20 major economies: 19 countries plus the EU. Additionally, India and China are members of the BASIC group of countries (BRICS sans Russia), a group of four large developing countries. They are also the two most populated countries in the world, sharing a long and respected history of early civilisations and a colonial past that became independent around the same time: India in 1947 and China in 1949. In the 1950s, they were in the forefront of the Non-Aligned Movement (NAM) and proposed the five principles of peaceful coexistence or

'Panchsheel'. These five principles are the cornerstone of India's and China's foreign policy.

The 'Asian Drivers' have turned to Africa and Africa's economy stands to be impacted in various ways due to the increasing interaction with the 'Asian Giants' (Goldstein *et al.*, 2006; Broadman and Isik, 2007). India and China have turned to Africa to quench their thirst for natural resources, especially oil,[2] to fuel their industrialisation process and catch up with the West (Rocha, 2007), new markets and commercial opportunities and for political and economic influence in Africa (Lake *et al.*, 2006; Brookes, 2007). Tables 2.1, 2.2 and 2.3 depict the production, consumption and proven oil reserves of India and China respectively from 2001 to 2014. Tables 2.1 and 2.2 show that although oil production in India and China has increased over the time period 2001–14, consumption has increased at a much faster pace. The shortfall in production had led to an increase in oil imports in both India and China. India, the fifth largest importer of oil in 2013, became the third largest oil importer[3] (next only to the United States and China) in June 2015 (Kennedy, 2015) and imports approximately 70–75 per cent of its oil consumption (BMI, 2016). China, on the other hand, is the second largest consumer of oil after the United States (Kennedy, 2015) and imports approximately 50–60 per cent of its oil consumption. Moreover, according to Table 2.3, the proven oil reserves of India have declined and China's oil reserves have risen at a very slow pace since 1994. The reserves to production ratio (R/P) illustrate that if India and China keep producing at the present rate, they will exhaust their oil reserves in approximately 18 years and 12 years, respectively. However, demand is forecast to keep growing in India and at a slower pace in China due to decline in economic growth. Both India and China

Table 2.1 Oil production in India and China from 2001 to 2014

Country/year (thousand barrels per day)	India	China	World
2001[a]	727	3310	74,767
2002[a]	753	3351	74,493
2003[a]	756	3406	76,860
2004	773	3486	80,938
2005	737	3642	81,963
2006	760	3711	82,417
2007	768	3742	82,220
2008	803	3814	82,847
2009	816	3805	81,149
2010	882	4077	83,190
2011	916	4074	83,980
2012	906	4155	86,150
2013	906	4216	86,579
2014	895	4246	88,673

Source: BP (2015: 8).

Note
a BP (2012: 8).

Table 2.2 Oil consumption in India and China from 2001 to 2014

Country/year (thousand barrels per day)	India	China	World
2001[a]	2228	4859	77,245
2002[a]	2376	5262	78,187
2003[a]	2420	5771	79,686
2004	2556	6740	83,107
2005	2606	6923	84,411
2006	2737	7437	85,238
2007	2941	7817	86,741
2008	3077	7937	86,115
2009	3237	8212	85,066
2010	3319	9266	87,867
2011	3488	9791	88,974
2012	3685	10,231	89,846
2013	3727	10,664	91,243
2014	3846	11,056	92,086

Source: BP (2015: 9).

Note
a BP (2012: 9).

Table 2.3 Proven oil reserves of India and China from 1994 to 2014 (thousand million barrels)

Country	At the end of 1994	At the end of 2004	At the end of 2013	At the end of 2014	Share of total reserves (%)	Reserves to production (R/P) ratio
China	16.3	15.5	18.5	18.5	1.1	11.9
India	5.8	5.6	5.7	5.7	0.3	17.6
World	1118.0	1366.2	1701.0	1700.1	100	52.5

Source: BP (2015: 6).

rely heavily on the Middle East for oil. The growing turmoil and political instability in the Middle East has necessitated that India and China look for alternative sources of oil in other parts of the world, especially West Africa.

India and China both vie for political influence in Africa, albeit for different reasons. Both seek the support of African countries in their pursuit of a multipolar world, in their fight against US hegemony (Volman, 2009). Africa's 54 nations make up more than one-fourth of the 192 UN member states and the African Union (AU) is an emerging important player in the international arena. The continent is the largest single regional grouping of states which have a propensity for 'bloc voting' in multilateral institutions like the UN and its multifarious agencies. African states have extended support for China's multilateral diplomacy. For instance, China is against Japan becoming a permanent member of the UNSC and, in 2005, China was able to prevent Japan from becoming a permanent member of the UNSC using AU's support. During the election of new Director General for the World Health Organization (WHO) in 2006, nine African countries among the 34 countries on the WHO Executive Board voted in favour of Dr Margaret Chan, a Chinese national, and Dr Chan was elected as the Director General of the WHO (Zhang, 2011).

However, India and China also differ in certain respects. India aspires to become a permanent member of the UNSC and sit at the high table as a major global power. China, on the other hand, seeks political support of African countries to shield itself against Western criticism of its human rights record (Cheng and Shi, 2009). During the past decade, African states that hold 15 of the 53 seats at the UN Commission on Human Rights have played a prominent role in frustrating efforts by some Western countries to bring about a formal condemnation of China's human rights record in the Commission 11 times (Zhang, 2011). It also seeks the support of African countries for equal status as a major power and to promote its status as a key player in world affairs (Cheng and Shi, 2009).

II

Africa has regained significance since the beginning of the new millennium because of its increasingly important role as a global supplier of oil, gas and non-fuel minerals, and nations vying for economic and political influence to access these resources (Rocha, 2007). The region has regained significance in the last decade not only because of oil and natural gas reserves but the quality and commercial advantages that it offers to IOCs (Frynas and Paulo, 2007).

According to Table 2.4, the countries in the Middle East contain approximately 48 per cent of the proven global oil reserves, i.e. approximately 810.7 billion barrels of oil. Africa, on the other hand, constitutes 7.6 per cent of proven global oil reserves or around 129.2 billion barrels, and West Africa has around 55 billion barrels or approximately 45 per cent of total African reserves. While oil reserves in Persian Gulf states eclipse the reserves in African states, the proven oil reserves of Libya (48.4 billion barrels) and Nigeria (37.1 billion barrels) are larger than those of China (18.5 billion barrels), Brazil (16.2 billion barrels) and India (5.7 billion barrels), and dwarf those of the UK (3.0 billion barrels) and many important petro-states such as Qatar (25.7 billion barrels), Mexico (11.1 billion barrels) and Azerbaijan (7 billion barrels).

Another reason for Africa's importance is that proven oil reserves have expanded at a higher rate relative to the rest of the world and especially countries in the Middle East. Table 2.4 illustrates that proven reserves in Africa have increased from 65.0 billion barrels in 1994 to 107.6 billion barrels in 2004 and to 129.2 billion barrels in 2014. This represents a 65 per cent increase from 1994 to 2004 and approximately 20 per cent increase from 2004 to 2014. In contrast, the world proven reserves have increased at a very slow rate from 1118.0 billion barrels in 1994 to 1366.2 billion barrels in 2004 and a faster rate to 1700.1 billion barrels in 2011. This represents a 19.5 per cent increase from 1994 to 2004 and a 24.5 per cent increase from 2004 to 2014.[4] The rate of growth of

Table 2.4 Total proven oil reserves from 1991 to 2014 in billion barrels

Country	Proven oil reserves				
	At end of 1994	At end of 2004	At end of 2013	At end of 2014	Share of total (%)
US	29.6	29.3	48.5	48.5	2.9
Canada	48.1	179.6	172.9	172.9	10.2
Mexico	49.8	14.8	11.1	11.1	0.7
Brazil	5.4	11.2	15.6	16.2	1.0
Venezuela	64.9	79.7	298.3	298.3	17.5
Russia	115.1	105.5	105	103.2	6.1
Azerbaijan	1.2	7.0	7.0	7.0	0.4
UK	4.3	4.0	3.0	3.0	0.2
Iran	94.3	132.7	157.8	157.8	9.3
Iraq	100.0	155.0	150.0	150.0	8.8
Kuwait	96.5	101.5	101.5	101.5	6.0
Oman	5.1	5.6	5.0	5.2	0.3
Qatar	3.5	26.9	25.1	25.7	1.5
Saudi Arabia	261.4	264.3	265.9	267.0	15.7
Syria	2.7	3.2	2.5	2.5	0.1
UAE	98.1	97.8	97.8	97.8	5.8
Yemen	2.0	3.0	3.0	3.0	0.2
Other Middle East	0.1	0.3	0.3	0.2	<0.05
Total Middle East	**663.6**	**750.1**	**808.7**	**810.7**	**47.7**
Algeria	10.0	11.8	12.2	12.2	0.7
Angola	3.0	9.0	12.7	12.7	0.7
Chad	–	0.9	1.5	1.5	0.1
Rep. of Congo (Brazzaville)	1.4	1.5	1.6	1.6	0.1
Egypt	3.9	3.6	3.9	3.6	0.2
Equatorial Guinea	0.3	1.8	1.7	1.1	0.1
Gabon	1.4	2.2	2.0	2.0	0.1
Libya	22.8	39.1	48.4	48.4	2.8
Nigeria	21.0	35.9	37.1	37.1	2.2
Sudan	0.3	0.6	1.5	1.5	0.1
South Sudan	–	–	3.5	3.5	0.2
Tunisia	0.3	0.7	0.4	0.4	<0.05
Other Africa	0.6	0.6	3.7	3.7	0.2
Total Africa	**65.0**	**107.6**	**130.1**	**129.2**	**7.6**
Total World	**1118.0**	**1366.2**	**1701.0**	**1700.1**	**100**

Source: BP (2015: 6).

proven reserves is much slower in the Middle East countries, with reserves growing at 11.5 per cent from 1994 to 2004 and at 8 per cent from 2004 to 2014. Analysts assert that there is a possibility of the existence of significant undiscovered oil reserves in Africa. According to Goldwyn (2009) and Hanson (2008), oil production in Africa can increase significantly in the next 20 years if the continent is able to fully realise its potential. Thus Africa can be a major global provider of oil and enhance energy security by diversifying sources of energy supply.

Even though approximately 48 per cent of the world's proven oil supplies are located in the Middle East, access to the nationalised oil resources in Saudi Arabia (267.0 billion barrels – Table 2.4) has been restricted for decades and a large chunk of the proven reserves are likely to remain underexploited for some time to come. Consequently, approximately 75 per cent of the world's oil reserves are closed to foreign equity investment. Additionally, countries with major oil reserves like Russia and Venezuela have also limited the opportunities for foreign investors to invest in their oil industries (Downs, 2007). In contrast, African states, especially countries in West Africa like Nigeria, Angola, Gabon, Ghana, Equatorial Guinea, Chad and others, have been keen on developing oil production at a fast speed and have allowed multinational firms to enter, which is demonstrated by the projected increases in African oil production.

According to an estimate provided by the US Department of Energy, during 2002–2025, oil production in Africa is to increase from 8.6 to 16.4 million barrels per day (mbpd), i.e. an increase of approximately 91 per cent. "While the world oil production capacity is predicted to grow by 53 per cent between 2002 and 2025, from 80 to 122.2 mbpd" (cited in Klare and Volman, 2006: 611), oil production in Africa will be growing faster relative to the rest of the world.

Table 2.5 illustrates that oil production globally has risen by approximately 18.6 per cent. It has increased to approximately 88.68 mbpd in 2014 from 74.8 mbpd in 2001. On the other hand, oil production in Africa increased by approximately 22 per cent from 7.9 mbpd to 10 mbpd. With respect to West African countries, oil production has increased at a much faster pace until 2010, although there has been a decline in oil production from 2010 to 2014. From 2001 to 2014 in Angola, oil production has increased from 742,000 barrels per day (tbpd) to 1.712 mbpd, a rise of nearly 130 per cent, and in Equatorial Guinea from 171 tbpd to 281 tbpd, an increase of approximately 64 per cent. In Chad, oil production has increased by approximately 225 per cent, increasing from 24 tbpd barrels to 78 tbpd.

Verma (2012a) avers that

> West Africa has also become attractive due to the predominance of new off-shore discoveries. Deep water drilling is exorbitantly expensive and risky. This has restricted development to a handful of companies with the techno-logy and wherewithal to manage the exploration risks. Offshore drilling also partly mitigates political risk, especially in conflict-ridden Africa, by enabling the operator to conduct business miles away from the host country's mainland. In Nigeria, all new discoveries and production are offshore and Angola's oil and gas reserves are offshore.

According to Goldwyn (2009), it is estimated that offshore oil production will account for the overall oil production in Sub-Saharan Africa, and Nigeria's and Angola's contribution will be approximately 85 per cent. Oil companies are

Table 2.5 Oil production from 2000 to 2014 in thousand barrels per day

Country	Year														
	2001[a]	2002[a]	2003[a]	2004	2005	2006	2007	2008	2009	2010	2011	2012	2013	2014	2014 share of total (%)
US	7669	7626	7400	7250	6897	6827	6860	6784	7260	7556	7861	8904	10069	11644	12.3
Canada	2677	2858	3004	3080	3041	3208	3290	3207	3202	3332	3515	3740	3977	4292	5.0
Mexico	3568	3593	3795	3830	3766	3869	3479	3165	2978	2959	2940	2911	2875	2784	3.2
Brazil	1337	1499	1555	1543	1713	1809	1833	1899	2029	2137	2193	2149	2114	2346	2.9
Azerbaijan	301	311	313	309	405	646	856	895	1014	1023	919	872	877	848	1.0
Russia	6989	7622	8460	9335	9598	9818	10044	9950	10139	10366	10516	10640	10777	10838	10.7
Venezuela	3142	2895	2554	3305	3308	3336	3.23	3.222	3.033	2.838	2.734	2.704	2.687	2.719	3.3
UK	2476	2463	2257	2064	1843	1666	1659	1555	1477	1361	1116	949	867	850	0.9
Iran	3825	3580	4002	4201	4184	4260	4303	4396	4249	4352	4373	3742	3525	3614	4.0
Iraq	2523	2116	1344	2030	1833	1999	2143	2428	2452	2490	2801	3116	3141	3285	3.8
Kuwait	2181	2027	2362	2523	2668	2737	2663	2786	2511	2562	2915	3172	3135	3123	3.6
Oman	960	904	824	783	777	738	710	757	813	865	885	918	942	943	1.1
Qatar	754	764	879	1082	1149	1241	1279	1449	1416	1655	1850	1968	1998	1982	2.0
Saudi Arabia	9158	8877	10,107	10,458	10,931	10,671	10,268	10,663	9663	10,075	11,144	11,635	11,393	11,505	12.9
Syria	581	548	527	487	448	421	404	406	401	385	353	171	59	33	<0.05%
UAE	2551	2390	2695	2836	2922	3099	301	3026	2723	2895	3325	3406	3648	3712	4.0
Yemen	455	457	448	424	421	387	341	315	307	306	241	190	150	145	0.2
Other Middle East	47	48	48	48	185	182	194	192	192	192	201	183	207	213	0.2
Total Middle East	**23,547**	**21,710**	**23,236**	**24,873**	**25,518**	**25,734**	**25,305**	**26,417**	**24,727**	**25,777**	**28,088**	**28,502**	**28,198**	**28,155**	**31.7**
Algeria	1562	1680	1852	1921	1990	1979	1992	1969	1775	1689	1642	1537	1485	1525	1.6
Angola	742	905	870	1103	1404	1421	1684	1901	1804	1863	1726	1784	1799	1712	2.0
Chad		—	24	168	173	153	144	127	118	122	114	101	83	78	0.1
Rep. of Congo (Brazzaville)	234	238	217	217	239	271	221	235	269	294	302	289	281	281	0.3
Egypt	758	751	749	701	672	679	698	715	730	725	714	715	714	717	0.8
Equatorial Guinea	177	230	266	351	358	342	350	347	307	274	252	272	267	281	0.3
Gabon	301	295	240	273	270	242	246	240	241	255	254	245	236	236	0.3
Libya	1427	1375	1485	1623	1745	1816	1820	1820	1652	1656	479	1509	988	498	0.6
Nigeria	2274	2103	2263	2430	2502	2392	2265	2113	2211	2509	2450	2395	2302	2361	2.7
Sudan	217	241	265	291	294	356	483	457	475	462	291	103	115	109	0.1
South Sudan												31	99	159	0.2
Tunisia	71	74	68	71	73	70	97	89	83	80	68	67	61	53	0.1
Other Africa	134	135	138	165	172	224	193	190	183	167	232	227	254	252	0.3
Total Africa	**7897**	**8028**	**8436**	**9313**	**9891**	**9945**	**10,194**	**10,203**	**9849**	**10,095**	**8524**	**9275**	**8684**	**8263**	**9.3**
Total World	**74,767**	**74,493**	**76,860**	**80,938**	**81,963**	**82,417**	**82,220**	**82,847**	**81,149**	**83,190**	**83,980**	**86,150**	**86,579**	**88,673**	**100**

Source: BP (2015: 8).

Note
a BP (2012: 8).

likely to invest approximately US$485 billion in E&P during 2005 to 2030. It is estimated that West Africa will account for nearly 45 per cent of the gross capital expenditures for deepwater oil development worldwide. "Gross deep-water capital expenditure in West Africa between 2008–15 will exceed that spent in Latin America, the Gulf of Mexico, the North Atlantic, and the Asia-Pacific" (Goldwyn, 2009: 70). Another reason why West African oil is attractive is the absence of Organization of the Petroleum Exporting Countries (OPEC) quotas. Gabon, Equatorial Guinea, Chad and other countries are not OPEC members. Consequently, IOCs can sell any amount of crude they want as stipulated in the agreement with the government in the host country (Goldwyn and Morrison, 2004).

III

This section discusses some key aspects of the existing literature on China in Africa, India in Africa, China in West Africa and India in West Africa. It also discusses India and China in Africa and in West Africa in a comparative perspective.

China in Africa

Tomes of literature and scholarly work are dedicated to China's presence in Africa and little attention has been given to India's interaction in Africa, or it has simply been bypassed in the wake of the Chinese juggernaut. There are myriad books, journal articles and reports from think-tanks on China in Africa. In the past, scholarly work on China and Africa has focused on the role played by China and its support in championing the cause of freedom struggles, liberation movements and the fight against imperialism in Africa, to promote China's multipolar world view, defending the PRC's positions in the international forum such as the UN, and its stance against US global dominance. Scholarly work also discussed Chinese aid and large-scale projects undertaken by China as a mark of China–Africa solidarity as members of 'Third World'.[5] It also dealt with the Sino-Soviet rivalry in Africa and attempts by China to isolate Taiwan diplomatically in Africa under the aegis of 'Dollar Diplomacy'.

Since the beginning of the new century, a vast literature on China in Africa focuses on the developmental impact of China in Africa, whether it is a coloniser, partner or a competitor. The emphasis has been on China's interaction with African countries in the resource extractive sector, mainly oil, minerals and timber. Scholars, policy-makers, commentators and journalists have debated and denounced China's callous destruction of the environment and exploitation of natural resources, especially oil and minerals (Farooki, 2011; Zhang, 2011). Yet for centuries such practices had been the norm for the US and Western colonial and imperialist powers (Marks, 2007; Bräutigam, 2009a; Taylor 2009). Numerous scholars have discussed the impact and costs and benefits of China's interaction on development and human rights in African countries in general and in different sectors in Africa, and the West's response to China's engagement in Africa. Alden (2007) investigates the expanding relationship between China and Africa and assesses the content and the nature of China's foreign policy in the continent – whether China is a partner, coloniser or a competitor. It also examines the response of African countries and society to Chinese presence and foreign policy, and the impact of Chinese activism in Africa on commercial and normative Western concerns. Alden contends that the three are not incommensurable and IR contains elements of both self and mutual interest. Bräutigam and Tang (2011) discuss Chinese efforts to construct economic co-operation zones in Africa and the rationale and background for their construction. Employing Egypt as a case study, the paper asserts that this provides a distinctive model of economic co-operation in Africa. Despite the fact that there are serious economic, social and political challenges, the unique co-operation may sow seeds for sustainable industrial growth. The edited book by Robert Rotberg (2008) explores China's overall strategy in Africa and China's interest in military and security relations, energy, aid and human rights concerns. The book has a pessimistic outlook. It elucidates that China's growing presence could be parasitic such that it might further augment China's economic power and exacerbate poverty and instability in Africa. The edited volume by Guerrero and Manji (2008) provides a perspective on the social, economic and environmental impact of China's expanding role in Africa. It also provides diverse views on the concomitant challenges faced by Africa as a result of China's rise as a global economic power. It explores and states that aid, trade and investments from China present opportunities and threats for both Africa and the 'global south'. Van Dijk (2009) discusses China's expanding sphere of activities in Africa, especially in Sub-Saharan Africa, and discusses China's development aid, investments and trade policy relative to Europe and the United States in oil-producing countries such as Angola, Nigeria and Sudan, and mineral-rich countries like Zambia. Foster *et al.* (2009) examine and compare China's growing role in financing infrastructure with Organisation for Economic Co-operation and Development (OECD) in Sub-Saharan Africa. They discuss the distribution of resources geographically, the different types of infrastructure employed, the size and the terms of finance for the projects, and the various methods through which the finance is procured. Sautman and Yang (2007) argue that whether it is the 'Beijing Consensus' or aid and migration, China's engagement with Africa makes China seem like a lesser evil compared to the West regarding the former's support for Africa's development and respect for African countries. They contend that, unlike the West, China is not obstructing development in the poor countries in Africa. Mol (2011) evaluates the present behaviour of myriad arms of the Chinese government and Chinese enterprises in Sub-Saharan Africa by employing the World-Systems Theory idea of 'environmentally unequal exchange' between rising global powers and marginal economies. Mol reaches the conclusion that the theory is only able to provide an incomplete explanation. Although environmental norms condition and guide the behaviour of Chinese government authorities and enterprises, it is too early for China to become the 'green' exemplar globally.

Scholars, policy-makers, journalists and the intelligentsia have chastised China for political and economic support for regimes responsible for crimes against humanity and for human right violations, for instance, Darfur in Sudan and in Angola, and dictatorial regimes like Zimbabwe. China (and India) follows a policy of non-intervention in the domestic affairs of other countries, which is welcomed by African countries. Taylor (2006) provides a comprehensive assessment of relations between China and Southern African countries. He avers that as China's demand for energy sources soars, a number of countries in Africa want a partner that does not want to or tries to impose political conditions on economic relations, and is not greatly affected by demands of transparency and democracy. Holslag (2011) argues that China did not perceive the five coups in Africa from 2003 to 2010 as a threat to its interests. However, Beijing accepted that instability was part and parcel of doing business in Africa. China remains sceptical of Western liberal democracy as a panacea for instability and was extremely suspicious of efforts by the West to promote liberal political standards. It seems that China is guided by the strategy of accepting political realities and adapting itself rather than trying to change them. Jakobson (2009) points out that, in Africa, there is a conflict between China's policy of non-intervention and its goal to be recognised as a responsible international stakeholder, and in the future, China will find it extremely difficult to reconcile the two. Thus, it is impossible for China to pursue a set of foreign policy goals that take into account all of its national interests in Africa. However, China's leadership is aware that its foreign policy is evolving and it is thinking of ways to overcome the non-interference conundrum.

Literature on China in Africa also focuses on Chinese aid in Africa, and whether it is malign or benign in its intent, implementation and political and economic consequences. Wang (2007), in an International Monetary Fund (IMF) working paper, provides an assessment of China's economic engagement in Africa and identifies the factors responsible for the burgeoning China–Africa relationship. The paper concludes that commercial ties between China and Africa trump Chinese aid because the volume of trade and investment has gained significance in volume terms relative to aid. Bräutigam (2009a, 2009b) undertakes a novel study of Chinese aid to Africa. She is sanguine regarding China's aid and postulates that although China's aid programme is large and growing, it is not enormous and still dwarfed by traditional Western donors. She contends that China's definition of foreign aid does not meet the paradigms of Official Development Assistance (ODA) set by the Development Assistance Committee (DAC) of the OECD. China's lack of transparency about its aid and export credits raises suspicions and concerns in the West but this is no different to the Western banks and corporations that have long maintained secrecy about their deals with African leaders. Nordtveit (2011) analyses China's novel approaches of aid to Africa in the education sector through a case study of Cameroon and notes, first, a strong shift from political engagement to more economic engagement by both countries since the Forum on China-Africa Cooperation (FOCAC) in 2000. Second, China's aid has increased significantly and it is becoming a substantial donor in the education sector in Cameroon but there are particular problems and weaknesses related to rapid growth in China's aid. Third, China seeks to enhance co-operation with other aid agencies and education donors in Cameroon like the DAC. It is willing to participate in information sharing, co-financing projects and co-ordinating with multilateral and bilateral initiatives. However, this is not the case in all African countries. In Kenya, China had a different discourse relative to other donors – a discourse of non-interference in internal affairs and mutual gain, and it was not interested in synchronising its procedures with other donors (King, 2010). According to King, only time will tell whether there is alignment in China's actions and vocabulary with the established donors or whether China will be able to maintain a divergent vocabulary.

Many scholars have also written on the China–Africa relationship with respect to China's own developmental experience and internal contradictions. Jiang (2009) asserts that China's own modernisation experience since 1978 is the guiding force behind individual entrepreneurs, Chinese companies and Chinese government actions in Africa. Thus, Chinese interactions with different African actors are reflective of China's contradictions during its development, and the disparate Chinese actors have multifarious incentives and objectives which affects their respective behaviour in Africa. Alden and Hughes (2009) expound the challenges faced by China in managing its convoluted relations with Africa, especially the structural factors that present disharmony and boost concord. The paper asserts that unlike traditional donors or investing countries which are influenced by non-governmental organisations (NGOs) and international NGOs, the leadership in China is unable to draw on the expertise of the NGOs and pressure groups because of the absence of a strong civil society. This explicates the inability of the leadership in China to find solutions to adverse criticisms of Chinese actions and engagement from the political opposition and civil society in Africa.

Literature on China in Africa also discusses the China–Taiwan battle for diplomatic recognition in Africa. Ever since the formation of China and Taiwan, the two have been divided by a fundamental and irreconcilable sovereignty dispute. An important objective of China's engagement with Africa was to isolate Taiwan diplomatically. Beijing aimed to achieve this through a diplomatic war and ending Taiwan's state-to-state relations with African countries (Zhu, 2010). This has been the underpinning of China's policy since 1963–4 when Premier Zhou Enlai toured Africa (Alden, 1997). The Chinese government's aim to deny space to Taiwan has been successful. The 'Dollar Diplomacy' employed by ROC that entailed financial support for friendly governments and modest aid and development programmes was dwarfed by China's willingness to use resources at its disposal to win the diplomatic war (Chao and Hsu, 2006). During 2006–13, only four countries in Africa – Burkina Faso, Swaziland, the Gambia and Sao Tomé and Príncipe – officially recognised Taiwan. In November 2013, Gambia severed relations with Taiwan but China did not establish formal ties with Gambia. However, China established relations with Gambia in March 2016. Some analysts say that China's rapprochement with Gambia has ended the diplomatic truce between PRC and ROC (Channel News Asia, 2016).

According to Taylor (2009), Alden *et al.* (2008), Tull (2008) and Beri (2007), the competition for international competition between Taiwan and Africa, although important in the past, has receded in significance for Beijing. According to Zhu (2010), since the diplomatic truce proposed by President Ma in 2008 and accepted by President Hu Jintao in 2009, the overt competition between China and Taiwan for international competition has ceased.

Another element of China in Africa focuses on how China may affect Western interests, particularly those of the United States. Some scholars aver that China's burgeoning economic and political engagement in Africa affects US economic and strategic interests (Brookes, 2007; Campbell, 2008; Cooke, 2008, 2009; Huang, 2008). This has translated into concerns in the United States about China's rise and Africa providing a new playing field where China and the United States are vying for economic, political and military supremacy.

However, some scholars argue that in Africa and in the oil industry in Africa, especially West Africa, the phrase 'Sino-US' rivalry is misleading. It is hyperbole, a misnomer and should be used with caution. This is because, first, China and the United States are not competing with each other politically and militarily in Africa and in the oil industry in Africa. Second, China does not have the intention and it is not in China's interests to compete politically and militarily with the United States globally. Third, even if China was competing with the United States politically and militarily, it is no match for the United States. China has a lot of catching up to do in Africa and in the oil industry in Africa as a whole and especially in West Africa.

Cooke (2009) asserts that not only are the aims and objectives of the United States and China in Africa (and in oil-producing African countries) different, but also the strategies to achieve those aims and objectives. In the new millennium, the principal source of US engagement in Africa has been its military. The main US objective in Africa is to provide assistance and security. Africa's economic potential and its trade or investment potential ranks second and a distant third respectively on its list of priorities in Africa (although the United States has a keen interest in the oil industry). Contrarily, China's economic strength is its principal basis of engagement in Africa and economic engagement is its primary means. Thus, the US military engagement in Africa far surpasses China's military presence in Africa (Pham, 2011).

Scholars like Lyman (2005) argue that despite the fact that China's activities do not threaten the United States, China's superlative economic growth alters the playing field in Africa in the economic and strategic realm. Cropley (2009) on the contrary points out that China still significantly lags behind the United States in its economic engagement in Africa. Although China narrowly eclipsed the United States to become Africa's largest trade partner in 2009, Chinese aid and investments in Africa are dwarfed by those of the United States and other OECD countries. Moreover, China neither has the intention nor the capacity to compete with the United States. Rather, China enjoys the stability provided by US military assistance programmes. Beijing aims to build a wide-ranging power base in Africa and obtain access to its strategic resources, and aims to avoid needless direct conflicts with the United States (Foot, 2006).

Scholars and policy-makers in Europe and the United States are alarmed and concerned by the rapid strides made by Chinese NOCs in the oil industry in Africa, particularly in West Africa. The conservative perception about China's NOCs in Africa is that they operate as a part of a very co-ordinated government strategy, and are able to gain access to oil in African countries because of the diplomatic, economic and political support from the government (Campbell, 2008; Chow, 2009).

Undoubtedly, Chinese investments in the oil industry in Africa and in West Africa have increased in the last two decades (Alessi and Hanson, 2012). Discerning fact from fiction, Goldwyn (2009) posits that Chinese NOCs are competing with, but not 'locking out', US (and Western) IOCs. Moreover, in terms of oil production, acreage and value of assets, Chinese NOCs lag behind the IOCs. Alessi and Hanson (2012) and Gill and Reilly (2007), among others, assert that contrary to prevailing perception, the operations of the Chinese NOCs are not reflective of a highly co-ordinated policy pursued by the Chinese government.

According to de Oliviera (2008), the notion of rivalry between Chinese NOCs and US IOCs is fallacious and has been exaggerated. China is not winning the competition, and lags behind the United States and Western countries in the hydrocarbon industry in Africa. Although the financial support provided by Beijing does give an advantage to Chinese NOCs, Beijing's support has not significantly altered the playing field in the oil industry in Africa. Additionally, even if China may threaten (not that it threatens) US interests in onshore E&P where less technical expertise is required, albeit by paying inflated prices for oil, Chinese NOCs are not competitive and do not pose a threat in the lucrative deep offshore areas. Chinese NOCs do not have the requisite cutting-edge technologies, large project management skills and capacity-building relative to IOCs. Thus, the IOCs are considered a more attractive option by African governments (Frynas and Paulo, 2007). Downs (2007) asserts that the NOCs backed by Beijing's financial muscle may test the IOCs if and when they acquire these capabilities or if they form a joint venture with companies that possess the technology and compete with the IOCs.

India in Africa

Relative to China in Africa, there is paucity of literature on India in Africa, but it is gaining currency. Various authors have focused on India–Africa co-operation in the struggle against colonialism, apartheid and other instances of political oppression. There is also a very rich literature examining South Asian Diasporas in East Africa and South Africa. Since the beginning of the twenty-first century, literature on India–Africa relations focuses on trade, aid and economic linkages and how it impacts the economic growth and development in Africa. Literature also exists on the Indian contribution to UN Peacekeeping Operations (UNPKO),

India's security focus on the Indian Ocean Rim (IOR) states and the Indian navy's anti-piracy operations in the Gulf of Aden. Beri (2003) avers that there is both transformation and continuity in India's policy towards Africa since the end of the Cold War. The policy is composed of five elements: enhancing economic co-operation; providing assistance to African armed forces; engaging with the Indian Diaspora; thwarting and fighting terrorism; and preserving peace. Beri opines that India should take advantage of its goodwill and employ a new partnership to further strengthen relations with Africa.

Since 2006, there has been a modest surge in writing on more contemporary interactions between India and Africa. Sheth (2008) examines the role of the Indian Diaspora, democracy and governance, the search for new markets and bilateral and multilateral co-operation in defence, maritime security, forestry, ship-building, pharmaceuticals, trade and commerce and knowledge industry in Indian–African relations. Mawdsley and McCann (2011) provide an overview of India in Africa and aver that India's role in Africa is going to increase. Drawing on a collection of case studies, they discuss India as an alternative development partner in the continent, India–East Africa economic linkages, identity and strategic instrumentality of the South Asian community in East Africa, civil society relations, diplomatic manoeuvring for energy security, development co-operation and aid, geopolitics, security and maritime strategy. Sinha (2010) opines that since the beginning of the new century, India and Africa are prepared more than ever to re-establish economic and political relationships to promote their mutual interests. The GoI attaches greater importance to economic relations as the basis of renewed India–Africa engagement. Moreover, India's recent experience in reducing its aid dependency and starting its own aid programme has played a central role in its foreign policy towards Africa and commercial interests have become rooted in assistance programmes offered by India.[6] Taylor (2012), in a similar vein, argues that the increasing salience of India's interest in Africa has important implications for Africa. He examines the historical, political and economic ties and India's aid to Africa, and asserts that this represents a further diversification of Africa's IR away from 'traditional' North–South linkages. This arguably provides a greater range of options for Africa.

Naidu (2010) asserts that India is in Africa to satisfy its resource needs which are vital to its industrialisation and modernisation. In the process, a new competition is being set in motion between India and China, on the one hand, and other Asian countries, on the other. Moreover, it is going to be hard to contain India because New Delhi represents what the West would like China to be. Modi (2010) examines the relationship between the publicly owned Export–Import (EXIM) Bank of India, the Indian state, the captains of major Indian corporations and the Indian private sector enterprises under the stewardship of the Confederation of Indian Industries (CII) in shaping the direction and content of India's growing engagement in Africa. Moreover, the influential Indian private sector is playing a critical role in India's engagement in Africa. Sharma and Mahajan (2007) scrutinise the key factors responsible for the growing engagement in the energy sector between India and China. They aver that India does not have a clearly defined energy policy with respect to Africa. Nonetheless, India's interests in the energy sector in the continent can be discerned at three levels, i.e. the geopolitical arena, trade and commerce, and foreign policy or diplomacy realm.

Vines and Oruitemeka (2007, 2008) and Vines (2011) chart the evolving relations between India and other African countries in the IOR. They aver that this strategy is expanding. Moreover, this strategy, in addition to commercial linkages as in other African countries, is also supported and strengthened by India's 2004 maritime doctrine. Due to concerns about China's expansion in recent years, India wants to expand its defence and commercial engagement with countries like Madagascar, Mozambique, the Seychelles and Mauritius. India's blocking of China's access to IBSA (group comprising India, Brazil and South Africa) is a part of this policy. Rooyen (2010) and other scholars discuss India's role and rationale in UNPKO in Africa. According to Verma (2012b), India, with 9300 peacekeepers, is the third largest contributor and has been a part of all the UNPKOs – in Sudan, DRC, Liberia, Ivory Coast, Burundi, Angola, Ethiopia, Namibia, Rwanda, Somalia and Mozambique. "In future, India may well develop criteria that require a greater return on investment than has been the case over the last half century. A more tempered approach particularly in view of India's global aspirations seems plausible."

India and China in Africa

Newspapers like the *Financial Times*, the *Guardian*, and newspapers in India, China and African countries and others, news channels like the BBC, and articles and reports by independent researchers, think-tanks and international organisations also touch on comparative analysis of India and China in Africa. Goldstein *et al.* (2006) give a detailed account of how India and China are influencing the growth patterns of African countries, particularly countries exporting oil and commodities.

Broadman and Isik (2007) take a benign view and aver that India and China are providing opportunities for African countries to supply goods and services, and process commodities to the two countries, which is in stark contrast to Africa's relations with the developed countries. Morrissey and Zgovu (2011) compare and contrast India's and China's trade with Sub-Saharan Africa, investigate the developmental impact and provide policy recommendations to enhance growth and development in Sub-Saharan Africa. Cheru and Obi (2010a) provide a detailed discussion of the disparate aspects of the varied roles assumed by India and China in Africa. The Pan-African and multi-sectoral coverage focuses on geopolitics of Indian and Chinese engagement with Africa and on investment, aid, trade and diplomacy. The book also examines the challenges and opportunities posed by their increasing presence in Africa and their impact and implication for African policy-makers and institutions like the AU, the New Partnership for Africa's Development (NEPAD) and regional economic consortia. They recommend that governments in Africa should negotiate with the two Asian giants from a position of strength and a more informed platform, and suggest recommendations to that effect. According to Cheru and Obi (2010b), over the long term, India will have a comparative advantage over China in Africa as a result of its Diaspora, strong educational system, its democratic tradition and proximity to the continent. McCarthy (2011) argues that both India and China have a policy of engagement with Africa aligned around respect for non-interference and non-intervention, which differentiates them from the traditional donors. He explores the internal developments in India and China, the influence of external developments, and the ideologies and principles that expounds the foreign policies of the two countries and their assistance to Africa.

Beri and Sinha (2009) compare and contrast India and China with respect to energy security in Africa. The book makes a concerted attempt to present energy security as a global problem there by going beyond state-centric perceptions of energy security and linking it with local perceptions on energy resources. It employs case studies to explore Africa's role as a provider of energy and the myriad consequences of a plethora of oil producers in Africa. It also highlights India's manifold approach to Africa compared to China. In Mawdsley and McCann (2011), contributors point out that India and China have similarities in their interests and compete with each other. Moreover, Africa is strategically more important, especially with respect to energy security, for India than China. India, like China, has a 'no strings attached' policy, but it is seen in positive light compared to China, and its non-interference policy has escaped criticism so far. This is because India, unlike China, does not have a 'go global policy' for its corporates (both in the public sector and in the private sector) to encourage them to enter international markets. Moreover, India is arguably engaged in a kind of 'globalisation slipstream' behind China in Africa.

China in West Africa

Little has been written about India's and China's engagement with West Africa as a region although scholars have worked on India's and China's interaction in individual West African countries as case studies, especially in the oil industry. Campos and Vines (2008) and Utomi (2008) explore China's trade and diplomatic ties, financial engagement, motives and strategy, engagement in the oil sector and developmental impact on Angola and Nigeria respectively. Alves (2010) explores the role played by oil in the Sino-Angolan relationship. She discusses the evolution of the relations between the two countries since China's intervention in the civil war in Angola. The paper also analyses how trade and commerce, including oil exports from Angola to China, have become the defining feature of the bilateral relationship and discusses the reasons why China has been so successful in the oil industry in Angola. Ferreira (2008) provides a multi-layered analysis of China–Angola relationship. Analysis focusing on China's engagement in Angola is more nuanced than just access to natural resources. Ferreira contends that all is not quiet on the China–Angola front and raises important questions regarding the long-term nature of Angolan–Chinese 'perfect marriage of convenience'.

Using Senegal as a case study, Gaye (2008) takes a holistic view of Sino-

African relations in general and West Africa in particular. He asserts that China appears to act as a partner, competitor and coloniser in Senegal, West Africa and Africa. China faces a tough task if it does not adhere to African needs and a 'win–win' relationship. Berto *et al.* (2009) examine briefly how West Africa's and Economic Community of West Africa States' (ECOWAS) economic and political development path is influenced by their interconnection with other areas of the world, especially China–Africa relations. An anthology of 'Occasional Papers', 'Policy Briefings' and articles have also been published by the South African Institute of International Affairs (SAIIA) on China's engagement with some natural-resource-rich West African countries in general and in the oil sector. For instance, Mthembu-Salter (2009) examines the operations of Chinese NOCs in Nigeria and Alves (2008) and Dittgen (2011) examine Chinese NOCs in the oil industry in Gabon.

India in West Africa

Vasudevan (2010) avers that India–Nigeria relations, like relations with the African continent, have transformed from historical and political connections and have an increasing economic focus. Vasudevan takes a holistic perspective and explores the pertinence of the bilateral relationship between the two countries. The paper asserts that India–Nigerian relations can act as a catalyst to reshape India–Africa relations. Vittorini and Harris (2011) trace the historical roots of Indian and West African relations since the NAM Conference in Bandung in 1956. They explore India's diplomatic and corporate global strategy in West Africa, especially Indian engagements in Liberia and Ghana, and contend that India's engagement with West Africa – Francophone, Anglophone or Lusophone – will increase in the future. Beri (2010), on the other hand, avers that although Indian oil companies have gained access to the Nigerian oil industry due to the historical relations between the two countries, the future is circumspect due to increasing insecurity and change in government. She promulgates that as India's investments increase, India needs to perform a dual act: first, a long-term strategy is required to cope with the increasing insecurity, and second is to strengthen relations with African countries. A compendium of 'Occasional Papers' and articles have also been published by SAIIA on India's interaction with some West African countries in the energy sector.

India and China in West Africa

India and China have also been compared and contrasted in West Africa. Singh (2007) discusses India's relations with West Africa in a wide historical context. The Chatham House paper discusses India's energy needs and highlights the regions significance for India. It also compares and contrasts India's and China's engagement in the region. It explicates that trade and economic framework is the key to the growing relationship between India and West Africa and outlines the broad framework with which India can engage the region. It contends that

India's involvement in West Africa is expanding beyond its traditional Commonwealth partners. Vines *et al.* (2009) and Wong (2009) provide a comparative perspective of the effect of Asian oil companies, especially Indian and Chinese oil companies, on Angola and Nigeria respectively. They elucidate the very divergent fortunes of Asian oil companies in the two countries. Wong (2009) concludes that Asian companies that were able to gain a footing in the oil industry in Nigeria as a quid pro quo for investing in downstream and infrastructure projects did not comprehend the politics in Nigeria. Vines *et al.* (2009) explain why China's oil strategy has been extremely successful in Angola relative to oil companies from other countries. Vines and Campos (2010) compare India and China in oil-rich Angola and assert that China plans to be present in Angola for a long period of time. Although it is a symbiotic economic relationship, it also raises new policy challenges for Angola. Although India is trying to catch up with China, it is unable to do so because it cannot match China's financial muscle. Aguilar and Goldstein (2009) compare and contrast India and China in Angola with respect to oil, trade, Angola's problems with financing and the role played by India and China, and the political economy of the relationship between Angola and the Asian Giants.

IV

This section states the limitations in the existing literature with respect to India's and China's role in the oil industry in West Africa and provides a rationale for undertaking the research and the empirical contribution that the study makes to the existing literature. Although there is an ever increasing literature comparing India and China in Africa, few scholars have tried to provide an answer for the difference in the interaction of India and China in the upstream sector of the oil industry in Africa. Even fewer have tried to explain the difference in India's and China's interaction in West Africa in general – their ability to mobilise resources, especially oil. Scholars have pointed out that India in Africa (and in West Africa) is spearheaded by the private sector followed by the public sector comprising SOEs, unlike China where the SOEs are the flag bearers. However, they do not explain the reason for the phenomenon.

There is no comprehensive study of acquisition of oil blocks by Indian and Chinese oil companies in West Africa. Vines *et al.* (2009), Wong (2009) and Beri and Sinha (2009) examine the competition between Indian and Chinese NOCs and mention that Chinese NOCs have outbid Indian companies in the oil industry in Angola. However, Vines *et al.* (2009) and Wong (2009) only examine the Indian and Chinese NOCs and do not study the Indian private sector oil companies in detail. Scholars like Beri and Sinha (2009), Dadwal (2011), Sharma and Ganeshan (2011) and others do mention the Indian private sector oil companies but they do not provide an explanation of how Indian oil companies like Essar Oil, Oil India Limited (OIL) and Indian Oil Corporation Limited (IOCL) have acquired oil blocks in West Africa. Singh (2007) states that the OIL–IOCL combine have acquired an oil block in Gabon through a 'farming in' offer. However, the study does not examine the quality of the oil block and its commercial potential. Alao (2011a, 2011b) discusses the acquisition of oil blocks by Indian and Chinese oil companies in Nigeria. However, Alao only discusses the competition between Oil and Natural Gas Corporation (ONGC), ONGC Videsh Limited (OVL) and ONGC (Mittal Energy Limited (MEL) (OMEL)) on the one hand and Chinese NOCs on the other. The study discusses and explains how and why all the Indian oil companies – ONGC, OVL, Essar Oil, OIL and IOCL – have acquired oil blocks in Nigeria.

Moreover, no studies have been undertaken on the acquisition of oil blocks by Chinese oil companies in other countries in West Africa apart from Nigeria, Angola and Gabon. The study breaks ground and makes an empirical contribution to the existing literature on India's and China's interaction in the upstream sector of the oil industry in West Africa by examining the acquisition of oil blocks by Chinese and Indian oil companies in 11 West African countries and provides an explanation for why China has greater outreach in the oil industry in West Africa relative to India. The study also makes an empirical contribution to the existing literature on India and China in the oil industry in West Africa by providing a more comprehensive explanation for the ability of the Chinese oil companies to outbid their Indian counterparts. It examines not only the bids that Chinese and Indian oil corporations place for the oil blocks and the quality of the oil blocks acquired by the oil companies from the two countries, but also tries to explain the reason why they are able to place those bids. It examines the rate of return on capital/investment, rate of interest on loans and the ease of availability of loans or finance, the difference in the level of technology and ability to acquire technology, project management skills, risk aversion and the difference in the economic, political and diplomatic support received by the Chinese and Indian oil companies from their respective governments. It also mentions the reasons why the Chinese NOCs are preferred as partners by African oil companies and IOCs and examines the relative commercial viability or relative quality of the oil blocks acquired by Indian and Chinese oil companies. Additionally, it is the most updated study and examines the time period from 2001 to 2015. This is discussed in greater detail in Chapter 4 and illustrated empirically in Chapters 5, 6 and 7.

Conclusion

The chapter provided a broad overview of the existing literature on India and China in Africa and in West Africa. It also highlighted the comparative perspective on India's and China's interaction in Africa and West Africa and also in the oil industry in the Africa and West Africa. The chapter mentioned the empirical gap in the existing literature and provided a rationale for undertaking the research. It explained the rationale for comparing India and China and the reasons for their new-found interest in Africa and West Africa. Africa has gained significance as an important oil supplier to the world. Although its oil reserves constitute approximately 8 per cent of the global oil reserves and its reserves are marginal relative to the Middle East, Africa, especially West Africa, can play a more important role. It is estimated that there will be more offshore oil discoveries in the West African countries, especially Nigeria and Angola, in the near future, which will not only increase the oil reserves but accentuate the ever increasing oil production in the region. West Africa also provides various commercial advantages and business opportunities and its high quality light sweet oil is in high demand.

Notes

1 Growth rates in China have declined to approximately 7 per cent since 2013.
2 Both India and China are following a strategy of acquiring equity oil blocks globally and in West Africa to enhance their energy security. Indian and Chinese oil companies sell 90 per cent of their equity oil (from their global assets) in the international market. This is because of three reasons. The first is technical. Indian and Chinese oil companies are unable to refine the oil and have to sell it in the international market. Second, the domestic oil industry is subsidised. This implies that Indian and Chinese oil companies incur a loss when they sell oil in the domestic market. The oil companies also swap their equity oil in the international market for oil that they can refine. The companies bring the swapped oil to their respective country, refine it and sell it in the domestic market. It is debatable whether selling oil in the international market enhances energy security. The opinion is divided. Some experts suggest that it allows the oil companies to get valuable foreign exchange. It also saves precious foreign exchange because it reduces the amount that the governments have to spend on buying oil. Others are of the opinion that the equity oil strategy does not enhance energy security. On the other hand, it creates political risks. Moreover, this policy is not feasible and will fail in the long term.
3 In the last few years, India has surpassed Japan multiple times to become the third largest importer of oil. Analysts are of the view that the two countries may trade places again in the very short term, but in medium term, India will be the third largest importer of oil (Kennedy, 2015).
4 A significant proportion of the absolute increase and percentage increase in global oil reserves is due to shale gas revolution in the United States and new reserves discovered in Venezuela (Table 3.4).
5 The 'Three World theory' was postulated by Mao Zedong. The theory had a three world configuration: the first world comprised of the two superpowers, the United States and the Soviet Union; the second world consisting of Australia, Canada, Europe and Japan; and the 'Third World' or the 'new' south comprising Asia (except Japan), Africa and Latin America.
6 Like China, India does not subscribe to the OECD definition of foreign aid or ODA (Sinha, 2010).

References

Aguilar, R. and Goldstein, A. (2009). The Chinisation of Africa: The Case of Angola. *World Economy*, 32 (11), pp. 1543–1562.

Alao, Abiodun (2011a). Nigeria and the BRICs: Diplomatic, Trade, Cultural and Military Relations. Online. Occasional Paper No 101, South African Institute of International Affairs. Available at: www.saiia.org.za/occasional-papers/nigeria.html (accessed 10 January 2013).

Alao, Abiodun (2011b). Nigeria and the Global Powers: Continuity and Change in Policy and Perceptions. Online. Occasional Paper No 96, South African Institute of International Affairs. Available at: www.saiia.org.za/occasional-papers/nigeria-and-the-global-powers-continuity-and-change-in-policy-and-perceptions (accessed 10 January 2013).

Alden, Chris (1997). Solving South Africa's Chinese Puzzle: Democratic Foreign Policy Making and the "Two Chinas" Question. *South African Journal of International Affairs*, 5 (2), pp. 80–95.

Alden, Chris (2007). *China in Africa*. London and New York: Zed Books.

Alden, Chris and Hughes, Chris (2009). Harmony and Discord in China's Africa Strategy: Some Implications for Foreign Policy. *The China Quarterly*, 199, pp. 563–584.

Alden, Chris, Large, Daniel and Soares de Oliviera, Ricardo (eds) (2008). *China Returns to Africa: A Rising Power and a Continent Embrace*. New York: Columbia University Press.

Alessi, Christopher and Hanson, Stephanie (2012). Expanding China-Africa Oil Ties. Online. Backgrounder, Council on Foreign Relations, 8 February. Available at: www.cfr.org/china/expanding-china-africa-oil-ties/p9557 (accessed 15 June 2015).

Alves, Ana Cristina (2008). China and Gabon: A Growing Resource Partnership. Online. China in Africa Project Report no. 4, Johannesburg: South African Institute of International Affairs. Available at: www.saiia.org.za/research-reports/267-china-africa-policy-report-no-4-2008/file (accessed 15 June 2015).

Alves, Ana Christina (2010). The Oil Factor in Sino-Angolan Relations at the Start of the 21st Century. Online. Occasional Paper No. 55, China in Africa project, South African Institute of International Affairs, February. Available at www.saiia.org.za/occasional-papers/the-oil-factor-in-sino%E2%80%93 angolan-relations-at-the-start-of-the-21st-century (accessed 15 November 2015).

Beri, Ruchita (2003). India's Africa Policy in the Post-Cold War Era: An Assessment. *Strategic Analysis*, 27 (2), pp. 216–232.

Beri, Ruchita (2007). China's Rising Profile in Africa. *China Report*, 43 (3), pp. 297–308.

Beri, Ruchita (2010). Prospects of India's Energy Quest in Africa: Insights from Sudan and Nigeria. *Strategic Analysis*, 34 (6), pp. 897–911.

Beri, Ruchita and Sinha, Uttam Kumar (eds) (2009). *Africa and Energy Security: Global Issues, Local Responses.* New Delhi: Academic Foundation in association with Institute of Defence Studies and Analyses.

Berto, Massimiliano, Appolloni, Omar, Izquierdo, Juana Bustamante, De Angelis, Francesco, Lelli, Edoardo and Vesenjak, Slavko (2009). China and the Different Regional Approaches in Africa. *Transition Studies Review*, 16 (2), pp. 404–420.

BMI (Business Monitor International) (2016). India: Oil and Gas Report Q2 2016. Online. Part of BMI's Industry Report & Forecasts Series. Available at: www.businessmonitor.com (accessed 18 April 2016).

BP (British Petroleum) (2012). Statistical Review of World Energy 2012. Online. June 2012. Available at: www.laohamutuk.org/DVD/docs/BPWER2012report.pdf (accessed 2 January 2013).

BP (British Petroleum) (2015). Statistical Review of World Energy 2015. Online. June 2015. Available at: www.bp.com/content/dam/bp/pdf/energy-economics/statistical-review-2015/bp-statistical-review-of-world-energy-2015-full-report.pdf (accessed 2 January 2016).

Bräutigam, Deborah A. (2009a). *The Dragon's Gift: The Real Story of China in Africa*. Oxford and New York: Oxford University Press.

Bräutigam, Deborah A. (2009b). China's Challenge to the International Aid Architecture. *World Politics Review*, 1 (4), pp. 1–10.

Bräutigam, Deborah A. and Tang, Xiaoyang (2011). African Shenzhen: China's Special Economic Zones in Africa. *Journal of Modern African Studies*, 49 (1), pp. 27–54.

Broadman, Harry G. and Isik, Gozde (2007). *Africa's Silk Road: China and India's New Economic Frontier*. Washington, DC: World Bank.

Brookes, Peter (2007). Into Africa: China's Grab for Influence and Oil. Online. Heritage Lecture 1006, The Heritage Foundation, 26 March. Available at: www.heritage.org/Research/Africa/hl1006.cfm (accessed 18 April 2012).

Campbell, Horace (2008). China in Africa: Challenging US Global Hegemony. In: Firoze M. Manji and Stephen Marks, eds. *African Perspectives on China in Africa*. Oxford: Fahamu, pp. 119–137.

Campos, Indira and Vines, Alex (2008). Angola and China: A Pragmatic Partnership. In: Jennifer G. Cooke, ed. *U.S. and Chinese Engagement in Africa: Prospects for Improving U.S.-China-Africa Cooperation*. Washington, DC: CSIS Press, pp. 33–48.

Channel News Asia (2016). With Gambia Move, China Ends Diplomatic Truce with Taiwan. Online. 17 March. Available at: www.channelnewsasia.com/news/asiapacific/with-gambia-move-china-e/2612146.html (accessed 20 May 2016).

Chao, Chien-min and Hsu, Chih-chia (2006). China Isolates Taiwan. In: Edward Friedman, ed. *China's Rise, Taiwan's Dilemmas and International Peace*. London and New York: Routledge, pp. 41–67.

Cheng, Joseph Y.S. and Shi, Huangao (2009). China's Africa Policy in the Post-Cold War Era. *Journal of Contemporary Asia*, 39 (1), pp. 87–115.

Cheru, Fantu and Obi, Cyril (eds) (2010a). *The Rise of China and India in Africa: Challenges, Opportunities and Critical Interventions*. London and Uppsala: Zed Books and Nordiska Afrikainstitutet.

Cheru, Fantu and Obi, Cyril (2010b). Introduction-Africa in the Twenty-First Century: Strategic and Development Challenges. In: Fantu Cheru and Cyril Obi, eds. *The Rise of China and India in Africa*. London and Uppsala: Zed Books and Nordiska Afrikainstitutet, pp. 1–9.

Chow, Edward C. (2009). China's Soft Power in Developing Regions: New Major Player in the International Oil Patch. In: Carola McGiffert, ed. *Chinese Soft Power and its Implications for the United States: Competition and Cooperation in the Developing World, A Report of the CSIS Smart Power Initiative*. Washington, DC: CSIS Press, pp. 91–96.

Cooke, Jennifer G. (ed.) (2008). *U.S. and Chinese Engagement in Africa: Prospects for Improving U.S.-China-Africa Cooperation*. Washington, DC: CSIS Press.

Cooke, Jennifer G. (2009). China's Soft Power in Africa. In: Carola McGiffert, ed. *Chinese Soft Power and Its Implications for the United States: Competition and Cooperation in the Developing World, A Report of the CSIS Smart Power Initiative*. Washington, DC: CSIS Press, pp. 27–44.

Cropley, Ed (2009). China Shunts U.S. into Second Place in Scramble for Africa. Online. Reuters, 7 August. Available at: http://blogs.reuters.com/africanews/2009/08/07/china-shunts-us-into-second-place-in-scramble-for-africa/ (accessed 20 April 2012).

Dadwal, Shebonti Ray (2011). India and Africa: Towards a Sustainable Energy Partnership. Online. Occasional Paper No 75, Emerging Powers and Global Challenges Programme, China in Africa Project, Johannesburg: South African Institute of International Affairs. Available at: dspace.cigilibrary.org/jspui/.../saia_sop_75_dadwal_20110222.pdf (accessed 10 January 2013).

Dittgen, Romain (2011). To Bélinga or not to Bélinga? China's Evolving Engagement in Gabon's Mining Sector. Online. Occasional Paper No 98, China in Africa Project,

Johannesburg: South African Institute of International Affairs. Available at: www.saiia. org.za/occasional-papers/to-belinga-or-not-to-belinga-china-s-evolving-engagement-in-gabon-s-mining-sector.html (accessed 30 December 2012).

Downs, Erica S. (2007). The Fact and Fiction of Sino-African Energy Relations. *China Security*, 3 (3), pp. 42–68.

Farooki, Masuma (2011). China's Structural Demand and Commodity Prices: Implications for Africa. In: Christopher M. Dent, ed. *China and Africa Development Relations*. Abingdon: Routledge, pp. 121–142.

Ferreira, Manuel Ennes (2008). China in Angola: Just a Passion for Oil?. In: Chris Alden, Daniel Large and Ricardo Soares de Oliveira, eds. *China Returns to Africa: A Rising Power and a Continent Embrace*. New York: Columbia University Press, pp. 295–317.

Foot, Rosemary (2006). Chinese Strategies in a US-Hegemonic Global Order: Accommodating and Hedging. *International Affairs*, 82 (1), pp. 77–94.

Foster, Vivien, Butterfield, William, Chen, Chuan and Pushak, Nataliya (2009). *Building Bridges: China's Growing Role as Infrastructure Financier for Sub-Saharan Africa*. Washington, DC: World Bank/Public-Private Infrastructure Advisory Facility.

Frynas, Jedrzej G. and Paulo, Manuel (2007). A New Scramble for African Oil? Historical, Political, and Business Perspectives. *African Affairs*, 106 (422), pp. 229–251.

Gaye, Adama (2008). China in Africa: After the Gun and the Bible: A West African Perspective. In: Chris Alden, Daniel Large and Ricardo Soares de Oliveira, eds. *China Returns to Africa: A Rising Power and a Continent Embrace*. New York: Columbia University Press, pp. 129–141.

Gill, Bates and Reilly, James (2007). The Tenuous Hold of China Inc. in Africa. *The Washington Quarterly*, 30 (3), pp. 37–52.

Goldstein, Andrea E., Pinaud, Nicolas, Reisen, Helmut and Chen, Xiaobao (eds) (2006). *The Rise of China and India: What's in it for Africa?* Paris: Organisation for Economic Co-operation and Development.

Goldwyn, David L. (2009). Pursuing U.S. Energy Security Interest in Africa. In: Jennifer G. Cooke and Stephen J. Morrison, eds. *U.S. Africa Policy beyond the Bush Years: Critical Challenges for the Obama Administration*. Washington, DC: CSIS Press, pp. 62–90.

Goldwyn, David L. and Morrison, Stephen J. (2004). *Promoting Transparency in the African Oil Sector: Recommendations for US Foreign Policy. A Report of the CSIS Task Force on Rising US Energy Stakes in Africa*. Washington, DC: CSIS Press.

Guerrero, Dorothy-Grace and Manji, Firoze (eds) (2008). *China's New Role in Africa and the South: A Search for a New Perspective*. Oxford: Fahamu.

Hanson, Stephanie (2008). China, Africa and Oil. Online. Council on Foreign Relations, Backgrounder, 9 June. Available at: www.washingtonpost.com/wp-dyn/content/article/2008/06/09/AR2008060900714.html (accessed 12 April 2012).

Holslag, Jonathan (2011). China and the Coups: Coping with Political Instability in Africa. *African Affairs*, 110 (440), pp. 367–386.

Huang, Chin-Hao (2008). China's Renewed Partnership with Africa: Implication for the United States. In: Robert I. Rotberg, ed. *China into Africa: Trade, Aid, and Influence*. Washington, DC: Brookings Institution Press, pp. 296–312.

Jakobson, Linda (2009). China's Diplomacy toward Africa Drivers and Constraints. *International Relations of the Asia-Pacific*, 9 (3), pp. 403–433.

Jiang, Wenran (2009). Fuelling the Dragon: China's Rise and Its Energy and Resources Extraction in Africa. *The China Quarterly*, 199, pp. 585–609.

Kennedy, Charles (2015). India Becomes the 3rd Largest Oil Importer. Online. Oilprice.

com. Available at http://oilprice.com/Energy/Crude-Oil/India-Becomes-3rd-Largest-Oil-Importer.html (accessed 10 January 2016).

King, K. (2010). China's Cooperation in Education and Training with Kenya: A Different Model? *International Journal of Educational Development*, 30 (5), pp. 488–496.

Klare, Michael and Volman, Daniel (2006). The African "Oil Rush" and US National Security. *Third World Quarterly*, 27 (4), pp. 609–628.

Lake, Anthony, Whitman, Christine Todd, Lyman, Princeton N. and Morrison, Stephen J. (2006). More Than Humanitarianism: A Strategic US Approach Towards Africa. Independent Task Report No. 56. Council on Foreign Relations. Available at: file:///C:/Documents%20and%20Settings/Administrator/My%20Documents/Downloads/Africa_Task_Force_Web.pdf (accessed 20 November 2012).

Lyman, Princeton (2005). China and the US in Africa: A Strategic Competition or an Opportunity for Cooperation. Online. Council on Foreign Relations. Available at: www.cfr.org/content/thinktank/ChinaandUS_Africa.pdf (accessed 18 April 2012).

McCarthy, Tom (2011). Assessing China and India's New Role in Africa. Online. e-International Relations. Available at: www.e-ir.info/2011/07/26/assessing-china-and-india%E2%80%99s-new-role-in-africa/ (accessed 2 April 2012).

Marks, Stephen (2007). Introduction. In: Firoze M. Manji and Stephen Marks, eds. *African Perspectives on China in Africa*. Oxford: Fahamu, pp. 1–14.

Mawdsley, Emma and McCann, Gerrad (eds) (2011). *India in Africa: Changing Geographies of Power*. Cape Town: Pambazuka Press.

Modi, Renu (2010). The Role of India's Private Sector in the Health and Agricultural Sectors of Africa. In: Fantu Cheru and Cyril Obi, eds. *The Rise of China and India in Africa*. London and Uppsala: Zed Books and Nordiska Afrikainstitutet, pp. 120–131.

Mol, Arthur P.J. (2011). China's Ascent and Africa's Environment. *Global Environmental Change*, 21 (3), pp. 785–794.

Morrissey, Oliver and Zgovu, Evious (2011). *The Impact of China and India on Sub-Saharan Africa: Opportunities, Challenges and Policies*. London: Commonwealth Secretariat.

Mthembu-Salter, Gregory (2009). Elephants, Ants and Superpowers: Nigeria's Relations with China. Online. Occasional Paper No 42, China in Africa Project, Johannesburg: South African Institute of International Affairs. Available at: www.saiia.org.za/occasional-papers/elephants-ants-and-superpowers-nigeria-s-relations-with-china.html (accessed 30 December 2012).

Naidu, Sanusha (2010). India's African Relations: In the Shadow of China. In: Fantu Cheru and Cyril Obi, eds. *The Rise of China and India in Africa*. London and Uppsala: Zed Books and Nordiska Afrikainstitutet, pp. 34–49.

Nordtveit, Bjørn H. (2011). An Emerging Donor in Education and Development: A Case Study of China in Cameroon. *International Journal of Educational Development*, 31 (2), pp. 99–108.

de Oliviera, Ricardo Soares (2008). Making Sense of Chinese Oil Investment in Africa. In: Chris Alden, Daniel Large and Ricardo Soares de Oliveira, eds. *China Returns to Africa: A Rising Power and a Continent Embrace*. New York: Columbia University Press, pp. 83–109.

Pham, J. Peter (2011). AFRICOM from Bush to Obama. *South African Journal of International Affairs*, 18 (1), pp. 107–124.

Rocha, John (2007). A New Frontier in the Exploration of Africa's Natural Resources: The Emergence of China. In: Firoze M. Manji and Stephen Marks, eds. *African Perspectives on China in Africa*. Oxford: Fahamu, pp. 15–34.

Rooyen, Frank van (2010). Blue Helmets for Africa: India's Peacekeeping in Africa. Online. South African Institute of International Affairs Occasional Paper No 60, pp. 3–26. Available at: www.saiia.org.za/occasional-papers/blue-helmets-for-africa-india-s-peacekeeping-in-africa.html (accessed 2 April 2012).

Rotberg, Robert I. (ed.) (2008). *China into Africa: Trade, Aid, and Influence*. Washington, DC: Brookings Institution Press.

Sautman, Barry and Yang, Hairong (2007). Friends and Interests: China's Distinctive Links with Africa. *African Studies Review*, 50 (3), pp. 75–114.

Sharma, Devika and Ganeshan, Swati (2011). Before and Beyond Energy: Contextualising the India–Africa Partnership. Online. Occasional Paper No 77, Emerging Powers and Global Challenges Programme, China in Africa Project, Johannesburg: South African Institute of International Affairs. Available at: www.saiia.org.za/occasional-papers/before-and-beyond-energy-contextualising-the-india-africa-partnership.html (accessed 5 January 2013).

Sharma, Devika and Mahajan, Deepti (2007). Energising Ties: The Politics of Oil. *South African Journal of International Affairs*, 14 (2), pp. 37–52.

Sheth, V.S. (2008). *India-Africa Relations: Emerging Policy and Development Perspective*. Papers presented at the International Seminar on India Africa Relations: Emerging Policy and Development Perspectives, held at Mumbai during 23–25 July 2006. Delhi: Academic Excellence.

Singh, Sushant K. (2007). India and West Africa: A Burgeoning Relationship. Online. Africa Programme/Asia programme briefing paper, Chatham House, London. Available at: www.chathamhouse.org/publications/papers/view/108471 (accessed 2 April 2012).

Sinha, Pranay Kumar (2010). Indian Development Cooperation with Africa. In: Fantu Cheru and Cyril Obi, eds. *The Rise of China and India in Africa*. London and Uppsala: Zed Books and Nordiska Afrikainstitutet, pp. 77–93.

Taylor, Ian (2006). *China and Africa: Engagement and Compromise*. London; New York: Routledge.

Taylor, Ian (2009). China's Africa Policy in Context. In: Ian Taylor, ed. *China's New Role in Africa*. Boulder: Lynne Rienner Publishers, pp. 1–36.

Taylor, Ian (2012). India's Rise in Africa. *International Affairs*, 88 (4), pp. 779–798.

Tull, Dennis M. (2008). The Political Consequences of China's Return to Africa. In: Chris Alden, Daniel Large and Ricardo Soares de Oliveira, eds. *China Returns to Africa: A Rising Power and a Continent Embrace*. New York: Columbia University Press, pp. 111–128.

Utomi, Pat (2008). China and Nigeria. In: Jennifer G. Cooke, ed. *U.S. and Chinese Engagement in Africa: Prospects for Improving U.S.–China–Africa Cooperation*. Washington, DC: CSIS Press, pp. 49–58.

Van Dijk, Meine Pieter (ed.) (2009). *The New Presence of China in Africa*. Amsterdam: Amsterdam University Press.

Vasudevan, Parvathi (2010). The Changing Nature of Nigeria–India Relations. Online. Programme Paper: AFP 2010/02, Chatham House. Available at: www.chathamhouse.org/publications/papers/view/109543 (accessed 3 April 2012).

Verma, Raj (2012a). Can Africa Become the New Persian Gulf? Online. LSE Africa blog, 19 December. Available at: http://blogs.lse.ac.uk/africaatlse/2012/12/19/can-africa-become-the-new-persian-gulf/ (accessed 24 December 2012).

Verma, Raj (2012b). India and Africa: Towards Greater Cooperation and Growth. Online. LSE Africa blog, 11 April. Available at: http://blogs.lse.ac.uk/africaatlse/2012/04/11/india-and-africa-towards-greater-cooperation-and-growth/ (accessed 24 December 2012).

Vines, Alex (2011). India's Security Concerns in the Western Indian Ocean. In: Emma Mawdsley and Gerrad McCann, eds. *India in Africa: Changing Geographies of Power.* Cape Town: Pambazuka Press, pp. 187–202.

Vines, Alex and Campos, Indira (2010). China and India in Angola. In: Fantu Cheru and Cyril Obi, eds. *The Rise of China and India in Africa: Challenges, Opportunities and Critical Interventions.* London and Uppsala: Zed Books and Nordiska Afrikainstitutet, pp. 193–207.

Vines, Alex and Oruitemeka, Bereni (2007). Engagement with the African Indian Ocean Rim States. *South African Journal of International Affairs,* 14 (2), pp. 111–123.

Vines, Alex and Oruitemeka, Bereni (2008). India's Engagement with the African Indian Ocean Rim States. Online. Africa Programme Paper AFP P 1/08. Chatham House, London, UK. Available at: www.chathamhouse.org/publications/papers/view/108782 (accessed 2 April 2012).

Vines, A., Weimer, M. and Campos, I. (2009). Asian National Oil Companies in Angola. In: Alex Vines, Lillian Wong, Markus Weimer and Indira Campos, eds. Thirst for African Oil: Asian National Oil Companies in Nigeria and Angola. Online. A Chatham House Report, pp. 29–60. Available at: www.chathamhouse.org/sites/files/chatham-house/r0809_africanoil.pdf (accessed 18 May 2016).

Vittorini, Simona and Harris, David (2011). India Goes Over to the Other Side: Indo West-African Relations in the 21st Century. In: Emma Mawdsley and Gerrad McCann, eds. *India in Africa: Changing Geographies of Power.* Cape Town: Pambazuka Press, pp. 203–217.

Volman, Daniel (2009). China, India, Russia and the United States: The Scramble for African Oil and the Militarization of the Continent. Online. Current Africa Issues 43, Nordiska Afrikainstitutet. Available at: http://nai.diva-portal.org/smash/record. jsf?pid=diva2:272960 (accessed 12 April 2012).

Wang, Jian-Ye (2007). What Drives China's Growing Role in Africa. Washington, DC: International Monetary Fund, IMF Working Paper (WP/07/211).

Wong, Lillian (2009). Asian National Oil Companies in Nigeria. In: Alex Vines, Lillian Wong, Markus Weimer and Indira Campos, eds. Thirst for African Oil: Asian National Oil Companies in Nigeria and Angola. Online. A Chatham House Report, pp. 29–60. Available at: www.chathamhouse.org/sites/files/chathamhouse/r0809_africanoil.pdf (accessed 18 May 2016).

Zhang, Baohui (2011). Taiwan's New Grand Strategy. *Journal of Contemporary China,* 20 (69), pp. 269–285.

Zhu, Zhiqun (2010). *China's New Diplomacy: Rationale, Strategies and Significance.* Farnham: Ashgate.

Part III
India and China

3   India and China

Difference in power and political economies

This chapter discusses the independent variable, i.e. the difference in the relative power of India and China and the intervening variable, i.e. the difference in the political economy of India and China. The chapter is divided into five sections. Section I discusses in brevity Sino-Indian relations since the end of the Second World War. It provides the context which facilitates the comprehension of the subject matter, especially the role and the significance of the independent variable. Section II discusses the difference in the economic, political and military power of India and China. To gauge the difference in the economic power, it uses indicators like GDP, GNI and other development indicators like IMR, life expectancy, etc. To measure the difference in the political power, it uses the permanent membership of the UNSC as a dummy variable or parameter, and the perception of leaders, government officials and bureaucrats. Section III briefly discusses the different economic systems and the analytical framework chosen to distinguish the political economy of India and China. Sections IV and V discuss the difference in the political economy of India and China since their independence, the trajectory of reforms introduced in the two Asian neighbours and how it has transformed their economic and industrial structure.

I

Sino-India relations since the end of Second World War are characterised by a roller coaster ride: at their zenith until the mid 1950s, hitting the nadir in 1962, a slight recovery in the late 1970s, tensions of war in the late 1980s, an improvement in 1990s, greater engagement and upward trend in the new millennium, and spiralling down since 2006. The relations are marred by rivalry, distrust, conflict, insecurity, estrangement and containment. Since the new millennium, the relations are characterised by 'hot economics and cold politics' or 'co-opetition' – economic co-operation and political competition.

In the early 1950s, the discourse of China–India relations manifested itself in 'Third World' solidarity and their support for freedom movements and struggle against colonialism for countries in Asia and Africa. This culminated in the NAM summit in Bandung, Indonesia in 1955 with China and India at the forefront. China's invasion of Tibet in 1950 laid the groundwork for the souring of relations between India and China. Chairman Mao was resolute in bringing Tibet under China's direct administrative and military control and construed India's concerns over Tibet as the latter's interference in the internal affairs of China. In 1954, the two countries signed an eight-year agreement on Tibet. This provided the foundation for Sino-Indian relations in the form of the Five Principles of Peaceful Coexistence or Panchsheel. This culminated in the phrase 'Hindi–Chini bhai bhai' which means 'Indians and Chinese are brothers'.

In 1959, the spiritual leader of Tibet, the Dalai Lama, escaped from Tibet and took sanctuary in India. This antagonised China and led to a reversal in the relationship between the two countries. China declined to accept the McMahon Line and laid claims to certain parts in northeast India, namely the state of Sikkim, Arunachal Pradesh or South Tawang and Aksai Chin. This resulted in a short border war in 1962 in which India was defeated and no peace agreement was signed. To this date, the Indian elite and intelligentsia bear the psychological scars and believe that India was stabbed in the back. The relationship between the two countries deteriorated in the 1960s and early 1970s. China backed Pakistan in the Indo-Pak wars in 1965 and 1971 and provided military, economic and political support and nuclear assistance to Pakistan. There was very little state-to-state contact and diplomatic overtures to improve the relationship between the two countries were not undertaken. The period was also marred by minor border clashes leading to fatalities on both sides.

In 1977, there was an attempt by the new GoI to improve ties with China. In 1979, both nations officially re-established diplomatic relations. China altered its pro-Pakistan stance on Kashmir and also appeared willing not to raise a voice on India's assertion of Sikkim being an integral part of India and its special advisory relationship with Bhutan. However, tensions rose again in 1984 along the disputed border and in 1987 there were predictions of war. The situation was de-escalated after visits by the Indian prime minister and minister for external affairs to Beijing to negotiate a truce.

The trend towards warming of relations was facilitated by Indian Prime Minister Rajiv Gandhi's visit to Beijing in 1988. An agreement was reached to restore friendly relations and to arrive at a fair and mutually acceptable solution to the border dispute on the basis of the Panchsheel Agreement. The 1990s was characterised by improvement in the relations between the two countries and border trade resumed in 1992 after more than 30 years. Consulates were also opened in Shanghai and Mumbai. The period saw high-level visits from both sides and various rounds of talks were held to reduce strains on the disputed border by employing confidence-building measures. The nuclear tests conducted by India in 1998 led to a low point in relations between the two countries. The threat posed by China was provided as the rationale for conducting the tests. China was extremely critical of India's nuclear tests and its entry into the nuclear club. During the Kargil conflict in 1999, Beijing adopted cautious neutrality but did not condemn Pakistan.

In the new millennium, there was significant improvement of ties and economic engagement between India and China but the relations were clouded by suspicions and security concerns. There were high-level visits from both countries. China recognised Sikkim as an integral part of India and there was also a movement towards resolving the border disputes. Sino-Indian trade skyrocketed to US$39 billion by the end of 2007 from a modest US$332 million in 1992 (Sharma, 2010) and US$2.92 billion in 2000. At the end of 2008, it reached US$41.85 billion, making China India's largest trading partner in goods, replacing the United States (Embassy of India, Beijing, n.d.a). At the South Asian Association for Regional Cooperation (SAARC) Summit in 2005, China was accorded an observer status despite India's protests and India has shown reluctance to consider China for full membership in SAARC. On the other hand, China has vacillated on India's permanent membership to the UNSC, from negative to neutral but not an endorsement. In the Shanghai Cooperation Organisation (SCO), Russia endorsed India's candidature for the membership but China has been reluctant and stated that India could be a full member if and only if Pakistan was allowed to become a full member. China has also objected to India's membership to the Nuclear Suppliers Group (NSG).

An extremely significant element of the evolving relationship between India and China is based on energy. Both require access to energy sources for their industrial expansion and concomitant economic growth and are proactively trying to secure them by investing in the oilfields in the Middle East, Central Asia, Latin America and Africa. This entails competition, which has been evident recently in bids for oil blocks in different parts of the world. India lags behind China in this race. This fierce competition for energy resources has geostrategic implications. However, India and China have also cooperated in the energy sector in Sudan, Iran and Russia.

In 2006, China and India were embroiled once again in a verbal clash over the disputed border. China asserted that Arunachal Pradesh was an integral part of China. On the other hand, India alleged that China was occupying 38,000 square km of its territory in Kashmir. The matter was further aggravated in 2007 when China refused to grant a visa to an Indian Administrative Service officer in Arunachal Pradesh to attend a training programme because China considers Arunachal Pradesh as a part of its territory. Reciprocating China's action, the GoI prevented a 107-person delegation from travelling to China for the programme. India also extended an invitation to Ma Ying-jeou, then a presidential candidate in Taiwan, to visit the country (Sharma, 2010).

China's anti-satellite test in January 2007 concerned Indian officials and the strategic community in India. In January 2008, Indian Premier Dr Manmohan Singh visited China and held talks with Premier Wen Jiabao and President Hu Jintao. Bilateral discussions were also held on various issues like military, defence, commerce and trade, amongst others. In October 2009, the Asian Development Bank (ADB) approved a loan for a project in Arunachal Pradesh and formally acknowledged that the eastern state was an integral part of India. However, China opposed the loan by the ADB (Jain, 2010).

There have been frequent reports in the Indian media about escalating Chinese transgressions into Indian territory. The Indian military recorded 270 border violations and nearly 2300 instances of 'aggressive border patrolling' by China's People's Liberation Army (PLA) in 2008. India is also wary of China's 'string of pearls strategy' – a strategy of encirclement of India by mostly rudimentary maritime facilities in the Indian Ocean and countries surrounding India. China also enhanced economic, military and political ties and nuclear co-operation with India's arch enemy, Pakistan. Vikram Sood, the former head of India's external intelligence service, the Research and Analysis Wing, avers that "China is determined to keep us ... psychologically and strategically handicapped" (cited in Joshi, 2011: 159). He also warned that "while we may agonize over challenges across our land frontiers, we would be ignoring the new challenge in the Indian Ocean unless we plan counter measures now" (cited in Joshi, 2011: 159). According to Professor Srikanth Kondapalli, Jawaharlal Nehru University (JNU) (Interview, Appendix A) "China's ancient strategy of 'hexiao kongda' (cooperate with the small countries to counter the big) has been implemented in South Asia to counter India". However, others argue that the so-called 'string of pearls' idea is just a term for an unreal and imaginary threat posed by China to India.

India is trying to counter China's encirclement and invasion of its strategic space by employing and furthering its 'look East policy'. India is improving relations and has increased engagement and co-operation with ASEAN states especially Indonesia and Vietnam. It has also increased co-operation with Japan and South Korea (Rehman, 2009). Some analysts aver that the United States wants to use India as a counterweight to balance or contain China's rise (Gupta, 2006; Roehrig, 2009). However, it is debateable whether India is towing the US line. India's joint naval exercises with the United States, Australia and Japan in 2007 further stoked fears in China that a democratic alliance is targeting China. In 2012, India tested a missile capable of carrying a nuclear warhead to Beijing. This once again manifested the insecurity and mutual suspicion between the two countries.

In December 2010, Premier Wen Jiabao visited India. More than 400 Chinese business leaders accompanied Premier Wen to increase the economic engagement with India (BBC, 2010). It is estimated that Sino-Indian trade will cross US$100 billion by 2015 (*Economic Times*, 2012). Table 3.1 shows trade between India and China from 2011 to 2014. As can be seen, India has a significant trade deficit with respect to China (Embassy of India, Beijing, n.d.a). As per Chinese figures, cumulative Chinese investments into India until September 2014 stood at US$2.63 billion while Indian investments into China were US$0.55 billion (Embassy of India, Beijing, n.d.b). While investments have grown, they remain limited compared to the investment relationships that both China and India have with other countries.

President Xi Jinping accorded priority to India–China relations after coming to power in March 2013 and suggested that the boundary conflict could be resolved in the medium to long term. Consequently, Premier Li Keqiang planned to visit India in May 2013. Despite these public statements, tensions between the two countries re-surfaced in April 2013 when the PLA transgressed 19 kilometres into Indian territory in the Depsang Valley. President Xi Jinping's visit to India in

Table 3.1 Trade between India and China from 2011 to 2014

Year	India's exports to China (US$ billion)	China's exports to India (US$ billion)	India's trade deficit (US$ billion)	Total trade (US$ billion)
2011	16.54	52.83	36.28	69.37
2012	14.87	51.88	37.01	66.75
2013	14.50	51.38	36.88	65.9
2014	11.98	58.27	46.29	70.25

Source: Embassy of India. Beijing, China (www.indianembassy.org.cn/DynamicContent.aspx?MenuId=97&SubMenuId=0).

September 2014 also witnessed border transgressions by the PLA in Demchok and Chumar in Ladakh, which cast a dark and expansive cloud on the event. Indian Prime Minister Modi bluntly told Xi that China's intransigence on the border might affect bilateral ties. There were 228 border transgressions in 2010, 213 in 2011, 426 in 2012, 411 in 2013 and 334 transgressions by China until 4 August 2014. There were 11 border transgressions in 2015 and 16 in the first three months of 2016 (*India Today*, 2016).

During Xi's visit, 16 agreements and Memorandums of Understanding (MoUs) were signed between the two countries. China committed to investing US$30 billion in India, out of which US$20 billion would be for a fast train corridor and a new strategic road over a five-year period. Agreements and MoUs were also signed to enhance co-operation in outer space, civilian nuclear energy and cultural collaboration, among others. However, US$30 billion is well below the over US$100 billion suggested by Mumbai's Chinese general counsel before Xi's visit. China was keen to dwarf the US$35 billion committed by Japan when Modi visited Japan in September 2014. China is concerned that an investment relationship between India and Japan might lead to a full-blown 'democratic alliance' between the two countries. This may also lead to the 'democratic arc' comprising India, Japan, the United States and Australia, and may also include other Southeast Asian countries in the future. Additionally, almost all the MoUs are non-binding. Moreover, co-operation between India and China on civil nuclear energy is surprising because China has signed a nuclear deal with Pakistan to match India's nuclear deal with the United States, and raised objections to India's membership in the NSG.

According to the joint statement by India and China, China stated that it understands and supports India's aspiration to play a greater role in the UN, including in the UNSC. President Xi also reaffirmed that China wants India (and also Pakistan) to become a full member of the SCO rather than have observer status and in 2015 both countries were accorded membership status. However, at the November 2014 SAARC summit in Nepal, India has shown its reluctance for China's full membership and elevating its observer status.

The end result of Xi's visit was below expectations and intentions of either side due to the border dispute, mistrust and lack of understanding and respect for each other's mutual concerns. India outraged China when Prime Minister Modi made a remark on his trip to Japan. Modi stated that "Everywhere around us, we see an 18th century expansionist mind-set: encroaching on other countries, intruding in others' waters, invading other countries and capturing territory" (Roy, 2014). What is important is not only the statement but the fact that the statement was made in Japan. Both China and Japan lay claims to the disputed Senkaku/Diaoyu Islands and Modi's statement implicitly endorsed Japan's right to the islands. To make matters worse, President Pranab Mukerjee went on a official state visit to Vietnam a couple of days before Xi's India visit, which underlines India's new twin track diplomacy. President Mukherjee signed a slew of agreements, including one deal on oil exploration and deals on defence co-operation, which might lead to India selling offensive maritime strike systems like Brahmos to Vietnam. The deal on oil co-operation allows India's ONGC to explore oil and gas blocks around the Spratly Islands in the South China Sea. China and Vietnam both lay claim to the Spratly Islands.

Prime Minister Modi visited the United States after Xi's visit to India. According to the GoI, since 2011, the United States has surpassed Russia to become India's largest arms supplier. By 2011, India was the third-largest purchaser of US arms, accounting for some US$4.5 billion. By 2013, India had ordered or purchased sensor-fused bombs, Apache helicopters, P8-I surveillance aircraft, M-777 howitzers, C-130J and C-17 transport aircraft and a large amphibious transport dock. The United States now conducts more joint military exercises with India – approximately 50 per annum – than any other country including NATO allies. Although US–India partnership is based on myriad common interests and strong diplomatic and people-to-people exchanges, the driving force behind the strategic rapprochement is shared concerns about China's rise.

India has declined to re-affirm any 'One China' policy in joint statements or official documents until China conforms to 'One India' policy. China is aware that its 'land-sea' strategy to prevent closer relations between India and Japan is not going to be successful. China is therefore pushing for the Maritime Silk Road to create an interlocking commercial web in the Indian Ocean Region that can keep India occupied in its own maritime neighbourhood. India is cognisant of this new Chinese strategy. India is rolling out India-Pacific wide littoral initi-atives of its own, such as 'Project Mausam' to allow it to re-establish its ties with its ancient trade partners and re-establish an 'Indian Ocean world' along the littoral of the Indian Ocean.

Prime Minister Modi visited China on 14–16 May 2015. The visit opened up a new chapter in India–China relations. For the first time, President Xi travelled outside Beijing to receive a foreign leader, in Xi'an in his home province of Shaanxi. There were 24 agreements signed on the government-to-government side, 26 MoUs on the business-to-business side worth over US$22 billion and two joint statements, including one on climate change. The fact that India and China could come up with over 50 outcome documents in just eight months reveals the huge potential that exists between the two countries, as well as the efforts that have been made to elevate their partnership. Both sides decided to establish new consulates in each other's country, in Chengdu and Chennai and to expand their interactions at the sub-national level (Embassy of India, Beijing, n.d.b).

In the future, India and China will compete and co-operate on various issues. They will have similar concerns on terrorism emanating from Afghanistan, Pakistan and Central Asia and co-operate with each other on changing global order, the establishment of a just and fair new international order, climate change, economic development, tackling piracy and providing other global public goods There is even possibility of increased trade and commerce and investment between the two countries. There is an unlimited scope for cultural exchanges under the auspices of the 'Sino-Indian Year of Exchanges'. India and China will compete with each other in various fields especially energy security. China will remain concerned about presence of the Dalai Lama and other Tibetan leaders in India. India will have concerns over China's cyber espionage and Chinese dam construction on its side of the Brahmaputra river. Most importantly, they will compete with each other for strategic space and influence not only in South Asia and East Asia but also globally especially in international and regional organisations. The competition for strategic space will lead to a tense rivalry between the two neighbours and exacerbate the perennial security dilemma. This will lead to greater military expenditures by the two countries as China tries to bridge the gap with the United States and India tries to bridge the gap with China and hopefully try to surpass China.

II

In IR, power has multiple definitions. However, the most common definition of power is the ability to influence someone to do something which he or she would not normally do. This can be achieved by using hard power (economic, political and military) or soft power (Nye, 2008). There is also a lack of consensus regarding the measurement of power (Dowding, 2012). The study compares the difference in India's and China's economic, political and military power. To gauge the difference in economic power, indicators like GDP, GNI and other development indicators like IMR, life expectancy, etc. are used.

There is no consensus and uniformity in the definition and measurement of political power (Garst, 1989). As discussed in Chapter 1, a dilemma exists regarding the power status of India and China in the IR literature. Due to the ambiguity in the power status of India and China, the study compares India's and China's economic and military capabilities using Posen and Ross' (1996/7) definition of power dimension. Due to ambiguity in the definition and measurement of political power, the study employs Hedley Bull's (1977) conception of status as recognised by others. With this consideration in mind, to measure political power, the study uses permanent membership of the UNSC with veto power to illustrate the status of a country in the international system. The author conducted interviews with academics in India, China, the UK and Nigeria and experts in think tanks or the strategic community to confirm if permanent membership of the UNSC with veto power can be used to gauge the status of India and China in the international system. The interviewees agreed that permanent membership of the UNSC with veto power can be used as a parameter to gauge a country's status in the international system. Appendix A provides the list of people interviewed.

Economic power

India and China with their phenomenal growth rates are surging ahead as world economic powers. While China has experienced approximately double-digit growth rates since economic reforms were undertaken in 1978 under the leadership of Deng Xiaoping, India has lagged behind. India has been growing at an average of 6 per cent from 1991 to 2000 and approximately 7–8 per cent since from 2001 to 2015. China has made great strides in the economic realm and India is at least a decade behind China. It was estimated prior to the global financial crisis of 2008 that India would start growing at a faster rate relative to China by 2013. However, this did not materialise in 2013. In 2015, India's rate of growth of economy surpassed China. The Indian economy expanded by 7.5 per cent[1] compared to 6.9 per cent for China (BBC, 2016).[2] There is a broad consensus amongst economists and analysts that economic growth rates in India will be higher than growth rates in China in the short to medium term as China's economy slows. China is undertaking a process of economic restructuring as it tries to move from an investment-led export-oriented economic growth model to an economy based on domestic consumption and the services sector.

Despite India surpassing China in terms of economic growth rates in 2015, India lags behind China in every economic indicator (Table 3.2). China's GDP at US$10.3 trillion is more than five times the size of India at approximately US$2.0 trillion. In PPP terms, China's GNI is approximately US$17.9 trillion which is two and a half times more than India's at US$7.2 trillion. Moreover, China's per capita income (PCY) at US$7400 is almost five times India's PCY at US$1570, and in PPP terms, China's PCY at US$13,170 is more than double India's PCY at US$5630. According to the United Nation Development Programme (UNDP), China has a higher Human Development Index (HDI) rank of 90 compared to India's rank of 130. Adult literacy rates and life expectancy for both males and females are much higher in China than in India. China has a much lower IMR compared to India. The percentage of population and the actual number of people living below the poverty line and in extreme poverty is lower in China than in India.[3] Moreover, China has foreign exchange reserves of more than US$3.33 trillion compared to India's modest US$348.93 billion (*Trading Economics*, 2016). Thus, China is economically more powerful than India.

Table 3.2 Economic indicators of India and China

Economic indicators	China	India
GNY, Atlas Method (current US$) trillion	10.096	2.027
GNY per capita, Atlas Method (current US$)	7400.0	1570.0
GNY, PPP (current international US$) trillion	17.966	7.292
GNY per capita, PPP (current international US$)	13,170.0	5630.0
GDP at market prices (current US$) trillion	10.345	2.048
GDP, PPP (2011 PPP US$) trillion[a]	15.643	6.558
GDP growth (annual %) 2007, 2008, 2009, 2010, 2011, 2012, 2013, 2014, 2015[b]	14.2, 9.6, 9.2, 10.6, 9.5, 7.8, 7.7, 7.3, 6.9	9.8, 3.9, 8.5, 10.3, 6.6, 5.1, 6.9, 7.3, 7.5
Income level	Upper Middle Income	Lower Middle Income
Human Development Index (HDI) 2014[a]	High Human Development	Medium Human Development
HDI rank[a]	90	130
HDI value[a]	0.727	0.609
Life expectancy at birth (years): [a] female, male	77.3, 74.3	69.5, 66.6
Adult mortality rate (per 1000 people):[a] female, male	76,103	
Mortality rate – infant (per 1000 live births)[a]	10.9	41.4
Mortality under five (per 1000 live births)[a]	12.7	52.7
Child malnutrition (% under 5)[a]	9.4	47.9
Expenditure on health (% of GDP)[a]	5.6	4.0
Population below income poverty line (%) $1.25 a day (2002–12)[a]	6.3	23.6
Population below income poverty line (%) National poverty line (2004–14)[a]	–	21.9
Expected years of schooling (years):[a] female, male	13.2, 12.9	11.3, 11.8
Mean years of schooling (years):[a] female, male	6.9, 8.2	3.6, 7.2
Gross enrollment ratio, primary, both sexes (%) 2007, 2008, 2009, 2010, 2011, 2012, 2013	109.4, 113.0, 114.0, 112.5, 110.8, 110.1, 108.7	110.2, 110.9, 109.6, 109.2, 108.4, 109.8, 110.6
Gross enrollment ratio, secondary, both sexes (%) 2007, 2008, 2009, 2010, 2011, 2012, 2013	72.6, 76.7, 80.6, 84.9, 89.1, 92.1, 96.2	57.5, 60.6, 59.8, 63.3, 66.4, 69.2, 68.9
Gross enrollment ratio, primary and secondary, gender parity index (GPI) 2007, 2008, 2009, 2010, 2011, 2012, 2013	1.0, 1.0, 1.0, 1.0, 1.0, 1.0, 1.0	0.9, 1.0, 1.0, 1.0, 1.0, 1.0, 1.1
Mobile cellular subscriptions (per 100 people) 2007, 2008, 2009, 2010, 2011, 2012, 2013, 2014	41, 47.8, 55.3, 63.2, 72.1, 80.8, 88.7, 92.3	20.2, 29.5, 44.1, 62.4, 73.2, 69.9, 70.8, 74.5
Internet users (per 100 people) 2007, 2008, 2009, 2010, 2011, 2012, 2013, 2014	16, 22.6, 28.9, 34.3, 38.3, 42.3, 45.8, 49.3	4.0, 4.4, 5.1, 7.5, 10.1, 12.6, 15.1, 18.0
Improved sanitation facilities (% of population with access) 2007, 2008, 2009, 2010, 2011, 2012, 2013, 2014	67.2, 68.4, 69.6, 70.8, 71.9, 73.1, 74.2, 75.4	32.6, 33.6, 34.6, 35.5, 36.5, 37.5, 38.5, 39.5

Source: all figures are from World Data Bank (n.d.), unless stated.

Notes
a   UNDP (2015).
b   BBC (2016).

Political power

Permanent membership of the UNSC with veto power is a symbol of prestige and influence. According to Srinath Raghavan, Senior Fellow at New Delhi's Centre for Policy Research, "The key attribute of a great power is not just military or economic power, but the ability to set the agenda of international politics. The UNSC has a great deal of control over what is discussed" (cited in Wax and Lakshmi, 2010). All the interviewees (Appendix A)[4] agreed that China's membership of the UNSC[5] with a veto power elevates its political status and leverage vis-à-vis India because the latter is not a permanent member of the UNSC. All the interviewees also agreed that China is politically more powerful than India. According to Ambassador Maharaj K. Rasgotra, former Foreign Secretary, GoI, "Membership of the UNSC with veto power elevates China's status relative to India. China is perceived as a greater power relative to India by leaders globally, especially in Africa. The asymmetry in power favours China" (Interview, Appendix A). India aspires to become a permanent member of the UNSC and sit on the high table as a major global power. It has been trying to conjure support for its candidature for the permanent membership of the UNSC along with Germany, Japan and Brazil. However, its ambitions have been blighted to date. Opinion is divided whether India will become a permanent member of the UNSC and it seems it may take some time before India can sit on the high table as a great power.

Military power

According to Table 3.3, China expends more on defence expenditure than India. China has spent more on defence than India in the last decade. Table 3.4 illustrates that China has superior military prowess compared to India. The major arms supplier for both countries is Russia; although they have also acquired military equipment from France, Ukraine and Israel (India has also acquired military equipment from Germany and Great Britain and since 2010 from the United States), which facilitates the technological comparison of their military capabilities to a certain extent (*Military Balance*, 2012). Considering that the technological difference is minor in conventional military equipment, China has numerical superiority over India in almost all the indicators. India lags behind China as far as missile and nuclear weapons are concerned. Additionally, China,

Table 3.3 Defence expenditures of India and China from 2001 to 2015 (US$ billion)

Country	Year														
	2001	2002	2003	2004	2005	2006	2007	2008	2009	2010	2011	2012	2013	2014	2015
India	14	13	16	20	22	22	27	32	38	31	36	41	42	47	48
China	46	48	56	63	104	122	46	60	70	76	90	103	116	131	146

Source: *Military Balance* 2002–16, IISS.

Table 3.4 Military indicators of India and China

Indicator	Country	
	China	India
Defence budget (US$ billion) 2010, 2011, 2012, 2013, 2014, 2015	76.4, 89.8, 106.0, 116.0, 131.0, 146.0	29.7, 31.9, 41.9, 45.2 45.3, 48.0
Defence expenditure (market exchange rate US$ billion) 2010, 2011, 2012, 2013, 2014, 2015	76.0, 90.2, 102.6, 162.0, 178.0, 180	30.9, 36.1, 40.9, 41.9, 46.5, 47.9
Defence personnel		
(1) Active	2,333,000	1,346,000
Army	1,600,000	1,150,900
Navy	235,000	58,350
Air Force	398,000	127,200
Strategic Missile Forces	100,000	–
Coast Guard	–	9550
(2) Paramilitary	660,000	1,403,700
Reserve	510,000	1,155,000
Space Based Systems		
Satellites	77	2
(1) Communications	5	–
(2) Navigation/Positioning/Timing	18	–
(3) ISR	39	–
(4) ELINT/SIGINT	15	–
Anti-Satellite Capability	Yes	No
Strategic Missiles	467	54
(1) ICBM	62	Agni V[a]
(2) IRBM	16	Agni III[b], Agni IV[c]
(3) MRBM	146	12
(4) SRBM	189	42
(5) LACM	54	In development
Equipment by Type		
(1) Army		
(i) Main Battle Tank (MBT)	6540	2974+
(ii) LT TK	650	–
(iii) RECCE	250	110
(iv) AIFV	3950	1455+
(v) Armoured Personnel Carrier	5020	336+
(vi) Artillery	13,178+	9682+
(2) Navy		
(i) Submarines	61	14
(a) Strategic	4	0
(b) Tactical	57	14
(ii) Principal surface combatants	74	28
(a) Destroyers	19	13
(b) Frigates	54	13
(c) Aircraft carriers	1	2
(iii) Patrol and coastal combatants	199+	109
(iv) Mine warfare	49	6
(v) Principal amphibious ships	221	1
(3) Air Force		
(i) Aircraft	2306	881
(ii) Helicopters	53	441

Source: *Military Balance* 2012–16, IISS.

Notes
a Agni IV with a range of just over 5000 km was tested on 19 April 2012. However, more tests are required before serial production can be initiated.
b Entering service.
c In test phase.

unlike India, possesses anti-satellite capabilities. India is trying to acquire anti-satellite capabilities to match China and is playing catch-up with China.[6] Thus, it can be rightly argued that China is a greater military power relative to India.

All the interviewees in Appendix A stated unequivocally that China is economically, political and militarily more powerful than India. All the Indian and Chinese experts agreed that China's permanent membership to the UNSC with veto power makes China politically more powerful and influential relative to India. They also agreed that relative to India, China is perceived as a greater power by leaders globally especially in Africa. According to Professor Madhu Bhalla, Delhi University (Interview, Appendix A), "African leaders see how China uses its economic muscle against the US. Economic influence translates into political influence. It is this perception which favours China relative to India in their interaction with African countries". According to Professor Srikanth Kondapalli, JNU (Interview, Appendix A),

> Unlike China which is active in 49 countries in Africa and 48 heads of state or other senior officials attend the FOCAC Summit, only 24–25 heads of state or senior government officials attended the second India–Africa Forum in 2011.

China's economic and political muscle allows it to pursue strategies that India cannot match. It is widespread not only in West Africa but in the entire continent relative to India's selective approach. Thus, China's economic and political power enables it to have a greater and far-reaching diplomacy relative to India.

III

Different economic and political systems exist in different countries. Different political economies in different countries have a direct bearing on how the state mobilises and extracts resources from domestic society via its institutions (and other means like nationalism, and statist or anti-statist ideology) to achieve foreign policy objectives. Following Karl Marx, capitalism and communism are two systems at the opposite end of the spectrum with a combination of the two in varying degrees and forms lying between the two. For the sake of simplicity, the study mentions three different political and economic systems. First is the capitalist system where the means of production is in the hands of private enterprise as in the United States. Second is socialism/communism where the ownership of the means of production is in the hands of the state as in China before the economic reforms in 1979. Third is a mixed economy system where the state controls the means of production in the key and strategic industries (private enterprise entered these industries at a later stage of development) and the consumer goods industry is in the hands of private enterprise as in India. There is a consensus amongst scholars that the nature of economic system determines the composition of the non-agricultural sector and politico-legal institutions and the study adheres to this proposition. The debate regarding which economic system

– capitalism, socialism or mixed economy – translates into higher economic and social welfare is outside the scope of this study.

Political economy: an institutional framework

The analytical framework chosen to highlight the difference in the political economy of India and China, the reforms introduced in the two countries and consequently their different growth trajectories is the one suggested by economic historian and noble laureate Douglass North (1990, 1994). In this framework, the performance of the economies over time is determined by path-dependent responses of individual entrepreneurs and organisations to the changing incentive structure generated by the evolving institutional matrix consisting of mutually interacting formal and informal rules of the game in the social, economic and political domains. The critical role of path-dependence in this analytical framework prompts the discussion of the Indian and Chinese political economies with the post-independence economic development (strategies which were rooted in the pre-independence period) that aimed at transforming the respective under developed economies into dynamically growing economies with equitable distribution (Tendulkar and Bhavani, 2007).

The analytical framework offered by Douglass North (1990, 1994) provides a diagnostic comprehension of the evolution of economies over time. The key element of North's framework is the notion of 'institutional matrix' in a society characterised by an interconnected mesh of formal as well as informal rules of the game and their concomitant enforcement characteristics. Informal rules comprise of customs, ideological beliefs, traditions, conventions, widely accepted codes of conduct and other behavioural norms. Formal rules cover rules such as the constitution, statutes, common laws, individual contracts and any formally binding procedures in the social, economic and political realm. Rules governing the structure of polity, its functioning and basic decision-making processes fall in the political domain. In the economic domain, they fundamentally encompass rules relating to the ownership, exchange and transfer of private property rights. The social domain comprises rules relating to inheritance of property, marriage and family (North, 1990, 1994). In this framework, the rules governing the formal organs of the state, namely the legislature, executive and the judiciary, are taken to constitute the political contract accepted by the people for governance. The political contract in turn evolves from and is shaped by the ideology of the society as reflected in the commonly accepted set of shared beliefs, goals and practices enshrined in what may be termed as a social contract (Tendulkar and Bhavani, 2007).

Institutions together with the standard constraints of economics define the choice set and determine the transformation (production) and transactions costs, and thus the feasibility and profitability of engaging in different economic activities. Thus institutions provide the incentive structure in the society, i.e. opportunities for benefit in different realms in the society: social, political and economic. Institutions lay down the rules of the game according to which organisations and entrepreneurs act (North, 1994). For instance, if the institutional structure prevents the rise of entrepreneurship, then entrepreneurs will not rise (as in China from 1949 to 1978) or if it offers gains from unproductive activities such as procuring licenses to pre-empt competition, firms will spend their resources on these activities (as in India from 1947 to 1985). Thus the amalgamation of formal rules, informal norms and enforcement characteristics, i.e. the 'institutional matrix', shapes how an economy performs, and explicates the difference in the political economy of India and China.

IV

This section discusses the political economy of India in two different phases: pre-reform phase from 1947 to 1991; and post-reform phase from 1991 to present.

Political economy of India: pre-reform era (1947–91)

Although India and China achieved independence around the same time, they adopted different political and economic paths to achieve rapid economic growth. In India, the long-held beliefs in the ideologies of economic nationalism and Nehruvian socialism were firmly rooted in the suspicion of international trade, markets and private capitalists and a naive faith in the benevolence and omniscience of state. This posed prima facie formidable obstacles to economic reforms. India's economic underdevelopment at independence was attributed to the British colonial policy of laissez-faire and free trade by the political leadership at that time and this provided the rationale for economic nationalism (Srinivasan and Tendulkar, 2003).

Consequently, India, a democracy, adopted a 'mixed economy' system to attain the 'commanding heights of the economy' and to mitigate the social ills of capitalism rather than destroying it. This development strategy and the consequent economic policies led to a highly regulated market and private economic activities for more than four decades. This is because India inherited limited but expanding functioning markets and private enterprise in modern industries remained well entrenched due to the democratic political framework that provided constitutional sanctity to the private ownership of property. It is well documented that at independence, India had one of the most well developed private sectors in manufacturing in the 'Third World'. However, the potential positive contribution of these features to economic development was never recognised by the political leadership inclined to establish a socialist pattern of society (Tendulkar and Bhavani, 2007).

The Indian economy was characterised by the Soviet-inspired model of centrally planned heavy industrialisation under the aegis of the Mahalanobis Model. This was formulated in the Industrial Policy Resolution (IPR) 1956. The public sector comprising SOEs commanded strategic industries like railways, telecommunications, defence, coal, iron and steel, oil and gas, atomic energy, aircraft manufacture, generation and distribution of electric power among others. The private sector produced consumer goods like electronic goods, automobiles and garments to name a few. There was a third sector – a mix of public and private enterprise – in which the state would increasingly establish new units and the private sector could also play a role. For instance in road transport, machine tools, ferro-alloys, drugs, dyestuffs and plastics, etc. The constitutional guarantee of the fundamental right to private property was provided by the IPR 1948. According to IPR 1948, SOEs will also progressively participate actively in the spheres of activity of the private enterprise and will not hesitate to intervene whenever the progress of the industry in the hands of the private enterprise was unsatisfactory. The IPRs of 1948 and 1956 reflected the prejudice against the private sector. The embedded beliefs of socialism and nationalisation were thus responsible for almost four decades of development strategy focused on public sector domination in basic and heavy industries and autarky until the 1970s (Tendulkar and Bhavani, 2007).

The Industries Development and Regulation Act (IDRA) 1951 paved the way for the regulation of the private sector. The IDRA made government permission compulsory for private investment above a certain specified limit with a view to channel large-scale private investment in accordance with social priorities by preventing the diversion of scarce resources into non-priority areas and also preventing over-capacity in key and strategic areas (Marathe, 1986). The IDRA laid down elaborate rules for licensing giving rise to the famous 'License Raj' in India. To control the concentration of economic power in the hands of the private sector, IDRA restricted the entry of large business houses to only a small subset of scheduled industries (Tendulkar and Bhavani, 2007).

In the late 1960s and again in the early 1980s, the system of economic controls was re-examined and an attempt was made to limit controls to large firms to achieve economic and social egalitarianism. The Monopolies and Restrictive Trade Practices (MRTP) Act 1969, Foreign Exchange Regulations Act (FERA) 1973 and import and foreign exchange controls stifled the growth of the private sector. In 1968, Prime Minister Indira Gandhi nationalised the commercial banks and invoked the vote catching slogan of 'Garibi Hatao' (eradicate poverty). This was followed by an indiscriminate expansion of the public sector which continued unabated until the 1980s (Tendulkar and Bhavani, 2007).

According to Desai (1999), the development strategy followed a caste system in modern industry for according policy priorities. The highest caste or the most favoured were SOEs. Second in the hierarchy were the modern small-scale industries with the state providing protection and promotional concessions. These were followed by industries that needed government permission under the IDRA 1951 for undertaking domestic private investment exceeding a fixed pre-specified floor level. Fourth were the large-scale business houses represented by the private sector. At the bottom rung were the subsidiaries of foreign companies which were subject to stiffer conditions under the FERA 1973 (Tendulkar and Bhavani, 2007).

The IPR 1980 officially stated the popular disillusionment and disenchantment with the unsatisfactory state of the SOEs. There was recognition of the fact that the losses and lower profitability of the SOEs could no longer be camou-flaged under 'public interest'. It announced a decision to make the SOEs more efficient by taking corrective measures on an individual basis under the aegis of a time-bound programme. The two primary objectives were, first, maximise pro-duction and optimally utilise installed capacity, and, second, to enhance produc-tivity to achieve higher growth. In order to improve their financial performance, central SOEs were given limited autonomy through the instrument of MoU (Tendulkar and Bhavani, 2007). In the mid 1980s, some of the SOEs were granted special privileges and allowed to form joint ventures with foreign corpo-rations. Maruti Udyog Limited's deal with Suzuki of Japan in 1983 is an apt example.

Under the stewardship of Prime Minister Rajiv Gandhi in 1984, a de facto reasonably wide ranging domestic liberalisation was introduced but the govern-ment was cautious on the external trade front. Although IDRA remained intact, the private sector was allowed to enter into industries which were previously under the hands of the public sector. There was also considerable relaxation of restrictions on large-scale industrial houses falling under the MRPT Act. In external trade, rules for importation of technology were considerably liberalised in view of the earlier autarkic policy. These measures reflected a more positive attitude towards harnessing the role of the markets and private sector for development. Despite loosening of controls after 1985, there was strong momentum for expansion of the SOEs. The first candid official admission of the indiscriminate expansion of and serious problems afflicting the SOEs was stated in the statement of the IPR July 1991. Thus, on the eve of reforms, India was possibly the most comprehensively regulated market economy (Tendulkar and Bhavani, 2007).

Reforms were introduced in India in 1991 under the leadership of Prime Minister P.V. Narasimha Rao. The prevailing government policies and regulations created a private sector characterised by large family-owned business houses, i.e. concentrated family ownership of Indian business assets. The highly favourable domestic climate in the absence of foreign competition and strong monopolistic positions made the industrial houses increasingly inclined to operate in the shel-tered domestic market. To grow, Indian business groups pursued unrelated diversi-fication. For instance, the Aditya Birla Group operated in diverse industries such as textiles, dairy, tea, sugar, automobiles, steel, sanitary ware, shipping, cement and plastics. The PRG Group had interest in agribusiness, cable, carbon black, fin-ancial services, music, radio, electricity, engineering, tea, typewriters, fibreglass, etc. Some business houses found opportunities to expand business activities in emerging markets in Africa and Southeast Asia. The total FDI by Indian enter-prises rose exponentially from a mere US$2 million in 1970 to approximately US$100 million in 1980 (Kumar *et al.*, 2009).

Before 1991, the Indian private sector was characterised by poor quality and productivity. The 'Licence Raj' and lack of competition provided an environ-ment in which the Indian businesses flourished. However, they were globally uncompetitive and lacked comparative advantage because of lack of economies of scale and their inability to develop unique competencies. Thus, Indian companies in the public and the private sector were not geared to compete globally or against global competitors in the domestic markets (Kumar *et al.*, 2009).

Indian political economy: post-reform era (1991 to present)

Before discussing the post-reform era, it is pertinent to distinguish between privatisation, disinvestment and liberalisation. According to Thiemeyer, there are at least 15 different concepts of privatisation (cited in Chai, 2003: 235). In the Indian debates, there is no uniformity in the usage of the term privatisation. The entry of private sector units in the construction of physical infrastructural facilities has usually been described as privatisation. In recent times, this has also been coined as public–private partnership. According to Tendulkar and Bhavani (2007), a sale of minor equity stake in SOEs is decried as privatisation by the Left political parties in India. Chai (2003) avers that privatisation in most countries implies the sale of state-owned non-agricultural enterprises such that it reduces public ownership to less than 51 per cent and passes management control to commercially oriented private hands. This definition is used in this study. Disinvestment is defined as the establishment of a broad-based ownership through liquidating or selling government shares to retail and institutional investors or a collective or the workers and managers of the enterprise. Liberalisation on the other hand implies the relaxation of government restrictions especially in the economic and social sphere. An example of liberalisation is the Washington Consensus. Economic liberalisation is often associated with privatisation but the two can be quite separate processes.

In July 1991, India initiated systemic changes in its economic policies precipitated by the twin crises of fiscal deficits and defaults on foreign debt. The reforms introduced in 1991 involved a major shift in the development strategy towards greater integration with the world economy and liberalisation of restrictions on market transactions and private economic activities. This is not to say that the reform process has been smooth, internally synchronised, complete or fully successful (Kumar *et al.*, 2009).

Nonetheless, economic reforms in India in 1991 paved the way for the privatisation and liberalisation of the Indian economy according to the Washington Consensus. This led to changes in the industrial, financial and trade policy. The IPR 1991 mentioned serious problems affecting the SOEs which made the SOEs a burden rather than a national asset. It promised a review of existing portfolio of public sector units (Tendulkar and Bhavani, 2007). Corrective measures included disinvestment of up to 20 per cent equity in some SOEs to yield 0.4 per cent of the GDP and a cut of a 0.3 per cent in budgetary support to SOEs. However, India's experience with privatisation of SOEs was short lived and very few central and even fewer state level SOEs were privatised. This was due to opposition not only within the ruling party but also from the opposition political parties because of vested selfish interests. Disinvestment of some SOEs was carried out despite some political opposition (Mohan, 2005). Table 3.5 provides a breakdown of disinvestments in terms of the number of SOEs in which the equity was sold and broad description of modalities of disinvestments.

Table 3.5 Disinvestment in Indian SOEs from 1991–2 to 2015–16

Year	No. of companies in which equity sold	Modality
1991–2	47 (31 in one tranche and 16 in another)	Minority shares sold by auction method bundles of 'very good', 'good' and 'average' companies
1992–3	36 (in three tranches)	Bundling of shares abandoned. Shares sold separately for each company by auction method
1993–4	–	Equity of seven companies sold by open auction but proceeds received n 1993–4
1994–5	13	Sales through auction method in which NRIs and other persons legally permitted to buy, hold, or sell equity were allowed to participate
1995–6	5	Equities of four companies auctioned and government piggybacked on IDBI fixed price offering for fifth company
1996–7	1	GDR (VSNL) in international market
1997–8	1	GDR (MTNL) in international market
1998–9	5	GDR (VSNL)/Domestic offerings with the participation of FIIs (CONCOR, GAIL). Cross purchase by three oil sector companies i.e. GAIL, ONGC, and Indian Oil Corporation
1999–2000	4	GDR-GAIL, VSNL domestic issue, BALCO restructuring, MFILs strategic sale and others
2000–1	4	Strategic sale of BALCO, LJMC, KRL (CRL), CPCL (MRL)
2001–2	9	Strategic sale of CMC 51%, HTL 74%, VSNL 25%, IBP 33.58%, PPL 74% and other modes: ITDC, HCI, STC, MMTC
2002–3	5	Strategic sale of JESSOP 72%, HZL 26%, MFIL 26%, IPCL 25% and other modes: HCI, Maruti
2003–4	3	–
2004–5	–	IPO in NTPC, sale to employees of IPCL, and balance receipts of ONGC sale
2005–6	–	Sale of shares of MTNL to public sector financial institution and public sector banks and sale to employees.
2007–8	2	PGCIL and REC
2009–10	2	NHPC and OIL
2010–11	3	Coal India Limited, MOIL and SJVN
2011–12	2	PFC, ONGC
2012–13	8	HAL, NALCO, NBCC, NMDC, NTPC, OIL, RCF, SAIL
2013–14	12	BPCL, CPSE-ETF, EIL, HCL, IOCL, ITDC, MMTC, NFL, NHPC, NLC, PFC, STC
2014–15	2	Coal India, SAIL
2015–16		BDL, CONCOR, DCIL, EIL, HCL, IOCL, NTPC, NTPC[a], PFC, REC
Total	49[b]	

Sources: Tendulkar and Bhavani (2007: 132) from 1991–2 to 2005–6; Department of Disinvestment, Ministry of Finance, GOI, www.divest.nic.in/MinoritySale.asp from 2007–8 to 2011–16.

Notes
a Sale of Bonus debentures held with government to EPFO.
b Total number of companies in which disinvestment has taken place.

Liberalisation removed the fetters which had plagued the economy since independence. The reforms changed the environment in which the Indian businesses could operate. The IPR 1991 allowed private firms to operate in sectors which were previously the domain of the SOEs. However, the private sector was not allowed to operate in a small negative list of 18 industries, such as telecommunications, airways, energy, banking, etc. This list was justified for reasons of security, environment and balance of payments. Later, only four sectors related to security and strategic concerns were reserved for the SOEs. It also removed fetters like diversification of large conglomerates under the MRTP Act, and pre-entry inspection of investment decisions regarding new capacity, mergers and expansion. The government took measures to facilitate private business. The incentive structure for private enterprise – markets and institutions for property rights and rule of law – that were in place since independence were strengthened (Tendulkar and Bhavani, 2007). Import licensing restrictions were also eliminated for 80 per cent of the industries in 1991 alone (Rosser and Rosser, 2004). There was a reduction in import tariffs which declined from an average of 85 per cent to 25 per cent. Additionally, quantitative controls on imports were also reduced. Indian enterprises were allowed to issue Global Depository Receipts to raise capital in the international financial markets. Foreign institutional investors were permitted to invest in the Indian equity markets. Measures were undertaken to make procedures for foreign direct investment (FDI) approvals more efficient and there was automatic approval of projects in at least 35 industries if they were within the perimeter of foreign participation. Measures were also undertaken to increase FDI. For instance, foreign investment was allowed in priority sectors and the share of foreign investment in joint ventures was increased from 40 per cent to 50 per cent (Kumar *et al.*, 2009).

The reforms proved a boon in disguise for the private sector. Measures undertaken by the government diversified the sectors in which private enterprises could operate, providing them with new opportunities. It helped spur consolidation within industries and led to an increase in the size and power of the private enterprises, especially the well-established business houses like Reliance Industries Limited (RIL), Tata Group, Birla Group and Bajaj Group among others. Consequently, companies undertook tough corporate restructuring measures like focusing on core business, consolidating the management, strengthening the balance sheet and enhancing competitiveness to prepare them for the global marketplace. Competition with the MNCs also increased the competitiveness of the private sector (Kumar *et al.*, 2009). Liberalisation also ushered in entrepreneurship which led to the emergence of small but dynamic firms led by entrepreneurs who are willing to take greater risks and are connected to the global economy. These small firms also have creative managers which augurs well for the Indian economy (Engardio, 2007).

Unlike China, India did not attract considerable FDI. This is because private industry, large and small, which received protection from stringent import controls since independence, did not want FDI in competing areas. However, it advocated FDI mostly through the joint venture route (which was non-competing and beneficial for domestic capitalists) and in areas like physical infrastructure where it would be complementary (Tendulkar and Bhavani, 2007).

Reforms were also introduced in the SOEs to increase their operational efficiency. For instance, longer tenures for chief executives of SOEs, greater operational autonomy, MoUs between SOEs and their parent ministries, freedom for SOEs to raise resources from the market, etc. Despite the reforms, autonomy for the SOEs has remained elusive. Although the private sector has been freed from license permit restrictions, commercial SOEs remain shackled by the need to obtain administrative clearances from the procedure driven bureaucracy. The SOEs are also being squeezed by the significant reduction in budgetary support besides competing with the private sector.

In the face of completion – domestic and foreign – a few SOEs have managed to pull up their socks and increase operational efficiency; a few that had been running well have continued to do so, but a large number of the SOEs have sunk deeper into the red. There are 11 well performing SOEs, including ONGC, which account for more than 75 per cent of the profits of the SOEs. These are called the jewels of the Indian public sector (Navratan meaning nine jewels. Two were added later on to make it 11). The nine SOEs were chosen because of their potential to become global players based on their size, performance, nature of activities, future prospects, etc. The Navratans were delegated substantial powers like the freedom to incur capital expenditure without any monetary ceiling, entering into technology joint ventures, opening new offices in India and abroad, and the appointment of functional directors.

The transformation of Indian enterprises and industrial houses post-1991 was critical in preparing Indian corporations for the global marketplace. The private sector and public sector coexist, operate and compete with each other in the Indian economy and, since 1991, they also compete with the well-established and iconic MNCs in the domestic market in India and also globally. The increase in FDI is a direct consequence of the pursuit by Indian enterprises to be competitive globally (Kumar *et al.*, 2009). Table 3.6 lists some of the main sectors/ industries in which the private and public sector compete not only with each other but also with MNCs.

Indian firms in the public and the private sector have also appeared in the Fortune 500. Table 3.7 provides a breakdown of the list of Indian companies in the Fortune 500 from 2005 to 2012. The number of Indian firms has increased from five in 2005 to eight in 2010 and decreased to seven in 2015. There has been a gradual improvement in their ranking, especially RIL, which has moved from 415 in 2005 to 99 in 2012. However, its global ranking has declined since 2012. In 2015, out of the five public sector enterprises, four are in the hydrocarbon sector and one in the banking sector. These two sectors were the sole recourse of the SOEs from 1947 to 1991. The number of private sector enterprises in the list of Fortune 500 companies increased from one in 2005 to two in 2008 and three in 2010. In 2015, there are only two private sector enterprises in the Fortune 500 rankings. There are expectations that the number of private sector enterprises in the Fortune 500 will increase and there may also be an improvement in their ranking.

Table 3.6 Industries where the private sector, public sector and MNCs operate in the Indian economy

Industry	Private sector	Public sector	MNCs
Aviation – domestic	Spice Jet, Airlines, Air Deccan Airlines, Go Air, JetLite, Indigo, Alliance Air, Jagson Airlines, Paramount Airways	Air India and Indian Airlines	–
Aviation – international	Jet Airways	Air India	British Airways, Virgin Airlines, Air Emirates, Air Asia etc.
Commercial automobiles	Tata Motors, Mahindra and Mahindra	Maruti Udyog Limited (MUL) till 2007	General Motors, Nissan, Volkswagen, Mercedes, Ford etc.
Hotels and hospitality	Taj Group, Oberoi's, The Leela Palaces, Hotels and Resorts, ITC	Ashok Group of Hotels	Starwood Hotels & Resorts Worldwide (Le Meridien)
Mining	Vedanta, Hindalco, Dempo Mining Corporation Limited, Obulapuram Mining Company	NALCO, Hindustan Copper Limited	–
Oil and gas	Reliance Industries, Essar Oil, Videocon	ONGC, IOC, BPCL, HPCL, GAIL	BP, Chevron, Cairn, Royal Dutch Shell
Iron and steel	Tata Iron and Steel, Arcelor Mittal, Essar, Yash Birla, Kirloskar Group, Jindal Steel and Power Limited	SAIL, Bharat Refractories Ltd, KIOCL Ltd, Rashtriya Ispat Nigam Limited, Ispat Industries Limited	POSCO, POS-Hyundai Steel Manufacturing, Daido Kogyo, Ralco Steels Private Limited
Heavy manufacturing	L&T, Bharat Forge	BHEL, Braithwaite & Co. Ltd, Andrew Yule & Company Ltd, Bharat Bhari Udyog Nigam Ltd	Volvo Construction Equipment, Komatsu, Caterpillar, Hitachi Construction Machinery, CNH
Banking and finance	ICICI, HDFC, Yes Bank	SBI, P&B, Bank of Baroda, Andhra Bank	HSBC, Citi Group, RBS ABN Amro, Deutsche Bank
Consumer electronics	Videocon, Godrej, BPL	–	LG, Samsung, Sony, Philips
Wireless and telecommunications	Reliance Communications, Bharti Airtel, Idea, Tata DoCoMo	BSNL, MTNL, NICSI	Vodafone, Virgin Mobile
Pharmaceuticals	Ranbaxy, CIPLA, Dr Reddys	Bengal Chemicals & Pharmaceuticals Ltd, Bihar Drugs & Organic Chemicals Ltd	Pfizer, Novartis, Johnson & Johnson, GlaxoSmithKline
Shipping	Reliance Industries Limited, Essar Shipping Ports, Garware Offshore Services Limited, Great Eastern Shipping	Hindustan Shipyard Limited, Dredging Corporation Of India Ltd, Ennore Port Ltd, Sethusamudram Corporation Ltd	Maersk, The Mediterranean Shipping Company, etc.

Source: compiled from different ministries, GoI.

Table 3.7 List of Indian corporations in the Fortune 500 from 2005 to 2015

Company	Ownership	Industry	Rank in year										
			2005	2006	2007	2008	2009	2010	2011	2012	2013	2014	2015
Indian Oil	Public	Oil and gas	170	153	135	116	105	125	98	83	88	96	119
Reliance Industries	Private	Petroleum, diversified	417	342	269	206	264	175	134	99	107	114	158
Bharat Petroleum	Public	Oil and gas	429	368	325	290	289	307	272	225	229	242	280
Hindustan Petroleum	Public	Oil and gas	436	378	336	287	311	282	336	267	260	284	327
State Bank of India	Public	Banking, finance	–	498	495	380	363	354	292	285	298	303	260
Tata Motors	Private	Automobile	–	–	–	–	–	410	359	314	316	287	254
Oil and Natural Gas	Public	Oil and gas	454	402	369	335	402	413	361	357	369	424	449
Tata Steel	Private	Metals	–	–	–	315	258	442	370	401	471	–	–
Total			5	6	6	7	7	8	8	8	8	7	7

Source: compiled from Fortune Global 500, 2005–15.

Since the beginning of the twenty-first century, the Indian private sector has emerged as the flag bearer not only domestically but also globally. According to a report published on 26 June 2010 in *Business Standard*, a leading economics daily in India, from 2000 to 2010, net sales and net profits grew at a faster rate in the private sector relative to the public sector. During the period 2000–10, the share of the private sector in the net sales jumped from 48.33 per cent to 68.55 per cent. On the other hand, the share of the public sector fell from 51.17 per cent to 31.45 per cent. In similar vein, the share of private sector with respect to net profit in the secondary and tertiary sectors rose from 39.17 per cent to 63.86 per cent whereas the share of the public sector declined from 60.83 per cent to 36.14 per cent (*Business Standard*, 2010). In 2012, the private sector accounted for more than 75 per cent of the GDP. Since 1990, the share of the public sector in GDP growth remained stagnant at 6 per cent, whereas private sector GDP growth went up to 7.7 per cent in the 2000s from 5.7 per cent in the previous decade. During the same period, private corporate investments have increased from 10.3 per cent of GDP in 1990 to 17.3 per cent in 2010 (*The Hindu*, 2012). Thus, India's economy has become a private sector economy in the new millennium. Economic growth in India is being driven by entrepreneurs and business leaders whose firms have become competitive and operate globally.

Indian enterprises, especially the Indian private sector, undertook corporate restructuring programmes which instilled confidence in them. As a result, rather than being scared of global competition in the domestic market, they were transformed into buoyant players adept at building Indian MNCs. This led to the creation of a number of large private enterprises that compete with the best in the world. Moreover, most of these enterprises fall in the high segment or cutting-edge and knowledge-based industries. For example, pharmaceuticals and biotechnology powerhouses like Ranbaxy, Dr Reddy's Laboratories, CIPLA, Jubilant and software giants like Infosys, TCS and Wipro to name an illustrious few. These outsourcing companies progressed from a low-cost base and are slowly but steadily moving up the food chain to more sophisticated projects and are starting to challenge the prominent Western MNCs like EDS, IBM and Accenture. Consequently, the Indian government is being persuaded by the Indian enterprises to implement changes in its policies and move towards a more open domestic market and business environment.

Indian corporations, especially the private sector corporations, have also acquired enterprises abroad. For instance, in 2006, Tata Steel acquired the Anglo-Dutch Company Corus for US$12.98 billion to become the fifth largest steel producer in the world. Another Tata Group Company, Tata Motors, acquired Jaguar Land Rover for US$2.3 billion in 2008. The Tata Group has also acquired hotels across the globe. Tata Tea, the second largest branded tea company in the world, acquired Tetley based in the UK. Mittal Steel acquired Arcelor to become the largest steel producer in the world. Incidentally, Mittal is credited for consolidating the steel industry. Hindalco, a part of the Aditya Birla Group, made an all-cash US$6 billion purchase of Canadian Novelis in 2007 to become the world's largest aluminium company. In 2010, Bharti Airtel acquired

Zain Africa for US$10.7 billion. Other prominent Indian firms like Infosys, TCS, Wipro, Bharat Forge, Essel Propack, Vedanta, Mahindra and Mahindra, Hidesign, Marico, Godrej, VIP, United Breweries, TVS, Larsen and Toubro, Bajaj Auto, Piramal Enterprises, RPG Group and Suzlon among host of others have made acquisitions and/or are planning to make acquisitions abroad. Even smaller private sector firms have made foreign acquisitions abroad. For instance, Bennett Coleman acquired Virgin Radio Holdings for US$100 million in 2008. The relatively unknown Rain Group bought the US-based CII Carbon for US$595 million in 2007, which helped them to become the world's leading producer of calcine petroleum coke (Kumar *et al.*, 2009). Indian Overseas acquisitions by Indian drug makers in 2015 stood at US$1.5 billion, a five-year high, as against US$251 million in 2014. Indian pharmaceutical major Lupin has completed the acquisition of US-based GAVIS Pharmaceuticals in a deal worth US$880 million. Cipla Ltd, one of the major pharmaceutical and biotechnology companies has acquired two US-based generic drug makers, InvaGen Pharmaceuticals Inc. and Exelan Pharmaceuticals Inc. for US$550 million (IBEF, 2016).

V

This section discusses the political economy of China in two phases: pre-reform phase from 1949 to 1978 and post-reform phase from 1978 to present.

Political economy of China: pre-reform era (1949–78)

The PRC was proclaimed by Mao Zedong in 1949. In 1949, China was a poor country characterised by low PCY, significant pressure from population on arable land and other resources and an absence of institutions appropriate for economic development. China, a communist state, adopted Stalin's model of 'centralised planned economy', emphasising capital-intensive heavy industrialisation to the detriment of the agricultural sector with comprehensive state and collective property. However, there were substantive modifications from the Soviet model. The result was economic growth and development, which was interrupted when ideological and political factors gained supremacy over economic factors (Rosser and Rosser, 2004).

The period from 1949 to 1952 was a period of consolidation. The state had two important goals. First, the redistribution of land to individual households was implemented in preparation of collectivisation. However, collectivisation was not to be pursued in undue haste. China adopted the basic Soviet model of land reform and subsequent collectivisation in the 1950s. There were also differences between the two, which were sufficient to avoid some of the extreme negative consequences experienced in the Soviet Union. Second was nationalisation and consolidation of industry in preparation for national economic planning. Financial and educational reforms were also undertaken along with other changes deemed necessary to stabilise the economy in preparation for the beginning of the first five-year plan in 1953 (Gregory and Stuart, 1999).

During the early 1950s, there was a gradual transition from private industry towards socialist industry. The shift was targeted to be slow, though toward the latter part of the first five-year plan it became rapid. In 1955, Mao launched the full scale socialist 'transformation movement' which spelled the beginning of the end of private economic activities. The pattern of change was from private ownership to elementary state capitalism followed by advanced state capitalism, and finally to socialist industry. By 1965, 68 per cent of the gross value of output was accounted for by the state industry and only 16 per cent by joint state private enterprises. From 1953 to 1957, aggregate investment accounted for 20–25 per cent of the national product. Heavy industry in China absorbed on average approximately 85 per cent of industrial investment and only 8 per cent of state investment was devoted to agriculture. The figures suggest a relatively high rate of accumulation for a poor country like China with emphasis on industry in general and heavy industry in particular (Gregory and Stuart, 1999).

During 1956 to 1957, there was open discussion and criticism of the system. The Stalinist model was discarded and Mao proclaimed a policy of simultaneous development of agriculture and industry with the economy 'walking on two legs'. This was manifested in the 'Great Leap Forward' (1958–60). The 'Great Leap' was a massive resurgence of ideology which replaced rationality. Campaigns were instigated with revolutionary fervour to emphasise a new role for the peasantry, especially through small-scale industry in the countryside contrary to all economic principles of mass production and economies of scale, and the introduction of agricultural communes. Agriculture was organised into massive communes encompassing thousands of households. The disruptions of the 'Great Leap' were substantial. Although the 'Great Leap Forward' was abandoned by 1960, the commune system introduced in 1958 remained (Rosser and Rosser, 2004).

Like the 1950s, the 1960s is divided into two very different periods: moderation in the early 1960s and upheaval in the late 1960s. The early 1960s was a period of relative calm in which Chinese leaders looked towards balance in economic development, modernisation in the agricultural sector and recovery from the aftermath of the 'Great Leap'. During this period, substantial reforms were introduced in industry. The Chinese industrial structure was modified to suit Chinese conditions and modifications for the most part withstood late upheavals. Both central control and local initiative changed during this period. There was a movement away from overwhelming importance on gross output towards quality in production and the elimination of major deficiencies in the planning system. The centre tried to put pressure on enterprises to improve quality and efficiency and to enhance the role of technical expertise in the decision-making process. Many decisions, especially minor ones, were shifted to the local level. The 1960s witnessed a widespread educational campaign among the Chinese people which culminated in the 'Cultural Revolution' (1966–9). It had a devastating impact on the Chinese economy and populace. Although economic activity was substantially affected, the basic organisational agreements in industry and agriculture did not alter in significant ways (Rosser and Rosser, 2004).

The early 1970s was a period of recovery from the events of the Cultural Revolution. However, attempts to return to normalcy were interrupted by the death of Lin Biao, the then number two, in 1971 followed by the deaths of Zhou Enlai, the first premier of the PRC, in early 1976 and Mao in September 1976. Shortly thereafter, in October 1976, the 'Gang of Four', representing the revolutionary Left and espousing a continuation of the Stalinist mode of industrialisation were arrested amidst great ideological fervour. Mao's economic policies continued for two years after his death. By the end of the Mao era, China was devoting an unusually large share of its product to investment and focusing that investment on industry relative to other countries at similar levels of economic development. After Mao's death, reforms were initiated in 1978 under the leadership of Deng Xiaoping. Although the reform era took China along a very different path, the experience of the Soviet model remained influential, especially with respect to privatising large-scale industry (Gregory and Stuart, 1999).

China's political economy: post-reform era (1978 to present)

Before discussing the Chinese economy in the post-reform era, it would be pertinent to state that the definition of private sector and SOEs in China is blurred and fraught with difficulties. This can be attributed to a great extent to the reforms that have spawned a variety of hybrid and highly ambiguous ownership firms (Haggard and Huang, 2008). In China, there are officially seven different kind of enterprises based on ownership: individual ownership, private ownership, joint ownership, shareholding corporations, foreign ownership or Foreign Invested Enterprises (FIEs), collective ownership and state ownership. The most common measure in the literature is the non-state sector which some analysts have equated with the private sector. The first five ownerships comprise the private sector in China (Lin and Song, 2007).[7] Because FIEs are more privileged (discussed later in the chapter) relative to other constituents of the private sector, FIEs are not included in the definition of the private sector in China. The study contends that the first four ownerships comprise the private sector. The private sector and the FIEs, two separate constituents, constitute the non-state sector. Township and Village Enterprises (TVEs) are a part of the collective enterprises. According to Woetzel (2008):

> Many observers define a Chinese state owned enterprise as one of the approximately 150 corporations that report directly to the central government. Thousands more fall into a grey area, including subsidiaries of these 150 corporations, companies owned by provincial and municipal governments and companies that have been partially privatised yet retain the state as a majority or influential shareholder.

In 1978, Deng Xiaoping implemented the four modernisations: agriculture, industry, science and technology and national defence. The Deng reforms fundamentally altered the Chinese economic system while at the same time maintaining state and party control. Economic reforms introduced in China relative to India were different and had a different impact on the economy. China adopted the East Asian model of FDI induced growth. Special Economic Zones (SEZs) were created for foreign firms because institutions like the rule of law, property rights, etc. had not been established in China. China embarked on gradual and evolutionary reforms referred to as the 'Beijing Consensus'. Legal, fiscal, financial, price and wage reforms were introduced (Mantzopoulos and Shen, 2011). Market forces were introduced in a meaningful way. China maintained a complex and highly restrictive system of controls in the initial period of the reform to provide protection to domestic industry (Lardy, 2003). Although the Deng reforms introduced in 1978 were intended to be a gradual process termed as 'crossing the river by feeling the stones', in reality the reforms moved quickly, especially in the countryside. This was because the party and the state chose not to stop them and because they resulted from the unleashing of existing entrepreneurial forces. The Deng reforms made two important changes to the countryside: first allowing Chinese farmers to work for themselves rather than for the collectives; and, second, allowing townships to create TVEs (Gregory and Stuart, 1999).

After the initial moves in 1980, major enterprise reforms were introduced in 1984 when most firms were allowed to replace plan targets with responsibility contracts that enabled them to retain and freely dispose of surplus. The dual price system was extended to most of the economy thus creating a market economy beyond the contracted portion and a steadily declining share of the SOEs. Although industry and transportation remained under state control and ownership, the reforms allowed villages and townships to form their own enterprises. The TVEs are owned by the town or village governments (Rosser and Rosser, 2004). These enterprises which were concentrated initially in the services and the light industry, accounted for one-third of Chinese manufacturing by the mid 1980s. The TVEs were free to develop unencumbered by state planning and bureaucratic fetters. They were also free to form joint ventures with foreign partners, who supplied capital and export marketing expertise. The development of services and light manufacturing promoted the growth of services. From 1978 to 1981, the share of total investment devoted to heavy industry fell sharply from 54.7 per cent to 40.3 per cent (Gregory and Stuart, 1999). The average size of TVEs is relatively small compared to the SOEs. For example, in 1998, an average TVE in the industrial sector employed only 11 workers which was only 2.6 per cent of the level of employment in an industrial SOE (Chai, 2003).

To remedy China's lack of advanced technology and its shortages, the reform strategy decided to tap Western markets and Western capital to promote China's economic development. Considering that Chinese legal protection of property rights was weak and Chinese courts could not be counted on to enforce the property rights of foreigners, Chinese reformers set up various SEZs. Moreover, China liberalised its joint venture laws to encourage the creation of export oriented joint ventures in these zones. This led to a massive influx of Western capital after 1978. FDI led to the installation of technology and the creation of marketing savvy enterprises that permitted China to become the largest exporter in the world surpassing Germany in 2011. In the late 1970s, the regulations pertaining to foreign trade were relaxed and businesses were encouraged to import and export using decentralised market arrangements. Exportation has been especially important in developing agreements to encourage the sale of manufacturing goods in foreign markets and to stimulate FDI in China (Mantzopoulos and Shen, 2011).

The reform strategy retained state control and ownership of the key and strategic industries like heavy industry, banking, finance, aviation and transportation or the 'commanding heights' of the economy. The state economy is managed along the lines of an administrative command economy with a national economic plan. SOEs are required to fulfil the plan and if they sustain losses, they are bailed out by state subsidies or direct credits administered through state-owned banks. The Chinese system of credit is based on the savings deposits of frugal Chinese citizens and is directed by a state credit and finance plan exclusively to SOEs even if the rate of return on invested funds is extremely low especially when compared with private enterprise where the returns are much higher (Rosser and Rosser, 2004). About 70 per cent of SOEs make losses, and bad loans to SOEs account for 30 per cent of the GDP. The discussion about the privatisation of large SOEs was delayed until the summer of 1997 (Gregory and Stuart, 1999). The state sector accounted for two-thirds of manufactured output in the early 1980s, but by mid 1990, its share had fallen to 50 per cent. By 1992, the pure SOE was in a minority (Rosser and Rosser, 2004).

The hallmark of the late 1980s was the demonstration by students and workers in Tiananmen Square.[8] After a period of international disapproval, China resumed economic reforms in 1992, signalled by Deng's visit to Shenzhen, the prominent SEZ close to Hong Kong. Reforms spread to many provinces and rules and regulations on private enterprise were loosened. In 1993, the China's Communist Party (CCP) officially declared its desire to achieve a socialist market economy. In 1994, farmer demonstrations and resurgent inflation up to 20 per cent increased pressure for scaling back reforms (Rosser and Rosser, 2004). With Deng increasingly ill in early 1995, reforms were scaled back by President Jiang Zemin and Premier Li Peng. Before Deng died in 1997, the movement for more reforms asserted itself and the hard-line Premier Li Peng was replaced by reformist Zhu Rongji who promised to restructure the SOEs. The private sector was recognised as legitimate in the constitution in 1999 and China joined the WTO in 2001 (Mantzopoulos and Shen, 2011).

Privatisation, SOEs and the non-state sector

The performance of SOEs in China suffers from both political as well as agency costs. In the 1990s, reforms were introduced to address these issues. Two strategies were adopted: privatisation and corporatisation. The primary objective of corporatisation was to transform SOEs from solitary state proprietorships to modern-form corporations and imbibe in them a Western-style corporate governance structure without seriously diluting the dominant public but not necessarily state ownership (Xu *et al.*, 2007). Privatisation of SOEs in China is a very recent phenomenon (Lin and Song, 2007). There was no privatisation of SOEs in the initial reform period although reforms were introduced in the SOEs to increase their efficiency and productivity. One hundred large and medium SOEs at the central, and 2500 at the local, level were corporatised or converted into companies. Disinvestment of SOEs was also carried out but restrictions were imposed to prevent the state from losing control over them. By 1997, 1080 of the 2500 SOEs were transformed into limited liability or shareholding companies characterised by diversified equity ownership (Mohan, 2005).

China's overall policy still remains strong state control over a large proportion of industrial assets (Tian, 2007). The state has retained the larger and let the smaller enterprises go which implies state control over the top 500–1000 large firms and control over heavy industry, banks, railways, airlines and infrastructure. In 1997, the 500 largest SOEs had 37 per cent share of the assets of the SOEs, contributed 46 per cent of the tax collected on all SOEs and its share of total profits was 63 per cent (Yang, 2004). The transfer of ownership has occurred only in small-scale SOEs that account for a relatively small proportion of industrial assets and profits. This has not led to a significant reduction of state ownership or control over business enterprises. The larger corporatised SOEs are run either by state-owned asset management companies or the concerned supervisory departments as before. Until the first half of the 1990s, only 2–5 per cent of the 118,000 industrial SOEs had been transferred to the non-state sector and almost all of them were small firms (Mohan, 2005). Between 1997 and 2002, 21,000 small scale SOEs were privatised (Zheng and Yang, 2009).

According to a study conducted by the World Bank in 1997, reforms led to the increased efficiency of the SOEs but approximately 50 per cent of the industrial SOEs incurred net losses amounting to 1.3 per cent of GDP. Moreover, the SOEs absorbed 75 per cent of the credit and the rate of return of 6 per cent was lower compared to 8.4 per cent and 9.9 per cent earned by collectives and FIEs (Mohan, 2005). The SOEs suffer from a number of inefficiencies and rely considerably on state support in the form of subsidies for their operations. They take loans from the state commercial banks but do not have to repay the loans. Moreover, the government provides loans to SOEs at a much lower rate compared to the market rate (Lin, 2007). An ESRC-funded research led by Dr Jackie Sheehan of Nottingham University states that without subsidies, China's SOEs cannot compete internationally (ESRC, 2002).

China's private sector has grown dramatically since 1978 despite being constrained or even forbidden to develop. The boom in FDI in the 1990s reduced the political leadership's need to cater to the concerns of the private sector leading to somewhat of a stagnation in the growth of the private sector in the 1990s and 2000s relative to the 1980s. The private sector has begun to grow more rapidly since the reforms in 1993 with an apparent acceleration after 1997. Deng's speech in 1992, the Fifteenth National Congress of the CCP in 1997 and the Sixteenth National Congress of the CCP in 2002 encouraged the growth of the non-public sector including private enterprise. The number of individual owned businesses increased from 0.14 million in 1978 to 24.64 million in 2005. By the end of 2005, the number of private enterprises increased to 4.30 million employing 58.24 million employees. The economy was characterised as 'socialism with Chinese characteristics'. Table 3.8 depicts the proportion of private enterprises and their registered total from 2000 to 2005. Although the strictly private sector has expanded primarily in the SEZs, the biggest increase in absolute terms has been in the collective sector, especially the rural TVE sector. The TVEs provided an alternative to privatisation where it was unavailable because, until 1993, privatisation outside the SEZs continued to be limited. However, there has been a considerable expansion since 1993 when the TVEs were hit by a wave of privatisation which accelerated after 1997 (Zheng and Yang, 2009).

Compared to regular SOEs, TVEs with their greater flexibility and freedom from central control are able to fill niches where SOEs are limited, such as light industry. However, compared to centralised SOEs, TVEs face harsher budget constraints and operate in vigorously competitive markets. In 1989, three million TVEs either went bankrupt or were taken over by others. They also have an edge over strictly private firms because of their lower tax rates and they also have an advantage in negotiating with a still dominant government (Rosser and Rosser, 2004). FIEs have been preferred over the domestic private sector (Haggard and Huang, 2008). Thus it appears that there is a hierarchy in the industry with SOEs at the fore, followed by TVEs and FIEs, and private enterprise constituting the bottom rung of the ladder. By 1997, less than 7 per cent of the 25 million TVEs were collectively owned (Greenfield, 1997). In 1999, a study confined to Zhejiang and Jiangsu provinces demonstrated privatisation levels of 55.3 per cent and 59.5 per cent respectively, with much of the privatisation occurring in 1998 (Rosser and Rosser, 2004). Thus, the private sector comprises small and medium scale TVEs and SOEs which have been privatised. Generally, private businesses on average employ less than 15 employees per firm. They are concentrated in small-scale manufacturing, retail and other service industries, and are at a

Table 3.8 Proportion of private enterprises and their registered total (2000–5)

Year	SOE and collective enterprises (thousand)	Foreign invested enterprises (thousand)	Private enterprises (thousand)	Total enterprises	Proportion of private enterprises (%)	Proportion of registered capital
2000	5351	203	1762	7316	24.08	10.63
2001	4833	202	2029	7063	28.73	13.05
2002	4445	208	2435	7088	34.35	20.68
2003	4124	226	3006	7256	40.87	18.69
2004	3798	242	3651	7691	47.47	22.56
2005	3491	260	4301	8057	53.38	26.33

Source: Zheng and Yang (2009: 18).

relative technical and scale disadvantage compared to the SOEs and other firms (Chen and Li, 2007).

Scholars like Huang (2003) and Zheng and Yang (2009) aver that the private sector in China has been deliberately stifled. Continued support for SOEs in the form of subsidies and soft loans has restricted private sector access to markets and financing. Restrictions have been imposed on the private enterprise to prevent them from competing against the SOEs while FIEs enjoyed preferential clauses. Research carried out by the State Development Planning Commission showed that, until 2004, there had been restrictions to market access in nearly 30 industries within the non-public sector. In a certain coastal province, SOEs could enter into more than 80 industries, foreign-held firms more than 60 industries and private businesses could only access about 40 industries. The local government had refused more than 56 per cent of loan applications by small and medium sized enterprises while more than 70 per cent of the bank loans were made to SOEs. The private sector is subject to numerous takes, fees and levies from local governments and has less than 30 per cent of funding support despite accounting for 50 per cent of the country's GDP and 70 per cent of job opportunities (Zheng and Yang 2009). Loans to private enterprises have been subjected to higher interest rates relative to SOEs. In addition, private enterprises are denied access to stock markets in Shenzhen and Shanghai (Tian, 2007).

In one cross-country survey, private firms in China are the most constrained in the world in terms of their access to capital. Moreover, the share of the private sector in total fixed asset investment in the 1990s was less than it was in the 1980s (Haggard and Huang, 2008). Private firms lack access to relevant business information and face restrictions on direct access to foreign trade compared to SOEs. They are often discriminated against on the basis of uncertain and unclear rules, especially in the context of property rights leading to difficulties in protecting private property and contract rights (Tian, 2007). Commercial legislation requirements are not only expensive but also time-consuming and registered capital requirements for a private limited company in China are the highest in the world (Wagle *et al.*, 2000). Li Yining (cited in Zheng and Yang, 2009: 13) described the restrictions facing the private enterprise as a "glass door" which was holding entrants back. Officials of the National Development and Reform Commission (NRDC) had said that promoting non-state sector growth did not mean that private enterprises were to be encouraged, supported and developed independently, but that they should be taken into consideration within the context of improving the socialist market economy system (Zheng and Yang, 2009). Despite these limitations, the private sector has outpaced the state sector and the collectively owned TVEs. This has led to a significant shift in the composition of industrial output. Until 1990, SOEs produced almost 90 per cent of the gross industrial output. In 2004, industrial value of SOEs above designated size declined to 35 per cent of the industrial value added and other types of enterprises produced 65 per cent (Lin and Song, 2007).

As a result of the state's discriminatory policies, many private enterprises chose to put on a 'red cap' or a 'red hat' by being affiliated to SOEs or collective units, which allowed them to register as publicly owned or collective firms to enjoy the benefits that accrue to these enterprises (Haggard and Huang, 2008). Many resourceful private enterprises have converted to FIEs by registering overseas before coming back to compete with SOEs and real FIEs in their home market (Zheng and Yang, 2009). Thus, SOEs continue to be significant players in the Chinese economy and the growth of mixed property forms that maintain central or local government ownership and control has far outstripped the growth of private firms (Haggard and Huang, 2008).

According to Lardy (2014), the private sector is becoming more important in China's economy. The number of people employed in the private sector has increased substantially during 1978–2012. In 1978, employment in individual businesses was 150,000. It grew rapidly and reached 4.5 million in 1985 and 76 million in 2012. By 2012, individual businesses and private registered firms employed more than 132 million people, i.e. four and a half times more than those employed in 2000, and accounted for more than one-third of urban employment. This figure, according to Lardy, is an understatement due to limitations in the methodology used to compile employment data. The private sector has slowly but steadily eroded the SOEs and made encroachments in sectors which were predominantly the domain of the SOEs. The retreat of the SOEs in China's industry has been across almost all product lines. By 2011, there were only six of 40 branches of industry where SOEs produced more than 50 per cent of output. Moreover, in 24 branches of industry, the share of SOEs in total output was less than 15 per cent. Even this data overstates the role of SOEs since the output data excludes firms with sales with less than 20 billion yuan. This leads to exclusion of a lot of private firms. The role of SOEs has also declined in some of the nine key industries such as coal, iron and steel, natural gas and downstream oil industry, construction and water among others. The SOEs still completely dominate and control certain key components of the services sector. For instance, basic telecommunications, some forms of transportation such as rail, airlines and ocean shipping and finance which includes banking, insurance, securities and asset management. They also have a dominating presence in education, health, social security and social welfare. Thus, unlike in agriculture, manufacturing and construction, there has been no ownership transformation in large parts of the services sector in China (Lardy, 2014).

Steps have been taken by private enterprises to become globally competitive and efficient. The family-oriented management style has been further integrated into an expert-based management style. A large number of professional and technical workers have entered private enterprises, enhancing the quality of managers and ordinary employees. The private sector has optimised its industrial structure and has expanded into heavy industry, chemical industries and infrastructure fields. Their level of technology is increasing and product quality is improving. As and when restrictions to market access are relaxed, their share in these industries will increase. The innovation ability of enterprises is constantly improving, which is expected to result in technologies and products with proprietary intellectual property rights (Zheng and Yang, 2009). The Chinese government under the leadership of Hu Jintao and Wen Jiabao tried to improve the business environment for the private sector like property rights, security for private investors and more equal treatment between domestic private firms and FIEs in the sectors in which they can enter and invest (Haggard and Huang, 2008). Despite these measures, Chinese private enterprises have a long way to go before they can become competitive with global brand names or become large-scale enterprises to acquire corporations across the globe like the private enterprises in India.

The new government under the leadership of President Xi Jinping and Premier Li Keqiang are cognisant of the important role played by the private sector and the need for the reform of the SOEs. The CCP's Third Plenum in November 2013 laid out the groundwork for further price liberalisation and the relaxation of barriers to entry for private firms wanting to compete with SOEs in service-related industries such as finance, telecommunications, banking, energy and transportation. In March 2016, President Xi vowed that the government will help cope with challenges the non-public sector faces resulting from a distorted market system by striving to provide reliable, efficient and convenient funding services to small and medium-sized enterprises, and grant more market access to private capital. Measures will be undertaken to cut red-tape and fees in private investment management to reduce corporate burdens (Xinhua, 2016). Considering the slowing down in the Chinese economy, the government needs a dynamic sector to create jobs and weather the storm. Thus it is imperative for the government to undertake reforms that remove fetters on the private sector.

Table 3.9 provides a breakdown of the list of Chinese companies in the Fortune 500 from 2005 to 2015. It shows that the number of Chinese enterprises in the Fortune 500 has increased more than six times from 16 in 2005 to 98 in 2015, and the rankings of the Chinese enterprises has improved at a fast pace. The list is dominated by SOEs, especially large SOEs focusing on key and strategic industries like banking and finance, oil and gas, iron and steel, mining, infrastructure, telecommunications, power and energy and heavy industries like automobiles, shipping and aviation. From 2005 to 2015, only nine private enterprises are in the Fortune 500. Out of the nine, four are based in Hong Kong, three are based in the SEZs in China, one is a collective-owned enterprise and Zhejiang Geely Holding Group is the only private sector enterprise in mainland China. As mentioned above, privatisation was limited to the SEZs until the late 1990s. The private enterprises figured in the list after 2008. The Jiangsu Shagang Group made it to the list in 2009, the Huawei Investment & Holding in 2010 and the Zhejiang Geely Holding Group figured in the list for the first time in 2012.

In similar vein, the MNCs from China are dominated by SOEs (Larcon, 2009). The ten Chinese companies listed in the top 100 non-financial multinational enterprises from developing countries are SOEs or state-controlled enterprises. Non-governmental companies like Huawei Technologies and Wanxiang have followed SOEs in their internalisation process but they are much smaller in size relative to the SOEs (Li, 2009). Acquisitions by Chinese companies are a part of the government's 'go global' strategy to boost investment

Table 3.9 List of Chinese corporations in the Fortune 500 from 2005 to 2015

Company	Ownership	Sector	Rank in year										
			2005	2006	2007	2008	2009	2010	2011	2012	2013	2014	2015
SINOPEC Group	SOE	Oil and gas	31	23	17	16	9	7	5	5	4	3	2
CNPC	SOE	Oil and gas	46	39	24	25	13	10	6	6	5	4	4
State Grid	SOE	Utilities, energy	40	32	29	24	15	8	7	7	7	7	7
Industrial and Commercial Bank of China	SOE	Banking, finance	229	199	170	133	92	87	77	54	29	25	18
China Construction Bank	SOE	Banking, finance	315	277	230	171	125	116	108	77	50	38	29
China Mobile Communications	SOE	Telecommunications	224	202	180	148	99	77	87	81	71	55	55
Agricultural Bank of China	SOE	Banking, finance	397	377	277	223	155	141	127	84	64	47	36
Noble Group	Private Hong Kong	Diversified	—	—	—	349	218	242	139	91	76	76	77
Bank of China	SOE	Banking, finance	339	255	215	187	145	143	132	93	70	59	45
China State Construction Engineering	SOE	Engineering, construction	—	486	396	385	392	187	147	100	80	52	37
CNOOC	SOE	Oil and gas	—	—	469	409	318	252	162	101	93	79	72
China Railway Construction	SOE	Engineering, construction	—	485	384	356	252	133	105	111	100	80	79
China Railway Group/China Railway Engineering	SOE	Engineering, construction	—	441	342	341	242	137	95	112	102	86	71
Sinochem Group	SOE	Petrochemicals	287	304	299	257	170	203	168	113	119	107	105
China Life Insurance	SOE	Insurance, finance	212	217	192	159	133	118	113	129	111	98	94
SAIC Motors	SOE	Automobile	—	475	402	373	359	223	151	130	103	85	60
Dongfeng Motor Group	SOE	Automobile	—	—	—	—	—	182	145	142	146	113	109
China Southern Power Grid	SOE	Utilities, energy	316	266	237	226	185	156	149	152	134	115	113
China FAW Group	SOE	Automobile	448	470	385	303	385	258	197	165	141	111	107
China Minerals	SOE	Mining	—	—	—	—	—	—	—	169	—	—	—
CITIC Group	SOE	Finance	—	—	—	—	415	254	221	194	172	160	186
Baosteel Group	SOE	Metals	309	296	307	259	220	276	212	197	222	211	218
China North Industries Group	SOE	Aerospace and defence	—	—	—	—	—	348	250	205	161	152	144
China Communications Construction	SOE	Engineering, construction	—	—	—	426	341	224	211	216	213	187	165
China Telecommunications	SOE	Telecommunications	262	279	275	288	263	204	222	221	182	154	160

Company	Ownership	Industry											
China Minmetals	SOE	Metals	—	—	435	412	331	332	229	169	192	133	198
China Natural Resources	SOE	Retailing, diversified	—	—	—	—	—	395	346	233	187	143	115
Shenhua Group	SOE	Mining	—	—	—	—	—	356	293	234	178	165	196
China South Industries Group	SOE	Manufacturing	—	—	—	—	428	275	227	238	209	169	—
Ping An Insurance	SOE	Insurance, finance	—	—	—	—	—	383	328	242	181	128	96
China Huaneng Group	SOE	Power, energy	—	—	—	—	425	313	276	246	231	221	224
Aviation Industry Corp. of China	SOE	Aerospace and defence	—	—	—	—	426	330	311	250	212	178	159
China Post Group	SOE	Mail, freight	—	—	—	—	—	—	343	258	196	168	143
He Bei Iron & Steel Group	SOE	Metals	—	—	—	—	375	314	279	269	269	271	239
Jardine Matheson	Private Hong Kong	Diversified	—	—	457	437	411	382	320	275	266	277	282
China Metallurgical Group	SOE	Engineering, construction	—	—	—	480	380	315	297	280	302	354	326
People's Insurance Co. of China	SOE	Finance	—	—	—	—	—	371	289	292	256	208	174
Shougang Group	SOE	Metals	—	—	—	—	—	—	326	295	322	348	402
Aluminium Corp. of China	SOE	Metals	—	—	—	476	499	436	331	298	273	227	240
China National Aviation Fuel Group	SOE	Diversified	—	—	—	—	—	—	431	318	277	314	321
Wuhan Iron & Steel	SOE	Metals	—	—	—	—	—	428	341	321	328	310	500
Bank of Communications	SOE	Banking, finance	—	—	—	—	494	440	398	326	243	217	190
Jizhong Metallurgical Group	SOE	Mining, crude oil	—	—	—	—	—	368	458	330	311	304	315
China United Network Communications	SOE	Telecommunications	—	—	—	—	419	—	371	333	258	210	227
China Guodian	SOE	Energy	—	—	—	—	—	477	405	341	299	297	343
Jiangsu Shagang Group	Private, SEZ	Metals	—	—	—	—	444	415	367	346	318	308	274
China Railway Materials	SOE	Diversified	—	—	—	—	—	—	430	349	292	442	—
Huawei Investment & Holding	Private, SEZ	IT	347	259	—	—	281	397	352	351	315	285	228
Hutchison Whampoa	Private Hong Kong	Retailing	—	—	290	286	—	302	362	365	363	363	336
China National Building Materials Group	SOE	Building materials	—	—	—	—	—	—	485	365	319	267	270
Sinosteel	SOE	Metals	—	—	—	—	372	352	354	—	—	—	—
Sinomach	SOE	Industrials	—	—	—	—	—	—	435	367	326	278	288
China Datang	SOE	Energy	—	—	—	—	—	412	375	369	376	396	392
Lenovo Group	SOE	IT	—	—	—	499	—	—	450	370	329	286	231
China Ocean Shipping	SOE	Shipping	—	—	488	405	327	—	399	384	401	451	432

continued

Table 3.9 Continued

Company	Ownership	Sector	Rank in year										
			2005	2006	2007	2008	2009	2010	2011	2012	2013	2014	2015
Power China	SOE	Engineering, construction	–	–	–	–	–	–	–	390	354	313	253
COFCO	SOE	Food processing	434	463	405	398	335	312	366	393	357	401	272
Henan Energy and Chemical	SOE	Mining	–	–	–	–	–	–	446	397	404	328	364
Chem China	SOE	Chemicals	–	–	–	–	–	–	475	402	355	276	265
Tewoo Group	SOE	Diversified	–	–	–	–	–	–	–	416	343	185	146
China Electronics	SOE	Manufacturing	–	–	–	–	–	–	408	425	395	382	366
Zhejiang Materials Industry Group	SOE	Trading	–	–	–	–	–	–	484	426	364	345	339
China Huadian	SOE	Utilities	–	–	–	–	–	–	–	433	389	368	345
China Shipbuilding Industry	SOE	Industrials	–	–	–	–	–	–	463	434	417	403	371
Shandong Weiqiao Pioneering Group	SOE	Textiles	–	–	–	–	–	–	–	440	373	388	234
Shanxi Coal Transportation & Sales Group	SOE	Logistics	–	–	–	–	–	–	–	447	390	–	–
China Pacific Insurance (Group)	SOE	Insurance, finance	–	–	–	–	–	–	467	450	429	384	328
China Power Investment	SOE	Utilities, energy	–	–	–	–	–	–	–	451	408	393	403
Shandong Energy Group	SOE	Mining, crude oil	–	–	–	–	–	–	–	460	373	305	373
Ansteel Group	SOE	Metals	–	–	–	–	–	–	–	462	493	475	451
Zhejiang Geely Holding Group	Private/non-state	Automobile	–	–	–	–	–	–	–	475	477	466	477
Greenland Holding Group	SOE	Real estate	–	–	–	–	–	–	–	483	359	268	258
Xinxing Cathay International Group	SOE	Metals	–	–	–	–	–	–	–	484	406	365	344
Kailuan Group	SOE	Mining	–	–	–	–	–	–	–	490	415	394	400
China Merchants Bank	SOE	Banking, finance	–	–	–	–	–	–	–	498	412	350	235
China Development Bank	SOE	Banking and finance	–	–	–	–	–	–	–	–	–	122	87
Pacific Construction Group	SOE	Engineering, construction	–	–	–	–	–	–	–	–	–	166	156
Beijing Automotive Group	SOE	Automobile	–	–	–	–	–	–	–	–	336	248	207
Amer Internatuional Group	Private, SEZ	Electronics	–	–	–	–	–	–	–	–	387	295	247
Industrial Bank	SOE	Banking, finance	–	–	–	–	–	–	–	–	428	338	271
Sinopharm	SOE	Healthcare	–	–	–	–	–	–	–	–	446	357	276
China Minsheng Bank	SOE	Banking, finance	–	–	–	–	–	–	–	–	411	330	281

Company	Type	Industry	2005	2006	2007	2008	2009	2010	2011	2012	2013	2014	2015
Shanghai Pudong Development Bank	SOE	Banking, finance	–	–	–	–	–	–	–	–	460	383	296
Bohai Steel Group	SOE	Metals	–	–	–	–	–	–	–	–	–	327	304
Datong Coal Mine Group	SOE	Mining	–	–	–	–	–	–	–	–	432	369	341
CEFC China Energy	Private Collective	Energy	–	–	–	–	–	–	–	–	–	349	342
Jiangxi Copper	SOE	Mining	–	–	–	–	–	–	–	–	414	381	354
Shanxi LuAN Mining Group	SOE	Mining	–	–	–	–	–	–	–	–	430	372	358
Guangzhou Automobile Industry Group	SOE	Automobile	–	–	–	–	–	–	–	–	483	366	362
Shanxi Jincheng Anthracite Coal Mining	SOE	Mining, crude oil	–	–	–	–	–	–	–	–	435	386	379
Shaanxi Yanchang Petroleum	SOE	Mining, crude oil	–	–	–	–	–	–	–	–	464	432	380
Jinneng Group	SOE	Energy	–	–	–	–	–	–	–	–	–	309	382
China Nonferrous Metal Mining	SOE	Mining	–	–	–	–	–	–	–	–	482	398	390
China Energy Engineering	SOE	Engineering, construction	–	–	–	–	–	–	–	–	–	465	391
Yangquan Coal Industry Group	SOE	Mining	–	–	–	–	–	–	–	–	407	391	409
Shaanxi Coal & Chemical Industry	SOE	Mining	–	–	–	–	–	–	–	–	–	–	416
China Everbright Group	SOE	Banking, finance	–	–	–	–	–	–	–	–	–	–	420
China General Technology	SOE	Engineering, construction	–	–	–	–	–	–	–	–	–	469	426
China Aerospace Science & Technology	SOE	Aerospace and defence	–	–	–	–	–	–	–	–	–	–	437
China Poly Group	SOE	Real estate	–	–	–	–	–	–	–	–	–	–	457
HNA Group	SOE	Airlines	–	–	–	–	–	–	–	–	–	–	464
AIA Group	Private, Hong Kong	Insurance, finance	–	–	–	–	–	–	–	–	–	–	467
Bailian Group	SOE	Diversified	–	–	–	–	–	–	–	–	466	–	–
Shanxi Coking Coal Group	SOE	Mining	–	–	–	–	–	–	–	–	403	290	264
Total			16	20	24	29	37	46	61	74	89	94	98

Source: compiled from Fortune Global 500, 2005–15.

abroad. China has slowly started to invest abroad and this has been carefully controlled and encouraged by Beijing. TCL Corporation, a SOE, controls the venerable Radio Corporation of America brand. Exploits of other major SOEs like Baosteel, ChemChina, Sinomach, China Netcom, ZTE and others are well documented (Engardio, 2007). In March 2016, Starwood Hotels agreed to be acquired by Anbang, an insurance company, for US$14.3 billion. In February 2016, Ingram Micro, ranked 62 in the list of Fortune 500 companies, agreed to be acquired by Tianjin Tianhai Investment Development Co. for US$6.3 billion. In January 2016, General Electric Appliance Business agreed to be acquired by Haier for US$5.4 billion (Gandel, 2016).

There is a wide consensus that the emergence of the Chinese MNCs can be attributed to the role of the state because the SOEs have explicit or implicit backing from Beijing. Despite the coddling from Beijing, the Chinese SOEs have not yet matured into true world beaters (Engardio, 2007), although there are some exceptions. The CCP has provided protection from foreign competition and encouragement to the SOEs to consolidate in important industries in China's economy. According to an independent Chinese study, the majority of the SOEs would incur losses if it was not for the government's grants and hidden subsidies. SOEs hardly pay any dividends back to the government. The money is reinvested into SOEs rather than allocating it more efficiently. Consequently, it reinforces the strength of the SOEs and the fortunes of their bosses, and political and economic reforms have been opposed and stymied by these vested interests (*The Economist*, 2012).

There is a consensus amongst scholars that government support for SOEs has resulted in China's failure to create globally competitive firms. Chinese private enterprises especially small and medium sized enterprises face administrative difficulties in developing the internationalisation process compared to the SOEs. However, the government policy is changing to create the same conditions for all business enterprises (Li, 2009). This is not to say that Chinese private sector enterprises have no foreign acquisitions. For instance, Lenovo acquired the personal computer business of IBM in 2005. Zhejiang Geely Holding Group, a private enterprise headquartered in Hangzhou, acquired Volvo in 2010 (Reed and Ward, 2010). In 2012, the Wanda Group acquired AMC Entertainment for US$2.6 billion. AMC Entertainment operates the second largest movie theatre chain in the United States. In 2013, Wanxiang America, the Chicago based arm of Wanxiang, a privately owned company in China, acquired A123, a US firm, for US$257 million. Shuanghui International, a private company in China, acquired Smithfield Foods in 2013 for US$7.1 billion. In January 2016, a deal was reached for US$3.5 billion in which Dalian Wanda will acquire Legendary Entertainment Group. It is the largest China–Hollywood deal to date (Gandel, 2016). Overall, Chinese firms accounted for almost 40 per cent of cumulative Chinese direct investment in the United States from 2000 to the second quarter of 2012. Private firms from China are also investing in Europe where they accounted for almost 30 per cent of a cumulative US$15 billion in Chinese investment during 2000–2011 (Lardy, 2014).

Due to the intense domestic competition where rivals cut prices relentlessly and also competition from foreign firms, Chinese firms often venture out of China from a position of weakness rather than strength (Engardio, 2007). According to Darrell Rigby, partner at consulting firm Bain and Co.:

> The management tools the Chinese companies used to become the world's leading factory are not the same as those that they will need to lead global innovation.... That is one of the reasons Lenovo insisted that IBM executives stay on the board after it acquired IBMs PC business.
>
> (Cited in Engardio, 2007: 105)

According to McKinsey & Co., Chinese companies lack executives with international experience. China has 5000 executives with international experience but will need 75,000 in the next five years (Engardio, 2007). According to Yue (2012), although indigenous innovation has achieved some progress, it is far from successful. This can be explained partly due to policy incoherence and partly due to the intensifying liberalisation pressures from China's main trading partners. Economic growth alone is by no means the hard evidence of China's rise in any meaningful way. Globalisation has not made China any closer to an emerging industrial power and the prospects of catch-up remain remote.

The Indian case is quite the opposite, where the domestic firms invest abroad from a position of strength (Kumar *et al.*, 2009). Financial data of 340 publicly listed Indian companies during the period 1999 to 2003 from Standard & Poor's Compustat indicates that Indian enterprises – barring a few exceptions – have performed much better vis-à-vis Chinese businesses in two areas: returns on investment and return on equity. This is because Indian businesses have to respond to market pressures. Despite the fact that the Indian economy is heavily regulated, it is more or less a well-functioning market economy. On the other hand, China is not a completely free market economy because the economy is still dominated by colossal SOEs (Engardio, 2007). It is for this reason that the Chinese government wants the Indian private enterprises to participate in the privatisation of China's SOEs (Chandran, 2006).

Conclusion

The chapter discussed the differences in the economic, military and political power of India and China and the differences in the political economies. The study showed that China has greater economic and military prowess relative to India. India lags behind China in all the economic indicators and scholars aver that India is at least a decade behind China. China's permanent membership of the UNSC with veto power also elevates its status relative to India and makes the former politically more powerful than the latter. Scholars aver that perception matters and world leaders perceive China as a global power relative to India.

Both India and China adopted different economic and political course to achieve rapid economic growth. India adopted a mixed economy system and

China adopted Stalin's model of 'centralised planned economy'. In a mixed economy, the key and strategic industries are controlled by the state and private sector enterprises operate in the consumer goods industry. China undertook reforms in 1979 under the leadership of Deng Xiaoping. The state retained control of key and strategic industries and led to the creation of colossal SOEs which dominate these sectors. Although private enterprise has increased in importance, it is discriminated against and faces numerous restrictions. China is represented abroad by SOEs and to a less extent by private enterprises. Additionally, an overwhelming majority of the private sector enterprises are small and/or medium enterprises (SMEs). In India, reforms were initiated in 1991 which removed the fetters on the private sector. The private sector operates (except in some sectors such as defence) and plays an important role in all the sectors of the economy. Private sector enterprises are of different scale. Some are industrial conglomerates and others are SMEs and they are the global torchbearers for India. The difference in the political economy illustrates why India is represented predominantly by private sector enterprises abroad and China is represented by SOEs.

Notes

1 Economists and analysts have expressed concerns and doubts about the veracity of the recent economic growth rates in India. The scepticism stems from the change in the method for calculating GDP in January 2015. Economists and analysts are of the opinion that the Indian economy is expanding but not by the numbers provided by the official government statistics (BBC, 2016).
2 China's economic growth declined to 6.9 per cent in October–December 2015, less than the government's target of 7 per cent growth per annum. There is a broad consensus that the economic growth figures are incorrect. Some economists and analysts opine that the economic growth rate is in the range of 2–5 per cent. According to the Chinese government, the 'new normal' is 7 per cent. However, some analysts state that 5.5–6.0 per cent growth is more realistic (Noble, 2015; Tegler, 2015).
3 For an in-depth comparison of economic, human development, environmental and other indicators refer to the UNDP (2015) and World Data Bank (n.d.).
4 This question was not posed to James Byrne, Reporter, Interfax (Appendix A).
5 China was co-opted by the United States as a permanent member of the UNSC with veto power after the Second World War. The permanent membership was enjoyed from 1949 to 1971 by Taiwan until China took over in 1972.
6 For an in-depth comparison of the military power potential of India and China refer to *Military Balance* (2016).
7 For a detailed analysis of the problems in defining the private sector in China refer to Haggard and Huang (2008).
8 There was widespread belief amongst the intelligentsia that the four developments were to be supplemented by democracy – the fifth development. However, it should be pointed out that the demonstrators in the Tiananmen Square were not only demonstrating to get democracy but also against corruption, unemployment and living conditions among others.

References

BBC (2010). Chinese PM Wen Jiabao Begins Bumper Indian Trade Trip. Online. 15 December. Available at: www.bbc.co.uk/news/world-south-asia-11997221 (accessed 30 December 2012).

BBC (2016). India Outpaces China in 2015 Economic Growth. Online. 8 February. Available at: www.bbc.com/news/business-35519671 (accessed 1 May 2016).

Bull, Hedley (1977). *The Anarchical Society*. London: Macmillan.

Business Standard (2010). Enterprise India, 21st Century's First Decade Growth Driven by Private Sector. Online. 30 June. Available at: www.business-standard.com/india/news/enterprise-india/399818/ (accessed 24 July 2012).

Chai, Joseph C.H. (2003). Privatisation in China. In: David Parker and David Saal, eds. *International Handbook on Privatization*. Cheltenham: Edward Elgar, pp. 235–261.

Chandran, Bipin (2006). China Wants Indian Firms to Take Part in its Privatisation Process. Online. *Business Standard*, 21 April. Available at: www.business-standard.com/india/news/china-wants-indian-firms-to-take-part-in-its-privatisation-process/242711/(accessed 28 July 2012).

Chen, Aimin and Li, Peng (2007). Corporate Governance and the Development of Private Enterprise in China. In: Shuanglin Lin and Shunfeng Song, eds. *The Revival of Private Enterprise in China*. Aldershot and Burlington: Ashgate, pp. 237–255.

Desai, Ashok V. (1999). *Transition to an Open Market Economy: India's Policy Experience of Controls over Industry*. New Delhi: Sage.

Dowding, Keith (2012). Why Should We Care About the Definition of Power? *Journal of Political Power*, 5 (1), pp. 119–135.

Economic Times (2012). India-China Trade Expected to Touch $100 Billion by 2015. Online. Available at: http://articles.economictimes.indiatimes.com/2012-10-26/news/34750100_1_india-china-trade-china-international-auto-parts-bilateral-trade (accessed 30 December 2012).

Economist, The (2012). China's State Capitalism: Not Just Tilting at Windmills. 6 October.

Embassy of India, Beijing (n.d.a). Economic and Trade Relations. Online. Available at: www.indianembassy.org.cn/DynamicContent.aspx?MenuId=97&SubMenuId=0 (accessed 5 May 2016).

Embassy of India, Beijing (n.d.b). Political Relations. Online. Available at: www.indianembassy.org.cn/DynamicContent.aspx?MenuId=97&SubMenuId=0 (accessed 5 May 2016).

Engardio, P. (ed.) (2007). *Chindia: How China and India are Revolutionizing Global Business*. New York: McGraw-Hill.

ESRC (2002). Privatisation, Chinese Style: Can China's State Owned Enterprises Compete in International Markets. Science Blog. Available at: http://scienceblog.com/community/older/2002/F/20022414.html (accessed 29 July 2012).

Fortune (n.d.). Global 500. Online. Available at: http://fortune.com/global500/ (accessed 19 April 2016).

Gandel, Stephen (2016). The Biggest American Companies Now Owned by the Chinese. Online. *Fortune*. Available at: http://fortune.com/2016/03/18/the-biggest-american-companies-now-owned-by-the-chinese/ (accessed 10 May 2016).

Garst, Daniel (1989). Thucydides and Neorealism. *International Studies Quarterly*, 33, pp. 3–27.

Greenfield, Gerard (1997). Concerning Privatisation in China. Online. 20 November. Available at: www.hartford-hwp.com/archives/55/214.html (accessed 29 July 2012).

Gregory, Paul R. and Stuart, Robert C. (1999). *Comparative Economic Systems*, 3rd edn. Boston: Houghton Mifflin.

Gupta, Amit (2006). US.India.China: Assessing Tripolarity. *China Report*, 42 (69), pp. 69–83.

Haggard, Stephen and Huang, Yasheng (2008). The Political Economy of Private Sector Development in China. In: Loren Brandt and Thomas Rawski, eds. *China's Great Economic Transformation*. New York and Cambridge: Cambridge University Press, pp. 337–374.

Huang, Yasheng (2003). Selling *China: Foreign Direct Investment During the Reform Era*. Cambridge: Cambridge University Press.

IBEF (India Brand Equity Foundation) (2016). Indian Pharmaceutical Industry. Online. September. Available at: www.ibef.org/industry/pharmaceutical-india.aspx (accessed 5 May 2016).

India Today (2016). India Rejects China Claim of PLA Not Crossing Border, Says Transgression has Increased. Online. 15 March. Available at: http://indiatoday.intoday.in/story/india-rejects-china-claim-of-pla-not-crossing-border-says-transgression-has-increased/1/620757.html (accessed 10 May 2016).

Jain, Bharti (2010). India "Succumbs" to Chinese Pressure on Arunachal at WB Meet. Online. *The Times of India*, 6 March. Available at: http://articles.timesofindia.india-times.com/2010-03-06/india/28121047_1_arunachal-pradesh-world-bank-ed-china-shaolin-yang (accessed 30 December 2012).

Joshi, Shashank (2011). Why India Is Becoming Warier of China. *Current History*, 110 (735), pp. 156–161.

Kumar, N., Mohapatra, P. and Chandrasekhar, S. (2009). *India's Global Powerhouses: How They Are Taking on the World*. Boston: Harvard Business Press.

Larcon, Jean-Paul (2009). Conclusion: China's Unique Advantage. In: Jean-Paul Larcon, ed. *Chinese Multinationals*. Singapore and Hackensack: World Scientific, pp. 229–230.

Lardy, Nicholas R. (2003). Trade Liberalization and Its Role in Chinese Economic Growth, Prepared for an International Monetary Fund and National Council of Applied Economic Research Conference, A Tale of Two Giants: India's and China's Experience with Reform and Growth New Delhi, 14–16 November. Online. NR Lardy – Institute of International Economics. Available at: perjacobsson.org (accessed 27 July 2012).

Lardy, Nicholas R. (2014). *Markets over Mao: The Rise of Private Business in China*. Washington: Peterson Institute for International Economics.

Li, Zhaoxi (2009). China's Outward Foreign Direct Investment. In: Jean-Paul Larcon, ed. *Chinese Multinationals*. Singapore and Hackensack: World Scientific, pp. 49–75.

Lin, Shuanglin (2007). Resource Allocation and Economic Growth in China. In: Shuanglin Lin and Shunfeng Song, eds. *The Revival of Private Enterprise in China*. Aldershot and Burlington: Ashgate, pp. 33–50.

Lin, Shuanglin and Song, Shunfeng (2007). Introduction. In: Shuanglin Lin and Shunfeng Song, eds. *The Revival of Private Enterprise in China*. Aldershot and Burlington: Ashgate, pp. 1–8.

Mantzopoulos, V. and Shen, R. (2011). *The Political Economy of China's Systemic Transformation: 1979 to the Present*. New York: Palgrave Macmillan.

Marathe, Sharad S. (1986). *Regulation and Development: India's Policy Experience of Controls over Industry*. Sage: New Delhi.

Military Balance (2012). London: International Institiute for Strategic Studies.

Military Balance (2016). London: International Institiute for Strategic Studies.

Mohan, T.T. Ram (2005). *Privatization in India: Challenging Economic Orthodoxy.* Abingdon and New York: RoutledgeCurzon.

Noble, Josh (2015). Doubts Rise Over China's Official GDP Growth Rate. Online. *Financial Times*, 16 September. Available at: www.ft.com/cms/s/0/723a8d8e-5c53-11e5-9846-de406ccb37f2.html#axzz46WvqAahP (accessed 10 April 2016).

North, Douglass C. (1990). *Institutions, Institutional Change and Economic Performance.* Cambridge: Cambridge University Press.

North, Douglass C. (1994). Economic Performance through Time. *American Economic Review*, 84 (3), pp. 359–368.

Nye Jr., Joseph S. (2008). Public Diplomacy and Soft Power. *The ANNALS of the American Academy of Political and Social Science*, 616 (1), pp. 94–109.

Posen, Barry R. and Ross, Andrew L. (1996/7). Competing Visions for US Grand Strategy. *International Security*, 21 (3), pp. 5–53.

Reed, John and Ward, Andrew (2010). Geely Buys Volvo for $1.8bn. Online. *Financial Times*, 29 March. Available at: www.ft.com/cms/s/0/e6874a70-3a93-11df-b6d5-00144feabdc0.html#axzz21vW2tsTP (accessed 28 July 2012).

Rehman, Iskander (2009). Keeping the Dragon at Bay: India's Counter-Containment of China. *Asian Security*, 5 (2), pp. 114–143.

Roehrig, Terrence (2009). An Asian Triangle: India's Relationship with China and Japan. *Asian Politics & Policy*, 1 (2), pp. 163–185.

Rosser, Jr. J. Barkley and Rosser, Marina V. (2004). *Comparative Economics in a Transforming World Economy*, 2nd edn. Cambridge, MA: MIT Press.

Roy, Subhajit (2014). Day After, China Daily Says Modi Remarks for Media Hype. Online. *The Indian Express*, 3 September. Available at: http://indianexpress.com/article/india/india-others/day-after-china-daily-says-modi-remarks-for-media-hype/ (accessed 10 May 2016).

Sharma, Shalendra D. (2010). The Uncertain Fate of "Chindia". *Current History*, 109 (728), pp. 252–257.

Srinivasan, T.N. and Tendulkar, S.D. (2003). *Reintegrating India with World Economy.* Washington, DC: Institute for International Economics; New Delhi: Oxford University Press.

Tegler, Eric (2015). Are China's GDP Numbers Believable? Online. *The Diplomat*, 24 August. Available at: http://thediplomat.com/2015/08/are-chinas-gdp-numbers-believable/ (accessed 1 May 2016).

Tendulkar, Suresh D. and Bhavani, T.A. (2007). *Understanding Reforms: Post 1991 India.* New Delhi and New York: Oxford University Press.

The Hindu. (2012). Only Pvt Sector Investment Can Give Leg-Up to Economy: Crisil. Online. 17 July. Available at: www.thehindu.com/business/Economy/only-pvt-sector-investment-can-give-legup-to-economy-crisil/article3649282.ece (accessed 6 November 2012).

Tian, Xiaowen (2007). The Prospect of Private Economy in China In: Shuanglin Lin and Shunfeng Song, eds. *The Revival of Private Enterprise in China.* Aldershot and Burlington: Ashgate, pp. 271–283.

Trading Economics (2016). China Foreign Exchange Reserves. Available at: www.tradingeconomics.com/china/foreign-exchange-reserves (accessed 12 January 2016).

UNDP (2015). Human Development Report 2015: Work for Human Development. UNDP: New York.

Wagle, Dileep M., Gregory, Niel and Teney, Stoyan (2000). *China's Emerging Private Enterprises: Prospects for the New Century.* Washington, DC: International Finance Corporation.

Wax, Emily and Lakshmi, Rama (2010). Obama Supports Adding India as a Permanent Member of U.N. Security Council. Online. Washington Post Foreign Service, 8 November. Available at: www.washingtonpost.com/wp-dyn/content/article/2010/11/08/AR2010110800495.html?hpid=topnews&sid=ST2010110402773 (accessed 30 December 2012).

Woetzel, Jonathan R. (2008). Reassessing China's State-Owned Enterprises. Online. McKinsey Quarterly. Available at: www.forbes.com/2008/07/08/china-enterprises-state-lead-cx_jrw_0708mckinsey.html (accessed 27 July 2011).

World Data Bank (n.d.). World Bank. Available at: http://data.worldbank.org/indicator.

Xinhua (2016). China's Private Sector Put On Equal Footing. Online. 12 March. Available at: http://news.xinhuanet.com/english/2016-03/12/c_135181860.htm (accessed 1 May 2016).

Xu, Lixin C., Zhu, Tian and Lin, Yi-min (2007). Political Control, Agency Problems and Ownership Reforms: Evidence from China. In: Shuanglin Lin and Shunfeng Song, eds. *The Revival of Private Enterprise in China*. Aldershot and Burlington: Ashgate, pp. 199–221.

Yang, Yao (2004). Government Commitment and the Outcome of Privatisation in China. In: T. Ito and A.O. Krueger, eds. *Governance, Regulation and Privatisation in the Asia Pacific Region*. NBER–EASE Volume 12. Chicago: University of Chicago Press, pp. 251–275.

Yue, Jianyong (2012). What Does Globalization Mean for China's Economic Development? Online. *Global Policy*, 24 May. Available at: www.globalpolicyjournal.com/blog/24/05/2012/what-does-globalization-mean-china%E2%80%99s-economic-development (accessed 1 April 2013).

Zheng, Hongliang and Yang, Yang (2009). Chinese Private Sector Development in the Past 30 Years: Retrospect and Prospect, Discussion Paper 45. Online. China Policy Institute, The University of Nottingham. Available at: www.nottingham.ac.uk/cpi/documents/events/2008/ifccs/hongliang-zheng.pdf (accessed 25 July 2012).

4 Oil industry in India and China

This chapter is divided into four sections. Section I discusses the global oil industry, different sectors and the different type of oil companies which operate in the global oil industry. Section II discusses the oil industry in India and the operations of key players in the upstream and downstream oil sector in India. Section III discusses the oil industry in China and the operations of key players in the upstream and downstream oil sector in China. Section IV highlights the significance of the independent variable or the difference in the economic and political power between India and China and illustrates how it has led to differences in the scale and operations of oil companies from the two countries. It compares and contrasts the diplomatic, political and financial support received by Chinese and Indian oil companies from their respective governments, internal rate of return or the rate of return on capital/investment, rate of interest on loans and the ease of availability of loans or finance, the ability to take risks, the difference in the level of technology and ability to acquire technology and project management skills.

I

There are three major sectors in the oil and gas industry: upstream, midstream and downstream. The upstream industry discovers and produces crude oil and natural gas. It is generally referred to as the E&P sector. It comprises all the activities that are undertaken in the field like acquiring land and mineral rights, conducting public involvement, engineering and planning of servicing and drilling wells, fracturing and perforating wells, supplies, acquiring land and mineral rights, conducting public involvement, identifying prospects, shooting seismic surveys, cementing, drilling fluids and equipment and others.

The midstream sector undertakes activities like storing, processing, marketing and transporting commodities like natural gas, sulphur and oil and natural gas liquids like butane, propane and ethane. It serves as an important link between the consumers and producers in far off petroleum producing areas. The downstream sector on the other hand includes natural gas distribution companies, petroleum products distributors, oil refineries, retail outlets and petrochemical plants. It provides numerous products to the consumers like natural gas, gasoline or petrol, jet fuel, lubricants, fertilisers, pharmaceuticals, pesticides, plastics, heating oil and diesel among others. In industrial jargon, midstream activities are generally included in the downstream sector. The study adheres to this classification. Thus the oil industry is divided into two main sectors: upstream and downstream.

There are four different types of companies in the oil and gas industry. First, companies which produce crude oil. They are further classified into two categories: NOCs and integrated MNCs or IOCs. Some of the biggest NOCs are Saudi Aramco, Abu Dhabi National Oil Company, Kuwait Petroleum Corporation, Petronas, Sonangol, China National Petroleum Corporation (CNPC), Sinopec, CNOOC, PetroChina, ONGC and Gazprom among others. A recent phenomenon is the movement of NOCs outside their home countries and investing internationally both in the upstream and downstream sectors. NOCs which have invested in the downstream sector abroad include Saudi Aramco, Statoil of Norway, Petroleos de Venezuela, Pertamina of Indonesia, Pemex of Mexico, Petronas and Petrobras of Brazil among others (Patra, 2004). NOCs which have invested in the upstream sector abroad include ONGC, CNPC, Sinopec, PetroChina, CNOOC and Petrobras to mention a few.

The second type of oil producing company is IOCs. The IOCs have integrated operations, namely E&P, refining, marketing and trading. They are very powerful operators in the oil markets because of their scale of operations, volume of transactions and financial strength. Examples of such IOCs are ExxonMobil, Shell, BP, Chevron Texaco, Total, Conoco Phillips and Eni. These seven companies are also termed as 'Super Majors'.[1] They play multiple roles in the crude oil market. They are suppliers of crude oil because they bring equity crude oil in the market through E&P, buy crude oil for their own refineries and their trading wing buys and sells crude oil in the markets for profit (Patra, 2004). Table 4.1 provides the ranking of the seven major IOCs from 2005 to 2012. The extent of their operations, size and strength can be gauged by the fact that the above mentioned IOCs figure in the top 17 corporations in the world in 2012. Moreover, Shell, ExxonMobil and BP have figured in the top four until 2012 and in the top six from 2012 to 2015. The fall in the rankings is attributed to the decline in the price of oil since 2014.

Table 4.1 Global Fortune 500 ranking of the seven major IOCs from 2005 to 2015

IOCs	Rank in year										
	2005	2006	2007	2008	2009	2010	2011	2012	2013	2014	2015
Shell	4	3	2	2	1	2	2	1	1	2	3
ExxonMobil	3	1	3	3	2	3	3	2	3	5	5
BP	2	4	4	4	4	4	4	4	4	6	6
Chevron	11	6	7	6	5	11	10	8	11	12	12
Total	10	12	10	8	6	14	11	11	10	11	11
ConocoPhillips	12	10	9	10	7	17	12	9	16	19	23
Eni	33	27	26	27	17	24	23	17	17	22	25

Source: compiled from Fortune Global 500, 2005–15.

There is also a group of integrated IOCs which are smaller in size relative to the big seven and with less geographical reach. It consists of companies like Amerada Hess, Diamond Sharmock, Marathon, Occidental, Unocal and Ultramar. There are yet smaller companies most of whom specialise in single segment and are usually referred to as 'Independents'. They include Anadarko, Ramco, Saga and Talisman among others. The third category of companies in the oil market is trading companies. They play an intermediary role between the buyers and sellers across the world and make profit for themselves by taking advantage of price movements. The last 15 years has seen the emergence of a new kind of trader: the Wall Street refiners. These are investment banks which have set up oil trading arms to deal in oil derivatives in a way similar to the way they deal with other financial instruments. The fourth category is the refiners. They are users of crude oil and are the ultimate buyers. In certain cases, they can also be sellers of crude oil which they have bought. Refiners are not only interested in the price they pay for crude oil but also in the value of the crude they realise from the refined products that are produced from crude oil. Thus, a particular type of crude oil has an economic value for a particular refinery and some refineries specialise in the refining of a particular kind of crude (Patra, 2004).

II

The oil and gas industry in India is one of the six core industries and has extremely important forward linkages with the rest of the economy. As discussed in Chapter 3, after independence in 1947, India adopted a 'mixed economy' system to attain the 'commanding heights of the economy'. Before 1947, the oil industry was monopolised by private companies led by US companies Caltex and Standard-Vacuum, and Burmah-Shell (BS), a British-owned oil company. According to IPR 1948, the oil industry was reserved and would be the domain of the SOEs. It also stipulated that unless special permission was given, all new units should be owned by the government. Consequently, Indian Oil Company, OIL and ONGC were formed by the GoI in 1961. In September 1964, IOCL was formed by merging Indian Oil Company and Indian Refineries Ltd. IOCL was made responsible for the downstream sector i.e. marketing and refining, and ONGC was in charge of the majority of the upstream sector i.e. E&P and capacity marketing (IOCL, n.d.).

Around 1973, when the world witnessed the first oil shock, the Indian oil industry was passing through the phase of nationalisation, during the premiership of Indira Gandhi, which culminated in the formation of Hindustan Petroleum Corporation Limited (HPCL) and Bharat Petroleum Corporation Limited (BPCL). In 1976, the GoI acquired the Caltex refinery in Vizagapatnam and the BS refinery in Bombay. The BS refinery became BPCL's primary asset, and in March 1978, the Caltex Oil Refining (India) Ltd was merged with HPCL. On 1 October 1976, the GoI acquired Esso's 26 per cent stake and HPCL became a wholly-owned SOE. Burmah Oil's remaining share in the Assam Oil Company was nationalised on 14 October 1981 and its marketing and refining operations were acquired by IOCL. Thus six out of the 12 refineries in India belonged to IOCL. The other half belonged to other SOEs. Consequently, by 1981, the oil and gas industry comprised only of SOEs (Patra, 2004).

The turning point for the oil and gas industry came in 1991 when India embarked on the path of economic reforms, liberalisation and globalisation. The Indian oil industry was integrated into the world oil market. The oil market graduated from conditions of oligopoly to a state of monopolistic competition with the entry of the private sector. There were consolidations and mergers within the SOEs operating in the industry and companies underwent various shades of restructuring. Until 1993, the entire oil and gas industry was subjected to extensive regulation and controls. Both the upstream and the downstream sectors were centrally planned. The process of integrating the oil industry with the world oil market began in February 1993 when the GoI allowed the private sector to import and sell kerosene and Liquefied Petroleum Gas (LPG). Licenses were granted to private companies to set up refineries and foreign companies were allowed to invest in the equities of refineries. On the eve of total deregulation, by March 2001, a restructuring exercise of the NOCs was undertaken. Stand-alone or independent refineries were merged with integrated refineries and marketing companies by divesting the government shareholding in these refineries. Thus, Chennai Petroleum Corporation Limited (CPCL) and Bongaigon Refinery and Petrochemical Limited were made subsidiaries of IOCL. Kochi Refineries and Numaligarh Refineries were made subsidiaries of BPCL. IBP Limited, the stand-alone marketing SOE, was sold to IOCL through competitive bidding by the Ministry of Disinvestment (Patra, 2004). GoI disinvested its stake in SOEs like ONGC, Gas Authority of India Limited (GAIL), BPCL and HPCL from 1994 to 2005. GoI has plans to further disinvest in ONGC and IOCL (BMI, 2012a).

From April 2002, GoI allowed nine private companies to operate in the downstream sector, which led to a paradigm shift in retail selling. GoI introduced policies aimed at increasing domestic oil E&P. Indian basins were opened up and offered to private and foreign companies for investment. New Exploration Licensing Policy I (NELP-I) was announced in 1997 and NELP-II in 2000 to attract private and foreign investment in the E&P sector in India. NELP-II permitted foreign enterprises to have 100 per cent equity ownership in oil and gas projects. Since then, seven more licensing rounds have been introduced and NELP-IX was launched on 15 October 2010. During the licence round, in excess of 260 blocks were allocated. It is estimated that in the near future, four more licence rounds will be undertaken and investors will be allowed to bid for assets (PwC, 2012).

Table 4.2 provides a breakdown of the SOEs and private enterprises operating in the oil and gas industry in India. The table shows that the oil and gas industry is dominated by SOEs. SOEs are still the dominant players in the E&P sector and have the largest acreage despite the increasing role of the private enterprises (PwC, 2012). ONGC is the largest upstream-oriented oil company, dominating the E&P segment and accounting for roughly three-quarters of the country's oil output. OIL and IOCL are also active in the upstream sector. Domestic private companies and IOCs also operate in the upstream segment. Privately owned domestic conglomerate RIL

Table 4.2 SOEs and private enterprises operating in the oil and gas industry in India from 1991 to 2015

Company	Ownership	Sector
OIL	SOE	Upstream
ONGC and OVL	SOE	Upstream
IOCL	SOE	Upstream and downstream
RIL[a]	Private conglomerate	Upstream and downstream
Essar Energy[b]	Private conglomerate	Upstream and downstream
Gujarat State Petroleum Corporation	SOE[c]	Upstream
GAIL (India) Ltd	SOE	Downstream
BPCL	SOE	Downstream
Bongaigaon Refinery and Petrochemicals Limited[d]	SOE	Downstream
CPCL[d]	SOE	Downstream
Mangalore Refinery and Petrochemicals Limited[e]	SOE	Downstream
Petronet LNG	SOE	Downstream
Gujarat Gas Company	SOE	Downstream
HPCL	SOE	Downstream
IBP[f]	SOE	Downstream
Tata Petrodyne[g]	Private conglomerate	Upstream
Reliance Petroleum[h]	Private conglomerate	Downstream
Reliance Natural Resources Limited[i]	Private conglomerate	Downstream
Hindustan Oil Exploration Company Limited	Private	Upstream
Shiv-Vani Universal	Private	Downstream
Aban Offshore	Private with foreign equity stake	Upstream
Cairn India[j]	Private with foreign equity stake	Upstream
Casrol India	Private – part of BP Group	Downstream
Mahanagar Gas	Joint venture between GAIL, BP and state government of Maharashtra	Downstream
South Asia LPG Company Pvt Ltd	Joint venture between HPCL and Total	Downstream
Great Eastern Energy Corporation Limited	Private conglomerate	Upstream
Tata BP Solar	Joint venture between Tata Power Company and BP Solar	Downstream
Bharat Shell	Joint venture between BPCL and Shell	Downstream
Andhra Pradesh Gas Distribution Corporation	Joint venture between GAIL and Andhra Pradesh Gas Infrastructure Corporation[k]	Upstream and Downstream
Adani Group	Private conglomerate	Downstream
Ratnagiri Gas and Power	Joint venture between GAIL, NTPC[l] and Maharashtra government	Upstream and Downstream
HPCL-Mittal Energy Limited	Jont venture between HPCL and Mittal Energy Limited[m]	Downstream
Bharat Oman Refineries	Joint venture between BPCL and Oman Oil Company	Downstream

Sources: compiled from BMI (2012, 2016).

Notes
a   Part of Reliance Group.
b   Essar Oil is a subsidiary of Essar Energy and both are a part of Essar Group.
c   Owned by the state government of Gujarat.
d   Subsidiary of IOCL.
e   Subsidiary of ONGC.
f   Merged subsidiary of IOCL.
g   Part of Tata Group.
h   Subsidiary of RIL.
i   Subsidiary of Reliance Anil Dhirubhai Ambani Group.
j   Part of Vedanta Group.
k   It is owned by the state government of Andhra Pradesh.
l   SOE.
m   Part of Lakshmi N Mittal Company, Singapore.

participates in the Indian exploration and refining segments. BP in partnership with RIL seeks to be a key partner in the upstream sector in India.

Experts assert that onshore and shallow basins have been explored a lot in India, but the future of the oil industry is in the deepwater and ultra-deepwater oil and gas resources. This will allow India to meet its ever increasing energy needs. However, Indian NOCs are hampered by the lack of technology and experience and financial resources to carry E&P activities in these areas. This provides opportunities for IOCs with the requisite financial strength and monetary resources to enter into joint ventures with Indian NOCs and private enterprises to develop such areas. The IOCs have entered into joint ventures with both SOEs and private enterprises. Despite the opportunities and NELPs, IOCs are active on a relatively small scale with UK-based Cairn Energy, through its Mumbai-listed Cairn India subsidiary, the most successful foreign upstream investor. In January 2012, Vedanta Resources bid to purchase Cairn's Indian arm for US$8.5 billion was approved by the Cabinet Committee on Economic Affairs (CCEA) (BMI, 2012a). The three key players in the upstream sector in India are ONGC, OIL and Cairn India (BMI, 2016a).

India's downstream segment is also dominated by SOEs although private companies have increased their market share in recent years. IOCL operates ten out of 19 refineries in India (20 refineries if the Jamnagar complex is counted as two plants) and controls approximately 75 per cent of the domestic oil transportation network. RIL, which started the first privately owned refinery in India in 1999, has gained a substantial share of the market. The refining sector features a number of domestic companies, namely HPCL, CPCL, BPCL, RIL, IOCL and Essar Energy among others. Fuel distribution has traditionally been handled by IOCL, BPCL and HPCL. However, IOCL, RIL, ONGC and other domestic companies such as Essar have been building retail networks. Several IOCs are present in the Indian lubricants market with ExxonMobil, Shell and Caltex accounting for almost one-third of the market share. Although these operations are of relatively small scale, they have allowed the IOCs to study the Indian oil market and create brand recognition. Castrol India (subsidiary of BP) has a stronger lubricants market position compared to other IOCs. In 2004, the IOCs began to obtain government approval for the establishment of fuels retail networks[2] (BMI, 2016a).

Diversification of sources of crude procurement has been attempted to meet the soaring domestic demand (discussed in Chapter 2) and both the SOEs and private enterprises have been successful in this endeavour. For instance, OVL, IOCL, OIL and RIL have increased their efforts to secure crude acreage and equity in overseas oilfields in Indonesia, Vietnam, Myanmar, Sudan, Angola, Nigeria, Central Asia, Russia, Iraq, Iran, Libya, Gabon and other places. The GoI granted ONGC and IOCL 'Maharatna' (Maharatna or 'mega jewel' status is given to the country's largest SOEs) status in November 2010 to increase the SOEs competitiveness in acquiring international oil and gas assets, particularly as India increasingly sees itself in direct competition with China. The 'Maharatna' status will provide ONGC and IOCL five times more resources to spend on acquisitions, and will give more flexibility in negotiations and in adopting a more streamlined decision-making process. Indian oil companies have repeatedly found themselves outspent, particularly by China's large NOCs, in their search for international assets. According to Bloomberg, in 2009, Chinese NOCs spent US$32 billion in acquiring energy assets abroad compared with US$2.1 billion by ONGC (BMI, 2012a).

OVL has struggled to compete with China's NOCs in the race to acquire oil blocks, especially in Africa. The GoI directed ONGC and OIL to acquire one major international asset in every financial year starting from April 2010 to narrow the gap with NOCs from China. Furthermore, the Ministry of Oil and Gas has formally asked the Ministry of Finance to create a sovereign wealth fund (SWF) specifically for the purpose of acquiring energy assets abroad by employing funds from the country's Forex reserves. According to the *Telegraph*, a leading Indian newspaper, SWF would total around US$20 billion. Additionally, China's SWF, CIC would be studied carefully if the decision is taken to establish a SWF (cited in the *Telegraph*) (BMI, 2012a).

Analysts however argue that although a SWF for energy could help Indian NOCs acquire assets overseas, it will not be able to bridge the gap between NOCs from India and China. China was able to establish the CIC because of its Forex reserves of approximately US$3 trillion that dwarf those held by India (BMI, 2012a). CIC's reserves of US$420 billion (Interview, Executive from CNOOC, Appendix A) alone are currently greater than India's entire foreign currency reserves of approximately US$350 billion, making it impossible for India to create an SWF on the same scale. Thus, a SWF of US$20 billion would allow Indian NOCs to compete more effectively abroad especially when scouting for small targets. However, it would not help the Indian NOCs to compete with Chinese NOCs.

E&P operations and acquisition of assets by major Indian oil and gas companies

This part of the section discusses the E&P operations and acquisition of assets of three Indian SOEs and two Indian private enterprises globally and in India. The SOEs are ONGC (and OVL), IOCL and OIL, and the private enterprises are RIL and Essar Energy.

ONGC (and OVL)

ONGC was established on 14 August 1956 as a statutory body under the ONGC Act with the objective to develop petroleum resources and for selling petroleum products. Under the aegis of the Companies Act, 1956, ONGC was transformed into a Public Limited Company and from 1 February 1994, it was renamed as the Oil and Natural Gas Corporation Limited. ONGC has headquarters in Dehradun in India. It is one of the largest Asian oil and gas E&P corporations in the world. It was ranked 449 in the Fortune Global 500 list of the world's largest corporations for 2015 (Table 4.3). ONGC was ranked 21 amongst the Top 250 oil companies in 2014 by Platts[3] (Table 4.4).

Table 4.3 List of Chinese and Indian oil companies in the Fortune 500 from 2005 to 2015

Company	Country	Type	Rank in year										
			2005	2006	2007	2008	2009	2010	2011	2012	2013	2014	2015
Sinopec Group	China	SOE	31	23	17	16	9	7	5	5	4	3	2
CNPC	China	SOE	46	39	24	25	13	10	6	6	5	4	4
CNOOC	China	SOE	–	–	469	409	318	252	162	101	93	79	72
IOCL	India	SOE	170	153	135	116	105	125	98	83	88	96	119
RIL	India	Private	417	342	269	206	264	175	134	99	107	114	158
ONGC	India	SOE	454	402	369	335	402	413	361	357	369	424	449

Source: compiled from Fortune Global 500, 2005–15.

Table 4.4 Platt 2010–14 ranking of selected Chinese and Indian oil companies

Company	Country of origin	2010	2011	2012	2013	2014
Petrochina (subsidiary of CNPC)	China	4	4	9	8	7
Sinopec	China	8	8	12	10	9
CNOOC	China	15	15	13	12	12
ONGC	India	21	21	22	22	21
RIL	India	24	24	27	19	22
IOCL	India	42	42	82	80	43
OIL	India	n/a	n/a	n/a	n/a	208
Essar Energy	India	225	225	238	229	209

Source: compiled from Platts Top 250 Global Energy Company Rankings.

ONGC is GoI's main upstream vehicle. It is the largest acreage holder and producer of oil and gas in India, and is in an incomparable position to exploit India's upstream potential. GoI owns 74.14 per cent of the company which accounts for approximately 61 per cent of crude oil output and 71 per cent of natural gas output in India. It has been diversifying into refining and oil distribution while attempting to build an international upstream asset base. ONGC has struggled to raise recovery rates, maintain production and tap new discoveries. It is under considerable state pressure to enhance its performance and has set itself tough targets. ONGC has three major strategic aims: first to improve its recovery factor; second, to intensify its exploration activities and third, to increase involvement in foreign projects via OVL. ONGC's long-term goals include doubling its oil and gas reserves by 2020 and increasing its overseas production to 1.2 million barrels of oil equivalent per day by 2025 as well as strengthening its global recovery factor from 28 per cent to the global norm of 40 per cent over the next 20 years (BMI, 2012a).

ONGC's international operations are carried out through the group's wholly-owned subsidiary OVL. Hydrocarbons India Private Limited formed on 5 March 1965 was renamed as OVL on 15 June 1989. Since then, OVL has become the second largest E&P corporation domestically with respect to proven oil and gas reserves and oil production (OVL, n.d.a). Presently, OVL has more than 30 E&P projects in 15 countries: Vietnam, Myanmar, Russia, Azerbaijan, Bangladesh, New Zealand, Iraq, Syria, Mozambique, Libya, Sudan, South Sudan, Brazil, Colombia and Venezuela (OVL, n.d.b).[4] Table 4.5 provides a list of the countries in which Indian and Chinese oil companies undertake E&P activities. OVL's leading alliance partners are BP, Ecopetrol, Exxon, CNPC, Statoil Hydro, Eni, Petrobras, PDVSA, Petronas, Rosneft, Petro Vietnam, Shell, Repsol, Total, Sinopec and TPOC among others (OVL, n.d.a).

IOCL

IOCL has headquarters in New Delhi, India. According to the Fortune 500 global rankings, in 2015, it was the world's 119th largest corporation (Table 4.3). It is

Table 4.5 E&P activities of Chinese and Indian companies globally

Company	Countries in which they operate					
	Africa	Asia and the Pacific (except Middle East)	Middle East	Latin America and the Carribean	North America	Europe
CNPC[a]	Libya, Nigeria, Sudan, South Sudan, Niger, Chad, Tunisia, Algeria	Azerbaijan, Kazakhstan, Turkmenistan, Russia, Myanmar, Indonesia, Mongolia, Thailand, Uzbekistan	Iran, Iraq, Oman, Syria	Ecuador, Peru, Venezuela	Canada	–
PetroChina	Liberia	Australia, Kazakhstan, Iraq	–	Venezuela, Peru	Canada	
Sinopec	Algeria, Nigeria, Gabon, Cameroon, Angola, Sudan	Kazakhstan, Russia, Myanmar, Indonesia, Australia	Saudi Arabia, Syria, Iraq, Yemen	Ecuador, Columbia, Venezuela, Trinidad and Tobago, Brazil, Argentina	US, Canada	UK
CNOOC Ltd[b]	Uganda, Algeria, Equatorial Guinea Nigeria, Republic of Congo, Gabon[b]	Indonesia, Australia. New Zealand, Paupa New Guinea	Iraq	Brazil, Argentina, Trinidad and Tobago, Colombia	Canada, US	Iceland, UK
ONGC (OVL)[c]	Libya, Sudan, Mozambique, South Sudan	Vietnam, Myanmar, Russia, Azerbaijan, Bangladesh, New Zealand	Iraq. Syria	Brazil, Colombia, Venezuela	–	–
IOCL[d]	Libya, Gabon, Nigeira	–	Yemen	Venezuela	US, Canada	–
OIL[e]	Gabon, Libya, Sudan, Nigeria, Mozambique	Bangladesh, Russia, Myanmar	Yemen	Venezuela	US	–
RIL[f]	–	Myanmar	–	–	US	–
Essar Energy	Madagascar, Nigeria	Vietnam, Indonesia	–	–	–	–

Sources: compiled from OVL, OIL, IOCL, RIL, Essar Energy (Essar Oil), CNPC, Sinopec, PetroChina and CNOOC.

Notes

a CNPC no longer has operations in Equatorial Guinea, UAE and Mauritania.

b CNOOC no longer has E&P operations in Ghana, Kenya, Myanmar, Cambodia, Qatar and Venezuela.

c OVL no longer has E&P operations in Nigeria, Kazakhstan, Iran and Cuba.

d IOCL no longer has E&P operations in East Timor and Iran.

e OIL no loimger has E&P operations in East Timor and Iran.

f RIL no longer has E&P operations in Yemen, East Timor, Australia, Oman, Kurdistan, Peru and Colombia.

the national flagship oil corporation of India. It has operations encompassing the entire oil and gas industry like E&P. It was ranked 43 by Platts in its ranking of the top 250 oil companies in the world in 2014 (Table 4.4). IOCL is India's largest partially publicly listed company by sales. IOCL and its subsidiary CPCL hold a 48 per cent market share in petroleum products, 71 per cent share in the downstream sector pipeline capacity in India and a 34.8 per cent proportion of India's refining capacity. The group has a combined capacity to refine 1.3 million bpd and owns and operates 50 per cent of India's 20 refineries. GoI owns 78.9 per cent share of IOCL and plans to divest 10 per cent of its share. According to industry experts, the proceeds from privatisation may act as a catalyst for boosting investment (BMI, 2012a).

In E&P, IOCL's domestic portfolio includes 11 oil and gas blocks and two Coal Bed Methane (CBM) blocks. Its foreign portfolio comprises blocks in the United States, Libya, Gabon, Nigeria, Yemen, Canada and Venezuela (Table 4.5) (IOCL, n.d.a). IOCL and OIL have incorporated Ind-OIL Overseas Ltd, a Special Purpose Vehicle to acquire E&P assets abroad and increase E&P operations. It has also globalised its market operations and has diversified into natural gas. It plans to undertake huge global expansion and plans to enter into talks with Turkey to expand its presence in the country. It plans to use Turkish refineries to access the European markets (BMI, 2016a).

OIL

OIL was taken into full state ownership in 1981. It was previously part owned by the former Burmah Oil Company (now part of BP). OIL is responsible for onshore upstream oil and gas E&P, transport of oil and production of LPG. The majority of its acreage is situated in northeast India – where it has been active since 1959 – especially Assam and is responsible for the whole of its crude oil production and a major proportion of gas production. Ten per cent of OIL's gas production is accounted by Rajasthan (OIL, n.d.a). OIL has achieved a high success rate of 65 per cent in drilling exploratory oil wells employing its scientific and systematic exploration methods (OIL, n.d.b).

OIL has expanded domestically as well as internationally. It has moved into 11 Indian states since 1999 and now has assets onshore in Orissa, Andaman, Rajasthan, Uttar Pradesh and Brahmaputra, and offshore in Saurashtra. OIL's strategic focus is very much on the onshore upstream segment. In January 2010, OIL confirmed that it was looking to purchase producing assets abroad and singled out Africa, Latin America and Australia for potential investment. OIL had a budget of US$2.47 billion for acquisitions (BMI, 2012a). Oil has E&P projects in ten countries: Gabon, Libya, Sudan, Nigeria, Mozambique, Bangladesh, Russia, Myanmar, Yemen and Venezuela (Table 4.5). Although OIL has overseas exploration acreage, it only holds producing assets in India. With none of its overseas assets currently producing, OIL is eager to complete work commitments as quickly as possible with the hope of hitting commercial quantities of reserves and starting production from these assets. In order to reduce its risk exposure, OIL is not looking to expand its exploration acreage unless assets are 'very attractive, prospective and if possible bundle with a producing property', but it is specifically looking to buy into producing assets or companies with producing assets (BMI, 2012a).

RIL

The Reliance Group activities range from petrochemicals, oil and gas, marketing and refining of petroleum, textiles, retail, telecommunications and special economic zones (RIL, n.d.a). RIL is the energy and chemicals division of the Reliance Group. RIL is ranked 158 in the Fortune Global 500 2015 (Table 4.3) and is India's biggest private sector company (RIL, n.d.a). RIL was ranked 22 amongst the top 250 oil companies in 2014 by Platts (Table 4.4). RIL operates in the upstream and the downstream sectors, and is one of the most aggressive investors in the two sectors in India. It has 31 onshore and offshore blocks and is India's biggest private sector E&P enterprise. RIL has E&P operations in the United States and Myanmar. To reduce risk, in November 2009, RIL declared that it was seeking partners to 'farm out'[5] its overseas assets (BMI, 2012a). It no longer has operations in Yemen, East Timor, Australia, Peru, Oman, Kurdistan and Colombia (RIL, n.d.b, n.d.c). In 2010, RIL was exposed to US shale gas through three upstream joint ventures. Reliance's upstream joint ventures in US shale gas include a 45 per cent working interest (WI) partnership with Pioneer Natural Resources in the Eagle Ford shale play, a 40 per cent WI partnership with Chevron and a 60 per cent WI partnership with Carrizo Oil & Gas in the Marcellus Shale play. These joint ventures have positioned RIL as one of the leading players in the Marcellus and Eagle Ford plays. Eagle Ford shale remains one of the most competitive liquid shale plays in the United States and Marcellus is among the most competitive gas plays in the United States (RIL, n.d.c).

Essar Energy (Essar Oil)

The Essar Group was established by Shashi Ruia and Ravi Ruia 1969. The Essar Group is a diverse Indian conglomerate with operations in iron and steel, oil and gas, power, ports and projects, shipping, telecom, realty, information and technology, publishing and agribusiness (Essar, n.d.a). Essar Oil is a subsidiary of Essar Energy and part of the Essar Group of companies. Essar Group currently holds nearly 89 per cent of Essar Oil. Essar Oil has traditionally been a downstream company. In recent years it has emerged as an oil giant internationally because it decided to participate and expand operations in all aspects of the oil value chain. It has expanded rapidly both domestically and abroad in the E&P sector. It has a strong presence in the CBM acreage in India, which has provided it exposure to a sector with a high growth potential. It also specialises in unconventional gas which may also provide opportunities to expand especially if it is able to enter into CBM acreage abroad (BMI, 2012a). In 2014, Essar became India's largest CBM gas producer. Essar Energy was ranked 209 amongst the top 250 oil companies in 2014 by Platts (Table 4.5). Essar Oil through its affiliate Essar E&P has a wide portfolio of E&P stake in assets in Assam, West Bengal, Assam and Gujarat. The overseas E&P assets include three onshore oil and gas blocks in Madagascar and one offshore block each in Vietnam and Nigeria (Table 4.5).

III

Before China became independent in 1949, there was little scientific petroleum E&P albeit on a very small scale (Kambara, 1974). This was because of political instability, absence of knowledge among oil geologists regarding the petroleum geology relevant to the land deposit type of oilfields and apathy by the international oil industry. The largest oilfield in China before 1949 was in the Yumen field in Gansu province and modern mechanisms of oil exploration were employed after 1936. During 1907–49, there were a number of oil and gas discoveries in China but these were all small (Kambara and Howe, 2007).

As discussed in Chapter 3, after 1949, China adopted Stalin's model of 'centralised planned economy' with comprehensive state and collective property. Consequently, China received considerable assistance from the Soviet Union until the breakdown in relations in 1960. After the formation of the PRC, creation and enlargement of refineries, preservation and development of shale oil distillation factories and crude oil E&P were hastened. China received substantial material aid and technical assistance from the Soviet Union during the first five-year plan from 1953–7, but the government's primary focus was on exploration. Chinese techniques and their own ideas frequently took primacy over modern science, notwithstanding the fact that China made concerted attempts to study modern petroleum technology from the Soviet Union (Kambara, 1974).

In 1960, the petroleum industry in China entered into a crisis with the departure of all Soviet oil specialists following the Sino-Soviet split. Although the Chinese had acquired some knowledge of modern petroleum from the Soviets, their experience and knowledge was incomplete. Thus, by 1960, the Chinese were in total control of refinery maintenance and production control although they received some help from Soviet experts (Kambara, 1974). In 1960–1, priority was once again given to E&P of oil (Kambara and Howe, 2007). The Daqing oilfield[6] was found ten days before the tenth anniversary of the PRC. It was opened in 1960 and, in 1963, China claimed petroleum self-sufficiency, i.e. it was able to cope without importing oil from the Soviet Union.

In the late 1960s, the Cultural Revolution dislocated output and growth and hampered operations of refineries, distribution arrangements and transportation. Thus, the Cultural Revolution led to a decline in the oil and gas industry. There was resurgence in the 1970s because China became a permanent member of the UNSC with veto power which increased its stature globally as the leader of the 'Third World'. China's membership of the UN and the 'open door' policy are related to the Cultural Revolution. A key element of Cultural Revolution was disagreements relating to the utilisation of modern technology, and a new disposition to learn and employ Western technology was signified by the 'open door' policy (Kambara and Howe, 2007).

After Mao's death in 1976, the new chairman of the CCP, Hua Guofeng, embarked on plans that were strongly oriented towards heavy industry with significant contribution from the oil industry. Consequently, Hua Guofeng appointed Yu Qiuli, the leader of the so-called 'Oil Group', as the chairman of the State Planning Commission to herald industrial revival in China. This changed dramatically when Deng Xiaoping came to power. Deng rejected Hua's plans of heavy industrialisation in favour of agriculture and light industry and undertook institutional reforms. Deng's 'open door' policy changed the prospects of the oil and gas industry by allowing it to tap into foreign resources, by bringing China into the international oil and energy markets and revolutionising the organisation and management practices of the pre-reform industry. One of the most important features of the 'open door' policy was to allow and to obtain access to foreign technology and expertise for E&P. This is in sharp contrast to the die-hard opposition before 1978 of allowing foreign involvement in China's oil industry if it required any kind of foreign ownership or even access to China's resources. This issue was particularly important in the case of offshore E&P (Kambara and Howe, 2007).

The 1980s spells the start of the reformation era for the oil and gas industry in China. As early as 1982–3, measures were undertaken by the government which laid the framework for the contemporary oil and gas industry. The rules provided the most rudimentary Production Sharing Contracts (PSCs) in the shape of petroleum contracts. The objective of the mandates was to benefit China by obtaining FDI and gaining access to technology and industry acumen (Blumental *et al.*, 2009). Consequently, CNOOC was established in 1982. CNOOC was responsible for offshore exploration and joint contracts with foreign companies. Under CNOOC, four companies with specific geographical remit were established to provide specialised services to foreign companies. These were the Bohai Petroleum Corporation based in Tianjin, the South Yellow Sea Petroleum Corporation in Shanghai, the South China Sea East Petroleum Corporation based in Guangzhou and responsible in particular for the Pearl River Delta and the South China Sea West Petroleum Corporation based at Maoming. Further rounds of international bidding were conducted in 1984 and 1989. In the 1980s, more than 100 foreign companies participated in offshore ventures constructing more than 200 test wells. However, in the 1990s poor results discouraged almost all of them from undertaking further offshore search (Kambara and Howe, 2007).

The political change had important implications for the performance of the oil industry. The impact worked through both the resolution of co-ordination conflicts and the mechanism of investment allocation. Considering that the oil industry is of strategic significance, decision on major projects and financing was taken at very high levels. Before reform, this factor worked in favour of the industry. However, in the post-reform period, the oil industry could not win the national budgetary support that was needed by the industry (Kambara and Howe, 2007).

In the 1980s, at the lower level of planning and management, the responsibility for the upstream and downstream sectors was divided. China Petroleum Corporation (CPC) under the Ministry of Petroleum Industry (MPI) was responsible for the upstream sector. However, in 1988, this agreement changed when the CPC was replaced by the CNPC still under the MPI. In the downstream sector, the key entity was Sinopec under the Ministry for Chemical Industries. Neither CNPC nor Sinopec were allowed to issue blocks for offshore prospecting to foreign companies and this right was confined to CNOOC (Kambara and Howe, 2007).

During the 1990s, major transformation in the planning and administration of the oil industry was undertaken, reflecting the wider trend to convert an economy based on central planning and non-competitive administration into one in which independent units enhanced their efficiency and utility by reducing cost, innovation and ever increasing capabilities to conform to market needs. The oil industry proved to be a model that was followed by other large-scale and capital-intensive industries. The turning point in this successful process was the 1998 reform according to which all ministries were to be converted into bureaus and the entities below them to operate as commercial entities operating on the governance and operating principles of modern corporations (Kambara and Howe, 2007). The government reorganised the oil industry, merging most state-owned assets, which led to the creation of two enormous commercial entities, namely the China National Petroleum Corporation (the 'new' CNPC) and China National Petrochemical Corporation (the 'new' Sinopec). Each was assigned a primary geographical location with north and west China for CNPC and south China for Sinopec. The old agreement was changed and both operated and competed with each other in the upstream and downstream sectors although CNPC leans more towards upstream activities and Sinopec more towards the downstream, especially refining. The intention of this reform was to create two Chinese NOCs which would develop capabilities to compete within China and worldwide with the IOCs. Subsequently, CNPC, Sinopec and a reformed CNOOC were all converted into holding companies known as PetroChina, Sinopec Corporation and CNOOC Ltd, and were encouraged to establish further operating company subsidiaries. The three companies were listed in stock exchanges in Hong Kong, London and New York (Kambara and Howe, 2007).

The NDRC was established in 2003 and is the largest body governing the energy sector. It sets fuel prices and provides the required approval for large domestic and international investments. Every project in the oil industry and overseas expenditures exceeding US$200 million are reviewed by the NDRC and passed onto the State Council for final approval. The NDRC oversees the National Energy Administration, which is responsible for long-term energy security and development strategy (Downs, 2008). However, the NOCs have technical advantages over the energy bureaucracy because much of the technical expertise on issues related to energy remained within the companies after they were transformed from ministries. Moreover, government officials often consult the companies for establishing new policies and laws (Downs, 2011).

As discussed in Chapter 3, despite the fact that China has made rapid progress towards a market economy, public interest and public funds still play the central role. Table 4.6 provides a breakdown of the companies operating in the oil industry in China. In 2014, the largest of these companies measured by oil production was the wholly state-owned CNPC and partly privatised PetroChina (subsidiary of CNPC), followed by Sinopec and CNOOC (BMI, 2016b). Sinopec is the largest producer of refined oil products not only in China but also in Asia. The three companies combined have the major proportion of upstream and downstream oil/gas assets in China and have also entered into joint ventures with IOCs. According to an executive from CNOOC (Interview, Appendix A), the domestic oil sector in China is dominated by CNPC, Sinopec and CNOOC and China is primarily represented by these three SOEs (and their subsidiaries) abroad.

Shaanxi Yanchang Petroleum Group Company, a SOE, is the fourth largest oil company in China. It was established in 2005 by merging 21 private E&P companies and three refineries (Blumental *et al.*, 2009). Additionally, there are numerous oil companies owned by provincial governments. It is not surprising to see (Table 4.6) that almost all the companies are SOEs. As discussed in Chapter 3, private enterprises in China are small in size relative to the SOEs. This is also the case in the oil industry. This is not only because of the role of institutions and the Maoist legacy of the past, but also because E&P is a risky business, which fledging private capitalist corporations in China are less willing to undertake. There are numerous small private oil companies in China like Guangdong Jovo Group, Dalian Shide, Leiyu Industry, Boco Energy, Weihai Huayue, Central Asia Oil Company, United Energy Group Ltd (based in Hong Kong) and Oil China Company, among others, but they are very minor players unlike in the oil industry in India where the private sector oil companies play a major role. Xinjiang Guanghui Industry Investment Group Co. Ltd is the largest private energy company in the autonomous region of Xinjiang (Out-Law.com, 2014).

In December 2004, under the aegis of the Gongshanglian, the China Chamber of Commerce for the Petroleum Industry (CCCPI), 140 private oil companies formed an association. In June 2006, the largest private sector companies in China united to establish the Great United Petroleum Holding Co., Ltd (GUPC) under CCCPI's coordination. The conglomerate had approximately five billion yuan (US$603.9 million) as capital at the time of its establishment. GUPC is hopeful that it will be able to provide a platform for the private companies to compete with the large SOEs to expand operations domestically and acquire upstream projects overseas. However, it has not been successful (Blumental *et al.*, 2009). In June 2012, the Chinese government introduced guidelines to encourage the participation of private oil and gas companies in the upstream and downstream sectors of the oil industry. Analysts opine that it is part of a drive by the government to foster competition and break the monopoly of the three big NOCs in China's oil industry (Owen, 2012). However, Zhang Chun, Deputy Director Centre for West Asian and African Studies, Shanghai Institutes for International Studies (SIIS)

Table 4.6 Chinese companies operating in the oil and gas industry in China from 1978 to 2015

Company	Ownership	Sector
China Clean Energy, Inc	SOE	Downstream
CNPC	SOE	Upstream and downstream
PetroChina (subsidiary of CNPC)	SOE	Upstream and downstream
Fushun Petrochemical Company (subsidiary of Petrochina)	SOE	Downstream
CNOOC Ltd	SOE	Downstream
China United Coalbed Methane Corporation (subsidiary of CNOOC Ltd)	SOE	Upstream
China Oilfield Services (subsidiary of CNOOC Ltd)	SOE	Upstream
China Natural Gas	SOE	Downstream
China Petroleum & Chemical Corporation Limited or Sinopec Corp. or Sinopec (subsidiary of Sinopec Group)	SOE	Upstream and downstream
Sinopec Shanghai Petrochemical Company Limited (subsidiary of Sinopec)	SOE	Downstream
CITIC Resources Holdings Limited (subsidiary of CITIC Group)	SOE	Upstream
Shaanxi Yanchang Petroleum	SOE	Upstream and downstream
Shenergy Group (including its subsidiary Shenergy Company)	SOE	Downstream
Towngas China Company Limited	SOE	Downstream
Sinochem Group	SOE	Upstream and downstream
China ZhenHua Oil Co., Ltd (subsidiary of China North Industry Corporation or Norinco)	SOE	Upstream and downstream
BOCO Energy (subsidiary of Bright Oceans Corporation)	SOE	Upstream and downstream
Shandong Energy Group	SOE	Upstream
United Energy Group Ltd	Private – HK	Upstream
Guangdong Jovo Group	Private	Downstream
Central Asia Oil Company	Prvate	Downstream

Sources: compiled from BMI (2012b, 2016b); Blumental *et al.* (2009); Fortune (n.d.).

avers, "The three oil companies have great political influence and are able to influence China's policy on energy security. They have hijacked the government" (Interview, Appendix A). According to Zhu Ming, Centre for West Asian and African Studies, SIIS, "The private oil companies in China are not allowed to go abroad and invest. They are only allowed to buy oil from the top three NOCs" (Interview, Appendix A). They are sceptical that the private sector will play a bigger role in the oil industry in the near future. In August 2014, Xinjiang Guanghui Industry Investment Group Co. Ltd, a subsidiary of China's Guanghui Energy Co. Ltd, became the first private enterprise licensed to ship crude oil into the country. Under the terms of the licence, Guanghui can import crude oil directly from its own oil project in Kazakhstan and sell it to refineries in China. According to Lin Boqiang, director of the China Centre for Energy Economic Research with Xiamen University:

> This is an opportunity for private enterprises to enter the upstream sector of the oil industry. Granting the import licence to private companies shows serious consideration of national energy security, while opening up to private companies is conducive to industrial competition and improving national energy security.
>
> (Out-Law.com)

WTO membership led to the opening of the Chinese fuels market in 2004. IOCs have been participating in the upstream sector in China for many years, but they do not have a strong presence in that sector (BMI, 2016b). Chinese government has encouraged foreign co-operation in E&P activity globally and in China to acquire technological capability. Additionally, in the 2007 Catalogue of Foreign Investment Industries, investments linked to new technologies for petroleum exploration and development and investments in E&P of petroleum and natural gas are listed as encouraged industries. However, it is specifically mentioned in the catalogue that all E&P operations in China should be conducted in partnership with Chinese companies (Blumental *et al.*, 2009). Unlike the upstream sector, partnerships with the oil majors in the downstream industry, i.e. fuels distribution, gas transportation and petrochemicals, are a very recent development. BP, Shell, ExxonMobil, Chevron and Conoco Phillips, to name a few, are active in the upstream and downstream sectors, and Husky Energy, Statoil, Total, Caltex, Eni and the British Gas Group among others in the upstream sector in China. Major IOCs like BP, ExxonMobil and Shell are all building world-scale petrochemicals capacity in China in conjunction with Sinopec and PetroChina. However, the major Chinese companies are moving fast to establish a strong grip on the distribution system in order to minimise the risk of losing profitable market share to the IOCs (BMI, 2016b).

China's oil production growth can be attributed to the rapidly rising output from nine giant fields which accounted for some 80 per cent of the country's total production in 2010. Five of these fields are now declining, in particular the flagship Daqing and Shengli oilfields. Production growth in the future will be driven by the remaining four fields at which production is still expanding or has remained steady: Changqing, Xinjiang, Dagang and Tarim (BMI, 2016b). Since the late 1990s, diversification of sources of crude procurement has been attempted by CNPC, PetroChina, Sinopec and CNOOC. Consequently, Chinese NOCs have aimed at acquiring and expanding their E&P activities globally and purchasing equity oil stakes abroad to meet the ever increasing domestic demand. Consequently, China's SWF, CIC, the third largest SWF in the world with approximately US$746.7 billion of assets under management (SWFI, n.d.) was established in September 2007 following the issuing of 1.55 trillion yuan of special bonds. These bonds were used to acquire US$200 billion of China's foreign currency reserves. Although CIC is wholly state-owned, it claims that its investment decisions are based entirely on commercial considerations contingent on the way the capital was acquired. CIC has played an extremely significant role in the purchase of overseas energy assets. For instance, an 11 per cent stake in Kazakhstan's KazMunaiGaz E&P acquired in September 2009, a 14.9 per cent stake in Russia-based Nobel Oil Group and a 13 per cent stake in coal-producer South Gobi Energy Resources. CIC's reserves now stand at US$420 billion. Table 4.6 provides a list of the countries in which the Chinese NOCs have E&P operations.

E&P operations and acquisition of assets by major Chinese oil and gas companies

This part of the section discusses the E&P operations and acquisition of assets of four Chinese NOCs globally and in China. The SOEs are CNPC, PetroChina, Sinopec and CNOOC. Although CITIC Resources Holdings Limited, a subsidiary of CITIC Group and Shaanxi Yanchang Petroleum are also NOCs operating in the upstream sector in China, they are relatively small compared to the NOCs mentioned above and operate only in China.

CNPC

CNPC, with headquarters in Beijing, is wholly owned by the state. It is China's largest oil and gas producer and the second largest integrated oil and gas enterprise not only in China but also globally. It operates in segments like development of new energy, oilfield services, natural gas and pipelines, manufacturing petroleum equipment, E&P of petroleum, finance, capital management and insurance services among others (CNPC, n.d.a). CNPC was founded in 1988 and was restructured into an integrated oil company in 1998 during the overhaul of China's oil and gas sector (BMI, 2016b). CNPC is ranked fourth in the Fortune Global 500 list of the world's biggest corporations for the year 2015 (Table 4.3). Its total assets in 2014 amounted to 3,938.37 billion yuan with an operating income of 2,729.96 billion yuan. It has a presence in 38 countries across the globe (CNPC, n.d.a).

CNPC is a key player in implementing China's international oil strategy and its principal focus is on securing oil production outside the domestic market through international E&P projects. Most of its Chinese operations are conducted via its 90 per cent owned subsidiary PetroChina. Unlike PetroChina and Sinopec, CNPC is under no great pressure to boost efficiency and maximise profits. Since privatisation is not on the agenda, it can be expected to concentrate on growth rather than profitability (BMI, 2012b).

CNPC has E&P projects in offshore and onshore China. At present in China, CNPC operates onshore oil and gas fields in the northeast and northwest as well as a few shallow water blocks in northern Bohai Bay. After receiving approval from the Chinese government, CNPC started cooperating with the IOCs for joint

E&P of blocks in China. CNPC has oil and gas assets in 24 countries (Table 4.5). CNPC's focus is on increasing its international oil reserves, although it is also considering overseas downstream investments such as refineries and petrol stations. The corporation's strategy of overseas expansion is similar to that of the IOCs which generally derive 60–70 per cent of their total business from overseas operations. The company's strategy will focus on three main areas: increasing exploration of domestic oil and gas blocks, making progress on major refining projects and enhancing oil and gas transport and distribution infrastructure (BMI, 2016b).

PetroChina Company Limited or PetroChina

PetroChina Company Limited (PetroChina) has its headquarters in Beijing. CNPC owns 86.5 per cent of PetroChina (BMI, 2016b). It is a dominant player in the hydrocarbon industry in China and is the biggest oil and gas producer domestically. In 2011, PetroChina produced 2.43 mbpd and surpassed Exxon-Mobil (2.3 mbpd) to become the biggest oil and gas producer globally (Fontevecchia, 2012). On 5 November 1999, CNPC launched PetroChina as a joint stock company possessing limited liabilities (PetroChina, n.d.). It is the largest publicly traded Chinese oil corporation. PetroChina was the first NOC to be launched on the stock market in China and is still viewed as China's oil sector proxy (BMI, 2016b). On 6 April 2000, PetroChina's American Depositary Shares were listed on the New York Stock Exchange and on 7 April 2000 its 'H' shares were listed on the Hong Kong Stock Exchange Limited. On 5 November 2007, it was listed on the Shanghai Stock Exchange (PetroChina, n.d.). It was ranked seventh amongst the top 250 oil companies in 2014 by Platts (Table 4.4).

PetroChina has a wide spectrum of interests in all the sectors of the hydrocarbon industry. The lion's share of PetroChina's oil and gas reserves are situated in southwestern, northeastern, northwestern and northern China and the majority is in the Songliao Basin in the Jilin and Heilongjiang provinces which is the site for the Daqing oil region. For some time now, PetroChina's oil production in China has remained the same because most of its oilfields, including the Daqing, are becoming exhausted. PetroChina had few assets abroad until June 2005 when it acquired 50 per cent of the overseas assets of the parent company CNPC for US$2.5 billion. Currently, it has assets in several countries such as Peru, Venezuela and Kazakhstan (BMI, 2016b).

Sinopec Corp. or Sinopec

Sinopec is headquartered in Beijing. It is a listed corporation on domestic as well as international stock exchanges. On 25 January 2000, the enterprise was incorporated by Sinopec Group or CPC. On 18 October and 19 October 2000, 16.78 billion 'H' shares were floated by Sinopec in New York, London and Hong Kong stock exchanges, and on 16 July 2001, it issued 2.8 billion 'A' shares in the Shanghai Stock Exchange (Sinopec, n.d.a). As of 2012, Sinopec is 55.06 per cent owned by the wholly state-owned Sinopec Group (BMI, 2016b). It is ranked second in the Fortune Global 500 list of the world's biggest corporations for the year 2014 (Table 4.3) and is ranked ninth amongst the top 250 oil companies in 2014 by Platts (Table 4.4). In 2014, Sinopec reported revenues of 2.825 trillion yuan and net profit of 73.5 billion yuan. Revenues decreased by 1.9 per cent year on year and net profits declined by 24.1 per cent year on year. The results are due to the decline in the price of oil since 2014 (BMI, 2016b).

Sinopec has a wide array of interests in all the sectors of the hydrocarbon industry. China's best downstream petrochemical and oil assets were allocated to Sinopec during the reorganisation of the hydrocarbon industry in the 1980s. It has approximately a two-thirds share in China's fuel market and has 30,063 stations, making it the largest operator in the retail market for hydrocarbon products. It is the largest refiner and producer of petrochemicals in the country and has entered into major partnerships with IOCs, such as BASF, ExxonMobil and BP (BMI, 2016b).

Sinopec is also involved in the upstream segment globally and in China. It is the second largest oil and gas producer in China. It has oil and gas E&P zones in the south, east and west of China. It has 12 oil and gas subsidiaries (Sinopec, n.d.b). Sinopec is heavily involved in southwest China where its operations are carried out through Sinopec Southwest Oil & Gas Company (BMI, 2016b). Sinopec has overseas E&P operations in 24 countries across Asia, Middle East, Latin America and Africa (Table 4.5). Overseas external oil and gas co-operation is undertaken on behalf of Sinopec by the wholly-owned subsidiary of Sinopec Group, Sinopec International Petroleum Exploration and Production Corporation (SIPC). SIPC was established in January 2001 and is headquartered in Beijing. Major progress has also been made in the development of new projects and the Sinopec Group successfully acquired five projects including Addax Petroleum (AP) and partial equity of three blocks in Angola (SIPC, n.d.). Significant funds have been allocated to secure overseas oil and gas reserves. Out of the 321.73 million barrels of crude oil produced by Sinopec in 2011, 18.36 million barrels came from Africa and the remainder from China. There has been a reduction in crude oil produced in Africa. In 2009 and 2010, Sinopec produced 26.47 million and 25.67 million barrels of oil in Africa (Sinopec, n.d.b).

CNOOC Ltd or CNOOC

CNOOC Ltd is a subsidiary of the CNOOC Group and has headquarters in Beijing. CNOOC Ltd and the CNOOC Group were incorporated in Hong Kong in 1999. On 27 February and 28 February respectively, CNOOC Ltd was listed on the New York Stock Exchange and the Hong Kong Stock Exchange. In July 2001, it was also listed on the Hang Seng Index. The group is the biggest producer of natural gas and crude oil in offshore China. Its main operations are in the sale of oil and natural gas, development and E&P (CNOOC, n.d.a). CNOOC Ltd is the smallest of the privatised Chinese NOCs and specialises in offshore E&P. The Chinese government has a 70 per cent share in CNOOC Ltd. It is more efficient and focused relative to Sinopec and PetroChina. In 2014, CNOOC revenues from oil and gas sales amounted to 218.21 billion yuan, a decline of 3.6 per cent relative to 2013. Its net profit increased by 6.6 per cent to 60.2 billion yuan in 2014 compared to 2013 (BMI, 2016b). It is ranked 72 in the list of Fortune 500 companies (Table 4.3) and was ranked 12 amongst the top 250 oil companies in 2014 by Platts (Table 4.4).

CNOOC is undertaking diversification in a number of directions. It is making a concerted attempt to develop a portfolio of upstream assets internationally which may dilute its future investments in China. For instance, its desire to expand rapidly is well illustrated by its failed attempt to acquire Unocal in the United States. In 2001, CNOOC annulled an agreement with the parent company which bestowed the latter with the sole rights to operate, explore and produce oil and gas assets. Since 2001, CNOOC and its parent company share upstream projects. This highlights that the Chinese government is assuming a stronger role in CNOOC's activities and has decided to offer more political and financial support for acquisitions abroad in the future. The group's major activities are offshore China in Bohai, Western South China Sea, Eastern South China Sea and East China Sea (CNOOC, n.d.a).

CNOOC is diversifying in various directions. It has started to build an international upstream portfolio, which dilutes the China element of the investment story. Its acquisition of Canada's Nexen for US$15.1 billion reveals a desire to grow rapidly. CNOOC has E&P operations in 20 countries in Asia, Latin America, Africa, Middle East, Europe and North America (Table 4.5) (CNOOC, n.d.b). It aims (along with Sinopec and CNPC) to continue expanding rapidly abroad to meet China's growing energy needs. This is being done by flexing its financial muscle. According to CNOOC's General Manager Fu Chengyu, as part of CNOOC's plan to expand domestically and abroad, CNOOC is set to invest between US$121 billion and US$151 billion during 2011–15 (BMI, 2012b).

IV Indian and Chinese oil companies: a comparative perspective

This section examines the diplomatic, political and financial support received by the NOCs in the two countries due to the difference in the economic and political power, ability to take risk, difference in technology and project management skills.

Diplomatic, political and financial support

The ability of the governments in India and China to provide diplomatic, political and financial support to the NOCs is influenced and constrained by the difference in their economic and political power. The governments in the two countries played an extremely important role in perpetuating, propagating and supporting the NOCs. All the Indian oil companies, especially ONGC (and OVL), OIL and Essar Oil, which are active in the upstream sector and in the oil industry in West Africa, are smaller in size, market capitalisation and revenue compared to the three Chinese NOCs, namely CNPC (and PetroChina), Sinopec and CNOOC. This is evidenced by the fact that all the three Chinese NOCs are ranked higher in the Global Fortune 500 rankings compared to the three Indian oil companies mentioned above for the period 2005–15 (CNOOC is ranked lower than IOCL until 2013 and ranked lower than RIL until 2012). According to Professor He Maochun, Director of the Research Centre for Economic Diplomacy Studies, Tsinghua University (Interview, Appendix A), "The Chinese oil companies are rich enough to support themselves. They are richer than a bank. They have huge financial resources at their disposal. They are sitting on billions of US$". It should be noted that both Indian and Chinese NOCs have improved their respective rankings until 2012. After 2012, the ranking of the Chinese NOCs has improved but the ranking of Indian oil companies has declined (Table 4.3). The Chinese NOCs are also ranked higher than Indian oil companies in the prestigious Platt rankings (Table 4.4).

It can be argued that since China has a bigger economy than India, Chinese oil companies would be larger relative to their Indian counterparts. Chinese NOCs are bigger also because of the state support and subsidies that they receive relative to Indian NOCs. The CIC had US$300 billion at its disposal – $100 billion for NOCs, $100 billion for agriculture and $100 billion for infrastructure – until 2013 and has US$420 billion in 2015, which is larger than the foreign exchange reserves of India which stand at approximately US$348.93 billion. According to Ashok Dhar, Distinguished Fellow at the Observer Research Foundation (ORF) (Interview, Appendix A), "Chinese government facilitates business. The government knows how to use money to get business deals. They have used money across the globe especially in Africa to get business deals".

There is a broad consensus amongst the interviewees that China is able to provide more diplomatic and political support compared to India (Interview, Appendix A). According to Professor Keun-Wook Paik, Senior Fellow at the Oxford Institute for Energy Studies (OIES), "Chinese NOCs receive direct political and diplomatic support from the Chinese government under the aegis of the 'go global policy' introduced in 2000. It is very difficult for Indian oil companies to compete with Chinese NOCs" (Interview, Appendix A). Professor He Maochun, Tsinghua University, states that

> China will continue to support the NOCs financially, diplomatically and politically to invest abroad. India will not be able to match the Chinese NOCs in the short to medium term. Chinese government provides a lot of diplomatic and political support to the Chinese NOCs.
>
> (Interview, Appendix A)

According to Chinese experts, the heads of the NOCs are appointed by the central government. Executives in the NOC are appointed, dismissed and promoted by the Organisation Department of the CCP and all the decisions need to be ratified by the Politburo. According to Zhu Ming at SIIS:

The Vice President and member of the Politburo Standing Committee Zheng Qinghing had a background in the oil industry. Similarly, Wu Yi, Vice Premier and Politburo member has also worked in the oil industry. The former Chief Executive Officer of CNOOC, Wei Liucheng, was appointed the Governor of Hainan province (from 2003–7). The top leaders of the provincial governments in China are not only from the CCP but also from the SOEs. This is not the case in India.

(Interview, Appendix A)

In 2007, Jian Jemin, the head of CNPC, and Su Shulin, the head of Sinopec, were named alternate members of the Central Committee of the CCP. Later Su was made the Deputy Party Secretary and Governor of Fujian province. Fu Chengyu, President of Sinopec, replaced Su as the head of Sinopec and was also elected as a member of the Central Commission for Discipline Inspection. In 1998, Zhou Yongkang from CNPC and Sheng Huaren from Sinopec became members of Zhu Rongji's State Council (Downs and Meidan, 2011). Both individuals supported the business activities of their respective companies (Kong, 2010). Zhou became Minister of Land and Natural Resources in 1998 and in 1999, he was also named the Party Secretary of Sichuan province (Downs and Meidan, 2011). In 2004, he became a member of the Politburo and Minister of Public Security. In 2007, he became a member of the Politburo Standing Committee and was the ninth highest ranking member of the Politburo.

Chinese NOCs also receive significant financial support from the Chinese government. According to Professor Paik, OIES, in addition to the support from the CIC, Chinese NOCs also receive financial support from the State-owned Assets Supervision and Administration Commission (SASAC),[7] China Development Bank (CDB) and the Chinese EXIM Bank under the aegis of the 'go global policy' introduced in 2000. According to Dr Lu Bo, Ministry of Commerce, PRC, "China has much larger foreign exchange reserves than India. State banks are willing to lend to the SOEs especially the NOCs for investment abroad because they know the NOCs will return the money" (Interview, Appendix A). Dr Liu Feitao, Deputy Director for the Division for American Studies, Chinese Institutes for International Studies (CIIS), states:

Chinese NOCs and other SOEs are able to borrow at 0–1 per cent interest rate domestically. Chinese banks are willing to lend to the NOCs and SOEs because they are backed by the Chinese government. Chinese government will support them financially. India will not be able to match that.

(Interview, Appendix A)

Lydia Powell, Head, Centre for Resources Management, ORF asserts that:

Chinese oil companies have access to cheap capital. Indian oil companies do not have access to cheap capital. In India, NOCs are asked to borrow from the market at the market prevailing interest rate which is substantially higher than the rate at which the Chinese NOCs can borrow money from the state owned Chinese banks.

(Interview, Appendix A)

To quote an executive from OVL (OVL[a]), "The domestic cost of capital in India is 10–11 per cent. It is not possible to compete with oil companies from China. We are not in the same league" (Interview, Appendix A). According to executives from OVL, IOCL, OIL and Essar Oil, the availability of cheap capital makes it easier for Chinese NOCs to operate at a 3–4 per cent rate of return. Shebonti Ray Dadwal, Research Fellow at the Institute for Defence Studies and Analysis (IDSA), and Uma Shankar Sharma, former Joint Secretary, Ministry of Oil and Gas, GoI, now at ORF, assert that for Indian NOCs, the minimum rate of return is 10–11 per cent whereas for private sector oil companies, the minimum rate of return is in the range of 18–20 per cent. The IOCs operate at a margin of around 15 per cent (Interviews, Appendix A). To quote an executive from OVL (OVL[a]):

> In the international market, finance is available at 3–4 per cent but currency fluctuations are a problem. It also requires collateral like guarantees from the parent company (ONGC) or banks and/or sovereign guarantees are required which OVL will not be able to provide for very large sums. OVL has to bank on commercial capital which is not less than 4–5 per cent. It is difficult to work at 3–4 per cent. This puts OVL and other Indian companies at a disadvantage with respect to Chinese NOCs.

(Interview, Appendix A)

According to Ruchita Beri, Senior Research Associate, IDSA and Shebonti Ray Dadwal, IDSA, because China is economically more powerful than India, it can provide more financial support to NOCs relative to India. To quote Shebonti Ray Dadwal, "The purses of the Indian NOCs have increased manifold but they still cannot be compared to China and they still cannot beat them. Cash is a problem with India compared to China" (Interview, Appendix A). According to Ambassador Viswanathan, Distinguished Fellow, ORF and former High Commissioner to Nigeria, GoI,

> Chinese oil companies have extremely deep pockets. ONGC and OVL have deep pockets by Indian standards but not compared to Chinese oil companies. Indian oil companies are no match for Chinese oil companies. They cannot and should not be compared.

(Interview, Appendix A)

According to Ruchita Beri, IDSA, and Uma Shankar Sharma, ORF, and executives from IOCL and OVL, the 'signature bonus'[8] and royalty payments in some of the West African countries are too high, especially in Angola, too high even for the IOCs. However, the Chinese NOCs can afford it. Consequently,

Indian oil companies are unable to bid for oil blocks. According to executives from OIL, IOCL, OVL and Essar Oil, and Ashok Dhar, ORF, Indian oil companies cannot and could not have bought Nexen, a Canadian oil company which CNOOC acquired for US$15.1 billion. To quote an executive from OVL (OVL[a]), "It is out of our league. Chinese strategy is driven by finance and economic power. If you do not have the money, Chinese strategy is not going to work" (Interview, Appendix A).

According to Lydia Powell ORF, an executive from IOCL (IOCL[a]), and two executives from OVL (OVL[a] and OVL[b]), although GoI also provides diplomatic and political support to the NOCs in their quest for oil, Indian NOCs are unable to match the Chinese NOCs (Interview, Appendix A). According to Associate Professor Bonnie Ayodele, University of Ado Ekiti, the relative difference in economic and political power plays an extremely important role in the ability of the Chinese and Indian governments to provide economic, political and diplomatic support to their respective oil companies. Dr Ayodele avers that China's economic power and UNSC membership with veto power enables China to establish better diplomatic relations with countries in West Africa which also helps the Chinese NOCs to the detriment of Indian oil companies. To quote Dr Ayodele: "Chinese power even trumps India's historical relations with Africa. China has used its economic power to build more robust relations with African countries including countries in West Africa. China's political and economic diplomacy cannot be matched by India" (Interview, Appendix A). Uma Shankar Sharma at ORF states that "Perception matters. African leaders see how China uses its veto power" (Interview, Appendix A). Professor Li Anshan, Director of Centre for African Studies, Peking University, also agrees that perception matters. "Some African presidents and leaders trust China a lot. Diplomatic support and relations provided a good foundation for business development. It allowed Chinese companies to invest in Africa. When China asks for something, African leaders agree" (Interview, Appendix A). According to Ruchita Beri at IDSA, "China uses money to build state to state relations. India has been unable to do so. We are constrained by lack of financial resources compared to China" (Interview, Appendix A). Shebonti Ray Dadwal, IDSA, states that "China is a favoured partner because of economic and political power. India cannot match China's financial and diplomatic muscle. India is unable to establish diplomatic relations like China does, using its economic leverage" (Interview, Appendix A). Professor Li Anshan, Peking University, states that because China is able to give more aid to Africa, Chinese NOCs are preferred as partners over Indian oil companies. According to Sunjoy Joshi, director of ORF and one of the leading experts in India on the oil industry, "India has not been able to match the aid provided by China. There is not much leverage there" (Telephone interview, Appendix A). Professor Zhongying Pang, Renmin University, avers:

> 49 African leaders attended the FOCAC in Beijing. These leaders do not go to the UN General Assembly meeting in New York. This shows the

extent of the close relations between China and countries in Africa. China has been able to establish better diplomatic relations with Africa relative to India.

(Interview, Appendix A)

According to Zhang Chun at SIIS:

The decisions of the African countries to give oil blocks to Chinese oil companies are not only based on economics but also on political and diplomatic considerations. In the last two decades, China's relations with Africa have strengthened relative to India–Africa relations.

(Interview, Appendix A)

This illustrates the importance of China–Africa relations.

Risk

The gargantuan financial resources at the disposal of the Chinese NOCs enable them to take more risks, to bid for oil blocks in almost every country in West Africa and outbid Indian oil companies if and when they compete directly for an oil block. According to Lydia Powell at ORF and James Byrne, reporter at Interfax, a news agency, Chinese bidding does not make commercial sense (Interview, Appendix A). Shebonti Ray Dadwal, IDSA, avers that "India is extremely risk averse relative to China. India does not go in for a difficult asset" (Interview, Appendix A). Regarding India's foray into acquiring equity oil blocks abroad and especially in Africa, Mani Shankar Aiyar, former Minister of Oil and Gas, GoI stated:

Everything was frowned upon because of the extremely high risks being created. We find it difficult to compete with China and the majors in the normal course. Therefore it is only in some unsafe conditions that we have a chance of competing and if and when the situation stabilises we would build our reputation as a reliable partner. Therefore we should be much more aggressive in pursuing the external dimension of our energy security policy than has been the case earlier. But Indian oil companies and Indian government are very conservative.

(Interview, Appendix A)

According to Zhang Chun at SIIS, "Chinese companies are more risk oriented" (Interview, Appendix A). According to Professor Paik at OIES, "China is not concerned about the rate of return on investment. Chinese NOCs are concerned about the size of the oil reserves" (Interview, Appendix A). An executive from OVL (OVL[a]) commented:

Our offers have a strong weighting on realistic assumptions, upon the rate of return on the asset and the future potential of the asset. Chinese are not concerned about returns. They have too much money. The ground reality is that China and Chinese oil companies have more money and we have to survive with that. We are still surviving.

(Interview, Appendix A)

To quote Uma Shankar Sharma at ORF, "China can bid for anything. They have too much money" (Interview, Appendix A). According to an executive from IOCL (IOCL[b]), "IOCL wants to get into areas where there are verified reserves, where there is production and not much risk should be associated with production" (Interview, Appendix A).

Dr Lu Bo, Ministry of Commerce, PRC, asserts that "the Indian oil companies are more reasonable than Chinese companies in their investment decisions" (Interview, Appendix A). Although Dr Lu Bo agrees with the decision-making process of the Indian NOCs, he avers that:

It is difficult to forecast what will happen in 10–20 years. In order to win the bid, sometimes Chinese oil companies have to take risks, and forgo many things. We can only wait and see whether the decisions are good. It is too early to say whether Indian or Chinese oil companies are right in their decision-making process. Sometimes if you are too hesitant to take the risk, you will lose the opportunity. This is what Indian oil companies have done.

(Interview, Appendix A)

According to Ambassador Viswanathan, ORF, Chinese oil companies can afford a long gestation period whereas Indian oil companies have to be careful about returns on investment (Interview, Appendix A).

Technology and project management

Although both Indian and Chinese NOCs have more or less similar technological capabilities, according to Shebonti Ray Dadwal at IDSA, Uma Shankar Sharma and Sunjoy Joshi at ORF and executives from OVL, IOCL and OIL, India is at disadvantage because it is unable to buy the necessary technology that is required. Both India and China rely on outsourcing to third parties but China has an advantage as it is able to pay a higher price for technology because it has more money. According to Sunjoy Joshi:

Technological edge is there if a company is the "operator" in the oil block. OVL is not the operator but sometimes Chinese companies are. They are able and willing to pay higher amounts to become operators. Chinese NOCs are extremely aggressive in acquiring technology. The whole purpose of the joint venture is to acquire technology. Indian oil companies are limited in their ability to acquire technology.

(Interview, Appendix A)

According to an executive from OVL (OVL^a), IOCL and Ashok Dhar, Indian oil companies, especially RIL, have better skills to manage complex and difficult projects than Chinese oil companies. If India had more money, Indian oil companies would be ahead. However, despite better project management skills, Chinese oil companies are a preferred partner relative to Indian oil companies. Even IOCs prefer to have Chinese oil companies as a partner because the former want to have a strong financial partner (Interviews, Appendix A). According to Ambassador Ghanshyam, former Ambassador to Angola and High Commissioner to Nigeria, GoI (Interview, Appendix A):

> Oil industry is a very complex business. Having oil in the field or in the acreage is the first issue. How much oil is there is the second issue and how much of it can be recovered is the third issue. Before oil companies bid for concessions today, oil companies need to spend half a billion US dollars on seismic data which can provide information with high degree of accuracy whether there is going to be oil or not. Chinese oil companies have that kind of money to spend. Indian companies are constrained in this respect relative to Chinese NOCs.

According to executives from Indian NOCs, diplomats and industry experts, the support provided by the Chinese government enabled the Chinese NOCs to become extremely large and important players in the global oil industry. However, this has not been the case with Indian NOCs because the Indian government is unable to extend a similar kind of support. Table 4.7 illustrates the difference in the oil companies from the two countries.

Conclusion

The different political economies of India and China are reflected in the oil sector in the respective countries. In the post-reform period, the oil industry in India is characterised by dominant SOEs, a vibrant and fast emerging private sector and joint ventures between the SOEs, private enterprises and IOCs. China on the other hand has an oil industry represented by the SOEs with joint ventures formed with IOCs to increase the E&P activities in China. The oil sector is dominated by three oil companies: CNPC, Sinopec and CNOOC. Private sector oil companies are also present in the oil industry but they are extremely small in size relative to the major NOCs and are very minor players.

The difference in the relative power of India and China is also reflected in the oil sector. Chinese NOCs have more financial muscle relative to Indian oil companies. Chinese oil companies have greater market capitalisation and financial resources at their disposal relative to Indian oil companies. This is evident from the rankings of the Indian and Chinese oil companies in the Global Fortune 500 rankings and also in the prestigious Platt rankings of oil companies. All three major Chinese oil companies are ranked higher than their Indian counterparts in the Platt rankings. Moreover, Chinese NOCs are active in more countries

Table 4.7 Comparative perspective of Indian and Chinese oil companies

Indicator/measure	China	India
Financial support from the government	Substantial support provided by CIC, EXIM Bank, SASAC and state banks	Yes but significantly less than China
Forex reserves	Approximately US$3 trillion. CIC has US$140 billion at its disposal	Approximately US$350 billion
Political support	Substantial	Yes but significantly less than China.
Diplomatic support	Substantial. China's status as an emerging superpower with a permanent membership of the UNSC with veto power allows the Chinese government to provide substantial diplomatic support	Yes but significantly less than China. India is not a member of the UNSC. The asymmetry in power favours China vis-à-vis India
Financial strength	Extreme strong financially as illustrated by the Fortune 500 rankings	Extremely strong financially in India but financially weaker relative to Chinese NOCs as illustrated by the rankings
Rate of interest paid on loans	0–1 per cent	Can vary from 3–4 per cent to 10–11 per cent NOC: 10–11 per cent
Rate of return on investment	3–4 per cent	Private enterprises: 18–20 per cent
Ability to take risk	Less risk averse	More risk averse, conservative
Technological capability	Same	Same
Ability to acquire and access technology	Relatively easy access due to greater financial resources	Constrained by lack of financial resources
Project management	More or less as capable as Indian NOCs but less than RIL	Better project management skills especially RIL

Source: Appendix A.

globally and in Africa and in West Africa in particular. Chinese NOCs are able to take more risks and bid for even difficult oil blocks. They are less concerned about the rate of return, are willing to pay a higher price to access and acquire technology and are preferred as partners by both the IOCs and other oil companies relative to Indian oil companies. Chinese NOCs also receive greater diplomatic and political support relative to Indian oil companies. Thus China's economic and political power provides Chinese NOCs a substantial edge over Indian oil companies. Therefore, NCR explains the differences and relative success and failure of China and India in their respective efforts to mobilise oil in the oil industry in West Africa. The hypothesis that NCR explains the differences and relative success and failure in how India and China mobilise oil externally in the oil industry in West Africa is examined in Chapters 5, 6 and 7.

Notes

1 Refer to Patra (2004: 176–178) for the 'Super Major Theory'.
2 For a brief description of the upstream and downstream operations of IOCs like BP, Shell, BG Group, Total, Eni and Oilex, refer to BMI (2012b: 140–145).
3 Platts is a provider of benchmark price valuations in the physical energy markets and of energy and metals information.
4 For a detailed analysis of the various oil blocks, refer to Assets, ONGC Videsh Limited, www.ongcvidesh.com/assets/ (accessed 30 April 2016).
5 'Farm out' is an agreement which a company makes with a third party if the former wants to keep its share in the asset, and mitigate the risk or does not have the monetary resources required to undertake operations that are desirable for that asset. The third party is called the farmee and the company is called the farmor. The farmor receives a sum of money from the farmee for the asset. Additionally, the farmee promises to spend money to perform a specific activity related to the asset such as operating and/or oil exploration. The interest transferred by the farmor is a 'farm-out' whereas the interest received by the farmee is a 'farm-in'. Farmout, Investopedia, www.investopedia.com/terms/f/farmout.asp (accessed 15 January 2013).
6 In Mandarin, Daqing means 'big celebration'.
7 SASAC is the official government owner of China's NOCs and oversees NOCs and SOEs.
8 Signature bonus is like an entry fee. Whenever an oil company enters into acreage, the host government charges money and sometimes it can be as high as US$1 billion (Interview with OVL[b]).

References

Blumental, David, Chua, Tju Liang and Au, Ashleigh (2009). Upstream Oil and Gas in China. Industry Sector Reports, Doing Business in China. Online. Available at: www.velaw.com/.../VEsite/.../20-Vol. 3SecVCh3UpstreamOilandGas.p... (accessed 2 August 2012).

BMI (Business Monitor International) (2012a). India: Oil and Gas Report Q3 2012. Online. Part of BMI's Industry Report & Forecasts Series. Available at: www.businessmonitor.com (accessed 18 April 2016).

BMI (Business Monitor International) (2012b). China: Oil and Gas Report Q3 2012. Online. Part of BMI's Industry Report & Forecasts Series. Available at: www.businessmonitor.com (accessed 18 April 2016).

BMI (Business Monitor International) (2016a). India: Oil and Gas Report Q2 2016. Online. Part of BMI's Industry Report & Forecasts Series. Available at: www.businessmonitor.com (accessed 18 April 2016).

BMI (Business Monitor International) (2016b). China: Oil and Gas Report Q2 2016. Online. Part of BMI's Industry Report & Forecasts Series. Available at: www.businessmonitor.com (accessed 18 April 2016).

CNOOC (n.d.a). About Us. Online. Available at: www.cnoocltd.com/col/col7261/index.html (accessed 1 May 2016).

CNOOC (n.d.b). Key Operating Areas. Online. Available at: www.cnoocltd.com/col/col7321/index.html (accessed 1 May 2016).

CNPC (n.d.a). CNPC at a Glance. Online. Available at: www.cnpc.com.cn/en/cnpcataglance/cnpcataglance.shtml (accessed April 30 2016).

CNPC (n.d.b). CNPC Worldwide. Online. Available at: www.cnpc.com.cn/en/cnpcworldwide/cnpcworldwide.shtml (accessed April 30 2016).

Downs, Erica S. (2008). Business Interest Groups in Chinese Politics: The Case of the Oil Companies. In: Cheng Li, ed. *China's Changing Political Landscape: Prospects for Democracy*. Washington DC: Brookings Institution, pp. 121–141.

Downs, Erica S. (2011). China Development Bank's Oil Loans: Pursuing Policy and Profit. *China Economic Quarterly*, December, pp. 43–47.

Downs, Erics S. and Meidan, Michal (2011). Business and Politics in China: The Oil Executive Reshuffle of 2011. *China Security*, 19, pp. 3–21.

Ebel, Robert E. (2005). *China's Energy Future: The Middle Kingdom Seeks its Place in the Sun*. Washington, DC: The CSIS Press Center for Strategic and International Studies.

Energy Business Review (2012). African Petroleum Enters Investment Deal with PetroChina. Online. Exploration and Development News, 18 July. Available at: http://explorationanddevelopment.energy-business-review.com/news/african-petroleum-enters-investment-deal-with-petrochina-180712 (accessed 15 August 2012).

Essar (n.d.a). Corporate Profile. Online. Available at: www.essar.com/section_level1.aspx?cont_id=SD7sjPUVBkw= (accessed August 2012).

Essar (n.d.b). Essar Energy Business. Online. Available at: www.essarenergy.com/about-us/essar-business.aspx#business1 (accessed May 1 2016).

FICCI (2010). Oil and Natural Gas. Online. Available at: www.ficci-b2b.com/sector...pdf/OIL_AND_NATURAL_GAS.pdf (accessed 2 August 2012).

Fontevecchia, Agustino (2012). The End Of Exxon's Reign? PetroChina Now The Biggest Oil Producer. Online. 29 March. Available at: www.forbes.com/sites/afontevecchia/2012/03/29/the-end-of-exxons-rein-petrochina-now-the-biggest-oil-producer/ (accessed 6 August 2012).

Fortune (n.d.). Global 500. Online. Available at: http://fortune.com/global500 (accessed 19 April 2016).

IOCL (n.d.). Forays into E&P. Online. Available at: www.iocl.com/Aboutus/e_and_p.aspx (accessed 1 May 2016).

Kambara, Tatsu (1974). The Petroleum Industry in China. *The China Quarterly*, 60, pp. 699–719.

Kambara, Tatsu and Howe, Christopher (2007). *China and the Global Energy Crisis: Development and Prospects for China's Oil and Natural Gas*. Cheltenham and Northampton, MA: Edward Elgar.

Kong, Bo (2010). *China's International Petroleum Policy*. Santa Barbara: ABC-CLIO.

KPMG (2009). China's Energy Sector: A Clearer View. Online. Industrial Markets. Available at: www.kpmg.de/14427.htm (accessed 4 August 2012).

OIL (n.d.a). Profile. Online. Available at: www.oil-india.com/Profile.aspx (accessed 20 August 2012).

OIL (n.d.b). Exploration. Online. Available at: www.oil-india.com/Exploration.aspx (accessed 20 August 2012).

Out-Law.com (2014). China Issues First Oil Import Licence to Private Company. Online. 29 August. Available at: www.out-law.com/en/articles/2014/august/china-issues-first-oil-import-licence-to-private-company/ (accessed 1 May 2016).

OVL (n.d.a). About ONGC Videsh. Online. Available at: www.ongcvidesh.com/company/about-ovl/ (accessed 1 May 2016).

OVL (n.d.a). Assets. Online. Available at: www.ongcvidesh.com/assets/ (accessed 1 May 2016).

Owen, Charlotte (2012). China to Encourage Local Private Investment in Energy Projects. Business Strategy, Oil and Gas Technology. Online. 19 June. Available at: www. oilandgastechnology.net/business-strategy/china-encourage-local-private-investment-energy-projects (accessed 4 August 2012).

Patra, Debesh C. (2004). *Oil Industry in India: Problems and Prospects in Post-APM Era*. New Delhi: Mittal Publications.

PetroChina (n.d.). About PetroChina. Online. Available at: www.petrochina.com.cn/ptr/gsjj/gsjs_common.shtml (accessed 1 May 2016).

PwC (PricewaterhouseCoopers) (2012). Emerging Opportunities and Challenges: Oil and Gas. Online. WEC-IMC, 23 January. Available at: www.pwc.com/.../pdfs/business-opportunities-in-indian-oil-and-gas-s... (accessed 2 August 2012).

RIL (n.d.a). About Us. Online. Available at: www.ril.com/html/aboutus/aboutus.html (accessed 2 August 2012).

RIL (n.d.b). Exploration and Production. Online. Available at: www.ril.com/html/business/exploration_production.html (accessed 2 August 2012).

RIL (n.d.c). Exploration and Production. Online. Available at: www.ril.com/OurBusinesses/Exploration.aspx (accessed 1 May 2016).

Sinopec (n.d.a). About Sinopec: Our Company. Online. Available at: http://english.sinopec.com/about_sinopec/our_company/20100328/8532.shtml (accessed 1 May 2016).

Sinopec (n.d.b). Exploration and Oil Production. Online. Available at: http://english.sinopec.com/about_sinopec/our_business/exploration_oil_production/ (accessed 1 May 2016).

SIPC (Sinopec International Petroleum Exploration and Production Corporation) (n.d.). About SIPC. Online. http://sipc.sinopec.com/sipc/en/about_us/erp_profile/ (accessed 1 May 2016).

SWFI (Sovereign Wealth Fund Rankings) (n.d.). Largest Sovereign Wealth Funds by Assets Under Management. Online. Available at: www.swfinstitute.org/sovereign-wealth-fund-rankings/ (accessed 1 May 2016).

Xinhua (2012). MOC Encourages Private Oil Companies. Online. *China Daily*, 28 June. Available at: www.chinadaily.com.cn/bizchina/2012-06-28/content_15530126.htm (accessed 4 August 2012).

Part IV

Case studies

5   India and China in Angola

Chapter 5 examines whether NCR can explain the differences and relative success and failure of China and India in their respective efforts to mobilise oil in the oil industry in Angola. The chapter does a case study 'pattern matching' of Angola in West Africa. The chapter is divided into four sections. Section I provides a brief background of Angola and discusses the oil industry in Angola, the oil reserves and production and the problems plaguing the oil industry. Section II compares and contrasts the political, diplomatic and economic relations of India and China respectively with Angola. It highlights that India's economic, political and diplomatic engagement with Angola is dwarfed by China's engagement with Angola. Section III discusses the oil blocks bid for and acquired by India and China in Angola. It investigates if Chinese and Indian oil companies entered into direct competitive bidding for the oil blocks and if the former outbid the latter, the number of oil blocks that oil companies from the two countries have bid for and acquired and the nature or type of Indian and Chinese oil companies that are operating in the oil industry in Angola. It also examines the quality of the oil blocks acquired by oil companies from the two countries. Section IV provides a brief analysis of India's and China's interaction in the oil industry in Angola.

I

Angola gained independence from Portugal in 1975. It was embroiled in a 27-year civil war which ended in 2002. Three rival independence movements, Movimento Popular de Libertação de Angola (MPLA), Frente Nacional de Libertação de Angola (FNLA) and União Nacional para a Independência Total de Angola (UNITA) were involved in the civil war which ravaged Angola. This eventually gave way to Cold War logic with the MPLA government backed by Cuba and the Soviet Union, and the UNITA rebels backed by apartheid South Africa and the United States. Following the death of UNITA leader Jonas Savimbi in 2002, Angola has enjoyed peace. The war left the country at rock bottom. According to the UNDP, in 2002, Angola was well below the average for Sub-Saharan Africa in the HDI. However, Angola has been transformed since 2002 (Weimer, 2012).

Since early 2002, Angola has experienced high rates of economic growth due to a rapid increase in oil exports and high government spending. President Jose Eduardo dos Santos has been in power since 1979 and is Africa's second-longest serving head of state. He is credited with turning the country's formerly socialist economy into one of the world's fastest-growing economies. However, he is also accused of authoritarianism, staying in office for too long and failing to distribute the proceeds from the oil boom more widely. Much of Angola's oil wealth lies in Cabinda province, where a decades-long separatist conflict simmers. The government has sent thousands of troops to subdue the rebellion in the enclave, which has no borders with the rest of Angola. In August 2006, the government signed a peace deal with a separatist group in the northern enclave of Cabinda. Human rights groups have alleged abuses against civilians (BBC, 2016).

In 2008, MPLA won the country's first parliamentary elections for 16 years. A new constitution approved in 2010 substituted direct election of the president with a system under which the top candidate of the largest party in parliament becomes president. It also strengthened the presidency's powers, prompting the UNITA opposition to accuse the government of 'destroying democracy'. In March 2011, more than 20,000 people rallied in support for President dos Santos in response to a reported social media campaign calling on people to demonstrate against the government. Human Rights Watch accuses the government of a 'campaign of intimidation' to suppress anti-government protests. In the 2012 parliamentary elections, MPLA won a comfortable majority which gave another term for dos Santos. AU observers deemed the polls free and fair, despite allegations by opposition party UNITA about a lack of transparency (BBC, 2015).

In March 2014, anti-government protesters alleged that they were beaten and detained for demonstrating against the killing of three activists by security forces. In November 2014, Amnesty International accused security forces of extra-judicial killings and excessive force when suppressing dissent against the government. In 2015, prominent anti-corruption activist Rafael Marques was given a six-month suspended jail sentence for defaming army generals in a book about violence in the country's diamond mining industry. At the end of 2015, President dos Santos called for stricter regulation of the social media at a time when the government was cracking down on political dissidence and activism (BBC, 2015).

Despite being the third-largest economy in Sub-Saharan Africa (in terms of nominal GDP) and fifth largest in Africa, more than 30 per cent of Angolans live below the poverty line (less than US\$1.25 per day) and most of them live below US\$2 although that proportion has declined substantially from 68 per cent in 2001. The latest 2012 estimate indicates that only 30 per cent of Angolans have access to electricity, leaving 15 million people without access. Contrarily, the elite who enjoy close relations with the state and the polity and have been blemished by pervasive corruption have become tremendously wealthy. Although transparency has improved in recent years, billions of petrodollars have simply vanished and not reached the central bank. Angola has been plagued by the mismanagement of revenues from oil exports (US EIA, 2016). The president's daughter Isabel was named Africa's first billionaire in 2013 by Forbes (BBC, 2016). According to Doing Business Ranking 2012, out of 183 countries, Angola is the eleventh most difficult country in the world to do business in (Weimer, 2012).

Oil industry in Angola

Angola, an OPEC member since 2007, is one of the major oil-producing countries not only in West Africa but also in Africa. It is an important oil supplier for China and the United States. The first commercial oil discovery in Angola was made in 1955 in the onshore Kwanza (Cuanza) Basin. Since that discovery, Angola's oil industry has grown substantially despite the civil war. Currently, oil production comes almost entirely from offshore fields off the coast of Cabinda and deepwater fields in the Lower Congo Basin. There is small-scale production from onshore fields, but onshore exploration and production have been limited in the past because of conflict. The first deepwater field to come online was the Chevron-operated Kuito field (Block 14) in late 1999. Since then, IOCs, led by Total, Chevron, ExxonMobil and BP have started production at additional deepwater fields and are in the process of developing new ones (US EIA, 2016).

According to Table 2.4 and Table 2.5, respectively, Angola has the third largest oil reserves in Africa after Libya and Nigeria, and is the second largest oil producer in Africa after Nigeria. It has the eighteenth largest oil reserves in the world. New exploration data suggests that Angola's reserves may be larger than initially estimated (US EIA, 2016). According to Table 5.1, oil reserves in Angola have almost doubled from 2001 to 2014, increasing from approximately 5.4 billion barrels to 9.5 billion barrels in 2012 and decreasing to 9.1 billion barrels in 2014. According to BP, Angola's oil reserves were approximately 12.7 billion barrels at the end of 2014. Oil production in Angola has more than doubled from approximately 742 tbpd in 2001 to 1756 tbpd in 2014 (Table 5.2). There are expectations of further offshore oil discoveries in Angola.

The Angolan economy is completely dependent on oil. According to the IMF, in 2011, approximately 98 per cent and, in 2012, approximately 97 per cent of the government revenue came from the export of oil (IMF, 2014). Angola earned US$24 billion in net oil export revenue in 2014 (unadjusted for inflation), US$3 billion less than in 2013 because of decrease in production and the decline in

Table 5.1 Proved reserves of crude oil from 2001 to 2014

Country	Year (billion barrels)													
	2001	*2002*	*2003*	*2004*	*2005*	*2006*	*2007*	*2008*	*2009*	*2010*	*2011*	*2012*	*2013*	*2014*
Angola	5.4	5.4	5.4	5.4	5.4	5.4	8	9	9	9.5	9.5	9.5	10	9.1

Source: compiled from US EIA.

Table 5.2 Total oil production from 2001 to 2014

Country	Year (thousand barrels per day)													
	2001	*2002*	*2003*	*2004*	*2005*	*2006*	*2007*	*2008*	*2009*	*2010*	*2011*	*2012*	*2013*	*2014*
Angola	742	896	902	1054	1249	1420	1748	1955	1876	1908	1755	1787	1842	1756

Source: compiled from US EIA.

average annual crude oil prices. Angola's dependence on oil revenue makes it vulnerable to a decline in oil prices. According to the World Bank, during Angola's oil production boom from 2002 to 2008, GDP grew by an annual average of 15 per cent, GDP growth fell to 2.4 per cent in 2009 following the global financial crisis and the drop in oil prices but recovered to 5.2 per cent in 2012 and 6.8 per cent in 2013 as oil prices increased (World Bank, 2016). The decline in the price of oil since 2014 has had a tremendous negative impact on the Angolan economy, which is highly dependent on oil. The share of the non-oil sector has increased from 40 per cent of the economy in the mid 1980s to just below 70 per cent of the economy in 2016. Despite that, oil is still central and it dominates exports and government finances (Walker, 2016). Angola's GDP grew by just 4.5 per cent in 2014 and slowed further to 3.8 per cent in 2015 (Winsor, 2015). Efforts to diversify the economy are being made with a focus on agriculture, fisheries and mining. Fiscal reforms and controlling public spending are also being undertaken to ensure there is no budget deficit. The Angolan government cut spending in 2015, which was described as a timely move by the IMF (Walker, 2016). IMF has projected that the Angolan economy will grow at 3.5 per cent in 2016 and 2017 (McGroarty, 2015). Angola has been forced to seek help from the IMF in light of declining oil prices. According to Min Zhu, Deputy Managing Director of the IMF, "We have received a formal request from the Angolan authorities to initiate discussions on an economic program that could be supported by financial assistance from the IMF" (IMF, 2016).

The major proportion of oil reserves in Angola are situated offshore because the civil war constrained onshore exploration. Nonetheless, proven onshore reserves exist in the partly unstable Cabinda province and around Soyo, a city in northern Angola (US EIA, 2016). Angola has followed a policy of diversification in its energy relationships since 1968 when oil production commenced off the coast of Cabinda province. Angola's continental shelf was divided into blocks. Angola has six onshore and offshore, and nine deepwater oil producing blocks. Table 5.3 provides a breakdown of the oil-producing oil blocks. Angola also has 33 E&P oil blocks. It has ten onshore and offshore blocks, 13 deepwater oil blocks and ten ultra-deepwater E&P oil blocks. Table 5.4 provides a breakdown of the E&P oil blocks in Angola. Sonangol is a shareholder in almost all oil and natural gas exploration and production projects with the exception of a couple of deepwater producing projects, and it operates Angola's only oil refinery. Sonangol has 17 subsidiaries that operate throughout the oil and natural gas

Table 5.3 Onshore and offshore production activity in Angola

Type of oil blocks	Name of oil blocks
Onshore and Offshore	Block-0 (Area A,B), Block-2/85, Block-3 Canuku, Block-3/05, Block-3/91, FST Association, FS Association
Deepwater	Block-14, Block-15, Block-17, Block-18

Source: compiled from Angola Concessions-Sonangol, available at: www.sonangol.co.ao/English/ AreasOfActivity/Concessionary/Documents/GAD201501-DMC0001-I-A.pdf (accessed 20 April 2016).

Table 5.4 Onshore and offshore exploration activity in Angola

Type of oil blocks	Name of oil blocks
Onshore and Offshore	Block-0 (Area A,B), Cabinda Northern, Cabinda Southern, Block-2/05, Block-3/05A, Block-4/05, Block-5/06, Block-6/06, Block-8, Block-9/09
Deepwater	Block-14, Block-15/06, Block-16, Block-17/06, Block 18/06, Block-19/11, Block-20/11, Block-21/09, Block-22/11, Block-23, Block-24/11, Block-25/11, Block-26/06
Ultra deepwater	Block-31, Block-32, Block-33, Block-34, Block-35/11, Block-36/11 Block-37/11, Block-38/11, Block-39/11, Block-40/11

Source: compiled from Angola Concessions-Sonangol, available at: www.sonangol.co.ao/English/ AreasOfActivity/Concessionary/Documents/GAD201501-DMC0001-I-A.pdf (accessed 20 April 2016).

industry, performing functions such as exploration, production and marketing of crude oil, storage, and marketing of petroleum derivatives (US EIA, 2016).

IOCs from the United States and Europe lead oil and natural gas E&P in Angola. IOCs involved in Angola operate under joint-venture operations and PSAs with Sonangol. Major operators and shareholders include Total, Chevron, ExxonMobil, BP, Statoil and Eni, among others. Sinopec and CNOOC and the Hong Kong-based New Bright International Development also operate in Angola. China Sonangol, established in 2004, is a joint venture between Sonangol and New Bright International Development.[1] Sinopec and China-Sonangol have a joint venture called Sinopec Sonangol International (SSI). Sinopec has a 55 per cent share, China Sonangol 13.5 per cent and Dayaun International Development Ltd, a subsidiary of New Bright International Development, has a 31.5 per cent share. There have been questions about Sonangol and New Bright International Development's relationship and how the Hong Kong-based company has quickly become a dominant player in Angola's oil industry (Levkowitz *et al.*, 2009). New Bright International also formed a joint venture with Sonangol called China Sonangol International Holding Limited (CSIH).

II

This section compares and contrasts the political, diplomatic and economic relations of China and India with Angola respectively. The aim of the section is to highlight that China's greater political and economic power relative to India enables it to establish better diplomatic and economic relations with Angola.

China and Angola

Beijing's ties with MPLA were not always good. China's controversial involvement in Angola's liberation war in the 1960s and 1970s put a dent in its relations with MPLA. Although at first China approached the MPLA, the largest liberation movement, Beijing soon decided that it was too urban-based and pro-Soviet. As a result, in 1963 China switched its support to FNLA. Chinese relations with FNLA were strained by the fact that Chinese delegates were not allowed in Zaire (now Democratic Republic of Congo) where the movement was based. In 1964, China switched again and started supporting UNITA, formed by a rebel group that had split from FNLA. Its leader, Jonas Savimbi, underwent military training in China in 1964 and 1965 before the formal establishment of UNITA in 1966. However, in the early 1970s, China abandoned UNITA to approach first MPLA and then FNLA. After Angola's formal independence in 1975 and the onset of civil war, Beijing covertly supported both FNLA and UNITA in an effort to prevent the victory of the Soviet-backed MPLA (Alves, 2010).

Diplomatic relations were formally established in January 1983. In 1984, an inconsequential trade and co-operation agreement was signed and, in 1988, the mixed Economic and Trade Commission was set up, which remained mostly inactive until the turn of the century. In the 1980s and 1990s, due to Angola's volatile domestic situation, China–Angolan relations were dominated by military co-operation. In the 1990s, the relationship was rattled a few times by the discovery of Chinese arms in UNITA's possession. China always denied any involvement and UNITA seems to have confirmed an indirect acquisition. Due to the internal turmoil in Angola, official visits and exchanges between the countries prior to 2002 were not very frequent. However, some important state officials from China visited Angola. For instance, Minister of Foreign Affairs (MOFA) Qian Qichen visited Angola in August 1989, Vice Premier Zhu Rongji in August 1995 and MOFA Tang Jiaxuan in January 2001 (Alves, 2010).

China's 'go global' policy in 2000 and the end of the civil war in Angola in 2002 set the stage of strengthening and deepening economic relations between the two countries. Since 2002, the bilateral economic and political relationship has been intensified. This has been marked by an increase in state level visits, investment and trade. Vice Premier Zeng Peiyan in February 2005, Premier Wen Jiabao in June 2006, Minister of Commerce Chen Deming in January 2009, Vice Minister of Commerce Jiang Zengwei in March 2009 (Alves, 2010) and Vice President Xi Jinping in 2010 (Benazeraf and Alves, 2014) visited Angola.

Numerous delegations from Chinese banking institutions like China EXIM Bank and CDB also visited Angola. From the Angolan side, in addition to various state representatives, former Prime Minster F. Piedade dos Santos visited China in 2006. The importance of Sino-Angolan relationship can be gauged by the fact that, in 2008, President José Eduardo dos Santos visited China twice (Alves, 2010). The dormant Economic and Trade Commission established in 1988 was reactivated and meetings were held in 1999, 2001, 2007 and March 2009. China moved quickly to provide loans for post-war reconstruction in Angola contrary to the traditional Western donors who were reluctant to support an international donor's conference or finance post-war reconstruction (Vines *et al.*, 2009).

China's official co-operation with Africa is dominated by concessional loans that are granted by its major banks – EXIM Bank and CDB – to construct or rehabilitate infrastructure. In 2002, the China Construction Bank and EXIM Bank funded infrastructure projects such as the first phase of Luanda's railway rehabilitation and electrical grid projects in four cities, valued at over US$150 million. In mid 2003, the Chinese government proposed large concessional loans targeting infrastructure, backed by oil, which were implemented after the negotiations that started soon after. From 2004 to 2007, three loan agreements were signed between China EXIM Bank and the Angolan government amounting to US$4.5 billion. In 2004, China EXIM Bank signed a US$2 billion oil-backed infrastructure development loan. In July 2007, a loan of US$500 million was provided to finance complementary works required to finish the projects started under the first credit line. A third agreement was signed in September 2007 for another US$2 billion. The credit lines were given to finance the projects listed in the government's Public Infrastructures Programme. In August 2008, CDB signed a framework agreement with the Angolan government to provide a credit line. The amount involved has not been officially disclosed, but purportedly there will be an initial batch of US$1.5 billion, which is expected to be extended in the following years. Negotiations for a new credit line from EXIM Bank were concluded in August 2009 in Beijing (Alves, 2010) and led to an additional China EXIM Bank credit line of US$6 billion in July 2010 (Corkin, 2011). Thus Angola received loans of US$12 billion from China. Angola received loans from China amounting to at least US$13.4 billion (up to US$19.7 billion as per some estimates) by 2009 (Vines *et al.*, 2009). According to the terms of the loans, Chinese companies are largely contracted to undertake required projects and are paid directly by China EXIM Bank, which writes down the contract amount against the loan available to the Angolan government. The loan is repayable at London Interbank Offered Rate plus 1.5 per cent over 17 years, including a grace period of five years. These terms render a less expensive financing option than the oil-backed loans extended to the Angolan government by previous financiers (Vines *et al.*, 2009).

CDB has also earmarked a loan of US$1 billion for investment in Angola's agricultural sector and CDB's head, Chen Yuan, stated that this amount may be extended if necessary (Corkin, 2011). From 2004 until March 2011, China provided approximately US$14.5 billion in financial support to Angola. In the first official estimate of Chinese lending to Angola, Ambassador Zhang Bolun said that three state banks – the EXIM Bank of China, the Industrial and Commercial Bank of China, and the CDB – have extended US$14.5 billion in credit to the resource-rich country (Comarmond, 2011). According to Reuters estimates, China has lent US$20 billion to China during 2002–15 (Coroado and Brock, 2015).

China has gained a foothold in Angola's construction sector through the provision of 'resources for infrastructure' loans, also referred to as the 'Angola model' by the World Bank. The dominance of Chinese companies is particularly evident in mega projects such as railways, major transportation arteries, public buildings, etc. The Ango-Ferro 2000 project involves the rehabilitation of 3100 kilometres of railway, 8000 kilometres of extensions, 36 bridges, and the rehabilitation and construction of 100 stations and 150 new substations (Kiala, 2010). China is also involved in the construction of new urban centres on a scale unequalled by any other foreign partner. China is building new cities and housing districts close to Angola's main cities. Around Luanda alone, five new cities are under construction: Kilamba Kiaxi, Cacuaco, Zango, Km 44 and Capari. In August 2008, China International Trust and Investment Corporation and the Angolan government launched a US$3.5 billion housing project spanning 880 hectares of land in Kilamba Kiaxi (Kiala, 2010). In 2011, around 50 Chinese SOEs and 400 SMEs were involved in these construction contracts (Benazeraf and Alves, 2014). The largest hospital in the country, Hospital Geral da Província de Luanda, was rehabilitated with a grant from the Chinese government concessional loans. Chinese companies have been constructing and rehabilitating a large number of the existing health centres and hospitals in Angola. China has also provided numerous scholarships to Angolan citizens to study in China. A number of Angolan doctors are pursuing postgraduate studies in China with Chinese grants. An agreement was signed in 2005 with the Chinese Ministry of Health for China to send Chinese medical teams (18 doctors for terms of two years) and donate much-needed medicines (Alves, 2010).

Trade increased from a mere US$1.8 billion in 2000 to US$25.3 billion in 2008 (Vines *et al.*, 2009). In the six-year period, Sino-Angolan trade relations achieved a dramatic level of interdependency. China not only became Angola's major trading partner in Africa in 2006 but China also became Angola's largest trading partner by displacing the United States, which had occupied that position throughout Angola's modern history (Alves, 2010). In 2014, bilateral trade was approximately US$32.6 billion. China has a 61 per cent share of Angola's total exports and a 21 per cent share of total imports (OEC, n.d.).

India and Angola

India and Angola have had friendly relations dating back to the pre-independence era of Angola. India supported the Angolan freedom struggle against Portugal until Angola achieved independence in 1975. India also continued to support

MPLA after Angola's independence. India opened its embassy in Angola in 1986. However, Angola only reciprocated this diplomatic gesture in 1992 with the establishment of an embassy in New Delhi (Vines *et al.*, 2009). Bilateral diplomatic relations appeared to attain some momentum during the mid 1980s. Former Prime Minister Rajiv Gandhi visited Angola in 1986 and President dos Santos visited India in 1987. The most recent high-level meeting was on 10 July 2009 on the sidelines of the G8 meeting in L'Aquila, Italy when Prime Minister Manmohan Singh met President dos Santos (MEA, GoI, 2014).

Unlike China, India's engagement with Angola has been confined to lower level state visits. In May 2006, Angolan Minister for External Relations, Joao Bernardo de Miranda visited India and met the Ministers of Oil and Gas, Commerce and Industry and Minister of State for External Affairs Shri Anand Sharma. A Protocol on Foreign Office Consultations was signed during the visit. India and Angola also agreed in principle to sign Agreements for the Creation of Bilateral Commission for Cultural, Technical, Scientific and Economic Cooperation and Promotion and Protection of Investments. In June 2007, Anand Sharma, Minister of State for External Affairs visited Angola and had detailed discussions with the President of Angola, Petroleum and Geology & Mines, Secretary, Political Bureau of International Relations of the ruling MPLA, Ministers of External Relations, and President of Empresa Nacional de Prospecção, Exploração, Lapidação e Comercialização de Diamantes de Angola (ENDIAMA), Angola's state diamond company. In March 2008, Minister of State for Commerce Jairam Ramesh, accompanied by a ten-member delegation visited Angola and had discussions with Ministers of Geology & Mines, Oil, President of ENDIAMA, Vice Minister of External Relations and the National Director of the Ministry of Commerce. In January 2010, Murli Deora, Minister of Oil and Gas, accompanied by a delegation of oil and gas SOEs and others, visited Angola to enhance co-operation in the oil and gas sector between the two countries. Numerous delegations from Angola also visited India. For instance, during October 2006–April 2007, Joaquim Duarte da Costa David, Minister of Industry, Gilberto Buta Lutukuta, Minister of Agriculture, Aguinaldo Jaime, Assistant Minister in the Office of the Prime Minister of Angola, and Paulo T. Jorge, Secretary, Political Bureau of International Relations, MPLA, among others, visited India. Jose Eduardo Zu Du P. dos Santos (son of the president of Angola) visited India in May 2007 and February 2008 (MEA, GoI, 2014) and in October 2015, Georges R. Chikoti, Minister of External Relations, attended the India–Africa Summit in India (ANGOP, 2015).

India's trade with Angola has increased since 2002. Bilateral trade increased from approximately US$1.28 billion during 2007–8 to approximately US$4.87 billion in 2009–10. Bilateral trade was US$5.8 billion in 2010–11, US$7.07 billion in 2011–12 and US$7.64 billion in 2012–13. During 2012–13, India became Angola's second largest trade partner after China. India's share in Angola's total trade was 10.6 per cent. Bilateral trade during 2013–14 totalled US$6.51 billion. Angola remained the second largest source of crude oil for

India after Nigeria in Sub-Saharan Africa (MEA, GoI, 2014). Trade volumes are still small relative to China–Angola trade.

GoI provided a line of credit (LoC) of US$40 million to the government of Angola for the CFM Railway Rehabilitation Project, the first government–to-government initiative between the two countries. Rail India Technical and Economic Consultancy Services Limited, which started implementation of the project in 2005, handed the completed project over to the Angolan Minister of Transport on 28 August 2007. EXIM Bank of India extended three credit lines of US$5, US$10 and US$13 million for agricultural equipment and Indian tractors. The State Bank of India, which opened its representative office in Luanda in April 2005, also extended a commercial LoC of US$5 million for supply of tractors from India. Two additional LoCs of US$30 and US$15 million to construct a cotton spinning and ginning plant and an industrial park was approved by EXIM Bank in 2010. In June 2012, EXIM Bank extended a LoC of US$23 million to supply tractors, implements and related spares. On 6 December 2005, Ministry of External Affairs (MEA), GoI gifted five ambulances manufactured by Mahindra & Mahindra to Angola which were handed over to Andre Luis Brandao, Minister of Transport. Optimum utilisation of Indian Technical and Economic Cooperation (ITEC) scholarships slots occurred in 2010, leading to 60 Angolan officials being sent to India to attend various courses. Generally, ITEC slots remain unutilised or highly under-utilised. Only two slots were used in 2013–14 (MEA, GoI, 2014). However, all the measures are very small compared to investment and credit lines provided by China.

III

India and China expressed an interest in acquiring oil blocks in Angola. According to Table 5.5, Chinese oil companies bid for five oil blocks and acquired five blocks. All the oil blocks except Block 31 and Block 32 acquired by SSI produce oil. SSI produced 3.9 million barrels in 2007 worth US$340 million (Vines *et al.*, 2009). Table 5.6 shows the names and number of oil blocks that Indian oil companies bid for in Angola. It highlights that Indian oil companies bid for six oil blocks in Angola but did not acquire the oil blocks. OVL was unable to acquire Block 15(06), Block 17(06), Block 18(06); Block 18, Block 31 and Block 32 in Angola. OVL lost the bid for Block 31 to Indonesia's NOC PETRAMINA. OVL also lost the bids for Block 15(06), Block 17(06), Block 18(06) and Block 18 to Chinese NOC Sinopec. A joint venture between Sinopec and CNOOC outbid OVL for Block 32.

A licensing round was held in 2006 in Angola. The Angolan government assured a high level of transparency for the licensing round built on new laws that went into effect at the end of 2004. The licensing round yielded unprecedented signature boni in excess of US$3 billion for the ultra-deep Blocks 31, 32, 33 and 34. This was much higher than the signature boni paid in 1999 and 2000. AGIP-Eni made a world record bid of US$902 million to become operators in Block 15(06) due to strong Chinese competition for the block. This also led to a

Table 5.5 Oil blocks bid for and acquired by Chinese oil companies in Angola

Country	Company	Oil blocks bid for	Oil blocks acquired	Commercial viability
Angola	Sinopec	Block 15/06; Block 17/06; Block 18/06; Block 18; Block 31; Block 32	Block 15/06; Block 17/06; Block 18/06; Block 18; Block 31; Block 3(80–3/05 and 3/05A)	Block 15/06; Block 17/06; Block 18/06; Block 3 (80) and Block 18 produce oil. Block 31 has reserves of 553 million barrels and Block 32 of 650 million barrels
Angola	CNOOC	Block 32	–	Block 32 has reserves of 650 million barrels
Total		**Bid 5; acquired 5**		

Sources: compiled from Vines *et al.* (2009) and Alves (2010).

Table 5.6 Oil blocks bid for and acquired by Indian oil companies in Angola

Country	Company	Oil blocks bid for	Oil blocks acquired	Commercial viability
Angola	OVL	Block 15(06); Block 17(06); Block 18; Block18(06); Block 31; Block 32	–	n/a
Total	**Bid 6; acquired 0**			

Source: compiled from Vines *et al.* (2009).

world record bid of US$2.2 billion in Blocks 18(06) and 17(06) by SSI. OVL also offered US$1 billion for the deepwater blocks: 15(06), 17(06) and 18(06). This was less than the US$2.2 billion bid by SSI for non-operator rights for Block 17(06) and Block 18(06) – US$1.1 billion for each oil block. SSI also paid US$750 million for Block 15(06). In 2007, SSI proposed willingly to relinquish its stakes in Blocks 15(06), 17(06) and 18(06). This raised rumours about tensions in China–Angola relations. There were also reports in the Portuguese media that Galp Energia SGPS of Portugal was to take Sinopec's share in the three oil blocks. However, these claims were denied by the finance director of Sonangol Holdings, Francisco de Lemos. He stated that real commercial factors were responsible for SSI relinquishing the oil blocks. SSI relinquished the three blocks and China Sonangol acquired the three blocks. The three blocks are now called SSI Fifteen Ltd, SSI Seventeen Ltd and SSI Eighteen Ltd. China Sonangol acquired a 25 per cent stake each in Block 3(05) and Block 3(05A) (the two were together were previously known as Block 3(80)) in 2005. SSI holds a 40 per cent share in Block 18(06). SSI is split between CSIH (13.5 per cent), Sinopec (55 per cent) and Dayuan (31.5 per cent). Their respective shares in the equity from SSI oil are: Sinopec 22 per cent, CSIH 5.4 per cent and Dayuan 12.6 per cent. Total equity oil received by Sinopec through SSI is 13.75 per cent of Blocks 3(05) and 3(05A), 11 per cent of Block 15(06), 15.125 per cent of Block 17(06), 22 per cent of Block 18(06) and 27.5 per cent of Block 18 (Vines *et al.*, 2009).

OVL also wanted to acquire a stake in Blocks 15(06), 17(06) and 18(06). In 2005, OVL stated that it might take part in the Sonaref Lobito oil refinery project as a part of its bid to acquire stakes in the three oil blocks. In March 2007, when Jairam Ramesh, Minister for Commerce, GoI visited Luanda, India again indicated that it wanted to participate in a 30 per cent share in Sonaref. This was after the collapse of the SSI deal for the construction of Sonaref. When Anand Sharama, Minister of External Affairs, GoI visited Luanda in May 2007, a 30 per cent share was offered by President dos Santos in the Lobito oil refinery. However, India stated that OVL will deal with all oil-related issues in Angola. Minister of State for Commerce, GoI, Jairam Ramesh visited Angola from 28 March to 1 April 2008. During his meeting with Angola's Petroleum Minister, Desidério da Costa, he signalled that "India has again expressed its interest in participating in the refinery and we will expedite the process" (Vines *et al.*, 2009: 38). Jairam Ramesh also discussed OVL's bid of US$1 billion for the three oil blocks which SSI wanted to give up. He also proclaimed that a joint commission will be set up between the two countries to improve the bilateral relationship, especially in natural resources, oil and infrastructure. However, this did not materialise because the meeting scheduled in October 2008 never took place due to elections in Angola in 2008 and India in 2009 (Vines *et al.*, 2009).

SSI outbid OVL for Block 18 in deepwater Angola in 2004. OVL wanted to purchase Shell's 50 per cent stake in Block 18 and finalised an agreement with Shell in April 2004. OVL won the deal as a part of an Indian–Japanese oil consortium by outbidding CNOOC (Huang *et al.*, 2015). Since mid 2003 the Angolan government had been negotiating the first batch of the much-needed loan with China EXIM Bank, in which Sonangol obviously played a role, since the loan was to be oil-backed. Delegations of both parties (Sonangol was represented by Manuel Vicente, president of the company) were meeting on a regular basis in Luanda and Beijing. By mid 2004 it became public that Sonangol was going to exercise its pre-emptive rights on Block 18 and jointly explore it with Sinopec. It was for this purpose that SSI, a joint venture, was established between Sonangol and Sinopec in September 2004 (Alves, 2010). In December 2004, Sonangol supported by an executive decree (no. 148/2004 of 14 December) officially exercised its preventive right to purchase Shell's 50 per cent share in the oil block. This blocked ONGC's move to acquire Shell's stake (Singh, 2007). Mani Shankar Aiyar, formerly the Minister of Oil and Gas, GoI, stated:

Neither the seller nor the buyer had sought permission from the Angolan government for the change of ownership. Angola objected and did not recognise the transfer. I vaguely explored the possibility of visiting Angola to smooth out some ruffled feathers. Our own people were not keen on the visit. At the same time I found it was very difficult to schedule the visit because of various other commitments. So I met the Angolan Petroleum Minister, Manuel Vicente, when I visited Vienna for the OPEC meeting to deliver a keynote address in September 2004. I sought out the Angolan delegation and set up a meeting at the hotel. The meeting did not move in a fruitful direction from our point of view. Manuel Vicente said that the contractual obligation that Shell had with the Angolan government was broken by the unilateral decision to sell the stake to another company and that there was no question of Angola recognising the deal and that was the end of the matter. As there was no scope whatsoever of moving them on that point, I did not pursue the matter further. I had hoped that India's support in the liberation of Angola, which is freely acknowledged, and Rajiv Gandhi's close friendship with dos Santos might have contributed to the resolution of the Shell issue. But oil ministers are not freedom fighters.

(Interview, Appendix A)

During the same time period, President dos Santos refused to meet Mani Shankar Aiyar and refused India's invitation to go to New Delhi (Levkowitz *et al.*, 2009). However, according to Mani Shankar Aiyar, former Minister Oil and Gas, GoI:

I have absolutely no knowledge of this. It would not be the Minister of Oil and Gas GoI who would invite the Head of State. It would be breach of protocol. Petroleum Minister can invite Petroleum Minister and not the President.

(Interview, Appendix A)

Similarly, Ambassador Ghanshyam, former Ambassador to Angola and High Commissioner to Nigeria, GoI (Interview, Appendix A), is also not aware of President dos Santos refusing to meet Mani Shankar Aiyar and refusing an invitation to go to New Delhi in 2004.

Confirming the goodwill China had generated among the highest stakeholders of the Angolan political elite that controls the institutional framework, in February 2005, Desidério Costa, the Minister for Petroleum, formally sanctioned the transfer (Alves, 2010). The surrounding framework and the procedures involved in the acquisition process illustrate very clearly the critical role played by connections at the highest level. Some argue that Angola was influenced by China EXIM Bank's concessionary loan of US$2 billion since it was the first entry of a Chinese NOC into what was considered a strategic African country. China EXIM Bank is believed to have indirectly supported Sinopec's oil acquisition through the provision of the loan facility (Downs, 2007: 53). Furthermore, according to Lee and Shalmon (2008: 120), although there is no explicit link to China EXIM

Bank's loan to Angola and the awarding of oil blocks to Sinopec, "there is a strong suggestion that they are linked. The coincidence is too great". China's offer of US$725 million for infrastructure development surpassed India's offer of US$310 million (Vines *et al.*, 2009). Consequently, SSI acquired the concession. Estimates of China's aid to clinch the deal vary. According to Singh (2007), China offered US$2 billion for a variety of projects to Angola and India offered US$200 million for the developing railways.

Block 18 is an interesting model as it is evenly shared by BP (50 per cent) and SSI (50 per cent). The project had a new funding structure. It was the first time that China had co-operated with Western banks on a project finance agreement. Initially the project did not attract much collaboration but later it led to participation from a range of Chinese and Western banks. The huge Chinese participation in the oil blocks in Angola was seen to have mitigated the political risks of operating in the country. Oil production from the Greater Plutonio development area in the block started on 1 October 2007. The Greater Plutonio development area has five distinct fields in water depths of up to 1450 metres (Vines *et al.*, 2009). Block 18 has been a huge commercial success, so much so that, by 2011, Sinopec had recovered its investment and, by the end of 2014, it had earned approximately US$2.6 billion (Huang *et al.*, 2015).

India also considered joint co-operation with Chinese NOCs to get a footing in the oil industry in Angola. Murli Deora, Minister of Oil and Gas, GoI announced in August 2007 that "ONGC and CNPC are jointly pursuing opportunities to secure oil equities in Angola" (Vines *et al.*, 2009: 39). This is after ONGC and CNPC signed a MoU in 2006 when Mani Shankar Aiyer was in charge of the ministry and later in 2007 when Murli Deora was the minister. However, co-operation between India and China failed to materialise because of worsening of bilateral relationship. India signed a strategic partnership agreement with GALP, a Portuguese oil and gas company, in November 2007 to explore opportunities globally including in Angola (Vines *et al.*, 2009).

Sinopec lost a bid for Block 31 to PERTAMINA, Indonesia's state-owned oil company. PERTAMINA paid US$3.5 billion whereas OVL bid US$2 billion (Wang, 2011). The bid placed by SSI cannot be verified. However, SSI acquired a 5 per cent stake in 2011 from Total for US$1 billion. Block 31 has proven and probable reserves of 553 million barrels (Pfeifer, 2013). In 2013, Marathon Oil Corporation decided to sell its 10 per cent share in Block 31 to SSI for US$1.5 billion which increased SSI's share to 15 per cent (Marathon Oil Corporation, 2013).

Dr Su Shulin, Director and Chairman of the third session of Board of Directors, Sinopec Corporation, visited Luanda in April 2008. On 17 July 2009, it was revealed that CNOOC and SINOPEC had entered into an agreement with a subsidiary of Marathon Oil to acquire an undivided 20 per cent participating interest in the PSC in Block 32 for US$1.3 billion. This became effective from 1 January 2009. Marathon Oil retained a 10 per cent WI (Vines *et al.*, 2009). A joint venture between Sinopec and CNOOC outbid OVL by paying US$1.3 billion for a 20 per cent stake in ultra-deepwater Block 32 in 2009 (Alves, 2010). Block 32 has estimated reserves of 650 million barrels and production capacity of 230 tbpd (*Oil and Gas Journal*, 2014). But in October 2009, Sonangol as existing equity holder exercised its right of first refusal (RFR) and blocked the Chinese purchase by announcing its own intention to buy it (Corkin, 2011).

IV

India had warm and friendly relations with Angola even before the latter became independent. India supported Angola in its freedom struggle and also supported the MPLA during Angola's civil war. Despite India's long-standing ties, Chinese oil companies have so far crowded out Indian oil companies. One of the key factors for the success of Chinese NOCs in the oil industry in Angola is that China was able to interlink business with diplomacy. On 20 June 2006, Angola's President José Eduardo dos Santos stated, "We appreciate the cooperation between China-Sonangol, Sinopec and Unipec (subsidiary of Sinopec) and the efforts our two countries are making to rehabilitate basic facilities destroyed during the war in Angola" (Vines *et al.*, 2009: 31). In November 2007, President dos Santos stated that "China needs natural resources and Angola wants development" (Vines *et al.*, 2009: 31). According to Ambassador Ghanshyam:

> Less importance has been given by India to African leadership compared to other countries. India has to give more importance to Angola. However, with respect to China, language of money is more important than Portuguese language. In oil business, you have to build the equation. In Africa, friendship comes first and then business comes, while in other parts of the world it is the other way round. It takes time to build friendships. Indian prime ministers and dos Santos could never meet which did not facilitate business. Prime Minister Manmohan Singh was willing to travel from Pittsburgh, US to Luanda. He was willing to take an 18-hour flight to meet dos Santos. However, he would have reached on Sunday. Angolans are devout Catholics and go to Church on Sunday. The schedules did not match. The Angolans said that the meeting between the two can be arranged at 8 a.m. on Monday. Prime Minister Manmohan Singh had to be in India on Monday. If Prime Minister Singh had come, talks about at least one deal might have taken place. It is difficult to say that deals would have been finalised because deals are done on the basis of hardcore negotiations. India needs to link up politically with Angola. India has not been able to do so as of yet. India needs to do this to maximise its potential.
>
> (Interview, Appendix A)

Additionally, the partnership between Sonangol and Sinopec International – the partnership between Sinopec and Queensway Group – has been instrumental in allowing China to build a portfolio of joint ventures with the Angolan leaders transcending the oil sector and venturing into real estate, aviation and construction worldwide. Consequently, Sinopec was able to beat OVL and obtained a stake in deepwater oil blocks operated by BP through SSI. Later, China also got a stake in more oil blocks in Angola (Vines *et al.*, 2009).

Sinopec is still a marginal player in the oil sector in Angola relative to the oil majors, primarily because it is a latecomer and it still lacks the right ultra-deepwater drilling technology and expertise. Despite the limitations, it can be said that Sinopec has been quite successful in Angola since 2002. Beijing's oil diplomacy has been relatively successful and it has achieved its major goal of ensuring access to equity production in Angola. It should be noted that all four stakes acquired by Sinopec (through its 55 per cent share in SSI) are in deepwater blocks. This indicates Sinopec's determination to enter the most promising areas of the upstream sector in Angola and to acquire new and much-needed technological expertise in deep-sea exploration by paying exorbitantly for the oil blocks (Corkin, 2011).

The Angola experience was a lesson for the Indian oil companies, especially OVL. ONGC is the biggest player in the upstream segment in India and globally through its overseas arm OVL. It is a 'maharatana' or a 'mega jewel' and receives considerable support and privileges from GoI. ONGC and OVL were completely swept away by Chinese oil companies in Angola. It was also a hard learnt lesson for the Ministry of Oil and Natural Gas, GoI, so much so that Mani Shankar Aiyar, Minister for Oil and Natural Gas, GoI, stated:

> The Chinese were way well over the mark, way ahead of India in seeking exploration and production blocks in Angola and rest of Africa. They were placing very high bids. We could not compete. If Indian oil companies cannot compete with Chinese oil companies, the former should cooperate with the latter.
>
> (Interview, Appendix A)

It can be inferred that the Angola experience was the reason why Indian oil companies did not enter into competitive bidding with Chinese oil companies for oil blocks in West Africa.

It could also be argued that because of its financial clout, China was more able to meet Angolan needs for post-conflict reconstruction than other Asian countries. Indian investment in the development of Angola's infrastructure has been dwarfed by Chinese efforts. Although India's participation has increased recently, China is still at the top in terms of trade. China is in Angola for the long haul. Both Angola and China will benefit from the increased trade and commerce. This enhanced economic co-operation raises policy challenges for Angola. Angola has to ensure that it is not overly reliant on one partner, i.e. China. India might be able to get oil concessions in the future if Angola decides to diversify its oil industry (Vines *et al.*, 2009).

Conclusion

The chapter discussed the presence of Indian and Chinese oil companies in Angola. NOCs from both India and China bid for oil blocks. A private oil company, New Bright International Development Ltd (based in Hong Kong), also bid for and acquired oil blocks along with Sinopec. This is explained by the intervening variable or the difference in the political economy of India and China. Joint ventures between Chinese NOCs and joint ventures between Chinese NOCs and private sector companies outbid Indian oil companies when they bid for the same oil block so much so that Indian NOC was not able to acquire any oil blocks in Angola. NOCs from China have acquired oil blocks which are commercially viable and produce oil. This is explained by the difference in the economic and political power which allows China to establish closer, better and stronger diplomatic relations with Angola. This conforms to the hypothesis that NCR can explain the difference and the relative success and failure of India and China to mobilise oil in the oil industry in Angola.

Note

1 New Bright International Development is one of the 88 Queensway Group's companies. Queensway Group is a group of 30 Chinese companies which are headquartered at 10/F Two Pacific Place, 88 Queensway, Hong Kong. Most, if not all, of the companies operate in Angola.

References

Alves, Ana Christina (2010). The Oil Factor in Sino-Angolan Relations at the Start of the 21st Century. Online. Occasional Paper No. 55, South African Institute of International Affairs, February. Available at www.saiia.org.za/occasional-papers/the-oil-factor-in-sino%E2%80%93angolan-relations-at-the-start-of-the-21st-century (accessed 15 November 2015).

ANGOP (Agencia Angola Press) (2015). Angola/India Cooperation Agreement in Pipeline – Foreign Minister. Online. 30 October Available at: www.portalangop.co.ao/angola/en_us/noticias/politica/2015/9/44/Angola-India-cooperation-agreement-pipeline-Foreign-minister,4f05f547-fe3a-4cb7-a525-25d61429391c.html (accessed 1 May 2016).

BBC (2015). Angola Profile – Timeline. Online. 4 June. Available at: www.bbc.com/news/world-africa-13037271 (accessed 1 May 2016).

BBC (2016). Angola Country Profile. Online. 11 January. Available at: www.bbc.com/news/world-africa-13036732 (accessed 1 May 2016).

Benazeraf, David and Alves, Ana (2014). Oil for Housing: Chinese-Built New Towns in Angola. Online. Policy Briefing 88, April South African Institute for International Affairs. Available at: www.saiia.org.za/policy-briefings/507-oil-for-housing-chinese-built-new-towns-in-angola/file (accessed 1 May 2016).

Comarmond, Cecile de (2011). China Lends Angola $15bn, but Few Jobs are Created. Online. *Mail and Guardian*, 6 March. Available at: http://mg.co.za/article/2011-03-06-china-lends-angola-15bn-but-few-jobs-are-created (accessed 1 May 2016).

Corkin, Lucy (2011). Uneasy Allies: China's Evolving Relations with Angola. *Journal of Contemporary African Studies*, 29 (2), pp. 169–180.

Coroado, Herculno and Brock, Joe (2015). Angolans Resentful as China Tightens its Grip. Online. Reuters, 9 July Available at: www.reuters.com/article/us-angola-china-insight-idUSKCN0PJ1LT20150709 (accessed 1 May 2016).

Downs, Erica S. (2007). The Fact and Fiction of Sino-African Energy Relations. *China Security*, 3 (3), pp. 42–68.

Huang Kaixi, Wang Xiaobing and Yu Ning (2015). Auditors Probe Sinopec, Savvy Broker in Angola. Online. *Caixin Online*, 4 August. Available at: http://english.caixin.com/2015-08-04/100836237.html (accessed 1 May 2016).

IMF (2014). Angola: Selected Issues Paper. Online. IMF Country Report No. 14/275. Available at: www.imf.org/external/pubs/ft/scr/2014/cr14275.pdf (accessed 1 May 2016).

IMF (2016). Statement by IMF Deputy Managing Director Min Zhu on Angola. Online. 6 April. Available at: www.imf.org/external/np/sec/pr/2016/pr16155.htm (accessed 1 May 2016).

Kiala, Carine (2010). China–Angola Aid Relations: Strategic Cooperation for Development? *South African Journal of International Affairs*, 17 (3), pp. 313–331.

Lee, H. and Shalmon, D. (2008). Searching for Oil: China's Oil Strategies in Africa. In: Robert I. Rotberg, ed. *China into Africa: Trade, Aid and Influence*. Washington, DC: Brookings Institution Press, pp. 109–135.

Levkowitz, Lee, Ross, Marta McLellan and Warner, J.R. (2009). The 88 Queensway Group: A Case Study in Chinese Investors' Operations in Angola and Beyond. Online. Report US–China Economic & Security Review Commission, 10 July Available at: www.uscc.gov/Research/88-queensway-group-case-study-chinese-investors%E2%80%99-operations-angola-and-beyond (accessed 1 May 2016).

McGroarty, Patrick (2015). Angola's Boom, Fueled by China, Goes Bust. Online. *Wall Street Journal*, 28 October. Available at: www.wsj.com/articles/angolas-boom-fueled-by-china-goes-bust-1446072930 (accessed 1 May 2016).

Marathon Oil Corporation (2013). Marathon Oil Announces $1.5 Billion Sale of Interest in Angola Block 31. Online. 25 June Available at: http://ir.marathonoil.com/releasedetail.cfm?ReleaseID=773689 (accessed 1 May 2016).

MEA (Ministry of External Affairs), GoI (2014). India-Angola Relations. August. Available at: www.mea.gov.in/Portal/ForeignRelation/Angola_August_2014.pdf (accessed 2 May 2016).

OEC (Observatory of Economic Complexity) (n.d.). Angola. Available at: http://atlas.media.mit.edu/en/profile/country/ago/ (accessed 1 May 2016).

Oil and Gas Journal (2014). Total, Partners Reach FID for Kaombo Project Off Angola. Online. 14 April Available at: www.ogj.com/articles/2014/04/total-partners-reach-fid-for-kaombo-project-off-angola.html (accessed 1 May 2016).

Pfeifer, Sylvia (2013). Sinopec Pays $1.52bn for Stake in Angolan Field. Online. *Financial Times*, 24 June. Available at: www.ft.com/intl/cms/s/0/2425aa52-dcee-11e2-9700-00144feab7de.html (accessed 1 May 2016).

Singh, Sushant K. (2007). India and West Africa: A Burgeoning Relationship. Online. Africa Programme/Asia programme briefing paper Chatham House. London: Royal Institute of International Affairs, pp. 1–16. Available at: www.chathamhouse.org/publications/papers/view/108471 (accessed 2 April 2012).

US EIA (Energy Information Administration) (2016). Angola: Country Analysis Brief. Online. 1 May. Available at: www.eia.gov/beta/international/analysis.cfm?iso=AGO (accessed 20 April 2016).

Vines, A., Weimer, M. and Campos, I. (2009). Asian National Oil Companies in Angola. In: Alex Vines, Lillian Wong, Markus Weimer and Indira Campos, eds. Thirst for African Oil: Asian National Oil Companies in Nigeria and Angola. Online. Chatham House Report, London: Royal Institute of International Affairs, pp. 29–60. Available at: www.chathamhouse.org/sites/files/chathamhouse/r0809_africanoil.pdf (accessed 18 May 2016).

Walker, Andrew (2016). Angola Seeks IMF Help in Wake of Oil Price Falls. Online. BBC, 6 April Available at: www.bbc.com/news/business-35981850 (accessed 2 May 2016).

Wang, Ying (2011). Pertamina Edges Out Sinopec for Stake in Angolan Oil. Online. 5 November. Available at: www.chinadaily.com.cn/business/2011-05/11/content_12489760.htm (accessed 25 April 2016).

Weimer, Markus (2012). The Peace Dividend: Analysis of a Decade of Angolan Indicators, 2002–2012. Online. Chatham House, London: Royal Institute of International Affairs, pp. 1–19. Available at: www.chathamhouse.org/sites/files/chathamhouse/public/Research/Africa/0312pp_weimer.pdf (accessed 1 May 2016).

Winsor, Morgan (2015). Angola Economic Woes: Chinese Slowdown, Global Crude Glut Hit Angola's Oil-Dependent Economy. Online. 1 September. Available at: www.ibtimes.com/angola-economic-woes-chinese-slowdown-global-crude-glut-hit-angolas-oil-dependent-2077944 (accessed 2 May 2016).

World Data Bank (n.d.). World Bank. Available at: http://data.worldbank.org/indicator (accessed 20 April 2016).

6   India and China in Nigeria

Chapter 6 examines whether NCR can explain the differences and relative success and failure of China and India in their respective efforts to mobilise oil in the oil industry in Nigeria. As discussed in the introductory chapter, although both Nigeria and São Tomé and Principe have jurisdiction over the JDZ, the study discusses it with Nigeria because São Tomé and Principe is an extremely minor player in the oil industry in West Africa. Thus the chapter does a case study 'pattern matching' of one country in West Africa, namely Nigeria. The chapter is divided into four sections. Section I provides a brief background of Nigeria and discusses the oil industry in Nigeria, the oil reserves and production and the problems facing the oil industry. Section II compares and contrasts the political, diplomatic and economic relations of India and China respectively with Nigeria. It highlights that China's economic, political and diplomatic engagement with Nigeria far surpasses India's engagement with Nigeria. Section III discusses the oil blocks bid for and acquired by India and China in Nigeria and JDZ in Nigeria–São Tomé and Principe. It investigates if Chinese and Indian oil companies entered into direct competitive bidding for the oil blocks and if the former outbid the latter, the number of oil blocks that oil companies from the two countries have bid for and acquired and the type of Indian and Chinese oil companies that are operating in the oil industry in Nigeria. It also examines the quality of the oil blocks acquired by oil companies from the two countries. Section IV provides an analysis of India's and China's interaction in the oil industry in Nigeria.

I

Nigeria is one of the most important countries in Africa, especially West Africa. It is considered one of the African superpowers along with South Africa and is competing with South Africa for the permanent membership of the UNSC with veto power. It can make this claim because of various reasons. In 2014, Nigeria became the largest economy in Africa (after revising the method to calculate its GDP). It is the most populous country in the continent. Historically, Nigeria has been a prominent player in African politics through the UN, the ECOWAS, the AU and the NEPAD. Nigeria has also deployed troops in West Africa to end disorder in the region, especially in Liberia (BBC, 2016).

Despite its growing status as a major power in Africa, Nigeria is still an extremely poor country where 70 per cent of people live on less than US$1 a day. Although it has secured billions of dollars in oil revenue, Nigeria has an extremely low status in human development. Less than 50 per cent of the population in Nigeria has access to basic amenities like sanitation and drinking water, among others. The country's infrastructure is ineffective. Even by 'Third World' standards, there is lack of efficient transport. There is a severe shortage of electricity and medical services are poor. Nigeria is epitomised by 'islands of prosperity surrounded by seas of poverty'. In the last few years, Nigeria has also witnessed violence along ethnic and religious lines, and separatist aspirations have been growing in some parts of Nigeria (BBC, 2016).

Poverty and low human development is attributed to Nigeria's long-standing governance problems. Nigeria gained independence in 1960 and had its first coup d'état in 1966. It subsequently endured military rule under a succession of military dictators except for the civilian interlude of 1979–83. President Olusegun Obasanjo won the elections in 1999 and democracy was restored in Nigeria. In 2007, Umaru Musa Yar'Adua succeeded Obasanjo to the presidency. This was the first time that there was a transfer of power from one civilian administration to another since independence (Mthembu-Salter, 2009). Although the last decade has witnessed continuous civilian rule, there have also been allegations of electoral malpractice. However, the April 2011 elections were considered to be among the best ever conducted in the country (Alao, 2011a). President Goodluck Jonathan came to power in 2011.

A former military ruler, Muhammadu Buhari won the election in March 2015. He is the first opposition candidate to win a Nigerian presidential poll. He scored a major diplomatic success in June 2015 when neighbouring countries agreed to Nigeria commanding a joint force to counter Boko Haram. The Nigerian government faces the growing challenge of preventing the country from breaking apart along ethnic and religious lines. Thousands of people have died over the past few years in communal attacks led by the Islamic State-aligned Boko Haram. Separatist aspirations have also been growing and the imposition of Islamic law in several northern states has embedded divisions and caused thousands of Christians to flee. Nigeria's insecurity has added to its economic woes, hindering foreign investment (BBC, 2016). Nigeria is infested with corruption, especially in the oil industry. Nigeria National Petroleum Corporation (NNPC), Nigeria's NOC, is dysfunctional and has been misused as little more than a cash machine by successive Nigerian leaders. Moreover, the oil industry has been marred by inconsistency, uncertainty and confusion due to frequent changes between civilian and military rule.

Oil industry in Nigeria

Nigeria, an OPEC member since 1971, is the largest oil producer in Africa. The Nigerian economy relies heavily on the oil sector. According to the IMF, over 95 per cent of export earnings and about 40 per cent of government revenues can be attributed to Nigeria's oil industry. Nigeria's fiscal buffers, the Excess Crude Account and SWF include savings generated when oil revenues exceed budgeted revenues. However, those funds declined from US$11 billion at the end of 2012 to US$3 billion at the end of 2013 (US EIA, 2016).

According to Table 2.4, Nigeria has the second largest oil reserves in Africa after Libya and the largest reserves in Sub-Saharan Africa. According to Table 6.1, oil reserves in Nigeria have increased by more than 50 per cent from 23 billion barrels in 2001 to 37 billion barrels in 2014. It is expected that oil reserves will further increase as more oil discoveries are made in offshore Nigeria. Nigeria also has the largest natural gas reserves in Africa and is among the world's top five exporters of liquefied natural gas. It is unable to develop the natural gas sector due to lack of adequate infrastructure (US EIA, 2016).

According to Table 6.2, oil production in Nigeria has remained approximately around the 2.3 mbpd on average during 2001–14. In 2014, Nigeria produced about 2.4 mbpd of oil, which is almost 16 per cent less than its oil production capacity of over 3 mbpd. This is attributed to disruptions in production (discussed below) that have compromised parts of Nigeria's oil industry. Additionally, production suffers from supply disruptions, which have resulted in unplanned outages as high as 500 tbpd. Nigeria's 2014 production was slightly higher than in 2013 because of fewer supply disruptions but still lower than previous years. No major oilfields have started production since the 125 tbpd Usan deepwater field came online in February 2012. The 40 tbpd Bonga North West field came online in 2014, helping to offset production declines (US EIA, 2016).

Table 6.1 Proved reserves of crude oil from 2001 to 2014

Country	Year (billion barrels)													
	2001	2002	2003	2004	2005	2006	2007	2008	2009	2010	2011	2012	2013	2014
Nigeria	23	24	24	25	35	36	36	36	36	37	37	37	37	37
São Tomé & Principe	0	0	0	0	0	0	0	0	0	0	0	0	0	0

Source: compiled from US EIA.

Table 6.2 Total oil production from 2001 to 2014

Country	Year (thousand barrels per day)													
	2001	2002	2003	2004	2005	2006	2007	2008	2009	2010	2011	2012	2013	2014
Nigeria	2261	2123	2279	2332	2631	2442	2353	2169	2212	2459	2554	2524	2372	2427
São Tomé & Principe	0	0	0	0	0	0	0	0	0	0	0	0	0	0

Source: compiled from US EIA.

In 2005, oil production reached the peak of 2.63 mbpd in Nigeria. However, there was a decline in production because many companies were forced to withdraw staff and shut down production due to an increase in violence from militant groups. Since December 2005, there has been an increase in kidnappings, pipeline damage and militants taking control of oil resources in the Niger Delta. The oil rich Niger Delta Basin is in a fragile state due to local ethnic and religious tensions, tensions over revenue distribution, opaqueness of oil revenues and environmental damages from oil spills. The Movement for the Emancipation of the Niger Delta (MEND) is the most important militant group. It is attacking oil infrastructure to achieve political goals. MEND aims to achieve redistribution of oil wealth and have greater local control of the sector to foster development in the Niger Delta. Consequently, by 2009, oil production decreased by more than 25 per cent. After 2009, there was a rise in oil production because the militants reached an agreement with the government whereby they received cash payments and training opportunities in exchange for giving up arms (US EIA, 2016).

The slowdown in E&P in the oil and gas industry can also be attributed to the uncertainties in Nigeria's investment policies and regulatory structure. Consequently, there have been deferments in project development, including LNG projects. However, there is optimism that the Petroleum Industry Bill (PIB) (which has been delayed and has been expected for a long time) could provide an adequate regulatory framework and mitigate investment uncertainties in the oil and gas industry. Due to lack of support, especially from the IOCs, passage of the PIB has been stalled. The ongoing debate within the Nigerian government has further compounded the problem. However, after multiple rounds of revisions, IOCs have a more positive outlook of PIB. Concerns still linger and have been expressed by Shell recently (US EIA, 2016).

According to the Nigerian government, Nigeria is incurring a loss of US$7 billion annually due to illegal refineries, losses in official oil sales and oil theft. The Nigerian National Oil Spill Detection and Response Agency contends that sabotage, bunkering and poor infrastructure has led to nearly 2,400 oil spills during 2006–10 and approximately 260,000 barrels of oil has been spilled annually for the past 50 years. However, some believe that estimate is too high and may include the volume lost in oil spills. It is difficult to measure the volume of stolen crude oil because metering systems are usually at export terminals and, therefore, oil stolen between the wellhead and pipelines is not easily detected. Furthermore, IOCs do not collectively report volumes stolen, so there is no authoritative source for total volumes stolen (US EIA, 2016).

An extremely contentious issue in Nigeria is the distribution of oil revenue because all the receipts from the oil revenue like value-added tax, corporate tax, customs duties and production proceeds go directly to the coffers of the central government. Trust between state governments, local councils and the central government has been vitiated due to the twin evils of mismanagement of oil revenue and lack of transparency. As a result, a revenue sharing agreement was established by the 1999 constitution. According to the agreement, 13 per cent of the oil revenue from onshore production is shared by the nine oil-producing states in the Niger Delta. The National Priorities Services Fund receives 6.5 per cent, local councils 15.2 per cent, states 31.1 per cent and the federal government gets 47.2 per cent. The theft, sabotage and political tensions in the Niger Delta are due to the discord over the present revenue sharing agreement. There have been demands by groups to increase their share from onshore activities to 50 per cent and to also get a proportion of the revenue from offshore production. It is not clear how the PIB will impact the present revenue sharing agreement (US EIA, 2016).

The NNPC was created in 1977 to oversee the regulation of the oil and natural gas industry, with secondary responsibilities for upstream and down-stream developments. In 1988, the NNPC was divided into 12 subsidiary com-panies to regulate the subsectors within the industry (US EIA, 2016). The Department of Petroleum Resources, within the Ministry of Petroleum Resources, is another key regulator, focused on general compliance, leases and permits, and environmental standards. Currently, most of Nigeria's major oil and natural gas projects are funded through joint ventures between IOCs and NNPC, where NNPC is the majority shareholder. The rest of the projects are managed through PSCs with IOCs (US EIA, 2016).

NNPC has joint ventures and PSCs with Chevron, Eni, ConocoPhillips, Statoil Hydro, ExxonMobil, Total, AP, Petrobras and others. IOCs participating in onshore and shallow water oil projects in the Niger Delta region have been affected by the instability in the region. As a result, there has been a general trend for IOCs, particularly Shell, Total, Eni, Chevron and ConocoPhillips, to sell their interests in marginal onshore and shallow water oilfields, mostly to Nigerian companies and smaller IOCs, and to focus their investments on deep-water projects and onshore natural gas projects (US EIA, 2016).

Shell has been operating in Nigeria since 1936 and has the biggest crude oil production capability of approximately 1.2–1.3 mbpd. However, Shell has been affected the most by the instability in Nigeria. Most of its crude oil production capacity has been severely affected, with some facilities stopping production in 2006. ExxonMobil is the second largest IOC in Nigeria. It operates fields in a partnership with NNPC and produces 800 tbpd. Chevron produced 516 tbpd of oil on average in 2011 and is the third largest producer. It functions under its subsidiary Chevron Nigeria Limited. In joint partnership with NNPC, it has a 40 per cent stake in 13 concessions. A major proportion of its operations are onshore in the Niger Delta and in shallow water. It also has stake in deepwater oil blocks, particularly its largest deepwater oil block, Agbami. Total and Eni produced 179 tbpd and 96 tbpd respectively in 2011 in Nigeria, and are the fourth and fifth largest producers of oil. Total is the operator in one onshore and a number of offshore oil blocks. It is the operator of the Usan deepwater field and its production has not been hindered in recent years. On the other hand, Eni/Agip has experienced some incidents, especially at the Brass River terminal, that resulted in a decline in production since the end of 2006 (US EIA, 2016).

Oil trade figures in Nigeria have not changed much in the last several years despite the instability and shut-in production. This can be ascribed significantly to capacity additions and shifting world demand. Nigeria exports 45 per cent of crude oil to Europe, 18 per cent to India, 10 per cent to Brazil, 3 per cent to the United States and 7 per cent to South Africa. Energy Intelligence Group's International Crude Oil Market Handbook claims that Nigeria exports roughly 20 types of crude oil. Most of them are light, sweet grades with low sulphur content. The gravities range from American Petroleum Industry Standard 29–47 degrees and sulphur content from 0.05–0.3 per cent (US EIA, 2016).

II

This section compares and contrasts the political, diplomatic and economic relations of India and China with Nigeria. The aim of the section is to highlight that China's greater political and economic power relative to India enables it to establish better diplomatic and economic relations with Nigeria.

China and Nigeria

A pro-Western stand was adopted by governments in Nigeria in the early years of its independence. The relationship between China and Nigeria became strained during 1968–70 because China supported Ibo-dominated Biafra's bid to secede from the Nigerian federation. Diplomatic relations were established in 1971. In 1993, Sani Abacha became the president and initiated contact with the Chinese government. Consequently, the Nigerian–Chinese Chamber of Commerce was founded in 1994 and, in 1995, a US\$529 million contract to construct the railway system in Nigeria was awarded to China Civil Engineering Construction Corporation (CCECC). Relations were further strengthened in 1997 when Li Peng, the former premier of China's State Council, visited Nigeria. During his visit protocols were signed relating to power generation, steel and oil. However, nothing materialised until Obasanjo came to power in 1999 (Mthembu-Salter, 2009).

Since the beginning of the twenty-first century, Sino-Nigerian relations have deepened. Both China and Nigeria are undergoing significant changes. China, with its rapidly growing economy, has embarked on an aggressive pursuit of trade and investment across the world. Nigeria, for its part, has tried to bring about major domestic economic and political reforms and thus remove its negative image as an unstable and unreliable business partner. The desire for a symbiotic relationship forms the backbone for recent developments and future prospects of Sino-Nigerian economic relations. China is a major economic and political power that can positively complement Nigeria's desire to diversify its economic reliance on the West. China is also seen as a credible investor in Nigeria's major natural resource endowments and a country whose support can assist in Nigeria's international diplomacy. By 2006, the perception in policy circles was that the relationship between the two countries was founded on economic interests and both countries had developed a set of lucid policies to meet those interests. China has a three-pronged strategy towards Nigeria: expansion of the market for Chinese manufactured goods, to increase the share of Chinese MNCs in the Nigerian market and to increase the presence of Chinese NOCs in the oil industry (Mthembu-Salter, 2009).[1]

The diplomatic and economic relations have strengthened due to bilateral visits from heads of states and senior government officials and leaders from both countries, and increased trade and Chinese investment in Nigeria. The first ministerial conference of the FOCAC was held in Beijing in October 2000 and was attended by senior Nigerian representatives. Consequently, a contract to construct 5000 housing units for athletes taking part in the annual All-Africa games to be held in Abuja in 2000 was awarded to CEEC. CEEC built the housing units in due time. Agreements were also signed between the two countries in 2001, which led to the establishment of China Investment Development and Trade Promotion Centre in Nigeria and Nigeria Trade Office in China. During Obasanjo's second term, from 2003 to 2007, relations between the two countries were further strengthened. There were also frequent visits and meetings between senior leaders and officials from both countries. For instance, Wu Bangguo, Chairman of the National Peoples' Congress (NPC), visited Nigeria in 2004 and met President Obasanjo (FOCAC, 2004a), President of Nigerian Senate Adolphus Wabara and Speaker of House of Representatives Aminu Masari (FOCAC, 2004b). Obasanjo visited China twice – in 2005 and 2006 – and met President Hu Jintoa, Premier Wen Jiabao and Wu Bangguo (FOCAC, 2005a, 2005b). Wen Jiabao and Hu Jintao also visited Nigeria. In July 2005, Aliyu Mohammed Gusau, National Security Adviser to Nigerian President, met MOFA Li Zhaoxing in Beijing (FOCAC, 2005c). In 2006, the intergovernmental Nigeria–China Investment Forum was established and Obasanjo as the Minister of Petroleum awarded several major oil blocks to the Chinese companies. As a quid pro quo, Chinese companies were required to invest and build infrastructure across a wide range of sectors. This increased the presence of Chinese companies in number of projects in Nigeria (Wong, 2009). Bilateral relations were further strengthened by the visits of President Yar'Adua in 2008 (Reuters, 2008).

Although China obtained approximately 1.4 mbpd of crude oil or 22 per cent of its total oil imports from Africa in 2014, it secured less than 2 per cent from Nigeria (US EIA, 2015). However, during 2001–7, China invested nearly 45 per cent or US$4.8 billion in the oil industry in Nigeria out of a total of US$10.5 billion in the oil industry in Sub-Saharan Africa. Consequently, exports of Chinese-manufactured goods rose rapidly in Nigeria. Additionally, Chinese MNCs were awarded significant new contracts in key industries like construction, power, telecommunications and transport during this period, and China's total investment in Nigeria reached US$6 billion by the end of 2008. For instance, the 335 MW Olorunsogo (also known as Papalanto) gas-turbine power station in Ogun State where Electric Power Construction Corporation began construction in late 2005. The cost of the project is US$220.7 million, 35 per cent of which is financed by the Nigerian government and the balance from a credit facility provided by China EXIM Bank. Another example is the 335 MW Omotosho gas-turbine power station in Ondo State, completed by the China National

Machinery and Equipment Import and Export Corporation in 2007 and largely financed by China EXIM Bank. Also financed by China EXIM Bank but built by Germany's Siemens is the 138 MW Geregu gas-turbine power station in Kogi State. In February 2008, it was announced that the China National Electric and Equipment Corporation would build and run (for a time) a 115 MW coal-powered plant at Enugu, in Enugu State. CCECC rehabilitated the Ikot Akpaden–Okoroette road in 2003–4 for US$5.7 million, built a new US$16.7 million corporate headquarters for the Nigerian Communications Commission in Abuja in 2003–5, and is the main construction company at the Lekki Free Trade Zone near Lagos (Mthembu-Salter, 2009). In July 2011 Nigeria signed a US$874 million contract with the CCECC for the construction of the Abuja–Kaduna railway (Alao, 2011a).

In July 2013, President Goodluck Jonathan visited China and met President Xi and other Chinese leaders. A dozen cabinet ministers, including those for petroleum resources, trade and transport, as well as several state governors, senior government officials and business people, accompanied the president on his visit. During the visit, China agreed to give Nigeria a US$1.1 billion low-interest loan to build much-needed infrastructure. Chinese companies are building roads across Nigeria in contracts worth US$1.7 billion. Agreements were also being finalised for China to provide loans of US$3 billion to Nigeria at an interest rate of less than 3 per cent (Aljazeera, 2013). Reports suggest that President Jonathan's visit attracted US$25 billion of Chinese investment. Nigeria's Bauchi state signed a MoU with China Machinery Engineering Corporation for electricity provision at an estimated cost of US$260 million. There was also an agreement by China EXIM Bank to lend US$500 million to Nigeria to build airport terminals in Lagos, Abuja, Port Harcourt and Kano. The 20-year loan is at a 2 per cent interest rate. According to Nigerian Aviation Minister Stella Oduah, "It's free money, so we're happy" (Li, 2013).

In April 2016, President Muhammadu Buhari visited China and met his counterpart Xi Jinping, Premier Li Keqiang and Zhang Dejiang, the chairman of the standing committee of the NPC. The president led a huge delegation comprising ministers of transportation, power and housing, trade, industry and investment. The two leaders also witnessed the signing of six documents on economic, industrial, aviation, financial, scientific and technological co-operation (China. org.cn, 2016). Buhari's visit yielded additional investments to Nigeria exceeding US$6 billion. For instance, North South Power Company Limited and Sinohydro Corporation Limited signed an agreement valued at approximately US$478 million for the construction of a 300 MW solar power station in Shiriro, Niger State. Granite and Marble Nigeria Limited and Shanghai Shibang signed an agreement valued at US$55 million for the construction and equipping of a granite mining plant in Nigeria (*Daily Post*, 2016).

Trade between the two countries has increased from US$2 billion in 2005 to US$7.76 billion in 2010, making Nigeria the fourth-largest trade partner (after Angola, South Africa and Sudan) and second-largest export market of China in Africa (Alao, 2011b). Trade increased further from US$13 billion in 2013

(*China Daily*, 2014) to approximately US$15.5 billion in 2015. Nigeria became China's third largest trading partner in Africa in 2014 (Yusuf, n.d.). Nigeria was also the largest importer from China. Chinese imports to Nigeria amounted to US$10.2 billion in 2014, that is 29.2 per cent of Nigeria's total imports (Global Edge, n.d.). By 2015, China's total investment in Nigeria reached US$15 billion (Ojonugwa, 2015). In January 2014, Nigeria approved US$10 billion Chinese investment for oil exploration in the Bida Basin and China is also going to construct a refinery in Baro in Niger State (Daly, 2014). According to Lin Songrian, Director-General of African Affairs Department, China's Ministry of Foreign Affairs:

> By the end of 2015, the total volume of project contracts by Chinese companies in Nigeria reached US$77.3 billion and the bilateral trade volume reached US$15 billion, accounting for one-fourteenth of the total trade volume between China and Africa.
>
> (China.org.cn, 2016)

It is estimated that China's trade and investment with Nigeria will increase further in the near future as China diversifies its interests in Nigeria (Daly, 2014).

India and Nigeria

Nigeria and India have a long history of political friendship, economic relations and social interaction even before Nigeria gained independence in 1960. There are recorded cases of Indians trading in Nigeria as early as the 1890s. The depth of the relationship owes much to the similarity in colonial experience and some of the policies Britain adopted while overseeing the two countries. Both countries have been in the forefront of the worldwide anti-apartheid and anti-colonial struggle, and have collaborated in various international fora. In 1958, India established a diplomatic mission in Nigeria. Despite warm relations between the two countries, before 2007, there were only two official visits and one unofficial visit from an Indian prime minister to Nigeria. Prime Minister Jawaharlal Nehru visited Nigeria in September 1962. Nehru and Nigeria's first prime minister, Tafawa Balewa, developed mutual respect and admiration. In 2003, Prime Minister Atal Behari Vajpayee visited Nigeria to participate in the Commonwealth Heads of Government Meeting. In 2006, Somnath Chatterjee, the Speaker of Lok Sabha, accompanied by a large delegation, visited Abuja from 1–10 September to attend the 52nd Commonwealth Parliamentary Conference (MEA, GoI, 2014). The relationship has developed significantly in recent years heralded by greater trade and commerce. Economic connections range from oil exploration, telecommunications and transportation, to retailing, banking, power, education and military training. Of all these, however, the relationship between the two countries in oil and gas appears to be the most important in recent times. This is due largely to the importance of these resources for the economic development of both countries (Alao, 2011b). The Indian High Commission in

Nigeria estimated that as of October 2010, there are about 25,000 Indian nationals and about 10,000 persons of Indian origin holding other nationalities (High Commission of India, Nigeria, n.d.). This is not to mention the Indian Diaspora in Nigeria. Many Nigerians also live in India.

President Obasanjo's visit to India in 2000, followed by a number of lower level visits from Nigerian government officials, provided the momentum for India–China relations. On 3 November 2004, Obasanjo visited India again and had discussions with Indian Premier Atal Behari Vajpayee. The talks focused on the hydrocarbon industry and this was followed by visits from cabinet ministers from Nigeria to continue with the discussions (Singh, 2007). India's involvement in Nigeria falls under its wider outreach programme in Africa. Since the early 2000s, India has been extensively involved in wider investment in Africa and there have been visible demonstrations of friendship between the two countries. India launched Techno-Economic Approach for India Movement seeking cooperation with nine West African countries (initiative is called Team-9) like Chad, Côte d'Ivoire, Equatorial Guinea, Ghana, Mali, Senegal, Guinea Bissau and Burkina Faso (Alao, 2011a).

Diplomatic friendship is evident in several exchanges of visits between leaders of both countries. In 2007, Indian Prime Minister Manmohan Singh visited Nigeria as part of a high-level meeting to discuss strengthening relations between the two countries. It was the first official visit by an Indian prime minister to Nigeria in 45 years. This led to signing of the Abuja Declaration – 'Declaration of Strategic Partnership' – in October 2007, which signalled an important new phase in diplomatic links between Nigeria and India, and provided an institutional framework to support investments and commerce (Alao, 2011a). The declaration included four agreements, namely, two MoUs on promoting interaction between foreign office backed institutes, one MoU on defence co-operation and a protocol for foreign office consultations (Alao, 2011b). Following the declaration, the fifth joint session was held in March 2011 to review the state of relations between the two countries. Since then India has continued to be a leading trade partner for Nigeria (Alao, 2011a). In 2007, Vice President of Nigeria, Goodluck Jonathan, visited India to attend the Federalism Conference and, in November 2007, a high-level delegation attended the India–Africa Hydrocarbon Conference in New Delhi. In April 2008, Vice President Jonathan visited India to attend the India Africa Forum Summit in New Delhi. Ministers and government officials from the two countries also visited each other (MEA, GoI, 2014). Nigeria's desire to expand bilateral relations and economic ties was discussed during the visit to India in March 2011 by the Nigerian Foreign Minister, Odein Ajumogobia, when he attended the fifth session of the Joint Commission with India. The Joint Commission constitutes a legal framework of the collaboration between Nigeria and India. Under it, there is a whole range of activities, such as the bilateral air service agreement (Alao, 2011a).

India has had a history of extensive commercial links with Nigeria. Economic relations between India and Nigeria are in a range of sectors such as transportation, oil exploration, telecommunications, education, banking, retailing and military power. Nigeria's pharmaceuticals, steel and power transmission sectors are dominated by Indian companies. There are 15 Indian companies operating in Nigeria's power sector (High Commission of India, Nigeria, n.d.). Telecommunications is a major enterprise in Nigeria and the country provides the largest market in Africa. Indian companies have entered Nigeria's business quite forcefully, with Bharti Airtel investing US$600 million in Nigeria's mobile market when it purchased Zain Telecom's African business for US$10.7 billion. The country's involvement in Zain Telecom has made it possible for India to infiltrate other aspects of business in the information technology (IT) sector. For example, the National Institute of Information Technology, an Indian company, trains about 15,000 Nigerians annually in IT, which enables them to get jobs without much difficulty. A major link between Nigeria and India in the education sector is the Pan-African e-Network Project. The satellite and fibre network project is an initiative of Indian President Dr A.P.J. Abdul Kalam using Indian expertise in IT to benefit the healthcare and higher education sectors in African countries. It will provide effective communication and connectivity among the 53 African nations that are signatories to the project. The project's three components are tele-education, telemedicine and a video conferencing link. As one of the pilot countries, Nigeria introduced the project in February 2009. India is also interested in establishing a coal and gas power project in Nigeria. India's largest power producer, the National Thermal Power Corporation (NTPC), came up with this initiative. The arrangement involved Nigeria ensuring the yearly supply of three million tonnes of gas for NTPC projects in India. In return for the gas, NTPC was to build a 700 MW gas-fired power plant, a 500 MW coal-based plant and renovate a 200 MW unit at a 1300 MW plant. NTPC also offered to train 30 Nigerian engineers and set up a training institute in the country (Alao, 2011a).

According to the Nigerian Foreign Affairs Ministry, Indo-Nigerian trade reached a peak of US$10.2 billion during 2008–9, although the global financial crisis reduced this to US$8.7 billion in 2009–10. During the first part of 2010–11, trade between the two countries grew by more than 50 per cent relative to the same time period in 2009–10 (Alao, 2011a). In 2010–11, bilateral trade was US$13 billion and reached US$17.3 billion in 2011–12. Since then bilateral trade has decreased to US$16.5 billion in 2012–13, increased marginally to US$16.7 billion in 2013–14 and declined further to US$16.3 billion in 2014–15. Nigeria is India's largest trading partner in Africa and India is Nigeria's largest trading partner globally. On 22 May 2014, India and Nigeria signed an agreement in Kigali, Rwanda on the sidelines of a meeting of the African Development Bank in which EXIM Bank of India provided US$100 million LoC to Nigeria. The Nigerian side, with the concurrence of the Indian side, decided to utilize the credit for power sector projects in three states: Enugu – US$40 million, Cross River – US$30 million and Kaduna – US$30 million (High Commission of India, Nigeria, n.d.). Additionally, India has invested US$5 billion in Nigeria (Alao, 2011a). However, India's investment and loans are small relative to China in Nigeria.

After a gap of almost a decade, President Buhari, along with a high-level delegation comprising governors of some states, the national security advisor and permanent secretaries in some ministries, visited India for the third India–Africa Summit. Buhari was at the Defence Services College, Wellington, India from 22 July to 24 November 1975 (Iaccino, 2015). President Buhari held talks with Indian Prime Minister Narendra Modi, Minister for Oil and Gas Dharmendra Pradhan and other African and Indian officials. The discussions with Prime Minister Modi focused primarily on three areas: strengthening relations between the two countries, oil business and helping Nigeria and Africa to develop their potential. India wanted oil from Nigeria on a government-to-government transaction which will be considered by Nigeria (Ejiofor, 2015).

According to Ambassador Ghanshyam, former Ambassador to Angola and High Commissioner to Nigeria, GoI:

> Nigeria hold India in very high regard. India has tremendous goodwill in Nigeria. An entire generation of Nigerians was taught by Indian teachers, treated by Indian doctors and grew up watching Indian Bollywood movies. All the Nigerians in the late 1940s will remember their Indian teachers. India has a better image in Nigeria than any other country in East Africa or West Africa. After independence, Nigeria asked India for almost everything. India set up the Nigerian Defence Academy. The US, USSR and Britain amongst others wanted to establish National Defence Academy but Nigeria asked India to set it up. All the Nigerian generals have been trained by India. Nigerians believe that the solution to all the problems in Nigeria lie with India.
>
> (Interview, Appendix A)

III

This section discusses India and China in the oil industry in Nigeria and the oil blocks bid for and acquired by India and China in the upstream sector of the oil industry in Nigeria.

India and China in the oil industry in Nigeria

Before being cajoled by Obasanjo's administration to acquire equity oil blocks, India and China bought Nigerian oil through long-term contracts and from the spot market. PetroChina had annual deals with NNPC to supply 30 tbpd and Sinopec had contacts worth 100 tbpd. IOCL is NNPC's main Indian client. China and India were forced to hunt and acquire their own oil blocks because of their growing energy needs due to a rapidly growing economy. Both countries were sceptical of entering the oil industry in Nigeria for four reasons. First, it was dominated by Western oil companies. Second, there were concerns that contracts will not be honoured due to decades of military rule and incessant political instability. Third was the political risk due to rampant fraud and corruption in Nigeria. Fourth is insecurity in the Niger Delta. The Niger Delta has become an increasingly hostile environment since the beginning of the new millennium and militants from MEND have targeted officials of foreign oil companies. Insistent lobbying by Obasanjo since the middle of 2004 persuaded the Indian and Chinese NOCs to enter Nigeria. To mitigate their concerns, Obasanjo waived signature bonus or offered Indian and Chinese NOCs RFR at a discounted rate on oil blocks if the latter committed to investing in infrastructure projects and the downstream oil sector (Wong, 2009).

In 2005, the first bidding round under the aegis of 'oil for infrastructure' was undertaken and 77 oil blocks were offered. Many Western companies boycotted the bidding round for two reasons. First is because they opposed RFR. Second, there were concerns that bidders were required to enter into partnerships with local partners and most of them were political cronies. As a result, only 44 blocks were awarded and almost 50 per cent withdrew because winners of the bids defaulted on their payments. Chinese NOCs also did not take part in the auction. They were under the impression that they had already secured the oil blocks in earlier negotiations with the Nigerian government. India's OVL was the favourite to acquire OPL 323 and OPL 321 because it had been negotiating for more than six months with Nigerian officials. However, the blocks were awarded to the South Korean National Oil Company, KNOC. OVL bid for the block as an upstream company. On the other hand, KNOC bid as a consortium and was better disposed to provide infrastructure (Wong, 2009).

The Obasanjo government held another bidding round in May 2006 because of a plethora of confusions including those mentioned above. Companies which were willing to make significant infrastructure and downstream investments were allowed to participate in this auction. Chinese, Indian and other Asian NOCs all received RFR on pre-assigned blocks. Indian NOC, ONGC, entered into a joint venture with MEL. The joint venture, called OMEL, proved to be a more effective vehicle for India's entry into the Nigerian oil industry. OMEL was able to provide infrastructure projects and compete with other Asian NOCs. It was offered OPL 279, OPL 285 and OPL 216 but it bid for and acquired only OPL 279 and OPL 285. CNPC pledged to invest US$2 billion in the struggling Kaduna refinery and in return acquired four oil blocks: OPL 471 and OPL 298 in the Niger Delta and OPL 721 and OPL 732 in the Chad Basin and (Wong, 2009).

In May 2007, two weeks before the end of its term, the Obasanjo government undertook another bidding round to provide a last chance for Obasanjo's supporters to milk the cow. Forty-five oil blocks were offered, out of which 24 were pre-assigned to 12 companies on RFR basis. Four blocks were offered to CNOOC on RFR terms. This was in return for a US$2.5 billion loan from China EXIM Bank for constructing the Lagos–Kano railway and a hydro-electric power plant in Mambilla. One block was also offered to CNPC on RFR basis for investment in the Kaduna refinery. OMEL was offered one block. In return, OMEL was to undertake a feasibility study of a new railway between Aba and Lagos. However, the Indian and Chinese NOCs did not participate in the final bidding round due to extremely high political risk. Chinese NOCs also acquired oil blocks outside the purview of three auctions held during Obasanjo's two terms in office (Wong, 2009).[2] This is discussed in more detail below.

China in the oil industry in Nigeria

Sinopec acquired AP, a Swiss-based oil company, for US$7.24 billion in June 2009. Sinopec paid a 47 per cent premium for the acquisition of AP (Vanguard, 2009). Mirror Lake Oil and Gas Company Limited, an indirect wholly-owned subsidiary of SIPC – a subsidiary of Sinopec – completed the acquisition of AP on 2 October 2009 (Rigzone, 2009). AP was one of the biggest independent oil producers in West Africa and had extensive onshore and offshore operations in Nigeria. This was the first of the many overseas takeovers of oil companies by Chinese NOCs in Chinese corporate history and the largest acquisition by any Chinese company until 2009. In December 2012, CNOOC acquired Canadian oil company Nexen for US$15.1 billion, one of the largest ever acquisitions in the international oil industry. Nexen operates as a wholly-owned subsidiary of CNOOC. Three Chinese oil companies are operating in Nigeria: Sinopec and its subsidiaries AP and SIPC, CNOOC and its subsidiary Nexen and CNPC. According to Table 6.3, the Chinese NOCs bid for 24 oil blocks and obtained 23 blocks. Almost all the oil blocks acquired by Chinese NOCs and their subsidiaries produce oil.

CNPC in Nigeria

Nigeria and CNPC commenced their co-operation in the oil sector in 2006. The Nigerian government and CNPC signed an agreement to co-operate in the oil and gas industry. Consequently, CNPC bid for four oil blocks and won contracts for four blocks: OPL 721, OPL 298 (formerly OML 65), OPL 732 and OPL 471. Blocks OPL 732 and 721 are situated in the Chad Basin in the Borno province in northern Nigeria. OPL 732 is for risk exploration only. Blocks OPL 471 and 298 are offshore blocks situated in the Niger Delta with acreage of 1370 and 1012.4 square km respectively (CNPC, 2016).

CNPC paid US$10 million for OPL 471, US$510,000 for OPL 721 and US$510,000 for OPL 732. CNPC paid US$35 million for OPL 298 (Ugwuanyi, 2008). During investigations by the House of Representatives Adhoc Committee probing the oil sector, there were allegations that OPL 298 was sold to CNPC for US$5 million by some workers in the Directorate of Petroleum Resources. The estimated value of OPL 298 was US$2.28 billion. Further investigations revealed that CNPC paid US$30 million for OPL 298 and also committed to invest US$2.1 billion in important infrastructure projects in Nigeria, especially the Kaduna refinery (The Nation, 2008). CNPC also paid US$25 million for OPL 226 in partnership with Startcrest Group (Ojiabor and Oluwasegun, 2008). Allocation of OPL 226 was later revoked and it was awarded to Essar Oil in 2009 (Zee News, 2009). OPL 298 was producing 6 tbpd in 2008 (The Nation, 2008). Oil production from OPL 731, OPL 732 and OPL 471 cannot be ascertained.

Table 6.3 Oil blocks bid for and acquired by Chinese oil companies in Nigeria

Country	Company	Oil blocks bid for	Oil blocks acquired	Commercial viability
Nigeria	CNPC	OPL 298; OPL 471; OPL 721; OPL 732; OPL 226	OPL 298; OPL 471; OPL 721; OPL 732; OPL 226	Allocation of OPL 226 revoked; OPL 298 produces oil; oil production from other blocks cannot be ascertained
Nigeria	CNOOC	OML 130; OPL 229	OML 130; OPL 229	OML 130 has reserves of 600 million barrels; oil production from OPL 229 cannot be ascertained
Nigeria	CNOOC (Nexen)	OML 138, OPL 223	OML 138, OPL 223	Both blocks produce oil. Have proven and probable reserves of 500 million barrels
Nigeria	Sinopec	OML 64; OML 66	OML 64; OML 66	Oil discoveries made in both blocks. OML 64 produces oil
Nigeria	Sinopec (SIPC)	Stubbs Creek; OML138	Stubbs Creek	Stubbs Creek produces oil. Has reserves of 15 billion barrels
Nigeria	Sinopec (AP)	OML 123; OML 124; OML 126; OML 137; OPL 227; OPL 291; Okwok	OML 123; OML 124; OML126; OML 137; OPL 227; OPL 291; Okwok	OML 123, OML 124 and OML 126 produce oil. OML 137 is exploration block and has not produced oil to date. OPL 227 is not commercially viable. Oil discovery made is OPL291. In Okwok, production is suspended
Nigeria-São Tomé & Principe, JDZ	Sinopec	Block 1, Block 2	Block 1, Block 2	Oil blocks relinquished
Nigeria-São Tomé & Principe, JDZ	Sinopec (AP)	Block 1, Block 2, Block 3, Block 4	Block 1, Block 2, Block 3, Block 4	Oil blocks relinquished
Total		**Bid 24; acquired 23**		

Sources: compiled from CNPC (2016), Vanguard (2009), Rigzone (2009), Energy-pedia News (2004), Infield Rigs (2006), Seven Energy (n.d.), CNOOC (n.d.), Juan (2011) and Nexen (2015).

CNOOC in Nigeria

CNOOC bid for two blocks, OML 130 (previously OPL 246) and OPL 229, and acquired the blocks. OML 130 is located 200 kilometres offshore at depths ranging from 1100–1700 metres (Singh, 2007) and constitutes four oilfields: Preowei, Egina, Akpo and Egina South. CNOOC owns a 45 per cent interest in OML 130 (CNOOC, n.d.) and bought contractor rights for US$2.3 billion (Wong, 2009). OML 130 was CNOOC's biggest-ever foreign acquisition until it acquired Nexen. It had recoverable reserves of 600 million barrels of oil and 2.5 tcb of natural gas and was hailed as CNOOC's crowning achievement (Singh, 2007; Energy-pedia News, 2008). In March 2009, the Akpo oilfield started production. In 2014, net production from Akpo field reached approximately 56 tbpd (CNOOC, n.d.). According to a Nigerian journalist, it can be inferred that one of the reasons why the block has been a success is because one of CNOOC's partners is South Atlantic Petroleum (SAPTERO). SAPTERO is owned by TY Danjuma, the former Nigerian defence minister, and once a close friend and senior officer in Yar'Adua's administration (Mthembu-Salter, 2009). CNOOC and the operator undertook preliminary development work in 2011 on the three other oilfields, including the Egina field (CNOOC, n.d.).

OVL won the auction for OML 130 (previously OPL 246). OVL planned a US$2 billion deal to acquire a 45 per cent stake in Nigeria's Akpo field (OPL 246). It was one of the very few important deals in Africa where India was able to outbid China. However, the Indian CCEA prevented OVL's planned acquisition of the block. The Indian cabinet thought that the political risk involved was too high. "It has not been approved", stated Finance Minister Palaniappan Chidambaram. According to Jaspreet Singh, a senior analyst with Prabhudas Lilladher, "Nigeria is a very risky country to invest in, especially for state-owned companies like ONGC" (BBC, 2005).

OPL 229 is a shallow-water block with acreage of 1,376 square metres. It has water depth of less than 25 metres. It was upgraded into mining licence OML 141 in 2008 after significant yields were discovered in 2007 from exploration wells Barracuda and Dila. It was estimated that oil production would commence in 2009. It is next to Brass oil terminal and the planned Brass LNG terminal and is also adjacent to a major find by Shell. Shortly after acquiring OML 130 for US$2.69 billion, CNOOC ventured into OPL 229 (Chen, 2008).

CNOOC opted out of most of its 35 per cent stake in oil mining licence OML 141 despite the company's successful drilling of two wells because of allegations of corruption by individuals in Sinosure (Mthembu-Salter, 2009). In August 2008, CNOOC decided to return its stake in the block to Emerald Energy Resources Ltd, an independent Nigerian firm. In January 2006, CNOOC had paid $60 million for a share in the block, but it remains unclear if the company will reacquire any of that investment. The new agreement will allow CNOOC to remain invested in the project with a 5 per cent interest as collateral for an $80 million loan that helped fund exploration efforts (CNOOC, n.d.).

In 2012, CNOOC acquired Nexen, a Canadian oil company, for US$15.1 billion. Nexen Petroleum Nigeria Limited (NPNL), a subsidiary of Nexen, holds a 20 per cent share in OML 138 (OPL 222) and an 18 per cent share in OPL 223. OPL 222 was acquired in 2002 and OPL 223 in 2008. Both blocks are in the lucrative Usan oilfield with proven and probable reserves of 500 million barrels (Nexen, 2015). In 2010, a successful oil well Owowo South B-1 was discovered in OPL 223. The Usan oilfield commenced production in February 2012 and its production continued to increase. NPNL made a new discovery in the Usan area in 2014 (CNOOC, n.d.).

Sinopec, AP and SIPC in Nigeria and JDZ

SINOPEC

Sinopec has also acquired oil blocks in Nigeria through its subsidiary Henan Oil-field. In April 2004, an agreement was signed between Sinopec and NNPC to develop OML 64 and OML 66 in offshore Niger Delta. Five exploration wells were drilled in OML 64 and 18 in OML 66. One well in OML 64 and 12 wells in OML 66 encountered hydrocarbon reserves (Energy-pedia News, 2004). Nigerian Petroleum Development Company, the E&P arm of the NNPC, discovered oil in OML 64 in March 2009. The well was drilled to a total depth of 11,150 feet and encountered six major hydrocarbon intervals out of which three are bearing oil with a net thickness of about 50 feet. Current production lies between 1.284–3.11 tbpd and is of sweet light crude type (NNPC, 2015). Sinopec acquired a 29 per cent share in Block 1 in the Nigeria–São Tomé JDZ in 2006. A discovery was made in the Obo-1 exploration well in 2006 (Infield Rigs, 2006). However, the discovery was not commercially viable and the block has been relinquished by Sinopec.

SIPC

Sinopec also acquired oil blocks through its subsidiaries SIPC and AP. In 2003, SIPC acquired a 49 per cent share in Stubb Creek oilfield which has oil reserves of 15 billion barrels. Universal Energy, a 62.5 per cent owned subsidiary of Seven Energy, has a 51 per cent licence interest, and is the operator of the Stubb Creek Field (Seven Energy, n.d.). It produced 4 tbpd in 2004. Sinopec has asked Henan oilfield to further investigate Stubb Creek to raise production (Rigzone, 2004). Subsequently production declined to 2 tbpd. Attempts are being made to increase production to 8 tbpd. Stubbs Creek was classified as a marginal oilfield in 2002. Production at Stubb Creek is important because it marks the attainment of oil at one of the marginal fields allocated to indigenous companies (Oladun-joye, 2015). SIPC agreed to buy Total's 20 per cent stake and operating rights in OML 138 in the Niger Delta. It was willing to pay cash for the purchase of the block. According to the deal, Sinopec would have acquired the entire 20 per cent stake Total holds in the block. OML 138 lies in the Niger Delta Basin and has water depths ranging from 500 to 1000 metres. The deal was subject to regulatory approval. After acquiring OML 138, Sinopec would have had access to approximately 100 million barrels of recoverable reserves. The block started producing oil in February 2012. It produced 24 tbpd and the output is expected to rise to 26 tbpd (Juan, 2011). However, the deal with Total failed. The reason for the failure is not known. Total has put its stake up for sale again. The block is going to be difficult to sell because it is a deepwater exploration block which requires substantial investment. Additionally, the owner's returns would be limited if Nigeria raises taxes on profits of foreign investors under the PIB. According to a London-based broker, "Anything in Nigeria is a tough sell. And anything with capital expenditure is even tougher these days. Very few players would be willing to acquire assets that have big investment commitments attached" (ExpoGroup, 2014). However, SIPC was not only willing to buy the block but was willing to purchase it in cash.

AP

In 1998, AP started operations in Nigeria when it signed two PSCs with NNPC. The average annual production was 8.8 tbpd. Since Sinopec's acquisition of AP, the sine qua non for AP's growth has been to acquire oil assets which are deemed by other companies to have limited remaining production potential. AP has been able to increase production and reserves in an economically worthwhile manner due to its strong operational and technical expertise. AP has extensive onshore and offshore operations in Nigeria. AP has acquired 11 blocks in Nigeria (Table 6.3). AP had stakes in Block 1 in 2012 and in Block 2, Block 3 and Block 4 in the JDZ in 2010. Sinopec also acquired stakes in Block 2 in 2006 and later in Block 3 and Block 4 from AP in the JDZ. However, AP and Sinopec relinquished the blocks because they were not deemed to be commercially viable (PwC, 2014).

In 2015, AP has one onshore oil block and six offshore oil blocks in Nigeria. This includes 11 field complexes with approximately 60 production wells in OML 123, two fields with 20 producing wells in OML 124 and two fields with 14 production wells in OML 126. In 2011, the total output from OML 124 averaged 4.5 tbpd. It also contains several identified exploration prospects which have not been tested and drilled. OML 123 also contains three unapprised oil discoveries and several exploration prospects. Production from OML 126 started in 2005 and averaged 35 tbpd by 2011. The combined oil production is expected to increase from 75 tbpd to over 85 tbpd from OML 123, OML 124 and OML 126. OML 137, an exploration and appraisal block, has no production facilities and oil has not been produced from the block but it has four identified oil prospects (AP, 2016).

In October 2006, AP acquired a 72.5 per cent stake in and operatorship of OPL 291 from Starcrest Nigeria Energy Limited. A potentially significant prospect (Odoko) has been identified in addition to a number of leads in OPL 291. In June 2008, AP acquired a 40 per cent stake in OPL 227. Four wells were drilled which encountered hydrocarbons but were not commercially viable. In 2006, in Okwok, AP drilled three wells and a side track well out of which two wells were flow tested. On testing, the first well produced 0.40 tbpd. However, due to sand control problems, it was difficult to reach the actual flow potential of the well. The second well produced 1.2 tbpd. Due to potential tie-back to production, both wells are currently suspended (AP, 2016).

India in the oil industry in Nigeria and JDZ

India has three interests in Nigeria's oil industry: E&P and development in the upstream sector, refineries and purchase of crude oil (Singh, 2007). Although India may be looking towards Africa as a whole, Nigeria is its main target because Nigeria plans to significantly increase its oil production. Recently, Nigeria has been one of India's main sources of crude oil. In 2011, India imported approximately 13 million metric tonnes of crude oil from Nigeria annually (Alao, 2011a) and in 2014, Indian imports constituted 18 per cent of Nigeria's total crude oil export (US EIA, 2016). India's rapidly growing economy's thirst for oil led GoI to seek increased ownership of Nigerian oil reserves. India's interest in Nigerian oil was strongly encouraged by the Nigerian government when Obasanjo was the president (1999–2007). Obasanjo's government auctioned oil blocks in bidding rounds that required bidders to commit themselves to providing Nigeria with major infrastructural projects. After initial hesitation, India responded positively, coupling its investments with substantial involvement in construction projects in Nigeria (Wong, 2009).

India is represented by four oil companies: OVL, IOCL, OIL and Essar Oil. ONGC in a joint venture with MEL bid for two oil blocks in Nigeria and acquired the blocks. OMEL was also awarded an oil block on a discretionary basis. It did not bid for the block. However, the case is subjudice in Nigeria's Supreme Court. OVL also bid for two oil blocks but lost to the South Korean National Oil Company, KNOC. OIL and IOCL entered into a joint venture and acquired a stake in one oil block in Nigeria, although they did not bid for the oil block. Essar Oil did not bid for an oil block in Nigeria but acquired the oil block. OVL also bid for and acquired an oil block in Nigeria–São Tomé and Principe, JDZ (Table 6.4). Thus, the Indian oil companies bid for five oil blocks but acquired six oil blocks.

OVL in Nigeria and JDZ

OVL IN NIGERIA

In 2006, OMEL won two of the 18 oil blocks (OPL 279 and OPL 285) as a part of a strategic 'oil for infrastructure' deal. It paid a signature bonus of US$50 million for OPL 285 and US$75 million for OPL 279 (*Economic Times*, 2013). According to the deal, OMEL promised to invest US$6 billion to construct a new refinery that would produce 180 tbpd, building a 2000 MW power plant or

Table 6.4 Oil blocks bid for and acquired by Indian oil companies in Nigeria

Country	Company	Oil blocks bid for	Oil blocks acquired	Commercial viability
Nigeria	OMEL	OPL 279; OPL 285	OPL 279; OPL 285, OPL 297	OPL 279 and OPL 285 relinquished; no E&P activity has been undertaken in OPL 297
Nigeria	OVL	OPL 321; OPL 323		n/a
Nigeria	OIL & IOCL		OPL 205	Oil or gas reserves in excess of 200 million barrels
Nigeria	Essar Oil		OPL 226	Low commercial prospects
Nigeria-São Tomé & Principe, JDZ	OVL	Block 2	Block 2	Oil block relinquished
Total Bid 5; acquired 6				

Sources: compiled from OVL (2012), OIL (n.d.) and Essar (n.d.).

building an east–west railway or any other downstream project as may be determined by Nigeria's steering committee (Alao, 2011). The condition for investing in the refinery and infrastructure projects was that at least 120 tbpd or six million tonnes of crude oil should be produced per year (*Economic Times*, 2013). OMEL was also given the RFR on Block 250 in exchange for the execution of a feasibility study on a new railway (Alao, 2011). At the time of signing, the chairman of ONGC made it clear that the investment would be proportional to the scale of oil discoveries. This implied that no action would be taken on the downstream promises for many years. According to the chairman of ONGC, "The investment in infrastructure will depend on the joint venture's returns from the blocks" (cited in Wong, 2009: 21). Moreover, before signing the implementation deal on any downstream project, MEL had clearly stated that it wanted two billion barrels of reserves. The true nature of the OMEL was revealed later during a closed session of the Ad hoc Committee meeting appointed by Yar Adua administration to investigate the Obasanjo era 'oil for infrastructure' deals. An MEL representative revealed during the meeting that Obbasanjo had agreed that until the two oil blocks awarded to MEL produced 650 tbpd, MEL was under no obligation to fulfil any promises on the downstream projects. This was almost impossible to accomplish until and unless OMEL's concessions had a major discovery. Later a discretionary award of OPL 297 was made by Obasanjo to OMEL to help reach its production target. Later MEL also exposed that a mutual agreement was reached which changed the original agreement. Under the new agreement, MEL was to invest in one, instead of three, downstream projects (Wong, 2009). The three offshore oil blocks are discussed below.

OPL 279 is a deepwater offshore exploration block and has acreage of 1125 square km. The PSC was signed on 23 February 2007. OVL entered into a joint venture with MEL and bid and acquired the block. OMEL has a 45.5 per cent share in the block through its wholly-owned subsidiary, OMEL Exploration & Production Nigeria Ltd (OEPNL). EMO, a local Nigerian company, with a 40 per cent share and Total with a 14.5 per cent stake are the two other partners. The drilling of Kuyere-1 well in January–February 2010 led to the discovery of hydrocarbons in three pay zones. On the basis of post-drill analysis of G&G data, it was possible to identify some prospects in the deeper stratigraphic levels of the block. On 22 February 2012, the first phase of exploration expired. "However, the identified prospects do not offer a standalone discovery case for any viable commercial development. A notice of relinquishment was accordingly issued to NNPC on 21 November 2011" (OVL, 2012).

OPL 285 is a deepwater offshore exploration block. It has acreage of 1167 square kilometres. A PSC was signed on 23 February 2007. OMEL has a 64.33 per cent share in OPL 285 as the operator through its subsidiary OEPNL. EMO and Total are the other partners with a 10 per cent and 25.67 per cent share respectively. The commitment for the first phase of exploration for the block was completed. Initial exploration established only sub-optimal quantities of hydrocarbons in the block and OMEL was reluctant to enter Phase-II as downstream investments attached to it imposed unsustainable financial burdens (OVL, 2012; *Economic Times*, 2013). A decision was taken by OMEL to undertake a second phase of exploratory activity based on review of G&G data and post-drilling analysis. However, OMEL wanted the commitment for the downstream project to be waived by NNPC. On 24 November 2011, a letter was sent to NNPC to request a waiver. According to an executive from OVL, OVL was unable to fulfil its promise of investing US$6 billion for constructing a refinery because the block was not commercially viable. OVL relinquished the block and conveyed its position to the Nigerian government (Interview with OVL[b], Appendix A).

OMEL was also awarded OPL 297. OPL 297 has a controversial history. OPL 297 was carved out of OPL 130 (previously OML 246). OPL 246 was 60 per cent owned by SAPTERO, a Nigerian company. It was headed by a former defence minister, General T.Y. Danjuma. In 1998, the entire block was originally awarded to Danjuma by President General Abacha. President Obasanjo and Danjuma had a falling out due to the latter's public criticism of Obasanjo's style of government and his bid to get a third term in office. Obasanjo made attempts by invoking 'back-in' rights to reduce SAPTERO's ownership in the block to less than 10 per cent. However, this proved to be unsuccessful. OML 246 was divided into two blocks under existing regulations once oil was discovered in the block. The first part was rechristened as OML 130 and sold to CNOOC. The second part was named OPL 297 and given to NNPC. SAPTERO took NNPC to court over OPL 297 after NNPC confirmed CNOOC deal in April 2006. SAPTERO claimed that the contractual date for OPL 246 had not expired. In 2007, the Court of Appeal announced that NNPC had acted under the rules. SAPTERO then took the matter to the Supreme Court. In the mean while, OPL

297 was awarded to OMEL by Obasanjo on a discretionary basis. However, the entire case is subjudice. A court injunction was won by SAPTERO which prohibited any E&P activity on OPL 297 (Wong, 2009). At the time of writing, the case is still pending in the Supreme Court (Department of Petroleum Resources, Government of Nigeria, 2014).

OVL IN JDZ

OVL also acquired a deepwater exploration block, Block 2, in JDZ, which has acreage of approximately 1034 square kilometres. Following the 2004 licensing round in the JDZ, OVL as a part of a consortium got a stake in Block 2. OVL's subsidiary, ONGC Narmada Limited, which was incorporated in Nigeria, had a 13.5 per cent share in the block. Sinopec with a 43 per cent share (Sinopec had a 28.67 per cent share and AP had a 14.33 per cent interest), ERHC Energy Inc. with 22 per cent, Equator Exploration with 9 per cent, Amber 5 per cent interest, Foby 5 per cent and A & Hatman Ltd with a 2.5 per cent stake are the other partners. Sinopec was the operator. OVL wanted to be the operator of the block but lost a bid to Sinopec (Wong, 2009). A well was drilled in 2009 based on data analysed from the survey. Though the well showed the presence of hydrocarbons, the volumes were inadequate to warrant commercial development. OVL communicated its intention of relinquishing the block to the operator and JDA of JDZ Nigeria–São Tomé and Principe (Interview with OVL[b], Appendix A).

IOCL AND OIL IN NIGERIA

OIL and IOCL formed a joint venture and acquired a stake of 17.5 per cent each in OML 142 in 2005 (Table 6.4). The bock is located in the Anambra Basin in the Niger Delta and has acreage of 1295 square kilometres. OML 205 was converted to OML 142 (OIL, n.d.). The Nigerian government formally provided the block to the Indian NOCs, that is they did not bid for the block (Interview Executive OIL, Appendix A). OIL also farmed into a joint venture with Suntera for OPL 205. In 2005, Suntera acquired the block from Summit Oil, a Nigerian oil company. Summit Oil allocated a 70 per cent working and economic interest and a 40 per cent production interest from the joint venture to Suntera OIL, n.d.). OML 142 offers relatively low-cost and low-risk exploration and development opportunities. It contains Otien-1 gas-condensate discovery and has prospects which may contain oil or gas reserves in excess of 200 million barrels of oil equivalent. If oil is present in Otien, it is likely that the volumes will be large and lead to immediate development. This may also lead to an increase in the probability of finding oil in other prospects (Sun Group, n.d.).

ESSAR OIL IN NIGERIA

OPL 226 is an offshore block located in offshore central Nigeria and has acreage of 1250 square kilometres. It is in water depths ranging from 40 metres to 180 metres. In March 2010, a PSC was signed for the block. Drilling operations were undertaken by operators in the block and it highlighted the presence of good quantities of oil and gas according to the log and well data. Essar Oil is finalising the work programme for OPL 226 (Essar, n.d.). The case of Essar Oil is particularly interesting. In the 2007 bidding round, Essar Oil bid for OPL 226 and acquired the block. OPL 226 has estimated reserves in excess of 80 million barrels. It paid US$37 million as signature bonus (Pathak, 2010). On assuming office in 2007, President Yar'Adua's government revoked Essar Oil's acquisition in July 2008 because it had failed to meet the pre-qualification requirement (Wong, 2009). When Esasr Oil asked for the signature bonus to be refunded, OPL 226 was reinstated to Essar. Nigeria's Ministry of Petroleum Resources issued a letter dated 10 March 2009 stating that it had favourably considered Essar's representation on the revocation and has decided OPL 226 be reinstated to Essar Oil (Zee News, 2009). However, according to an executive from Essar Oil, the Nigerian government asked Shell to award the block to Essar Oil (Interview, Appendix A). I contacted Essar Oil in 2012, 2013 and 2014 to clarify the issue of acquiring the block. I wanted to meet the executives from Essar Oil in Mumbai. However, Essar Oil stated that it was not possible for their executive(s) to meet me. I was provided the information I needed by the Essar Oil executive in London. Shell had not been developing OPL 226 for some time because it did not think that the returns from the block would be commensurate with the investment. It is normal practice for a government of the host country to ask the oil company to give the block to another oil company if the block has been left barren for a long period of time (Interview, US IOC, Appendix A). Thus, the oil block that Essar Oil has acquired has a low prospect of producing oil.

IV

The essential tenet of the 'oil for infrastructure' deal propagated by Obasanjo was that Indian and Chinese NOCs and other Asian oil companies had to include and commit in their bids to build major infrastructural projects in Nigeria. The rationale behind the 'oil for infrastructure' deal was three-fold. First, the Nigerian government was disillusioned and frustrated with the lack of development in its co-operation with the West since independence. Second, the government was also exasperated with the cumbersome aid conditionalities placed by the West. Moreover, Obasanjo was extremely impressed with his first-hand experience of the rapid infrastructure development when he visited China (Mthembu-Salter, 2009).

Unlike in Angola, the 'oil for infrastructure' deal in Nigeria was unsuccessful due to the inability of the Obasanjo administration to administer the scheme. This is partly explained by politics. Nigeria has had nine different leaders since 1983. On the other hand, Angola has been ruled by the MPLA since independence and President José Eduardo dos Santos has been in power for more than 30 years. This resulted in greater uniformity in government policies and provided a durable and long established central government. Angola, like Nigeria, is also corrupt but the corruption in Nigeria is different from corruption in Angola. In Nigeria, apart from the presidency, there are other centres of power which can influence decision-making and the awarding of oil blocks. All the people in power want to deepen their pockets and their political base. Moreover, a change in government brings forth a new rent-seeking elite. There was a failure on the part of Asian oil companies, including Indian and Chinese oil companies, that were able to enter the Nigerian oil industry under the 'oil for infrastructure' model to comprehend the political context in Nigeria. Moreover, there was a complete absence of follow-up mechanisms to implement the agreements. The combination of these factors led to the failure of the 'oil-for-infrastructure' model. According to a South Korean official, the contrast between Nigeria and Angola is: "In Nigeria we found that a change of government results in a change of business partners" (cited in Wong, 2009: 4).

Since 2006, concerted attempts were made by Obasanjo to get a third term in office by changing the constitution, but in 2007, Yar'Adua was elected as president. A prompt investigation was launched by the new government to investigate the 'oil for infrastructure' deals signed between the Asian oil companies and the Obasanjo administration. Consequently, the contracts were either revoked or suspended.[3] The common belief was that the present government will revive some of the contracts if and only if the contracts are restructured, taking into account new political realities, i.e. until the present regime is able to profit from the 'oil for infrastructure' deals. The construction of the Mabilla power plant and the Lagos–Kano railway was suspended. The repair of the Kaduna refinery is also uncertain. Additionally, there are recommendations from an ad hoc committee of the House of Representatives investigating the 'oil for infrastructure' deals that CNPC should relinquish OPL 298. However, the committee agreed that CNPC should retain OPL 471, OPL 721 and OPL 732 (Wong, 2009).

There was a lot of uncertainty regarding China's Obasanjo-era deals. However, it is certain that the concept of 'oil for infrastructure' is dead because President Yar' Adua's administration and subsequent administrations had a new oil policy: 'oil for cash'. This implies that in future, oil blocks will be awarded to those who bid the highest. The Chinese leadership firmly believes that the change in government has burned them. However, China has resolved to engage with Nigeria because of its natural resources and the large size of the market (Wong, 2009). Officials from Chinese NOCs aver that the 'oil for infrastructure' setbacks are highly political. They opine that given the circumstances, the only option is to wait and see what happens with the 'oil for infrastructure' agreements. They have concluded that the state governments in Nigeria are safer to work with relative to the federal government because the former are more predictable in their political machinations and it is easier to work with the state bureaucracy (Mthembu-Salter, 2009). The suspension of the massive 'oil for infrastructure' deals by the Yar'Adua government was a major impediment to China's Nigeria policy and led to significant revaluation by China to find the best way to do business with Nigeria. China decided that the acquisition of Nigerian oil assets by purchasing established Western companies is a much better low-risk strategy rather than the cumbersome and lingering oil-for-infrastructure deals. The estimated US$7.22 billion acquisition in June 2009 of AP by Sinopec and US$15.1 billion of Nexen in February 2013 by CNOOC bears consonance with this strategy. Thus NOCs from China have adopted a new strategy of acquiring existing oil producers that have operations in Nigeria.

Moreover, Yar' Adua's administration policy of 'oil for cash' will bear consonance in Beijing. Beijing has extremely deep pockets and it is willing to flaunt its financial largesse to bid exorbitantly for oil blocks. India, on the other hand, is less pleased with the new policy for it is at a distinctive disadvantage vis-à-vis China in Nigeria because of its relative lack of political, diplomatic and financial muscle. Additionally, since India is more risk averse relative to China as evidenced in the acquisition process of OML 130/OPL 246, the new 'oil for cash' arrangement puts India at a further disadvantage relative to China. India did not try to acquire AP and would not have been able to match China's bid of US$7.24 billion to acquire AP (Interviews with Executives from OVL, IOCL, OIL, Essar Oil, and Ashok Dhar, ORF, Appendix A). It would be highly unlikely that India would be able to beat China in direct or indirect competitive bidding for oil blocks in Nigeria despite the fact that India procures approximately 18 per cent of its oil from Nigeria. "Nobody is going to give you a discount because they politically love you. If you are out bid, you are out bid" (Interview, Mani Shankar Aiyar, Appendix A).

Conclusion

In Nigeria, China is represented by NOCs and India is represented by NOCs and one private sector oil company. This is explained by the intervening variable or the difference in the political economy of India and China. Indian oil companies bid for five oil blocks and acquired six oil blocks. Chinese NOCs bid for 24 oil blocks and acquired 23 oil blocks. Thus Chinese NOCs bid for and acquired more oil blocks than oil companies from India. In Nigeria, Indian and Chinese oil companies did not bid for the same blocks except for OML 130/OPL 246. OVL bid the maximum amount of US$485 million to win the auction. However, GoI did not allow the planned acquisition to be completed due to the political risk involved. China, on the other hand, did not consider the investment risky and acquired the block after GoI directed OVL to withdraw. This shows that India is more risk averse than China. Additionally, Chinese NOCs have better quality oil blocks relative to Indian oil companies. China's financial and political muscle allowed it to establish better economic and diplomatic ties with Nigeria relative to India despite India's long engagement with Nigeria since the nineteenth century. India's investment and loans to Nigeria are dwarfed by China's investment and loans to Nigeria. India's advantages of speaking English, cultural affinity and other elements of soft power in Nigeria have been sidelined by China's economic and diplomatic prowess. China's relations with Nigeria are comparatively recent and underdeveloped compared with those of India. Despite India's historical ties, China's influence in Nigeria has increased rapidly vis-à-vis India. This is explained by the independent variable or the difference in the economic and political power of India and China. Thus NCR is able to explain the differences and the relative success and failure of India and China in mobilising oil in the oil industry in Nigeria.

Notes

1 The study focuses on the presence of Chinese NOCs in Nigeria.
2 For a detailed discussion of the different licensing rounds in the oil industry in Nigeria, refer to Wong (2009).
3 Refer to Wong (2009) for a detailed analysis of the oil for infrastructure deals and the revocation of the oil contracts.

References

Alao, Abiodun (2011a). Nigeria and the BRICs: Diplomatic, Trade, Cultural and Military Relations. Online. Occasional Paper No 101, South African Institute of International Affairs. Available at: www.saiia.org.za/occasional-papers/nigeria.html (accessed 10 January 2013).

Alao, Abiodun (2011b). Nigeria and the Global Powers: Continuity and Change in Policy and Perceptions. Online. Occasional Paper No 96, South African Institute of International Affairs. Available at: www.saiia.org.za/occasional-papers/nigeria-and-the-global-powers-continuity-and-change-in-policy-and-perceptions (accessed 10 January 2013).

Aljazeera (2013). Nigerian Leader Secures $1.1bn on China Trip. Online. 11 July. Available at: www.aljazeera.com/news/africa/2013/07/2013710171651692540.html (accessed 30 April 2016).

AP (2016). Nigeria: Operations. Online. Available at: www.addaxpetroleum.com/operations/nigeria (accessed 1 May 2016).

BBC (2005). India Blocks West Africa Oil Deal. Online. 16 December. Available at: http://news.bbc.co.uk/1/hi/business/4534412.stm (accessed 1 May 2016).

BBC (2016). Country Profile Nigeria. Online. Available at: www.bbc.com/news/world-africa-13949550 (accessed 1 May 2016).

Chen, Aizhu (2008). CNOOC in Surprise Exit of Nigeria Oil Block-Source. Online. Reuters, 18 August. Available at: http://uk.reuters.com/article/2008/08/18/cnooc-nigeria-idUKPEK25462220080818 (accessed 19 January 2013).

China Daily (2014). Nigeria, China Trade Volume Hits $13b in 2013. Online. 20 January. Available at: www.chinadaily.com.cn/business/2014-01/20/content_17244697.htm (accessed 30 April 2016).

China.org.cn (2016). Xi Jinping Meets Nigerian President Buhari in Beijing. Online. 13 April. Available at: www.china.org.cn/video/2016-04/13/content_38232661.htm (accessed 1 May 2016).

CNOOC (n.d.). Overseas: Key Operating Areas. Online. Available at: www.cnoocltd.com/encnoocltd/AboutUs/zygzq/Overseas/ (accessed 1 May 2016).

CNPC (2016). CNPC in Nigeria. Online. Available at: www.cnpc.com.cn/en/Nigeria/country_index.shtml (accessed 17 April 2016).

Daily Post (2016). Buhari's Visit to China Yielded Billions in Investments for Nigeria – Presidency. Online. 15 April. Available at: http://dailypost.ng/2016/04/15/buharis-visit-to-china-yielded-billions-in-investments-for-nigeria-presidency/ (accessed 30 April 2016).

Daly, John K.C. (2014). China's Bold $10 Billion Investment in Nigerian Hydrocarbons. Online. *The Diplomat*, 17 January. Available at: http://thediplomat.com/2014/01/chinas-bold-10-billion-investment-in-nigerian-hydrocarbons/ (accessed 30 April 2016).

Department of Petroleum Resources, Government of Nigeria (2014). Oil and Gas Industry Annual Report. Online. Available at: https://dpr.gov.ng/index/wp-content/uploads/2016/01/2014-Oil-Gas-Industry-Annual-Report-1.pdf (accessed 2 May 2016).

Economic Times (2013). ONGC-Lakhsmi Mittal JV Give Up Nigerian Oil Block. Online. 29 January. Available at: http://articles.economictimes.indiatimes.com/2013-01-29/news/36616167_1_signature-bonus-omel-opl-285 (accessed 2 May 2016).

Ejiofor, Clement (2015). Inside Story of Buhari's Trip to India-Adesina. Online. Available at: www.naij.com/623642-interesting-inside-story-president-buharis-trip-india.html (accessed 1 May 2016).

Energy-pedia News (2004). Nigeria: Sinopec Signs Oil Development Agreement. Online. 20 December. Available at: www.energy-pedia.com/news/nigeria/inopec-signs-oil-development-agreement- (accessed 1 May 2016).

Energy-pedia News (2008). Nigeria: CNOOC Sends Shockwaves Over Licence Exit. Online. 20 August Available at: www.energy-pedia.com/news/nigeria/cnooc-sends-shockwaves-over-licence-exit- (accessed 1 May 2016).

Essar (n.d.). Essar Energy Business. Online. Available at: www.essarenergy.com/about-us/essar-business.aspx#business1 (accessed 1 May 2016).

ExpoGroup (2014). Total Resumes $2.5bn Usan Deepwater Oil Block Sale. Online. 17 September Available at: www.expogr.com/kenyaoil/detail_news.php?newsid=353&pageid=2&t=Total%20resumes%20$2.5bn%20Usan%20Deepwater%20oil%20block%20sale (accessed 1 May 2016).

FOCAC (Forum on China-Africa Cooperation) (2004a). Nigerian President, China's Top Legislator Hold Talks on Bilateral Ties. Online. 9 November. Available at: www.focac.org/eng/zt/sbfw/t169441.htm (accessed 30 April 2016).

FOCAC (2004b). China's Top Legislator Meets Nigerian Parliamentarian Leaders. Online. 8 November. Available at: www.focac.org/eng/zt/sbfw/t169182.htm (accessed 30 April 2016).

FOCAC (2005a). Top Legislator Meets Nigerian President. Online. 21 April. Available at: www.focac.org/eng/zt/sbfw/t192563.htm (accessed 30 April 2016).

FOCAC (2005b). Wen Jiabao Meets Nigerian President. Online. 21 April. Available at: www.focac.org/eng/zt/sbfw/t192561.htm (accessed 30 April 2016).

FOCAC (2005c). Foreign Minister Li Zhaoxing Meets Nigerian National Security Adviser. Online. 20 July. Available at: www.focac.org/eng/zt/sbfw/t204273.htm (accessed 30 April 2016).

Global Edge (n.d.). Nigeria: Trade Statistics. Online. Available at: http://globaledge.msu.edu/countries/nigeria/tradestats (accessed 30 April 2016).

High Commission of India, Nigeria (n.d.). India-China Bilateral Relations. Online. Available at: http://hcindia-abuja.org/display_content.php?id=28 (accessed 1 May 2016).

Iaccino, Ludovica (2015). Nigeria's President Muhammadu Buhari Arrives in New Delhi for India-Africa Forum. Online. Available at: www.ibtimes.co.uk/nigerias-president-muhammadu-buhari-arrives-new-delhi-india-africa-forum-1526036 (accessed 30 April 2016).

Infield Rigs (2006). Obo-1 Discovery in Block 1 of the Nigeria Sao Tome and Principe Joint Development Zone Confirmed. Online. 30 May Available at: www.infield.com/rigs/news/obo-1-discovery-in-block-1-of-the-nigeria-sao-tome-and-principe-joint-development-zone-confirmed/288 (accessed 1 May 2016).

Juan, Du (2011). Sinopec Agrees Nigerian Oil Deal. Online. *China Daily*, 21 November. Available at: http://usa.chinadaily.com.cn/business/2012-11/21/content_15947643.htm (accessed 1 May 2016).

Li, Xiaokun (2013). New Deals for Prosperity. Online. *China Daily*, 19 July. Available at: http://africa.chinadaily.com.cn/weekly/2013-07/19/content_16799228.htm (accessed 30 April 2016).

MEA (Ministry of External Affairs), GoI (2014). India-Nigeria Relations. Online. August. Available at: www.mea.gov.in/Portal/ForeignRelation/Nigeria_Aug_2014.pdf (accessed 30 April 2016).

Mthembu-Salter, Gregory (2009). Elephants, Ants and Superpowers: Nigeria's Relations with China. Online. Occasional Paper No 42 South African Institute of International Affairs. Available at: www.saiia.org.za/occasional-papers/elephants-ants-and-superpowers-nigerias-relations-with-china.html (accessed 30 December 2012).

Nexen (2015). About Nexen: In West Africa. Online. June. Available at: file:///C:/Documents%20and%20Settings/Administrator/My%20Documents/Downloads/Nexen-WestAfricaFactSheet.pdf (accessed 1 May 2016).

NNPC (2015). NNPC Discovers More Crude Oil. Online. 6 August. Available at: www.nnpcgroup.com/PublicRelations/NNPCinthenews/tabid/92/articleType/ArticleView/articleId/152/NNPC-DISCOVERS-MORE-CRUDE-OIL.aspx (accessed 1 May 2016).

OIL (n.d.). JVs/PSCs/Alliances: Nigeria. Online. Available at: www.oil-india.com/JVs.aspx (accessed 2 May 2016).

Ojiabor and Oluwasegun, Victor (2008). Eight Oil Blocks "Sold Illegally" at N14b. Online. *The Nation*, 11 September. Available at: www.thenationonlineng.net/archive2/tblnews_Detail.php?id=62306 (accessed 1 May 2016).

Ojonugwa, Ugboja Felix (2015). Nigeria Economy: How China and US Battle for Relevance. Online. *Leadership*, 20 May. Available at: http://leadership.ng/features/434584/nigeria-economy-how-china-and-usa-battle-for-relevance (accessed 30 April 2016).

Oladunjoye, Phillip (2015). Nigeria: Seven Energy Begins Crude Oil Production From Stubb Creek. Online. *Daily Independent*, 1 May. Available at: http://allafrica.com/stories/201505010555.html (accessed 1 May 2016).

OVL (ONGC Videsh Limited) (2012). Africa: Assets. Online. Available at: www.ongc-videsh.com/Assets.aspx?tab=0 (accessed 4 December 2012).

Pathak, Kalpana (2010). Essar May Farm Out 37 per cent in Nigerian Block. Online. *Business Standard*, 9 September. Available at: www.business-standard.com/article/companies/essar-may-farm-out-37-in-nigerian-block-110090900093_1.html (accessed 3 May 2016).

PwC (PricewaterhouseCoopers) (2014). Nigeria Sao Tome and Principe, Joint Development Zone First EITI Report 2003–2013. Online. November. Available at: https://eiti.org/files/First%20Report%20%202003-2013%20(Nigeria-Sao%20Tome%20and%20Principe).pdf (accessed 1 May 2016).

Reuters (2008). China Offers Nigeria Export Credit Guarantees-FT. Online. 2 April. Available at: http://uk.reuters.com/article/china-nigeria-idUKPEK9950620080402 (accessed 30 April 2016).

Rigzone (2004). Sinopec Henan Oilfield in Study of Nigeria Oil Prospects. Online. 29 April. Available at: www.rigzone.com/news/oil_gas/a/12758/Sinopec_Henan_Oilfield_in_Study_of_Nigeria_Oil_Prospects www.rigzone.com (accessed 1 May 2016).

Rigzone (2009). Sinopec Acquires 100% of Addax Petroleum's Shares. Online. 6 October. Available at: www.rigzone.com/news/oil_gas/a/81087/Sinopec_Acquires_100_of_Addax_Petroleums_Shares (accessed 1 May 2016).

Seven Energy (n.d.). Upstream: South East Niger Delta. Online. Available at: www.sev-enenergy.com/operations/upstream/south-east-niger-delta (accessed 2 May 2016).

Singh, Sushant K. (2007). India and West Africa: A Burgeoning Relationship. Online. Africa Programme/Asia programme briefing paper. Chatham House. London: Royal Institute of International Affairs, pp. 1–16. Available at: www.chathamhouse.org/publications/papers/view/108471 (accessed 2 April 2012).

Sun Group (n.d.). Energy. Online. Available at: www.sungroup-global.com/english/sectors/suntera1.asp (accessed 2 May 2016).

The Nation (2008). $2b Block Sold at $5m in Oil Bazaar. Online. 31 July. Available at: www.thenationonlineng.net/archive2/tblnews_Detail.php?id=57584 (accessed 1 May 2016).

Ugwuanyi, Emeka (2008). DPR Clarify Deal on OML 65. Online. *The Nation*, 6 August. Available at: www.thenationonlineng.net/archive2/tblnews_Detail.php?id=62306 (accessed 30 April 2016).

US EIA (2015). China Country Analysis Brief. Online. Available at: www.eia.gov/beta/international/analysis.cfm?iso=CHN (accessed 1 May 2016).

US EIA (2016). Nigeria: Country Analysis Brief. Online. Available at: www.eia.gov/beta/international/analysis.cfm?iso=NGA (accessed 1 May 2016).

Vanguard (2009). Sinopec Acquires Addax for $7.2bn. Online. 25 June. Available at: www.vanguardngr.com/2009/06/sinopec-acquires-addax-for-72bn/ (accessed 1 April 2016).

Wong, Lillian (2009). Asian National Oil Companies in Nigeria. In: Alex Vines, Lillian Wong, Markus Weimer and Indira Campos, eds. Thirst for African Oil: Asian National Oil Companies in Nigeria and Angola. Online. Chatham House Report, Royal Institiute of International Affairs, pp. 29–60. Available at: www.chathamhouse.org/sites/files/chathamhouse/r0809_africanoil.pdf (accessed 18 May 2016).

Yusuf, Omotayo (n.d.). China to Import More Crude Oil from Angola. Online. NAIJ.com. Available at www.naij.com/762937-good-news-china-shows-interest-nigerian-oil.html (accessed 1 May 2016).

Zee News (2009). Essar Regains Oil Block in Nigeria. Online. 19 March. Available at: http://zeenews.india.com/home/essar-regains-oil-block-in-nigeria_516209.html (accessed 1 May 2016).

7 India and China in eight countries in West Africa

Chapter 7 examines whether NCR can explain the differences and relative success and failure of China and India in their respective efforts to mobilise oil in the oil industry in eight countries in West Africa. The countries are Gabon, Ghana, Chad, Equatorial Guinea, Cameroon, Mauritania, Niger and Liberia. The chapter does a case study 'pattern matching' of eight countries in West Africa. The chapter is divided into three sections. Section I examines the differences and the relative success or failure of India and China in their ability to acquire oil blocks in Gabon. It provides a brief background of Gabon and discusses the oil industry in Gabon, the oil reserves and production. It then compares and contrasts the political, diplomatic and economic relations of India and China respectively with Gabon. It highlights that India's economic, political and diplomatic engagement with Gabon is dwarfed by China's engagement with Gabon. In the end, it discusses the oil blocks bid for and acquired by India and China in Gabon and the nature or type of Indian and Chinese oil companies that are operating in the oil industry in Gabon. It also examines the quality of the oil blocks acquired by oil companies from the two countries. Section II provides a brief background of Ghana and discusses the oil industry in Ghana, the oil reserves and production. It then compares and contrasts the political, diplomatic and economic relations of India and China respectively with Ghana. It highlights that India's economic, political and diplomatic engagement with Ghana is dwarfed by China's engagement with Ghana. In the end, it discusses the oil blocks bid for and acquired by India and China in Ghana. Section III undertakes a case study 'pattern matching' of six countries in West Africa. The aim is to find out if Indian and Chinese oil companies have acquired oil blocks and the type of the oil companies from the two countries operating in the upstream oil industry in the six countries.

I

Gabon, a former French colony, became independent on 17 August 1960. The death of the first president, Leon M'Ba, in November 1967, brought Omar Bongo to power with the backing of the French government. Under the pretext of defending national unity against ethnic fragmentation, a one-party state was established immediately after Bongo's ascent to the presidency. Prompted by the democratisation wind that swept across West Africa after the end of the Cold War, a constitutional change reintroduced the multiparty system in 1990. The president's political party, Partie Démocratique Gabonais (PDG), won 66 of the 120 parliamentary seats in the first multiparty legislative elections in September 1990 and Omar Bongo, amid much political unrest, won the presidential elections held three years later (Alves, 2008).

Since then, President Bongo has astutely managed to retain and reinforce his grip on power through the expansion of his patronage network, by maintaining a policy of balancing the various ethnic groups in his government appointments and by co-opting the main opposition leaders. He won the last presidential election in November 2005 with 79 per cent of the vote (Alves, 2008). At the time of his death in 2009, President Bongo was the longest serving head of state. Elections were held in 2009 and Ali-Ben Bongo Ondimba, son of late President Omar Bongo and candidate for the incumbent PDG, became the new president. However, opposition supporters question the outcome (Petlane, 2009). In 2011, the main opposition candidate in the 2009 vote, Andre Mba Obame, declared himself the rightful winner in the 2009 election and legitimate president. President Bongo banned Obame's opposition National Union. In December 2011, PDG won 95 per cent of the seats in the parliamentary election amidst accusations of fraud from the opposition (BBC, 2015a). The ban on the National Union was lifted in 2015.

Although Gabon has achieved impressive stability and economic growth relative to other countries in the region, it is characterised by misuse and abuse of power, entrenched corruption, incompetence, lack of reliable opposition to depose the rulers and an entitlement to rule on the part of the incumbent rulers. The ruling elite have handled the political party and the state as conjoined entities. Consequently, although it has a higher GDP per capita than some of its neighbours, it is characterised by stark economic inequality and living conditions have deteriorated. The majority of the population does not have access to electricity (BBC, 2015a).

Oil industry in Gabon

Gabon is an established oil-producing country in the region. Gabon was a member of OPEC from 1975 to 1994 but it left the organisation because of high annual fees. According to the IMF, Gabon's economy is heavily dependent on its oil production. IMF states that in 2011, oil revenue accounted for nearly 56 per cent of total government revenue and hydrocarbon exports accounted for nearly 90 per cent of total export revenue in 2011. The government in Gabon is under pressure to increase economic diversification efforts because of ageing oilfields. Oil output has declined by approximately 34 per cent since it peaked in 1997. Consequently, Gabon has slid in the rankings of oil-producing countries in the region. Gabon is the fifth largest oil producer in Sub-Saharan Africa. It used to be ranked third but has slid in the rankings due to lack of adequate infrastructure. This has stymied Gabon's ability to exploit its natural resources (US EIA, 2014).

According to Table 7.1, Gabon has oil reserves of two billion barrels. It has the third largest oil reserves in Sub-Saharan Africa after Nigeria and Angola. Oil reserves have declined from 2.499 billion barrels in 2001–6 to two billion barrels in 2014. Table 7.2 shows that oil production in Gabon has declined steadily. From the peak of 314.8 tbpd in 2000, oil production has declined with marginal increase in production in 2005–6 and reached 240 tbpd in 2014. The rate of decline slowed in recent years, as IOCs invested in longevity projects at mature fields and brought online moderate levels of new production (US EIA, 2014).

Gabon has both onshore and offshore oilfields. The majority of Gabon's oilfields are located in the proximity of Port-Gentil. A pattern of oil production exists in Gabon. Historically, one large field is responsible for oil produc-

Table 7.1 Proved reserves of crude oil from 2001 to 2014 in eight countries in West Africa

Country	Year (billion barrels)													
	2001	2002	2003	2004	2005	2006	2007	2008	2009	2010	2011	2012	2013	2014
Gabon	2.5	2.5	2.5	2.5	2.5	2.5	2.0	2.0	2.0	2.0	2.0	2.0	2.0	2.0
Ghana	s	s	s	s	s	s	s	s	s	s	0.7	0.7	0.7	0.7
Chad	–	–	–	–	–	1.5	1.5	1.5	1.5	1.5	1.5	1.5	1.5	1.5
Equatorial Guinea	s	s	s	s	s	s	1.1	1.1	1.1	1.1	1.1	1.1	1.1	1.1
Cameroon	0.4	0.4	0.4	0.4	0.4	0.4	0.4	0.2	0.2	0.2	0.2	0.2	0.2	0.2
Mauritania	–	–	–	–	–	–	0.1	0.1	0.1	0.1	0.1	s	s	s
Niger	0	0	0	0	0	0	0	0	0	0	–	–	0.2	0.2
Liberia	0	0	0	0	0	0	0	0	0	0	0	0	0	0

Source: compiled from US EIA.

Notes
– = Not applicable.
s = Value is too small for the number of decimal places shown.

Table 7.2 Total oil production from 2001 to 2014 in eight countries in West Africa

Country	Year (thousand barrels per day)													
	2001	2002	2003	2004	2005	2006	2007	2008	2009	2010	2011	2012	2013	2014
Gabon	270	251	241	239	266	237	244	248	242	246	244	242	239	240
Ghana	7.2	7.4	7.5	8.6	7.4	7.1	7.7	7.2	6.9	8.5	78	80	99	106
Chad	0	0	36	171	177	158	144	127	119	123	115	104	98	103
Equatorial Guinea	181	213	206	368	375	363	369	359	346	323	299	310	291	269
Cameroon	77	70	67	66	83	87	83	82	77	66	62	64	63	81
Mauritania	0	0	0	0	0	31	15	13	11	8.2	7.7	6.6	6.8	6.0
Niger	0	0	0	0	0	0	0	0	0	0	6.7	20	20	20
Liberia	0	0	0	0	0	0	0	0	0	0	0	0	0	0

Source: compiled from US EIA.

tion in Gabon and smaller fields provide support to the largest field. As the largest field matured and production declined, another major field would emerge to substitute for the decline in production. Rabi is the largest oilfield in Gabon and led to a significant increase in output in the 1990s. It has matured and oil production reached its peak in 1997 at 217 tbpd. Production from the field has declined steadily to approximately 23 tbpd since 2010. A new large field has not yet emerged to balance the reduction in oil production from the Rabi oilfield because new exploration has led to only moderate discoveries (US EIA, 2012).

During 1987–2011, a NOC did not exist in Gabon because the previous NOC, Société Nationale Petrolière Gabonaise, was disbanded in 1987. During the same period, the Ministry of Mines, Energy, and Petroleum and the president's office were jointly responsible for the operations of the oil sector. In June 2011, the Gabonese government formed the Gabon Oil Company to enhance its involvement in oil production. It adopted a policy of equity oil in future awards of oil blocks. Foreign companies are allowed to operate in the oil industry in Gabon and have acquired large equity stakes in E&P through PSCs (US EIA, 2012).

The Gabonese government is in the process of deciding new regulatory rules to ease new deepwater exploration. The government is working on a new petroleum law. It was scheduled to be enacted in 2014 but was delayed to 2015. According to Platts, Gabon's NOC is expected to take a 15 per cent equity stake in all new projects, and the law is also expected to propose that at least 90 per cent of all jobs in the energy sector be held by locals, including executive positions. In October 2013, Gabon's Ministry of Energy awarded 13 oil and natural gas blocks to 11 companies, as part of a deepwater licensing round. Some of the winners included Ophir Energy, ExxonMobil, Eni and Repsol among others (US EIA, 2014).

Foreign oil companies dominate the oil industry in Gabon. Over 20 oil companies from ten different countries operate in Gabon: three French, six US, three Canadian, four South African, one Japanese, one Indian and two Chinese (Alves, 2008). Total has been operating in Gabon for more than 80 years. It is the largest operator in Gabon and, in 2009, it produced 71 tbpd. The second largest producers are Shell and its subsidiary Shell Gabon. Perenco, the third largest producer, produces 65 tbpd from its four offshore fields. AP is the fourth largest producer. AP has stakes in five PSCs in both onshore and offshore oil blocks (US EIA, 2012). Total Gabon and Shell Gabon account for two-thirds of total production (Alves, 2008).

The Gabonese government is introducing means to expand investment to extend the life of existing fields in order to mitigate the gradual decline in oil production. The measures are bearing fruit. In the Anguille oilfield, which is one of the largest oil producing fields, Total has increased investment to expand production. The government has also taken measures to encourage investment from smaller companies for the development of smaller fields. It is estimated that in the short term, the decline in production from larger fields will continue to be allayed by production in smaller fields. Nonetheless, in the long-run, successful new explorations, especially the prospects of deepwater, pre-salt fields, will play an important role in oil production in Gabon. Investors have been interested in the offshore Brazilian pre-salt discoveries in Gabon which were untapped until June 2011. Analysts aver that future discoveries in pre-salt fields could be instrumental in mitigating the decline in production from Gabon's large mature fields (US EIA, 2012).

China and Gabon

Gabon established diplomatic relations with Taiwan in 1960 and severed diplomatic relations in 1974. In April 1974, diplomatic credentials were formally exchanged between Gabon and PRC. Bilateral co-operation and trade developed gradually, encouraged by official visits exchanged over three decades of undisturbed diplomatic ties. President Omar Bongo visited China at least ten times over the last three decades and personally met all the members of the Chinese leadership since the 1970s, which represented a valuable political asset in bilateral relations. In March 2001, Ali Bongo, Gabon minister of national defence, visited China. In September 2002, a Chinese military delegation headed by Jiang Futang, political commissar of the Shenyang Military Zone, paid a visit to Gabon. In February 2003, René Ndemezo, Gabon minister in charge of the assembly, visited China and the following month, Martin Mabala, Gabon minister resident of the prime minister's office in charge of supervision, examination, anti-poverty and anti-corruption affairs, paid a visit to China (China.org. cn, 2004). High ranking Chinese officials visited Gabon with President Hu Jintao visiting Gabon in 2004 (Cabestan, 2014) and Deng Nan, vice minister of science and technology, visited Gabon in November 2002 (China.org.cn, 2004). President Ali Bongo and Prime Minister Paul Biyoghe Mba visited China in 2010 (Cabestan, 2014). In May 2013, Gabonese minister of digital economy, communications and post, Blaise Louembe, attended the Second Session of Beijing International Fair for Trade in Services and Global Services Forum-Beijing Summit in China (Ministry of Foreign Affairs, PRC, n.d.). In April 2016, Chairman of the National Committee of the Chinese People's Political Consultative Conference (CPPCC), Yu Zhengsheng, visited Gabon at the invitation of Senate Speaker Lucie Milebou of Gabon and met President Ali Bongo Ondimba, Prime Minister Daniel Ona Ondo and President of the National Assembly Richard Onouviet and also held talks with Senate Speaker Lucie Milebou (Ministry of Foreign Affairs, PRC, 2016).

As in Angola, Nigeria and other countries, China over the years has provided several aid packages to Gabon mostly aimed at infrastructure construction or rehabilitation. At the end of 2000, China granted Gabon a combined sum of US$73 million in interest-free and concessional loans to develop a number of co-operation projects. These were the new National Assembly building in Libreville (built by the Chinese Overseas Engineering Company and completed in 2002), two medical centres (including the sending of 12 medical teams), two primary schools, a pharmaceutical laboratory in Franceville, a factory for processing cassava and two timber-processing factories near Owendo port (Alves, 2008).

China entered the oil market in Gabon in 2004 in the wake of President Hu Jintao's visit to the country. China has helped and co-operated with Gabon in various sectors like health, education, agriculture and defence. Sino-Gabonese co-operation covers a wide range of areas of varying importance. Although China's direct investments in Gabon have increased from US$24 million in 2003 to US$128 million in 2012, it was only 3 per cent of the overall FDI in Gabon. This is close to the US level of 3.7 per cent, but way behind France at 41.7 per cent. During Hu Jintao's first state visit to Gabon in February 2004, two co-operation agreements were signed between the two countries to provide for a US$1.2 million grant for economic and technical assistance and an interest-free loan of US$6 million for co-operation projects (Alves, 2008). A number of projects have taken the Sino-Gabonese lending relations to a new level. These include the construction of the Senate House in 2005 (€24.5 million), the Grand Poubara hydroelectric dam (€292 million), a new radio and television complex ('Cité de l'information') in 2007 (€21 million) and the Stadium of Sino-Gabonese Friendship for the 2012 Africa Cup of Nations (€46 million) (Dittgen, 2011). In 2007, Huazhou Industrial and Commercial Mining Company received a licence to prospect and exploit manganese in the M'Bembélé Mountains. The Chinese investment amounted to US$420–US$560 million, including a US$84 million loan provided by its main shareholder, Huazhou Mining Investment Company at an interest rate of 6.5 per cent (Cabestan, 2014). The most important Chinese project is the €2.2 billion Bélinga project in the mining sector. The scale and impact of the Bélinga project far exceeds other projects launched by China in Gabon (Dittgen, 2011). In January 2008, China and Gabon signed a framework agreement for a US$83 million concessional loan to part fund a hydroelectric dam (Grand Poubara) linked to the Belinga mining development project. This soft loan is to be repaid over 20 years at an interest rate of 3 per cent and there is a grace period of seven years (Alves, 2008). In May 2012, China Harbour Engineering Company signed the Port Môle project worth US$450 million. Since 2008, China has become Gabon's third largest trade partner. According to the WTO, bilateral trade has increased from US$310 million in 2005 to US$951 million in 2012. In September 2013, the China Road and Bridge Company signed a contract to build the road from Port-Gentil to Libreville via Omboué and then Lambarene. The project is planned over a period of four years at a cost of US$723 million. It is primarily financed by China's EXIM Bank (95 per cent) and symbolically by the Gabonese government (5 per cent) (Cabestan, 2014).

Since 2008 China has become Gabon's second largest client ahead of France (with the United States as the largest) and is its third largest trade partner. According to the WTO, China–Gabon bilateral trade increased from US$310 in 2005 US$1.146 billion in 2011 and declined to US$951 million in 2012. China accounted for a 7.2 per cent (7.9 per cent according to Chinese statistics) share of Gabon's total volume of merchandise trade by 2012. China was still clearly behind the United States (44.8 per cent) and the EU as a whole (31 per cent), but closing up with France (9.1 per cent). In 2012, the United States had a 59 per cent share, EU 18 per cent, China 8 per cent and France 2.3 per cent of Gabon's exports (Cabestan, 2014).

China's provision of LoCs at preferential rates and financial assistance has led to a change in scale of the Sino-Gabonese relationship and to Gabon considering China as one of its privileged partners. Repeated attempts by Gabon to obtain debt relief from traditional donors did not materialise because of Gabon's' high PCY. Preferential or interest free loans from China were a welcome alternative. Gabon's government has often used diplomatic and political means in an attempt to persuade foreign businesses to invest in the country. It seems that in the long term, if President Ali Bongo wants to gradually exit the French fold and or reduce alliance on international financial institutions, Gabon may use China backed by its investments as a preferred partner because China's expansion of its interests in Gabon is compatible with Gabon's ambition for economic diversification. Moreover, China, like France, is a permanent member of the UNSC and has extremely deep pockets.

India and Gabon

India and Gabon have enjoyed warm and friendly relations dating back to Gabon's pre-independence period. Gabon has supported India's candidature at various international fora (MEA, GoI, 2013). India's diplomatic drive, aid and commercial relations are dwarfed by China commensurate with China's greater economic power. India–Gabon bilateral relations are confined to the ministerial level. Ministers in charge of mining, oil and communications portfolios have visited India during 2007–10. Ali Ben Bongo (the new president) visited India in 2007 and met Minister of Defence, GoI. There have also been visits by ministers and senior government officials from Gabon to India. For instance, Minister for Mining, Oil, Energy and Hydraulic Resources, Richard Auguste Onouviet, and Vice Minister of Foreign Affairs, Cooperation and Regional Integration, Jean Ping, visited India in May 2007. In 2011, the seventh CII-EXIM Bank Conclave on India Africa Project Partnership was held in New Delhi and the Deputy Minister for Foreign Affairs attended the conclave. On the Indian side, no senior minister has visited Gabon recently. In January 2011, talks were held between M. Paul Toungui, Minister of Foreign Affairs, Gabon when Joint Secretary (West), MEA, GoI visited Gabon (Gabon Embassy, India, n.d.).

Moreover, India's economic assistance and co-operation with Gabon are minuscule relative to China. Principal items of exports from India to Gabon are meat and meat products, pharmaceuticals, cotton, iron and steel. Imports from Gabon are wood and articles of wood, ores, slag and ash (Gabon Embassy, India, n.d.). In March 2007, an amount of US$14.45 million was provided as a LoC to construct 300 houses and four amenities in Libreville. The project consisted of construction of 300 houses and four amenities. EXIM Bank released US$4.35 million for this project. In June 2011, another LoC of

US$67.19 million was offered to upgrade broadcasting facilities in Libreville. During 2010–11, under the ITEC, Gabonese officials have been chosen to undertake training in short- and medium-term courses in India and, for 2011–12, 15 ITEC places were reserved. During the same period, under IAFS-I, Gabonese officials also received training in different disciplines in India. Tele-education, tele-medicine and 'Very Very Important Person' connectivity has been established in Libreville under the Pan African e-network project. In April 2008, during the first India Africa Forum Summit in New Delhi, a Plan of Action was agreed with the AU. Under the plan, proposals to establish a Vocational Training Centre/Incubation Centre have been completed. During 2012–13, 25 seats under the ITEC were allocated for Gabon but only four ITEC slots were utilised. Tata Chemicals (part of the Tata Group) along with Singapore-based Olam International has acquired 25 per cent stake (worth US$290 million) in a urea fertiliser project. Bilateral trade has increased steadily from US$53 million in 2004–5 to US$132 million in 2006–7 to US$345 million in 2010–11. In 2011–12, bilateral trade was approximately US$193 million with Gabon exporting US$146.26 million (MEA, GoI, 2013).

China in the oil industry in Gabon

Despite Chinese enterprises' strong interest in the oil sector in Gabon and the increasing aid and commercial assistance offered by China, Chinese NOCs still play an insignificant role in the Gabonese oil industry due to the poor performance of their concessions (Alves, 2008) as most of the profitable oilfields are dominated by French and US companies as mentioned above. Two Chinese oil companies are operating in Gabon: Sinopec and CNOOC. Sinopec operates in Gabon through its subsidiary AP. In 2012, AP was Gabon's fourth largest oil producer at 23 tbpd. This is way behind Shell at 64 tbpd, Total at 57 tbpd and Perenco at 55 tbpd. (Cabestan, 2014) Chinese NOCs bid for nine oil blocks and acquired the blocks (Table 7.3).

CNOOC in Gabon

CNOOC has acquired two exploration blocks – BC9 and BCD10 – in offshore Gabon from Shell China Exploration and Production Company Limited, a subsidiary of Shell. CNOOC will bear a part of the cost for future exploration and will compensate 25 per cent of Shell's specific exploration costs in the past (Petzet, 2012). In October 2014, a deepwater gas discovery was made in Leopard-1 well in BCD10. An appraisal programme is being undertaken to seek commercial viability (Shell, 2014).

SINOPEC AND AP IN GABON

Sinopec operates in Gabon through its subsidiary AP. In 2013, AP had interests in five onshore and offshore licence areas. Three fields were onshore and two

Table 7.3 Oil blocks bid for and acquired by Chinese oil companies in eight countries in West Africa

Country	Company	Oil blocks bid for	Oil blocks acquired	Commercial viability
Gabon	Sinopec (AP)	Maghena; Panthere NZE; Awoun; Kiarsseny and Etame	Maghena, Panthere NZE, Awoun, Kiarsseny and Etame	Koula in Awoun licence area started producing oil in 2010. In Etame licence area, oil produced by Etame Marine since 2001, Avouma since 2005 and Ebouri since 2006
Gabon	Sinopec (AP)	Dinongra, Irondou	Dinongra, Irondou	Oil production and discovery cannot be ascertained
Gabon	CNOOC	BC9; BCD10	BC9, BCD10	Gas discovery made in BCD10
Ghana	CNOOC	Jubilee Oil Field	–	n/a
Chad	CNPC	Block H	Block H	Bongor Basin produces oil; Naramay basin produces 1000 tonnes of oil per day
Equatorial Guinea	CNPC	Block M	Block M	Block relinquished
Equatorial Guinea	CNOOC	Block S	Block S	Hyrdocarbons discovered in S-3 exploration well and Cretaceous Santonian interval in Block S
Cameroon	Sinopec (AP)	Rio Del Rey basin (6), Lokele (4), Dissoni, Ngosso and Iroko	Rio Del Rey basin (6), Lokele (4), Dissoni, Ngosso and Iroko	AP gets 6 tbpd from Mokoko Abana in Lokele and 7.3 tbpd from Rio Del Rey
Mauritania	CNPC	Block Ta13; Block Ta21; Block 12; Block 20	Block Ta13; Block Ta21; Block 12; Block 20	Oil blocks relinquished
Niger	CNPC	Block Bilma; Block Tenere, Agadem block	Block Bilma; Block Tenere, Agadem block	Discoveries made in block Bilma; significant discoveries made in Agadem block
Liberia	Petro China	Block LB-09[a]	Block LB-09	Block relinquished[b]

Total Bid 34: acquired 33

Sources: compiled from CNPC (n.d.a, n.d.b, n.d.c, n.d.d), AP (2013, 2016a, 2016b), Cabestan (2014) and Kosmos Energy (n.d.).

Notes
a *Energy Business Review* (2012).
b McLellan (2015).

were offshore. The onshore licence areas comprised of three licence areas, namely Panthere NZE, Maghena and Awoun, which had three oil-producing fields (Koula, Obangue and Tsiengui). AP was the operator for the Tsiengui and Obangue fields and Shell was the operator for the Koula field. Damier, a near-field discovery, was attached to Koula. Additionally, Autour, which was on the Panthere licence, was being developed (AP, 2016a).

In 2013, AP lost the right to exploit Obangue field. It was accused by the Gabonese government of bad management, damage to the environment, corruption and tax evasion and more generally having failed to fulfil its contractual obligations. Later it was revealed that the main reason was tax evasion. AP was targeted for having reported underestimated production results, thereby avoiding paying some US$400 million of royalties to the Gabonese treasury. After negotiations had failed, Sinopec decided to sue the Gabonese government before the Paris-based international Chamber of Commerce's arbitration court but lost its case in September 2013. Negotiations were held and a new ten-year PSC was signed by AP and Gabon in January 2014 but only on three fields including Obangue. It was later revealed that AP paid US$400 million in compensation to the Oil Ministry in Gabon under Etienne Ngoubo due to an estimated loss to Gabon of US$1 billion (Cabestan, 2014).

In 2014, AP had interests in four PSCs in onshore and offshore Gabon. The onshore licence areas are Dinongra, Irondou and Koula/Damier, which is part of the Awoun licence area. The offshore licence areas are Etame and Kiarsseny Marin. Etame comprises of Etame Marin, Avouma and Ebouri licences. Dinonga and Irondou were acquired in 2014 and are APs principal producing licences. A subsidiary of AP is the operator and holds an 88.75 per cent working share. In Awoun licence area, AP has a 40 per cent working share in the Koula/Damier licence. Production from Koula started in May 2010. In Etame licence area, Etame Marin has been producing since 2001, Avouma since 2005 and Ebouri since 2006. AP has a 31.36 per cent WI in these licences. AP also has a 33.90 per cent interest in Etame licence, which is one of two non-operated exploration licence of AP in Gabon. Kiarsseny licence area has the Kiarsseny exploration licence operated by Tullow Oil Gabon. Oil has not been produced from Kiars-seny licence area (AP, 2016a).

India in the oil industry in Gabon

OIL and IOCL in Gabon

Two Indian NOCs, OIL and IOCL, formed a joint venture and acquired one oil block, Shakthi (FT-2000), an onshore oil block in Gabon in 2006 (Table 7.4). OIL is the operator in the block. The government in Gabon offered the block to the two Indian NOCs through a 'farm in' offer (OIL, n.d.), that is the NOCs did not bid for the oil block. As discussed in Chapter 4, OIL is an onshore upstream company whereas IOCL specialises in the downstream sector. US$12.5 million will be spent by the consortium to acquire the stake

Table 7.4 Oil blocks bid for and acquired by Indian oil companies in eight countries in West Africa

Country	Company	Oil blocks bid	Oil blocks acquired	Commercial viability
Gabon	IOCL and OIL	–	Shakthi (FT-2000)	Oil discovered; prospects of commercial viability low
Total Bid 0; acquired 1				

Source: compiled from OIL (n.d.).

and another US$50 million to develop it (Singh, 2007). The consortium partners are OIL and IOCL with a 45 per cent share each, and Marvis Petroleum from Singapore with a 10 per cent stake (*The Hindu*, 2012). A discovery was made in the third well which produced oil and gas. Two appraisal wells – Lassa-2 and Lassa-3 – were drilled, of which Lassa-2 was completed as an oil producer. This is the first instance that OIL has made a discovery in an overseas operated block. OIL is in the process of developing Block Shakthi (OIL, 2015).

Analysis

As in Angola and Nigeria, Chinese financial muscle and political prowess has not only strengthened Sino-Gabon relations but allowed China to access and play an important role in the oil sector in Gabon. China has employed two instruments to gain access in the oil sector in Gabon. First is interlinking of business and diplomacy and second is infrastructure construction/rehabilitation. Chinese oil companies have so far crowded out other Indian oil companies.

The Shakthi (FT-2000) block was offered to two Indian NOCs through a 'farm in' offer by the Gabonese government. The two NOCs did not bid for the oil block and have little experience in the oil sector abroad. OIL is the smallest NOC in the upstream business in India and IOCL specialises in the downstream sector. OVL, India's flagship NOC, either individually or in a joint venture with any other oil company, did not bid for or try to acquire an oil block in Gabon. Neither RIL nor Essar Oil bid for the block or ask the Gabonese government to be included in the 'farm in'. Chinese NOCs (especially CNPC, which specialises in onshore E&P), which are gobbling up oil blocks in Gabon and other countries in West Africa, and which are more concerned about the size of the asset rather than the return from the asset, also did not bid for the block or were not interested in the block. Moreover, as discussed above, in recent years, no major oil discoveries have been made in Gabon. Thus, it can be inferred that the oil block is of low commercial value, i.e. the amount of oil that can be harvested from the block is low and/or the rate of return on the investment is inadequate to warrant interest from other oil companies.

Ghana

Since gaining independence from Britain in 1957, Ghana has been very proactive in originating and implementing development programmes, for which it has received substantial donor support, especially since the 1980s. Democratic Ghana is a relatively more stable country in West Africa. It has a sound record of peaceful transition of power. In recent years, it has recorded history by hosting a sequence of fair and free elections. On two occasions, the incumbent has respected democracy and stepped down from office after the opposition won the elections. Ghana possesses a free media which operates without fear of retaliation and a strong civil society which augurs well for democratic consolidation. Compared to neighbours like Nigeria, Ghana is not a resource-abundant country, but it is endowed with some natural resources like gold, timber and cocoa (which are its leading exports), and enjoys a favourable coastal position. It is the second largest producer of gold after South Africa and the second biggest producer of cocoa after Ivory Coast.

Although Ghana depends mainly on the primary sector for economic growth, it has followed stable and prudent economic policies which have resulted in strong rates of growth. Consequently, between 2003 and 2008, poverty has declined from 53 per cent to 28 per cent. It is one of the few countries in Africa which is ahead of schedule to meet its millennium development goals. Despite the advances, approximately 80 per cent of the population still lives on less than US$2 per day. It is one of the fastest growing economies in Africa and Africa's newest oil producer. Until recently Ghana was hailed as a model for African growth but, since 2013, its economy has endured a growing public deficit, high inflation and a weakening currency. This is attributable mostly to the fall in the price of oil and to a less extent the fall in the price of cocoa, Ghana's third largest export after oil and gold (Natural Resource Governance Institiute, 2015). In April 2014, the IMF had to step in to bail out Ghana. Since 2014, public unrest has increased due to the mishandling of the economy by the government and allegations of corruption. In December 2015, 20 judges were sacked after being implicated in a high profile bribe taking scandal.

Oil industry in Ghana

Ghana is a fringe player in the oil industry in West Africa. According to Table 7.1 and Table 7.2, its oil reserves of 0.7 billion barrels in 2014 are small relative to Chad and Equatorial Guinea despite the major offshore oil discoveries in the Jubilee oilfields in 2007. Because of the Jubilee oilfields, oil reserves have more than quadrupled from 0.015 billion barrels to 0.7 billion barrels in 2014. Consequently, oil production also increased from 7.2 tbpd in 2001 to 106 tbpd in 2014 but it is still small relative to Chad and Equatorial Guinea. Jubilee oilfield produces light sweet crude oil. Technical challenges at the Jubilee field have prevented it from reaching its expected production plateau of 120 tbpd. In July 2015, Jubilee's production was almost halved because of problems with gas compression systems on its Kwame Nkrumah floating production, storage, and offloading vessel. Production returned close to its previous rate a month later. It is estimated that oil production will increase in the future. There are also expectations of major oil finds in the Jubilee oilfields in the near future (US EIA, 2015a).

China–Ghana relations

China and Ghana established diplomatic relations on 5 July 1960. Since then, relations between the two countries have been deepened by strong personal relationships between the political elites of the two countries, especially during the era of Nkrumah and Premier Zhou Enlai. In the twenty-first century, there have been high-level official visits, including visits by Ghana's President John Kufuor to China in 2002 and China's President Hu to Ghana in 2003. The governor of the People's Bank of China, Zhou Xiaochuan, visited Ghana in 2005 accompanied by Chinese businessmen in search of new business opportunities. There have also been political exchanges between members of Ghana's Parliament and officials of the CPPCC. In 2007, Jia Qingling, the chairperson of the CPPCC, visited Ghana and signed agreements that included a US$30 million concessional loan for the Dedicated Communications Project for the security agencies. In 2007, Premier Wen Jiabao visited Ghana, which resulted in the signing of six agreements, including an agreement to build a malaria centre and a primary school in Ghana, and a US$66 million loan agreement to expand and upgrade Ghana's telecommunications network. Over the decades, Ghana has provided critical diplomatic support to China, while China has reciprocated with material support for development (Idun-Arkhurst, 2008). In December 2015, President Xi Jinping met President Mahama during the Johannesburg Summit of the FOCAC which charted a new course for the development of China–Ghana relations. In April 2016, Yu Zhengsheng, chairman of the CPPCC, visited Ghana along with Vice Chairman and Secretary-General of the CPPCC National Committee, Zhang Qingli, and Vice Chairman of the CPPCC National Committee, Liu Xiaofeng. Yu Zhengsheng met President Mahama and speaker of the parliament Edward Korbla Doe Adjaho among others. He added that China is willing to work with Ghana to promote the implementation of the ten major plans for the China–Africa co-operation, which was announced by President Xi in December 2015 (Consulate General of PRC in Johannesburg, 2016).

Like in Angola, Nigeria and Gabon, in Ghana, Chinese economic and financial power strengthened Sino-Ghana relations. China has provided economic assistance to Ghana and made vigorous efforts to promote the development of co-operation between the two countries. Aside from writing down debt owed to it by Ghana since 1985 amounting to US$25 million, China has provided much-needed additional loans to assist Ghana to overcome its development challenges. China has invested in construction, mining, steel industry, building materials industry, chemical industry, the pharmaceutical sector, food processing, fisheries, agriculture, slate production and power plants among others in Ghana (Gyasi

Jnr, 2014). China's recent assistance to Ghana includes a US$562 million loan from the China EXIM Bank for the construction of a US$622 million dam at Bui. China provided a concessionary loan of US$30 million to support the first phase of Ghana's National Communication Backbone and E-Government Project. Additionally a US$28 million interest-free loan for the reconstruction of the 17 km Ofankor–Nsawam road and a US$99 million interest-free loan for the construction of landing sites has been provided by China (Idun-Arkhurst, 2008). China has also assisted Ghana in the construction of the National Theatre, the Afife Irrigation Project, the Dangme East District Hospital, the Teshie General Hospital, the Police and Military Barracks, the Ofankor-Nsawam stretch of the Accra-Kumasi Road, the Kumasi Youth Centre, the Office Block of Ministry of Defence, several rural basic schools, the Complex of Ministry of Foreign Affairs and Regional Integration. The newest projects granted by the Chinese government, such as the Sports Complex in Cape Coast, the campus of the University of Health and Allied Sciences in Ho and the New Century Career training Institute Expansion Project in Accra started in 2013 while those supported and contracted by the Chinese side such as Bui Hydro-electric Dam, Kpong Water Supply Expansion Project, Atuabo Gas Project are all in full progress. A number of newly registered Chinese investment projects topped Ghana's FDI list in 2012. The Sunon Asogli Power Plant invested by China–Africa Development Fund and Shenzhen Energy Group has been combined to the national grid of Ghana in 2011 and now accounts for around 14 per cent of Ghana's electricity generation (Embassy of the PRC in Ghana, n.d.). According to an official from the Ghana embassy in Beijing, China's total direct investments in Ghana increased to over US$500 million by the end of 2012. In 2012, China had the maximum number of registered projects in Ghana and was ranked sixth in terms of value of registered projects (Gyamerah, 2014). In 2014, China was the fifth largest investor in Ghana (Larry, 2015).

In 2013, China eclipsed the United States to become Ghana's largest trading partner (Amanor, 2013). According to China's ambassador to Ghana, Sun Baohong, bilateral trade has increased from less than US$100 million in 2000 to US$5.6 billion by the end of 2014. Ghana's exports to China have also increased significantly – by 86.7 per cent – and reached US$1.4 billion in 2014 (Government of Ghana, n.d.). China has provided cheap and unconditional loans to Ghana to meet its development needs and goals. CDB and China EXIM Bank have signed agreements worth US$13 billion with Ghana, which is approximately one-third of Ghana's GDP. For instance, US$3 billion for the Western Corridor gas commercialisation project with CDB and US$9 billion for dams, roads and railways with China EXIM Bank and a US$250 million deal for the rehabilitation of the Kpong water works (Amanor, 2013).

India–Ghana relations

India and Ghana have maintained warm and friendly ties for more than 100 years. The strong foundation of the bilateral relations was laid by India's first prime minister, Jawaharlal Nehru, and Ghana's first president, Kwame Nkrumah. The two leaders also enjoyed a close friendship. Until the end of the twentieth century, three presidents of Ghana visited India. There were several ministerial visits, including that of the Foreign Minister for the NAM Ministerial Conference in April 1986. In the twenty-first century, the bilateral relationship is based less on ideology and more on economic and strategic aspects. There were numerous visits by the president of Ghana and senior government officials to India. In August 2002, accompanied by a high-level delegation, President Kufuor visited India and four bilateral agreements were signed. In March 2008, Vice President of Ghana Alhaji Ali Mahama led a large Ghanaian delegation to the CII conclave held in New Delhi. In April 2008, President Kufuor visited India to participate in the India–Africa Forum Summit held in New Delhi. In March 2010, Vice President John Mahama accompanied by Minister of Trade and Industry Hanna Tetteh visited India to participate in the CII-EXIM Bank Conclave. In November 2014, Vice President Kwesi Bekoe Amissah-Arthur along with Minister of State for Private Sector Development Rashid Pelpuo visited India to attend the World Economic Forum Summit in New Delhi. He also met Vice President Mohammad Hamid Ansari and participated in an interactive session with the captains of Indian industry. Visits by GoI to Ghana have been confined to the Ministerial level. Indian prime ministers and presidents have not visited Ghana since Prime Minister Narasimha Rao's visit to Ghana in 1995. There have been regular ministerial and official visits from India. In 2006, Minister of State for External Affairs, Anand Sharma, led a high-level delegation to Ghana and visited Ghana again in 2007. In September 2010, Anand Sharma, Minister of Commerce and Industry, visited Ghana, leading the delegation for the India–Ghana CEOs Round Table. In 2012, he led a high-level official and business delegation to Ghana (MEA, GoI, 2015).

Just as India's diplomatic relations and engagement with Ghana is weaker relative to China's diplomatic engagement with Ghana, India's economic ties and commercial relations with Ghana are also substantially weaker relative to China's. In recent years, India–Ghana relations have been enriched by enhanced South–South co-operation efforts. Ghana was included as one of the nine West African countries under the GoI's TEAM 9 initiative launched in 2004. India has been participating in Ghana's development by providing assistance in setting up projects through the provision of LOCs and grants. Until June 2015, India extended LOCs amounting to US$228.73 million to Ghana for various developmental projects. In 2011, a MoU on GoI's financial and technical assistance of approximately US$860,000 to the India–Ghana Kofi Annan Centre for Excellence in IT was signed. GoI has also provided LoCs for various projects. For instance, US$21 million for a Fish Processing Plant at Elmina, US$35 million for the construction of the Komenda Sugar Factory in the Central Region of Ghana and US$24.5 million for sugarcane development and irrigation project. A MoU was signed on 6 July 2010 between the two countries for the setting up of a US$1.2 billion joint venture fertiliser project. According to Ghana Investment Promotion Centre, Indian companies have invested in more than 600 projects with total investment of US$998 million between September 1994 and September 2014, making India the second largest foreign investor country in Ghana in terms of number of projects. India was ranked ninth in terms of FDI in Ghana. There were 57 projects registered under Indian FDI in 2013 (MEA, GoI, 2015).

Although bilateral trade between India and Ghana has increased significantly in the new millennium, it is still substantially less than China's trade with Ghana. In 2003–4, total trade was US$212.8 million and increased to US$947.62 million in 2007–8 (The High Commission of Ghana in India, n.d.). It increased further from US$739.52 million in 2010–11 and in 2011–12 reached US$1.204 billion. In 2014–15, total bilateral trade was US$1.623 billion. India's imports from Ghana totalled US$1.257.6 billion and India's exports to Ghana amounted to US$680.39 (MEA, GoI, 2015).

India and China in the oil industry in Ghana

Both India and China expressed interest in acquiring oil blocks in the offshore Jubilee oilfields. Neither China nor India has acquired an oil block in Ghana. Ghana's NOC, the Ghana National Petroleum Corporation (GNPC) and CNOOC entered into a joint venture and placed an unsuccessful joint bid of US$5 billion for a 23.5 per cent stake in Dallas-based Kosmos Energy LLC's block in the Jubilee field and assets situated close by. ExxonMobil had expressed interest in the block and previously talked with Kosmos Energy. It was willing to pay US$4 billion but withdrew its offer after objections were raised by the government of Ghana. Moreover, Kosmos Energy believed that the offer of US$4 billion was undervalued because it estimated its worth at approximately US$6.75 billion. That is also the reason why it rejected the joint bid by CNOOC and GNPC (Sharma and Ordonez, 2010). Kosmos Energy did not sell its stake in the Jubilee field (Kosmos Energy, n.d.).

OVL also expressed an interest in acquiring Kosmos Energy's stake in the Jubilee oilfields. It wanted to enter into a joint venture with GNPC to bid for the stake. GNPC holds a 10 per cent stake in Jubilee oilfields. OVL was willing to match CNOOC's offer if it were to tie up with GNPC. However, GNPC decided to enter into a joint venture with CNOOC (Shrinate, 2009). GNPC preferred CNOOC over OVL because a loan of US$3 billion was provided for the development of the hydrocarbon sector by CDB, and in September 2010, the China EXIM Bank also provided a loan of US$10.4 billion for the development of infrastructure (Sharma and Ordonez, 2010).

Chad

Chad, a former French colony, is Africa's fifth largest nation. Although it is still under French influence, it has been trying to come out of it for years. It suffers from inadequate infrastructure and internal conflict. Since independence, Chad has been marred by violence and instability, arising primarily from tensions between the mainly Christian and animist south and predominantly Arab-Muslim north. President Deby has held office since 1990. He gained office for the fifth consecutive time in general elections held in April 2016. Several groups have taken up arms against the government and the situation has been further complicated by Sudanese incursions. President Deby survived coup attempts in 2006 and 2013. Chad is one of the most corrupt countries in the world. Since Exxon-Mobil opened the Kone oilfield in 2003, US$10 billion from oil exports has been spent on purchasing arms and making superficial changes to the capital. The income from oil exports has not been used to improve the livelihoods of the people. Even by West African standards, poverty is widespread in Chad and health and social conditions are below the regional average. Very few households in Chad have access to electricity (Hicks, 2015).

Oil industry in Chad

Conflict-ridden and conflict-prone Chad is a relatively new player in the oil industry in West Africa. According to Table 7.1 and Table 7.2, Chad has the maximum amount of oil reserves of 1.5 billion barrels in the eight countries in West Africa covered in this chapter. It ranks as the tenth-largest oil reserve holder among African countries. Chad came into prominence in 2003 when significant quantities of oil were produced. From 2003 to 2011, oil production had fluctuated in Chad. Oil production reached a peak in 2005 at 177 tbpd. Since then, production has declined significantly to reach 103 tbpd in 2014 with some years in which production has increased by very small amounts relative to the previous year. Almost all the oil is exported via the Chad–Cameroon pipeline (US EIA, 2013).

China in the oil industry in Chad

Since diplomatic ties resumed between China and Chad in 2006, relations between the two countries have enlarged and strengthened. China's development activities, especially the Rônier refinery project, epitomises the expanding relationship between the two. China gained ascendancy in Chad after N'Djamena rejected Chad's relations with the West by annulling the Chad–Cameroon pipeline project led by the World Bank. The hallmark of China–Chad relations will be epitomised by China's engagement in the oil industry in Chad despite the recent turbulence (Dittgen and Large, 2012).

CNPC is active in Chad. In December 2003, CNPC entered into a deal with Cliveden, a Swiss company, to purchase stake for the risk exploration of Block H (Table 7.3). The block constitutes the whole area or part of the area of seven depositional basins: Erdis, Doseo, Bongor, Chad Lake, Doba, Salamat and Madiago. In 2005, CNPC was able to prove the presence of three different groups of reservoirs: top, middle and bottom. CNPC was able to obtain 100 per cent equity on Block H in 2006. In the Bongor Basin of the block, it discovered Baobab and Ronier-1 and other new oil-bearing structures (CNPC, n.d.a).

Continuous exploration in the Mimosa and Ronier areas in the Bongor Basin in 2009 led to the finding of new reserves. Additionally, substantial advances were made in the exploration of Baobab and Prosopis. In Bongor Basin, CNPC made important discoveries. In 2010, a successful formation test was attained in Cassia N-1, a risk exploration well situated in the Naramay area of Block H. The well produced 1000 tonnes of oil per day. In Block H in Bongor Basin in Chad, a hydrocarbon play was discovered in 2011. In 2013, significant discoveries were made in the Bongo Basin leading to high-yield flows. Additionally, substantial advances were made in the exploration of Prosopis. In 2010, a successful formation test was attained in Cassia N-1 in the Naramay area of Block H. The well produced 1,000 tonnes of oil per day. In 2014, an oil reserve of 100 million tonnes was identified in the Bongor Basin (CNPC, n.d.a).

India in the oil industry in Chad: Indian oil companies did not bid for and have not acquired oil blocks in Chad.

Equatorial Guinea

Equatorial Guinea is characterised by widespread inequalities in income and wealth. It is a rich country of poor people and is a textbook case of the resource curse. It has the lowest HDI rank of all the countries in the world. According to the UN, only 50 per cent of the people have access to clean drinking water and IMR is extremely high. It is infested with nepotism and cronyism, and the oil money has been used by the rulers to increase their own wealth and expend on defence rather than on development projects for the populace (BBC, 2015b).

Since independence, Equatorial Guinea has not been well governed. Obiang Nguema seized power in a coup by executing his uncle in 1979. President Obiang has been in power for more than three decades and oil money has made his regime increasingly paranoid. Although Equatorial Guinea is a multiparty democracy, elections have generally been considered as a sham. Like his predecessor, President Obiang has arranged periodic crackdowns against the opposition and his regime is infamous for human right violations. The president ridicules Western notions of transparency. He opines that oil revenues are a state secret and how much money his government earns from oil is nobody's business. According to Transparency International, Equatorial Guinea is one of the 12 most corrupt countries in the world. A US Senate investigation in 2004 discovered that President Obiang's family was the recipient of large sums from US oil corporations like Hess and ExxonMobil. In 2008, Equatorial Guinea met the candidature of the Extractive Transparency Initiative (ETI)[1] but failed to meet an April 2010 deadline. In October 2014, President Obiang's son Teodorin, a minister in the government, was forced to relinquish more than US$30 million of assets in the United States. According to US authorities, stolen money was used to buy the assets (BBC, 2015b).

Oil industry in Equatorial Guinea

Equatorial Guinea is a substantial player in the oil industry in West Africa not only because of its oil reserves but also oil production. According to Table 7.1, oil reserves have increased from a paltry 0.0120 billion barrels in 2001 to 1.1 billion barrels in 2014. Table 7.2 illustrates that oil production has also increased substantially. It increased from 181 tbpd in 2000 to 375 tbpd in 2005. Since then it has declined and reached 269 tbpd in 2014, although there was a marginal increase in oil production in 2012 relative to 2011. It is expected that the recent operationalisation of the Aseng oil and gas-condensate field may revive the production of liquids in 2012. The Zafaro field has been the mainstay of Equatorial Guinea's hydrocarbon industry. However, recently, its present output has decreased by almost 50 per cent. Consequently, Equatorial Guinea has been eager to commence production from new assets (US EIA, 2015b).

According to the IMF, Equatorial Guinea's economy is heavily reliant on its oil and natural gas industry, which accounted for almost 95 per cent of its GDP and 99 per cent of its export earnings in 2011. Equatorial Guinea's declining oil and natural gas production, coupled with a decline in global oil prices, is adversely affecting its economy, and has resulted in lower, and at times negative, GDP growth. Emphasis on the oil and natural gas industries has also led to the lack of development in non-hydrocarbon sectors (US EIA, 2015b).

The Zafiro field, operated by ExxonMobil, is the country's most prolific oilfield, but its current output has more than halved since its peak, leaving the country eager to start production from new fields. Despite the recent start of the Alen field, which produces natural gas condensate, new production is not enough to offset natural declines. Equatorial Guinea does not have any refining capacity. The country consumed 2.1 tbpd of petroleum in 2014, all of which was imported. The government has announced plans to open a 20 tbpd refinery in Mbini, but the project has been slow to develop. NOC, GEPetrol, manages the government's interest in PSAs and joint ventures with IOCs. GEPetrol is also responsible for marketing, oil licensing and hydrocarbon policy implementation. The largest foreign investors in Equatorial Guinea are US companies, particularly ExxonMobil, Hess, Marathon and Noble Energy, although European and Chinese companies have started to play a role in Equatorial Guinea's hydrocarbon sector (US EIA, 2015b).

China in the oil industry in Equatorial Guinea

Chinese SOEs CNPC and CNOOC have an oil block each in Equatorial Guinea (Table 7.3). In 2006, CNPC moved into Equatorial Guinea and its major oil asset is in Block M. The block has acreage of 2703 square kilometres and is situated in the Rio Muni Basin. CNPC and Fruitex signed a Simplified Purchase Agreement for the block on 15 May 2006 and on 20 July 2006, the government of Equatorial Guinea signed an E&P agreement for the block. Santa Isabel

Petroleum Company (SIPCL), a subsidiary of CNPC, is the operator and has a 70 per cent share in Block M (CNPC, n.d.a). In 2011, SIPCL withdrew from Block M and Fruitex resumed as operator (Ministry of Mines, Industry and Energy, Republic of Guinea, n.d.). Thus, SIPCL has relinquished the block.

In 2006, CNOOC Africa Limited, a subsidiary of CNOOC, GEPetrol and the Ministry of Mines, Industry and Energy in Equatorial Guinea, were signatories for a PSC for Block S (Rigzone, 2006). The block is situated offshore in south Equatorial Guinea and has acreage of nearly 2,287 square kilometres. It is in water depths ranging from 30–1500 metres (Rigzone, 2006). In 2015, the ministry announced that CNOOC has discovered hydrocarbons in the S-3 exploration well on Block S in the Cretaceous Santonian interval. CNOOC is evaluating the results to assess commercial viability (African Energy, 2015).

India in the oil industry in Equatorial Guinea: Indian oil companies did not bid for and have not acquired oil blocks in Equatorial Guinea.

Cameroon

Cameroon came into existence in 1961 when two former colonies from France and Britain were unified. It is one of the most diverse countries in Africa with more than 200 different linguistic groups. Cameroon has struggled to come to terms with a multiparty system from a one-party system since it was created with severe restrictions on the freedom of expression. President Biya has been in power since 1982. He is one of Africa's most entrenched presidents. It was during his tenure that a move was made towards multiparty democracy due to local discontent. In April 2008, a controversial amendment to the constitution by Cameroon's parliament enabled President Biya to run for a third term of office in 2011. He won another seven-year term amidst allegations of widespread fraud by opposition parties (BBC, 2016a). Cameroon has favourable agricultural conditions and modest oil resources. This has provided Cameroon with one of the best endowed primary commodity economies in the continent. It has one of the highest literacy rates in Africa. It faces many serious problems like stagnant PCY, inequalities in income, a bureaucratic civil service, endemic corruption and a climate which is unfavourable for business (CIA, n.d.).

Oil industry in Cameroon

Table 7.1 and Table 7.2 illustrate that Cameroon is a relatively small player in the oil industry in West Africa. The oil reserves in Cameroon are marginal, amounting to only 0.2 billion barrels in 2014. This puts Cameroon in the middle of the table out of the eight countries. Proven oil reserves in Cameroon have fallen from 0.40 billion barrels in 2001 to 0.20 billion barrels in 2014. Oil production was 77 tbpd in 2001. This declined substantially until 2004. It rose again in 2005 and peaked at 87 tbpd in 2006. Since then, production has declined steadily. However, production increased significantly in 2014.

China in the oil industry in Cameroon

Sinopec has operations in Cameroon (Table 7.3). It operates in Cameroon through its subsidiary AP. In May 2011, SIPC, through its wholly-owned subsidiary AP, entered into an acquisition agreement with Shell, under which SIPC would take over all of the 80 per cent stake of Pecton Cameroon Company (PCC) held by Shell and Cameroon National Petroleum Corporation would hold the remaining 20 per cent. PCC holds 12 E&P offshore blocks in the Rio Del Rey Basin and operates two of them. Subsequently, PCC was rechristened as Addax Petroleum Cameroon Company LLC (APCC). APCC has stakes in one oil block in Ngosso, five oil blocks in Lokele, six oil blocks in Rio Del Rey and one in Dissoni (AP, 2013).

The government of Cameroon and AP signed a contract in December 2002 for the Ngoso licence area. AP has a 60 per cent share in the block and is the operator. The Ngosso licence area is situated offshore west of Cameroon in the hydrocarbon rich Rio del Rey Basin. It is adjacent to the shore in deep water of approximately eight metres. It has acreage of 117,100 acres or 474 square kilometres. There has been no exploration activity in the block in the last two decades although it contains a number of hydrocarbon discoveries. In 2008, there was a discovery in Ngosso licence but stand-alone development was not deemed commercially viable. In the Ikoro licence area, oil has not been produced to date (AP, 2016b).

Lokele consists of five oil blocks. AP has a 40 per cent share in Mokoko Abana, a 25 per cent stake in South Asoma, a 32.25 per cent share in Lipenja, and a 27.6 per cent stake in Erong North. Lokele has 11 existing oil-producing platforms. Mokoko Abana produces 18 tbpd and AP's share is 6 tbpd. Rio Del Rey has six oil blocks. AP has a 24.5 per cent share in Bavo-Asoma, Ekoundou Marine, Kole Marine, Boa-Bakassi and Kita Edem, and 25 per cent in Sandy Gas. Rio Del Rey produces approximately 70 tbpd and AP's share is 18 tbpd. Dissoni has one oil block. AP has a 37.5 per cent share in Dissoni North. Oil has not been produced to date. APCC signed an agreement with the government in Cameroon in 2002 and acquired a 60 per cent stake in Ngosso and a 100 per cent share in Ikoro licence areas (AP, 2016b).

India in the oil industry in Cameroon: Indian oil companies did not bid for and have not acquired oil blocks in Cameroon.

Mauritania

Mauritania is one of the poorest countries in the world. It is relying on revenue from its offshore oil and gas reserves for future prosperity. It is expected that millions of barrels of oil will be produced by the Chinguetti and Tiof fields. President Taya's 20 years of authoritarian rule were ended by a coup in 2005. A move towards democracy was initiated in March 2007 but it was short-lived. There were also coups in 2008 and 2009. Mohamed Ould Abdelaziz, the initiator of the coup in 2008, became the president in 2009. In 2014, he gained another five-year term in the general election. The election was boycotted by most of the opposition parties. Slavery still exists in Mauritania. The country is severely affected by Islamic terrorism and is viewed by the West as a key ally in the fight against terrorism. Mauritania was suspended from the African Peer Review Mechanism (APRM) following the coup d'état in August 2008 and also from the AU. Mauritania was not officially readmitted to the APRM although its suspension from the AU was revoked in 2009. However, during the 14th Summit of the Committee of Participating Heads of State and Government (known as the APR Forum) held in Addis Ababa, Ethiopia in January 2011, Mauritania was readmitted into the APRM (BBC, 2015c).

Oil industry in Mauritania

Mauritania is a very small and new player in the oil industry in West Africa. According to Table 7.1 and Table 7.2, its oil reserves and oil production are marginal. It has oil reserves of approximately 0.10 billion barrels in 2014. Oil production started in 2006 and has declined since then. It produced 30 tbpd in 2006 and production declined every year to 6 tbpd in 2014.

China in the oil industry in Mauritania

CNPC no longer has operations in Mauritania. It used to operate in the E&P activities and also provided oilfield services. In 2004, CNPC operated four exploration projects in Mauritania (Table 7.3). CNPC and the Ministry of Industry and Mining of Mauritania entered into an agreement for the E&P of four oil blocks: Block 12, Block Ta13, Block 20 and Block Ta21. The exploration period was set to be nine years, together with a 25-year development period. Blocks Ta21 and Ta13, situated in the Taoudeni Basin, have acreage of 15,292.45 square kilometres and 19,778.5 square kilometres respectively. Block 20 and Block 12 are situated in the coastal basin and the latter has acreage of 10,339.05 square kilometres. CNPC has conducted comprehensive geological research, formation testing and drilling in the four blocks (CNPC, n.d.c).

In 2005, the Mauritanian National Assembly approved PSCs for Blocks 12, Ta21 and Ta13. In the same year, CNPC entered into a 'farm out' agreement with Brimax Petroleum Limited and became the operator of Block 20. The 'farm out' agreement was ratified by the Mauritanian National Assembly on 18 August 2005. In the first exploration well, Heron-1 assigned in Block 20, oil and gas show was observed in 2006. Oilfield services like well drilling, well logging and geophysical prospecting were also provided by CNPC (CNPC, n.d.c). CNPC has relinquished all four oil blocks because they were not commercially viable.

India in the oil industry in Mauritania: Indian oil companies did not bid for and have not acquired oil blocks in Mauritania.

Niger

Niger gained independence from France in 1960. Since independence, it has experienced numerous coups and political instability. Tuareg insurgency emerged in 2007 in north Niger after one decade. Niger is one of the poorest and also one of the most undeveloped countries in the world. It has the lowest literacy rates in the world. It has a basic healthcare system and disease is widespread. Niger is ranked bottom in the annual UNDP report in 2014. However, it is rich in natural resources like minerals (uranium and gold) and oil. Although slavery was banned in 2003, according to anti-slavery organisations, thousands of people still live in slavery. The best route to economic power in Niger is through political office. In 2009, using unconstitutional measures in an attempt to extend his political office, President Tandja suspended a democratic constitution that limited the president's term in office. The polity in Niger aggrandise their personal wealth to the detriment of the people by receiving kick-backs and misusing revenues from lucrative mining contracts. Niger typifies 'islands of prosperity surrounded by seas of poverty'. Moreover, political parties also receive support from countries which have invested heavily in Niger due to strategic reasons. For instance, France, which receives uranium imports from Niger for its nuclear energy, has a vested interest in Niger. President Tandja was ousted in a coup in 2010. Polls to restore civilian rule were held in January 2011. In 2011, Mahamadou Issoufou was sworn in as the president and was re-elected in 2016 in an election boycotted by supporters of his opponent, Hama Amadou (BBC, 2015d).

Oil industry in Niger

Niger is a very small player and a newcomer in the oil industry in West Africa. According to Table 7.1 and Table 7.2, its oil reserves and oil production are marginal. It started producing oil in 2011 and produced 6.7 tbpd. Since then, oil production has almost tripled to 20 tbpd (Table 7.2). In Table 7.1, '0 billion barrels' implies that oil reserves are in single-digit million barrels or even less. It has paltry oil reserves of 0.2 billion barrels.

China in the oil industry in Niger

In 2003, CNPC started its oil and gas operations in Niger. It operates in upstream and downstream sectors. It operates a refinery in a joint venture. It is the operator in two E&P ventures and also provides oilfield services. CNPC owns and operates two E&P blocks: Tenere and Bilma (Table 7.3). CNPC signed a deal with the government in Niger on 23 November 2003 for E&P licence for the two blocks. In Block Tilma, CNPC has a 100 per cent ownership. In Block Tenere, CNPC has an 80 per cent share and TG World of Canada has a 20 per cent stake. Block Tenere and Block Bilma are situated in the vicinity of the Sahara desert and cover an area of approximately 71,155 square kilometres and 60,884 square kilometres respectively. In 2005, integrated studies and 2D seismic data acquisition were initiated in Block Tenere. The first exploration well, Saha-1 in Block Tenere, was spudded in October 2006. In 2012, progressive exploration led to new discoveries in Block Bilma (CNPC, n.d.d).

Niger and CNPC were signatory to combined upstream and downstream ventures in Agadem block in June 2008. This involved the construction of a refinery as a joint venture, constructing and operating a long-distance pipeline and exploration and development of oilfields. According to the terms of the contract, within a three-year period, CNPC was to finish the first stage of construction and make the refinery, pipeline and oilfield operational. In 2009, substantial progress was made in the exploration of the Agadem project. In the Dibella site, situated east of Agadem, formation test resulted in high yield flow from three exploration wells in 2010. In 2013, significant discoveries were made from risk exploration in the Fana-Koulele reservoir in the Agadem Block (CNPC, n.d.d). Agadem project has estimated reserves of 320 million barrels (Burgis, 2010).

India in the oil industry in Niger: Indian oil companies did not bid for and have not acquired oil blocks in Niger.

Liberia

Liberia is the oldest republic in Africa. However, it became infamous in the last decade of the twentieth century for its protracted and devastating civil war and the role played by President Charles Taylor in the civil war in Sierra Leone. First polls were undertaken in 2005 after the end of the civil war and Ellen Johnson-Sirleaf came to power. She is Africa's first female president. Charles Taylor, the former president of Liberia, was convicted of war crimes in Sierra Leone by the International Criminal Court. The infrastructure in Liberia is in ruins. President Johnson-Sirleaf has been praised for upholding the rule of law and stability in Liberia. She has also managed to obtain forgiveness from international lenders for Liberia's huge national debt. This has enabled Liberia to be financially stable and has also made the country much more attractive to foreign investors. However, she has also been criticised for being ineffective against corruption and for favouring nepotism. At the fourteenth ARF Forum held in Addis Ababa, Ethiopia, in 2011, Liberia voluntary acceded to the APRM. Johnson-Sirleaf was re-elected as president in 2011 in elections with a low turnout and boycotted by Winston Tubman, her main rival. She was awarded the Nobel Peace Prize in 2011 for securing peace, strengthening the position of women and promoting social and economic development (BBC, 2016b).

Oil industry in Liberia

Like Niger, Liberia is a very small player, and a newcomer in the oil industry in West Africa. According to Table 7.1 and Table 7.2, oil reserves and oil production in Liberia is relatively small.

China in the oil industry in Liberia

In 2012, PetroChina International Investment Company, a subsidiary of PetroChina, clinched a deal with Africa Petroleum for a strategic investment in some of its oil and gas exploration activities in West Africa. The deal gives PetroChina an exclusive period to decide if it wants to invest in nearly 20 per cent in Block LB-09. It also gives PetroChina the right to invest up to 20 per cent in at least one exploration block in Sierra Leone, Liberia, Côte d'Ivoire, Senegal and the Gambia (*Energy Business Review*, 2012). The option PetroChina had to pick up a stake in Liberia from African Petroleum Corp. has expired. African Petroleum stated that it is continuing to negotiate with the Chinese firm in good faith (Petroleum Africa, 2012). PetroChina has decided not to renew the deal and has no stake in the oil block (McLellan, 2015).

India in the oil industry in Liberia: Indian oil companies did not bid for and have not acquired oil blocks in Liberia.

Conclusion

The chapter discussed the presence of Indian and Chinese oil companies in eight countries in West Africa and the number of oil blocks that each country has in those countries. The case studies and pattern matching in eight countries demonstrates that both China and India are represented by SOEs in the upstream sector of the oil industries in West African countries. This is due to the difference in the political economy of the two countries. It also highlights that Chinese oil companies are preferred as partners to enter into joint ventures to develop oil blocks relative to Indian companies, as in Ghana. Moreover, Chinese oil companies bid for more oil blocks relative to India in Gabon and acquired more oil blocks relative to Indian oil companies. Additionally, Chinese oil companies had bid for and acquired oil blocks in seven countries while India acquired an oil block in only one country, that is Gabon. Chinese oil companies also have better quality oil blocks, that is the oil blocks are commercially viable relative to the oil block acquired by Indian oil companies. This is explained by the independent variable or the difference in their economic and political power which allows China to establish closer, better and stronger diplomatic relations with oil-producing countries in West Africa. This conforms to the hypothesis that NCR can explain the difference and the relative success and failure of India and China to mobilise oil in the oil industry in countries in West Africa.

Note

1 ETI is an international project intended to promote openness about government oil revenues.

References

African Energy (2015). Equatorial Guinea: Block S Discovery for CNOOC. Online. 17 April. Available at: http://archive.crossborderinformation.com/Article/Equatorial+Guinea+Block+S+discovery+for+CNOOC.aspx?date=20150417 (accessed 21 April 2016).

Alves, Ana Cristina (2008). China and Gabon: A Growing Resource Partnership. Online. China in Africa Project Report No 4, Johannesburg: South African Instituite for International Affairs. Available at: www.saiia.org.za/research-reports/267-china-africa-policy-report-no-4-2008/file (accessed 15 June 2015).

Amanor, Samuel (2013). Chinese Money for Ghana's Natural Resources: The Real Cost. Online. *Modern Ghana*, 12 August. Available at: www.modernghana.com/news/484254/chinese-money-for-ghanas-natural-resources-the-real-cost.html (accessed 21 April 2016).

AP (2013). Operations: Gabon. Online. Available at: www.addaxpetroleum.com/operations/cameroon (accessed 11 January 2013).

AP (2016a). Operations: Gabon. Online. Available at: www.addaxpetroleum.com/operations/gabon (accessed 20 April 2016).

AP (2016b). Operations: Cameroon. Online. Available at: www.addaxpetroleum.com/operations/cameroon (accessed 20 April 2016).

BBC (2015a). Gabon Country Profile. Online. Available at: www.bbc.com/news/world-africa-13376333 (accessed 3 May 2016).

BBC (2015b). Equatorial Guinea Country Profile. Online. Available at: www.bbc.com/news/world-africa-13317175 (accessed 3 May 2016).

BBC (2015c). Mauritania Country Profile. Online. Available at: www.bbc.com/news/world-africa-13881985 (accessed 3 May 2016).

BBC (2015d). Niger Country Profile. Online. Available at: www.bbc.com/news/world-africa-13943663 (accessed 3 May 2016).

BBC (2016a). Cameroon Country Profile. Online. Available at: www.bbc.com/news/world-africa-13146029 (accessed 3 May 2016).

BBC (2016b). Liberia Country Profile. Online. Available at: www.bbc.com/news/world-africa-13729504 (accessed 3 May 2016).

Burgis, Tom (2010). China to Expand Niger Operations. Online. *Financial Times*, 20 May. Available at: www.ft.com/intl/cms/s/0/3eac7388-5d17-11df-8373-00144feab49a.html (accessed 23 April 2016).

Cabestan, Jean-Pierre (2014). Gabon-China Relations: Towards a More Cautious Partnership. *African East-Asian Affairs*, 2, pp. 6–37.

China.org.cn (2004). China–Gabon Relations. Online. 18 Janaury Available at: www.china.org.cn/english/features/phfnt/85075.htm (accessed 3 May 2016).

CIA (Central Intelligence Agency) (n.d.). The World Factbook: Cameroon. Online. Available at: www.cia.gov/library/publications/the-world-factbook/geos/cm.html (accessed 12 January 2016).

CNPC (n.d.a). CNPC in Chad. Online. Available at: www.cnpc.com.cn/en/Chad/country_index.shtml (accessed 22 April 2016).

CNPC (n.d.b). CNPC in Equatorial Guinea. Online. Available at: www.cnpc.com.cn/en/Chad/country_index.shtml (accessed 22 April 2016).

CNPC (n.d.c). CNPC in Mauritania. Online. Available at: www.cnpc.com.cn/en/cnpc-worldwide/mauritania/ (accessed 12 January 2016).

CNPC (n.d.d). CNPC in Niger. Online. Available at: www.cnpc.com.cn/en/Niger/country_index.shtml (accessed 22 April 2016).

Consulate General of PRC in Johannesburg (2016). Yu Zhengsheng Pays Official Goodwill Visit to Ghana. Online. 19 April. Available at: http://johannesburg.chineseconsulate.org/eng/xwdt/zgyw/t1357309.htm (accessed 3 May 2016).

Dittgen, Romain (2011). To Bélinga or not to Bélinga? China's Evolving Engagement in Gabon's Mining Sector. Online. Occasional Paper No 98 South African Institute of International Affairs. Available at: www.org.za/occasional-papers/to-belinga-or-not-to-belinga-china-s-evolving-engagement-in-gabon-s-mining-sector.html (accessed 30 December 2012).

Dittgen, Romain and Large, Daniel (2012). China's Growing Involvement in Chad: Escaping Enclosure? Online. Occasional Paper 116 South African Institute for Internatonal Affairs. Available at: www.saiia.org.za/occasional-papers/chinas-growing-involvement-in-chad-escaping-enclosure (accessed 15 April 2016).

Embassy of the PRC in Ghana (n.d.). Introduction of China-Ghana Relations. Online. Available at: http://gh.chineseembassy.org/eng/zjgx/zzwl/t177920.htm (accessed 22 April 2016).

Energy Business Review (2012). African Petroleum Enters Investment Deal with PetroChina. Online. Exploration and Development News. 18 July. Available at: http://explorationanddevelopment.energy-business-review.com/news/african-petroleum-enters-investment-deal-with-petrochina-180712 (accessed 15 August 2012).

Gabon Embassy, India (n.d.). India-Gabon Ties: Warm and Friendly. Online. Available at: www.gabonembassynewdelhi.com/index.php?option=com_content&view=article&id=26&lang=en (accessed 15 January 2016).

Government of Ghana (n.d.). Ghana–China Trade is More than $5 Billion. Online. Available at: www.ghana.gov.gh/index.php/media-center/news/1579-ghana-china-trade-is-more-than-5-billion (accessed 21 April 2016).

Gyamerah, Emmanuel Adu (2014). China's Investments in Ghana Increase. *Business News*, 22 March. Available at: http://business.peacefmonline.com/pages/news/201403/193742.php (accessed 21 April 2016).

Gyasi Jnr, Stephen (2014). Ghana and China, Friends for Life? (Part 1). Online. *New African*, 14 April. Available at: http://newafricanmagazine.com/ghana-and-china-friends-for-life-2/ (accessed 21 April 2016).

Hicks, Celeste (2015). Is Chad Managing to Beat the "Oil Curse"? Online. *Guardian*, 14 April. Available at: www.theguardian.com/global-development/2015/apr/14/chad-oil-curse-africa-challenge-negative-impact (accessed 22 April 2016).

Idun-Arkhurst, Isaac (2008). Ghana's Relations with China. Online. Report No. 3 South African Institute of International Affairs. Available at: www.saiia.org.za/research-reports/china-in-africa-policy-reports.html (accessed 11 January 2016).

Kosmos Energy (n.d.). Operations: Jubilee Field. Online. Available at: www.kosmosenergy.com/operations-ghana-jubilee-field.php (accessed 22 April 2016).

Larry, Dasmani (2015). Ghana–China Trade Surpasses $5 Billion. Online. *The Africa Report*, 3 July. Available at: www.theafricareport.com/West-Africa/ghanas-china-trade-surpasses-5-billion.html (accessed 21 April 2016).

McLellan, Amy (2015). African Petroleum Lands Funding as it Advances Farm-Out Talks for its "Big Company Portfolio". Online. 24 February. Available at: http://masterinvestor.co.uk/uncategorized/african-petroleum-lands-funding-as-it-advances-farm-out-talks-for-its-big-company-portfolio/ (accessed 23 April 2016).

MEA, GoI (2013). India–Republic of Gabon Relations. Online. May. Available at: http://mea.gov.in/Portal/ForeignRelation/Republic_of_Gabon.pdf (accessed 15 April 2016).

MEA, GoI (2015). India–Ghana Relations. Online. June. Available at: www.iafs.in/down-loads/Ghana.pdf (accessed 15 April 2016).

Ministry of Foreign Affairs, PRC (n.d.). China and Gabon. Online. Available at: www.fmprc. gov.cn/mfa_eng/wjb_663304/zzjg_663340/fzs_663828/gjlb_663832/2989_663994/ (accessed 1 May 2016).

Ministry of Foreign Affairs, PRC (2016). Yu Zhengsheng Pays Official Goodwill Visit to Gabon. Online. Available at: www.fmprc.gov.cn/mfa_eng/zxxx_662805/t1355715. shtml (accessed 1 May 2016).

Ministry of Mines, Industry and Energy, Republic of Equatorial Guinea (n.d.). Exploration History. Online. Available at: www.equatorialoil.com/Petroleum_Exploration_ history.html (accessed 22 April 2016).

Natural Resource Governance Institute (2015). An Analysis of Ghana's 2005 Oil Revenue Performance: Testing the Model. Online. 17 December. Available at: www.resource-governance.org/blog/analysis-ghanas-2015-oil-revenue-performance-testing-model (accesed 20 April 2016).

OIL (n.d.). JVs/PSCs/Alliances: Gabon. Online. Available at: www.oil-india.com/JVs. aspx (accessed 20 April 2016).

OIL (2015). Chairman's Address. Online. Available at: www.oil-india.com/CAddress. aspx (accessed 20 April 2016).

Petlane, Tsoeu (2009). Gabonese Election Aftermath Confirms Worrying Trends in African Politics. Online. Diplomatic Pouch: South African Institute of International Affairs. 10 December. Available at: www.saiia.org/za/diplomatic-pouch/gabonese-election-aftermath-confirms-worrying-trends-in-african-politics.html (accessed 15 January 2013).

Petroleum Africa (2012). PetroChina's MoU for Liberia Stake Expires. Online. 4 September. Available at: www.petroleumafrica.com/en/newsarticle.php?NewsID=14175 (accessed 12 January 2016).

Petzet, Alan (2012). Gabon: CNOOC Joins Shell on Two Offshore Blocks. Online. *Oil and Gas Journal*, 25 July. Available at: www.ogj.com/articles/2012/07/gabon-cnooc-joins-shell-on-two-offshore-blocks.html (accessed 20 April 2016).

Rigzone (2006). CNOOC Inks Deal for Block S in Equatorial Guinea. Online. 17 February. Available at: www.rigzone.com/news/oil_gas/a/29548/CNOOC_Inks_Deal_for_ Block_S_in_Equatorial_Guinea (accessed 21 April 2016).

Sharma, Rakesh and Ordonez, Isabel (2010). Bid for Ghana Oil Field Rebuffed: Kosmos Energy of U.S. Rejects $5 Billion Offer From CNOOC and GNPC. Online. 2 November. Available at: http://online.wsj.com/article/SB10001424052748704141104575588111375730330.html (accessed 6 January 2016).

Shell (2014). Shell Announces Gabon Deep-Water Gas Discovery. Online. 22 October. Available at: www.shell.com/media/news-and-media-releases/2014/shell-announces-gabon-deep-water-gas-discovery.html (accessed 20 April 2016).

Shrinate, Supriya (2009). Ghana Blocks in ONGC Crosshairs: OVL in Talks with GNPC to Bid for Kosmos Energy's Stake In Giant Offshore Jubilee Field. Online. *The Economic Times*, 9 November. Available at: http://epaper.timesofindia.com/Default/ Layout/Includes/ET/ArtWin.asp?From=Archive&Source=Page&Skin=ET&BaseHref= ETD%2F2009%2F11%2F19&ViewMode=HTML&PageLabel=16&EntityId=Ar0160 1&AppName=1 (accessed 25 April 2016).

Singh, Sushant K. (2007). India and West Africa: A Burgeoning Relationship. Online. Africa Programme/Asia programme briefing paper Chatham House. London: Royal Institute of International Affairs, pp. 1–16. Available at: www.chathamhouse.org/pub-lications/papers/view/108471 (acessed 2 April 2012).

The High Commission of Ghana in India (n.d.). Trade and Investment. Online. Available at: www.ghana-mission.co.in/hcg.php?id=trade1 (accessed 16 April 2016).

The Hindu (2012). Oil India Starts Drilling Operation in Gabon, Africa. Online. 1 November. Available at: www.thehindubusinessline.com/companies/oil-india-ltd-commences-drilling-operation-in-gabon-africa/article4054855.ece?ref=wl_opinion (accessed 20 April 2016).

US EIA (2012). Gabon: Country Analysis Brief. Online. Available at: www.eia.gov/beta/international/analysis.cfm?iso=GAB (accessed 15 January 2013).

US EIA (2013). Chad: Country Analysis Brief. Online. Available at: www.eia.gov/beta/international/analysis.cfm?iso=TCD (accessed 21 April 2016).

US EIA (2014). Gabon: Country Analysis Brief. Online. Available at: www.eia.gov/beta/international/analysis.cfm?iso=GAB (accessed 3 May 2016).

US EIA (2015a). Ghana: Country Analysis Brief. Online. Available at: www.eia.gov/beta/international/analysis.cfm?iso=GHA (accessed 21 April 2016).

US EIA (2015b). Equatorial Guinea: Country Analysis Brief. Online. Available at: www.eia.gov/beta/international/analysis.cfm?iso=GNQ (accessed 21 April 2016).

Part V
Conclusion

Conclusion

The concluding chapter revisits the core argument and research question before discussing the theoretical and empirical contribution to the existing literature on NCR and India and China in the oil industry in West Africa. This is followed by a discussion on the findings. It provides a short analysis of competition between Indian and Chinese oil companies to mobilise oil in the oil industry in West Africa, distilling some insights and offering some policy implications moving forward. The study concludes by offering some direction for future research.

Debate and the research question revisited

India and China, the 'Asian Drivers', have turned to Africa to diversify their sources of energy and meet their energy security due to increasing instability in the Middle East. Although oil production in India and China increased during 2001–14, consumption has increased at a much faster pace. The shortfall in production had led to an increase in oil imports in both India and China. Africa, especially West Africa, has regained significance since the beginning of the new millennium because of oil and natural gas reserves, the quality of the reserves and commercial advantages that it offers to foreign oil companies.

Tomes of literature have been written on China's engagement with Africa. Recently, there has been a growth in literature in India's interaction in Africa but it still lags behind the literature on China and Africa. India and China have also been compared and contrasted extensively in Africa from different prisms. India's and China's engagement has also been discussed in West Africa and they have also been compared and contrasted in West Africa. Scholars have also undertaken research on India's and China's engagement in the oil industry in West Africa. Although there is an ever increasing literature comparing India and China in Africa, few scholars have tried to provide an answer for the difference in the interaction of India and China in Africa. Even fewer have tried to elucidate the divergence in India's and China's interaction in West Africa in general and the oil industry in particular.

The aim of the study is to provide an explanation for the differences and the relative success and failure of how India and China mobilise oil externally in the oil industry in West Africa. The study uses NCR as the theoretical construct to explain the above phenomena. Thus the research question is 'Can NCR explain the differences and relative success and failure of China and India in their respective efforts to mobilise oil in the oil industry in West Africa?' With respect to India's and China's interaction in the oil industry in West Africa, the driving force is economic relations, to mobilise oil, a key resource, and foreign policy has been driven by economic imperatives. In other words, economic motives are driving political and diplomatic factors. There are three differences in the interaction of India and China in the oil industry in West Africa. First, Chinese oil companies operate in more countries in West Africa relative to Indian oil companies. Second, Chinese oil companies outbid Indian oil companies in acquiring oil contracts when they directly bid for the same oil block, have more and better quality oil blocks relative to their Indian counterparts and are preferred as partners by African oil companies and other oil companies. Third, China is represented by SOEs in the oil industry in West Africa whereas India is represented by SOEs and/or private enterprises.

Theoretical contribution

NCR was coined by Gideon Rose in 1998. It is a theoretical paradigm which explains foreign policy outcomes of states. It provides a theoretically-inspired framework which explains the foreign policies of a state over different periods in time or states facing comparable external limitations. It incorporates elements of both neorealism and classical realism. It has three variables: the independent or the systemic variable, the intervening or the domestic variable and the dependent variable or the foreign policy outcome. The independent variable signifies the difference in the relative power in an anarchical international system. Neoclassical realists aver that the scale and aspiration of a country's foreign policy is driven by its relative material power capabilities in an anarchical international system. Thus, as the relative material power capabilities of a country rises in an anarchical international system, its aims, objectives and the ability to achieve the objectives will also rise. They further argue such power capabilities have an indirect and convoluted influence on foreign policy. This is because pressures exerted by the system must be interpreted through intervening variables at the unit level. Proponents of NCR state that it incorporates first, second and third image variables. It has been debated recently whether NCR should be considered as a theory of foreign policy. Lobell *et al.* (2009) posit that, contingent on (1) clarity of threats and (2) clear information on policy responses, NCR not only explains foreign policy puzzles but is also a theory of foreign policy. They add that NCR is 'theories of foreign policy' because there is no single theory of foreign policy. The study adheres to this classification.

NCR is in an embryonic stage. It is gaining momentum as a theoretical paradigm and literature on NCR has been expanding since the 1990s. Although tomes of literature have been written on political economy and international political economy, there is a paucity of literature on NCR and political economy. In recent years, literature on NCR and political economy has increased where the latter has been used either directly or indirectly. However, much of the initial literature has focused on either structural outcomes like polarity or balancing or deviations from neorealism like under-balancing.

While Mastanduno *et al.* (1989) were not postulating NCR, they emphasised the role of political economy as a domestic variable to achieve international objectives. However, they did not emphasise that domestic variable should be used as an intervening variable while retaining the primacy of the systemic variable. Moreover, they discuss internal mobilisation of resources by a state to increase its wealth and power. This study uses NCR as a theoretical construct to discuss external mobilisation. The study explains the differences and the relative success and failure of how India and China mobilise oil externally in the oil industry in West Africa. The rationale is regime survival as well as augmenting both absolute and relative power.

This study uses political economy as an intervening variable in NCR. The study asserts that the independent variable or the difference in the relative power of India and China explains why Chinese NOCs have operations in more countries in West Africa relative to Indian oil companies, Chinese NOCs are able to outbid Indian oil companies in acquiring oil contracts when they directly bid for the same oil block, and/or Chinese NOCs have more and better quality oil blocks relative to their Indian counterparts and/or Chinese NOCs are preferred as partners by IOCs and African oil companies. The difference in the political economy or the intervening variable explains why China is represented by SOEs in the oil industry in West Africa whereas India is represented by SOEs and/or private enterprises. Thus the study provides a theoretical contribution to the existing literature on NCR in general and NCR and political economy in particular, and extends NCR's research design because in the past NCR as a theoretical construct has been employed by scholars to explain either structural outcomes like polarity or balancing, or deviations from neorealism like under-balancing or lack of polarity.

Empirical contribution

Scholars have observed that China relative to India has greater outreach in Africa and Chinese SOEs outbid Indian SOEs and/or private enterprises because Indian enterprises do not have deep pockets relative to the Chinese SOEs. However, there is no comprehensive study of acquisition of oil blocks by Indian and Chinese oil companies in West Africa as a region. Additionally, there is no comprehensive study of Indian oil companies in Nigeria apart from OVL. This study makes an empirical contribution to the existing literature because it examines the acquisition of oil blocks by Chinese and Indian oil companies in 11 West African countries and provides an explanation for why Chinese NOCs operate in the oil industry in more countries in West Africa relative to India. The study is also path-breaking because it explains how and why three Indian oil companies, Essar Oil, OIL and IOCL, have acquired oil blocks in Nigeria which has not been discussed in the existing literature. Additionally, it provides a more comprehensive explanation for the ability of the Chinese oil companies to outbid their Indian counterparts. It examines not only the bids that Chinese and Indian oil corporations place for the oil blocks and the quality of the oil blocks acquired by the oil companies from the two countries, but also tries to explain the reason why they are able to place those bids. It examines the internal rate of return or the rate of return on capital/investment, rate of interest on loans and the ease of availability of loans or finance, the difference in the level of technology and ability to acquire technology, project management skills, risk aversion and the difference in the economic, political and diplomatic support received by the Chinese and Indian oil companies from their respective governments. It also mentions the reasons why the Chinese NOCs are preferred as partners by African oil companies and IOCs and examines the relative commercial viability or quality of the oil blocks acquired by Indian and Chinese oil companies. Additionally, it is the most updated study and examines the time period from 2001 to 2015.

Findings

The study adopted case study pattern matching in 11 countries in West Africa to verify the hypothesis. Since the empirical pattern in the 11 countries coincides with the predicted pattern, the result helps to strengthen the internal validity of the hypothesis. The study discovered that in all 11 countries, China is represented by SOEs in the upstream sector of the oil industry. CNOOC, CNPC and Sinopec are SOEs. On the other hand, India is represented either by SOEs like OVL, IOCL and OIL and/or private enterprise Essar Oil in the oil industry in West African countries. Thus, the difference in the political economy of India and China or the intervening variable explains one of the three differences.

The study established that Chinese oil companies have operations in the upstream sector of the oil industry in more countries in West Africa relative to Indian oil companies. Chinese NOCs bid for and acquired oil blocks in 11 countries in West Africa whereas Indian oil companies bid for oil blocks in only three countries – Angola, Nigeria and JDZ, and Gabon acquired oil blocks only in Gabon, Nigeria and JDZ. Chinese NOCs have bid for and acquired more oil blocks than Indian oil companies in the 11 countries in Africa. Chinese oil companies bid for 63 oil blocks and acquired 61 oil blocks. Indian oil companies bid for 11 oil blocks but acquired only seven oil blocks.

In Angola, Sinopec bid for five oil blocks and acquired five oil blocks. Four out of the five blocks are producing oil. OVL bid for six oil blocks but did not acquire any oil blocks. Chinese NOCs outbid OVL in five of the six oil blocks that the latter bid for. In Cameroon, AP, a subsidiary of Sinopec, bid for and acquired 12 oil blocks. AP gets 6 tbpd from Mokoko Abana in Lokele and 7.3 tbpd from Rio Del Rey. In Equatorial Guinea, both CNPC and CNOOC bid for one oil block and acquired the oil block. CNPC has relinquished the oil block. CNOOC has discovered hydrocarbons in Block S. In Liberia, PetroChina, a subsidiary of CNPC, bid for one block and acquired the block. Later it relinquished the block. In Niger, CNPC bid for and acquired three oil blocks. CNPC made discoveries in block Bilma and significant discoveries were also made in Agadem block. In Mauritania, CNPC bid for four oil blocks and acquired the oil blocks respectively. The blocks were relinquished by CNPC because they were not commercially viable.

In Nigeria, the three Chinese NOCs bid for 24 oil blocks and acquired 23 oil blocks. Sinopec operates in Nigeria through its subsidiaries SIPC and AP. Sinopec and its subsidiaries bid for 12 oil blocks and acquired 11 blocks. Most of the blocks produce oil and are commercially viable. Sinopec and its subsidiary AP also bid for four oil blocks and acquired the oil blocks. However, the blocks were relinquished because they were not commercially viable. CNPC bid for four oil blocks and acquired the oil blocks. Oil block OPL 298 produces oil. Oil production from other blocks cannot be ascertained. CNOOC and its subsidiary Nexen operate in Nigeria. CNOOC bid for two oil blocks and acquired the oil blocks. OML 130 has oil reserves of 600 million barrels. Oil production from OPL 229 cannot be ascertained. Nexen bid for two oil blocks and acquired the oil blocks. Both oil blocks have proven and probable reserves of 500 million barrels. CNOOC and AP, a subsidiary of Sinopec, operate in Gabon. CNOOC bid for two oil blocks and acquired the oil blocks. A gas discovery has been made in block BCD10. AP bid for seven oil blocks and acquired the seven blocks. Majority of the oil blocks are producing oil and are commercially viable.

In Nigeria, Indian oil companies bid for five oil blocks and acquired six blocks. OMEL bid for two oil blocks and acquired three oil blocks. The two oil blocks bid for have been relinquished. The acquisition of the third oil block is subjudice in Nigeria's Supreme Court. OVL bid for two oil blocks but failed to acquire the oil blocks. The joint venture between OIL and IOCL acquired an oil block. It was offered to the two Indian NOCs by the Nigerian government, i.e. they did not bid for the oil block. The block is estimated to have oil or gas reserves in excess of 200 million barrels of oil equivalent. Essar Oil did not bid for OPL 226. The Nigerian government offered it to Essar. IT can be inferred that the block has low commercial prospects. OVL also bid for and acquired a block in Nigeria–São Tomé and Principe, JDZ. The block was relinquished because it was not commercially viable. Indian NOCs, IOCL and OIL, did not bid for the oil block in Gabon. The Gabonese government offered the block to the joint venture between the two NOCs through a 'farming-in' offer. Although oil has been discovered in Block Shakthi, prospects of commercial viability are low.

The study discovered that Chinese NOCs are preferred as partners relative to Indian oil companies in West Africa. In Ghana, although there was no direct competition for oil blocks in the Jubilee oilfields between Indian and Chinese oil companies, GNPC, the Ghana NOC, preferred CNOOC as a partner over OVL for a 23.5 per cent stake in Ghana's Jubilee oilfield. Although GoI also provides subsidies and diplomatic and political support to the NOCs in their quest for oil, Indian NOCs are unable to match the Chinese NOCs. This is because China being a permanent member of the UNSC has greater political clout relative to India. China is able to provide more subsidies and financial help to Chinese

NOCs because it has greater financial muscle compared to India. China's economic power and UNSC membership with veto power enables China to establish better diplomatic relations with countries in West Africa, which also helps the Chinese NOCs to the detriment of Indian oil companies. This also makes the Chinese NOCs preferred partners for African NOCs and other oil companies. Thus the difference in the economic and political power of India and China in an anarchical international system or the independent variable is able to explain the remaining two differences.

The study established that Chinese oil companies are less risk averse relative to Indian oil companies in Nigeria and Gabon. In Nigeria, Indian and Chinese oil companies did not bid for the same oil blocks except for OML 130/OPL 246. OVL bid the maximum amount of US$485 million to win the auction for OML 130/OPL 246. However, the Indian government did not allow the planned acquisition to be completed because it deemed the acquisition extremely risky due to the political risk involved. China, on the other hand, did not consider the investment as risky and acquired the block after the Indian government directed OVL to withdraw. Henceforth, China won the auction for OML 130/OPL 246.

The study also established that Chinese NOCs operate at a lower rate of return on investment or the internal rate of return compared to Indian oil companies. Whereas the Chinese NOCs operate at margins of 3–4 per cent in general, the Indian NOCs operate at a margin of 10–11 per cent. Indian private enterprises like Essar Oil and RIL operate at margins close to 18–20 per cent. The IOCs operate at margins of 15 per cent. The Indian NOCs and the private sector oil companies did not have the financial resources to acquire Nexen, a Canadian oil company acquired by CNOOC for US$15.1 billion. They also would not have been able to bid US$7.2 billion to acquire AP, a subsidiary of Sinopec. Because of their financial muscle, Chinese bidding does not make commercial sense. Chinese NOCs are not concerned about the rate of return. They are more concerned about the size of the asset. Although Indian and Chinese oil companies possess similar level of technological capabilities, Chinese NOCs are able to pay more to acquire technology relative to Indian oil companies because of their extremely deep pockets. Moreover, Chinese NOCs have greater access to technology because they are operators in more oil blocks relative to Indian oil companies.

Chinese NOCs also have access to cheap capital. Indian oil companies have no access to cheap capital. In India, NOCs are asked to borrow at the market prevailing interest rate which is substantially higher than the rate at which the Chinese NOCs can borrow money from the state-owned Chinese banks. SOEs in China can obtain loans from the Chinese state-owned banks at a rate of 0–1 per cent. Moreover, the state banks in China lend to the NOCs because they know that the NOCs will not default on the loan. Indian oil companies can also access finance in the international market at 3–4 per cent. However, fluctuations in the currency pose a major problem. Additionally, this would require collateral from the parent company or banks and/or sovereign guarantees which Indian oil companies including the flagship Indian NOC ONGC/OVL cannot provide.

Consequently, it is difficult for Indian oil companies to operate at a margin of 3–4 per cent unlike the Chinese NOCs.

As far as the oil industry in West Africa is concerned, the signature bonus and royalty payments in some of the West African countries are too high especially in Angola, high even for the IOCs. However, China can afford to pay the high amount as evidenced by the world record breaking bids by Chinese NOCs for oil blocks in Angola. It can be inferred that India learned from the Angolan debacle and did not enter into direct bidding for oil blocks in other countries in West Africa vis-à-vis China.

The study also discovered that the European and US oil companies are still the dominant players in the oil industry in Nigeria, Angola, Gabon, Equatorial Guinea and other countries in West Africa. The former have better quality oil blocks, more oil blocks and greater acreage despite the recent rapid strides made the Chinese NOCs. Thus Chinese NOCs lag behind Western IOCs globally and in West Africa.

China has been successful in forging diplomatic, political, economic and business ties with nascent democracies, authoritarian regimes and dictatorships in conflict prone and conflict ridden countries in West Africa. The United States and the European countries and Western oil companies have provided support to authoritarian regimes and dictators in these countries and have little moral ground to chastise China in this regard. India, like China, also follows a policy of non-intervention. The non-intervention policy is the cornerstone of the foreign policies of these two countries. However, despite the same principle, India has not been as successful as China in forging diplomatic, political, economic and business ties with countries in West Africa. Despite following similar policies employed by China, India has so far escaped criticism because of three reasons. First, unlike China, India is a democracy. Second, India is in China's slipstream in West Africa and in Africa. India's trade and investment in West Africa and Africa is significantly less relative to China. Third, India, unlike China, is not perceived as a peer competitor by the United States and the West.

The deep and substantial inroads made by Chinese corporations have meant that despite its long-standing ties with Africa, India has taken a backseat to China in Africa and in West Africa. This perception was strengthened when Indian and other international oil companies lost to Chinese NOCs in their quest for oil wherein the latter linked business with diplomacy to acquire oil assets in Africa and West Africa. The Chinese strategy of establishing joint ventures that extend beyond the oil sector to infrastructure development, construction and others has served Chinese companies well. In many respects, India's strategies for accessing Africa's (and West Africa's) upstream oil sector are similar to those of China, offering economic and infrastructure assistance in exchange for access to oil.

On the diplomatic front too, India lags behind China. Indian strategic thinker C. Raja Mohan avers that, "Africa has generally been neglected in India's foreign policy over the decades" and "West Africa was virtually a blind spot" (cited in Singh, 2007: 10–11). According to C. Raja Mohan, there is a consensus among West African countries that in the past "India got in touch with West

African chancelleries only when it needed votes in international fora" (cited in Singh, 2007: 11). Ambassador Ghanshyam, former Ambassador to Angola and Indian High Commissioner to Nigeria, GoI, states that it is true Africa and West Africa have been neglected.

> India needs to focus more on Africa. This requires a change in mindset in New Delhi. Some of the best diplomats and officers in the Ministry of External Affairs, GoI do not want to go to Africa. People who implement foreign policy in India are arrogant. They look down upon people from other countries. They should realise that there are different kinds of people: some who are better than us, some who similar to us in capabilities and some who are less capable than us.
>
> (Interview, Appendix A)

In West Africa, India is represented by only five small missions responsible for all the countries in the region – in Ghana (Niger, Togo, Burkina Faso and Central African Republic), Senegal (Mauritania, Mali, Cape Verde, the Gambia and Guinea Bissau), Nigeria (Chad, Equatorial Guinea, Benin, Cameroon and Sao Tomé and Príncipe), Côte d'Ivoire (Sierra Leone, Liberia and Guinea) and Angola. Regarding embassies, Ambassador Ghanshyam states that "Physical presence is important. Ninety per cent of the job is to be physically present in the country to avail a business opportunity or strike a deal" (Interview Ambassador Ghanshyam, Appendix A). "Until 2003, in the Ministry of External Affairs, Government of India, there was only one joint secretary to oversee the entire African continent. The Ministry of External Affairs is extremely understaffed and the least understaffed all the ministries in Government of India" (Interview Ambassador Ghanshyam, Appendix A).

Since the beginning of the new century, India's African focus has changed. There has been a reawakening in India regarding improving diplomatic relations with countries in West Africa. India now has three joint secretaries representing three Africa divisions: Southern and East Africa, West Asia and North Africa, and Central and West Africa. The restructuring in the MEA has been undertaken with the aim of substantially increasing India's presence and role in Africa. This has helped in sharpening India's focus and an improvement in assessing factors such as economic performance, political stability and energy issues. However, the recent Indian diplomatic surge in West Africa pales in significance relative to China's diplomacy in Africa. China is represented in all the countries in West Africa and 49 out of 53 countries in Africa. It has more representatives in its Foreign Ministry dealing with Africa or on issues related to Africa compared to India. China's permanent membership of the UNSC and its new-found economic muscle gives China a substantial leverage relative to India in West Africa. The change in policy has paid in delivering dividends. India's bilateral trade with Africa and countries in West Africa has increased. India's investments in Africa and in West Africa have also increased. However, compared to China's trade and investment with Africa and West Africa, India is a long way behind and is trying to catch up to China.

India's energy linkages with West Africa are still in their formative years and the presence of other developed countries such as the United States, Italy, the UK, France, the Netherlands and developing countries such as China in West Africa's energy market in the future is a reality that India has to contend with. India and China are locked in a competitive quest for energy resources in West Africa. India's trade and investment in West Africa (and in Africa) is substantial but dwarfed by China's trade with West Africa. Therefore, the fact that India and China both have energy needs that compel them to turn increasingly to energy imports and that China is far superior to India in terms of its political and financial capabilities and diplomatic and economic ties with West Africa has meant that the two countries (especially India) have had to contend with each other more and more.

Policy implications and recommendations

As discussed in Chapters 3 and 4, and as evidenced in Chapters 5, 6 and 7, the asymmetry in power is in China's favour vis-à-vis India. Under these circumstances, what should India do to improve its competitive edge with respect to China not only in acquiring oil blocks in countries in West Africa but also in Africa, and globally, and in other sectors?

As evidenced, China has a multi-pronged strategy of economic, political and diplomatic engagement with countries in West Africa. To meet China's challenge, first and foremost, India has to put its house in order and undertake a second round of economic reforms. Economic reforms are necessary to remove the fetters on economic growth in order for the economy to grow at 8–9 per cent per annum for at least two more decades. This will increase India's economic power and commensurate political clout in the international system. This will also allow GoI to not only increase the purses of the Indian NOCs but would also be able to leverage greater political and diplomatic support for the Indian SOEs across different sectors. The formation of a SWF on lines similar to the CIC or other SWFs will increase the financial resources at the disposal of the NOCs.

In addition to providing more resources to the Indian NOCs and other SOEs, the Indian government should also provide more autonomy in decision-making to these corporations. This will facilitate faster decision-making and cut bureaucratic red tape. However, accountability should not be compromised for the sake of greater autonomy in decision-making. Additionally, the Indian NOCs and other SOEs should enhance their technical and managerial competence and be at par with IOCs and other major corporations across the globe.

In the short term, India should have a more focused strategy. Like China, it should have a multi-pronged strategy. India should increase its political and diplomatic relations with countries in West Africa. Rather than indulging in niche diplomacy, India should engage with all the countries in West Africa and improve and strengthen diplomatic relations to provide more leverage to Indian NOCs, other SOEs and also the private enterprises. According to Ambassador

Kishan Rana, Honorary Fellow, Institute of Chinese Studies and Ambassador Shu Zhan, Senior Research Fellow, Centre for African Studies, Zhejiang Normal University, China has approximately 5000–7000 diplomatic personnel in its foreign service whereas India has approximately 500–700 personnel (Interviews, Appendix A). Like China, the number of officers in the Indian Foreign Service cadre focusing on countries in West Africa and in Africa should increase substantially. India should open high commissions, embassies and consulates in all the countries in West Africa to enhance its diplomatic and political relations with these countries. There should be more state-to-state visits of heads of state, senior ministers and trade delegations, among others. Thus, India needs to revamp the MEA and recruit, train and commission more officials and diplomats to countries in West Africa and Africa. However, Ambassador Ghanshyam points to a downside regarding increasing the number of personnel in the MEA:

> There is increasing need to co-ordinate with the actors in all the different ministries. It is a Herculean task. If the numbers in Ministry of External Affairs increase, the task will be even more difficult. Thus it is important to improve co-ordination. Additionally, what needs to be done is to give a set of instructions and space for officers for innovation. If you are not able to give them space, then you are not going to get the best out of the officers.
>
> (Interview, Appendix A)

India should use its historical relations with African countries and goodwill that these countries have for India. India should present an alternative model of development to countries in West Africa, especially countries which are fledgling democracies and countries which are in a transition phase. India should highlight its soft power by providing infrastructure, dams, electricity, schools and medicines to mention a few. Unlike China, it should play a role in human capital formation by providing education, training and vocational courses aimed at generating employable skills catering for the domestic economy of the countries concerned.

India should also have a coherent policy to meet its energy insecurity. It should have a coherent policy to acquire energy assets abroad and should employ oil diplomacy as a tool to acquire assets abroad. According to Mani Shankar Aiyar, former Minister of Oil and Gas, GoI:

> India has genuine resources constraints and there are also genuine concerns about the security of these investments. I am deeply convinced about the cultivation of political dimension to external oil policy. In other words, the deployment of oil diplomacy would give us very satisfactory results. Obviously, the main player would continue to be the commercial element. The Government of India in its totality is unpersuaded that this is the way to go about energy security. I think they believe we should be tapping the market. Getting involved in a risky situation abroad which would not add to the quality of oil and gas we get into India but might get us into serious trouble

is not welcome. We were completely outbid by China because we never operationalised the cooperative mechanisms that I had in mind. I do not think that the external policy on oil has been fully determined and carried on from generation to generation. I was effecting an innovation, which while it looked interesting and exciting during that period (which was ten years ago), has not caught the imagination of these in charge subsequently.

(Interview, Appendix A)

Avenues for future research

Political economy and neoclassical realism: a positive science

The study illustrated that political economy can be used as a domestic or intervening variable to clarify the divergence and the relative success and failure of how India and China mobilise oil externally in the oil industry in West Africa. The study compared and contrasted the political economy of India and China in Chapter 3. As discussed in Chapter 1, according to Karl Marx, capitalism and communism are two systems at the opposite end of the spectrum with a combination of the two in varying degrees and forms lying between the two. For simplicity, the study mentioned three different political and economic systems: capitalism where the means of production are in the hands of private enterprise as in the United States, socialism/communism where the ownership of the means of production are in the hands of the state, as in China before the economic reforms in 1979, and a mixed economy system where the state controls the means of production in the key and strategic industries and the consumer goods industry is in the hands of private enterprise, as in India.

The manner in which political economy is incorporated in NCR in the study highlights an extremely important aspect of political economy. Political economy as the intervening variable in NCR highlights the positivistic element or aspect of political economy. First and second image variables that have been incorporated in NCR like ideas, role of the leaders and their beliefs, perceptions, the nature of the executive and the legislature, among others, change and have changed. For instance, beliefs, ideas, values, morals, perceptions may change with time. Similarly, leaders change and a change in leadership may or may not usher change in policy.

Since there are three kinds of economic systems, albeit varying in their degree of capitalism, socialism/communism and mixed economy, these three systems will remain the same (until and unless there is a revolution and the old economic system is replaced by a new one as in Russia in 1917 or in China after 1949 or there is large-scale nationalisation of private sector enterprises by the government or the new government which comes to power). For instance, during the time period 1978–2015, China has been characterised by the same system and there is a wide consensus that it will remain so in the foreseeable future although the contribution of the state sector and the private sector to the GDP might change. Similarly, India has been characterised by the same system, as a mixed economy from 1947 to 2015, and will be so in the foreseeable future although the contribution of the private sector and the state sector to the GDP might change. In India, the private sector contributes more to the total GDP relative to the state sector for the first time in 2010–11. The same can be said about the United States. The United States has had a capitalist economic system for a long period of time. What is evident is that although the relative power capabilities of the countries have changed over time, their economic systems have remained the same although there have been some changes in the composition of the systems. For instance, reforms introduced in India led to privatisation, disinvestment, deregulation, and liberalisation and globalisation which removed the fetters for the private sector. This did not imply that the SOEs ceased to exist. Similarly, in China attempts have been made to increase privatisation and improve the functioning of the SOEs but this does not mean that the SOEs have and will become extinct. On the contrary, there is a wide consensus that SOEs are going to play an even greater role in the Chinese economy in the near future. Unlike the boiling point of water, which is different at the poles and at the equator, the economic system remains the same, although its constituent parts may undergo variations over time.

This implies that political economy can be used as an intervening variable not only to elucidate the difference in the ability of India and China to mobilise resources externally, as in the oil sector in this study, but also in other sectors especially the key and strategic sectors such as mining, heavy manufacturing, international aviation, iron and steel, chemicals and defence among others. Not only India and China can be compared but because of the difference in the economic systems, political economy can be used as an intervening variable to compare and contrast the mobilisation of resources by India and the United States, China and the United States, and other countries, as long as the economic systems determined by their political economies are different. For instance, the manner in which the United States and China mobilise resources externally is different and it can be explained by the difference in their political economy. In the oil industry in West Africa, the United States is represented by private enterprises like Chevron Texaco, ExxonMobil, ConocoPhillips and others. China, as discussed in the study, is represented by SOEs. This is due to the difference in the political economy of the two countries. In a similar vein, comparisons can be made between France, India and China, or the UK, India and China, or the UK and China and other countries. Thus, political economy as an intervening variable gives rise to a multitude of combinations to compare and contrast the manner in which countries mobilise resources externally in different sectors in the economy. This can be done not only between and among countries but also in different sectors. Hence, political economy as an intervening variable in NCR can be used to explain the mobilisation of resources externally by a country or countries and extends NCR's research design.

Empirical research

The study compares and contrasts the ability of India and China to mobilise resources externally in West Africa in the oil industry using political economy as the intervening variable in NCR. Further research should be undertaken to compare and contrast India and China in the oil industry not only in West Africa but also in other countries and regions in Africa: North Africa, East Africa, Central Africa and Southern Africa. The research can and should be extended to compare and contrast India and China in other countries and parts of the world like Latin America, North America, Central Asia, the Persian Gulf, Southeast Asia and other regions and continents.

This study examines competition for a key and scarce resource, oil, between India and China. Research should be undertaken to show sectors in which India and China have co-operated to mobilise key and scarce resources like oil, metals and minerals, chemicals, etc. For instance, India and China co-operated in the upstream oil sector in Sudan. Furthermore, the study highlights the fact that Chinese oil companies outbid Indian oil companies when they compete directly, as in Angola, or are the preferred partners for other oil companies, as in Ghana and other countries in West Africa. Research should be undertaken to find cases and explain the reasons for Indian oil companies outbidding Chinese oil companies, as in Libya. Research should examine what factors enabled India to mobilise resource externally in the oil sector in Libya? Was it a domestic factor in Libya and what was that factor? That is to say that the agency is in the hands of either a first or second image variable in Libya. What was the enabling factor for India and/or what was the debilitating factor for China? This gives rise to a comparative case study analysis of India and China in Angola on the one hand and India and China in Libya on the other.

As discussed above, political economy can be used as an intervening variable in NCR to compare and contrast different countries in different sectors. Thus, further research should be undertaken with or without using NCR to compare and contrast and to highlight cases where two or more countries compete and co-operate in the same sector or different sectors. This creates a goldmine of comparative case study analysis of different countries and if NCR is used, it extends its research design.

Neoclassical realism and foreign policy analysis

As discussed in Chapter 1, NCR is 'theories of foreign policy' and it explains the foreign policy outcomes of states. Recently there has been a focus on explaining the foreign policy outcomes of MPs like Canada, SPs like South Korea, major powers like Germany, India, China, Russia and the global hegemon, the United States. NCR is gaining steam in explaining foreign policies of all types of powers. FPA literature as a part of IR has a lot in common with NCR. Both aim to explain the foreign policy outcomes of states. Both NCR and FPA examine the first and second image variables. NCR employs the first and second image as the intervening variable while retaining the primacy of the independent variable or the third image. FPA also studies the systemic variable but does not state that the third image is more important then the first and second image. Another difference is that FPA employs the categorisation of states into GP, MP and SP to highlight the difference in the states behaviour, NCR employs the difference in the relative power of states in the anarchical international system. What is important for NCR is that one state has more or greater power than the other or vice versa. The categorisation of states is not important. Additionally, the categorisation of states gives rise to definitional dilemmas. As discussed in Chapter 1, the systemic variable limits the ambitions or goals and objectives of countries and the means to achieve the objectives. As the relative power of a state increases, the state will seek more influence abroad and vice-versa. This highlights the salience of the independent variable in NCR and distinguishes it from FPA.

FPA studies and employs first and second image variables such as the role of the leader, the beliefs, values and cognition of the leader, public opinion, role of media, bureaucratic politics, rational actor model, structure of the state especially the executive and the legislature and state–society relations and economic statecraft among others to explain foreign policy outcomes. Research must be undertaken to employ similar variables in NCR to explain foreign policy outcomes. Additionally, further research must be undertaken to bridge or amalgamate the existing gap between NCR and FPA. The differences in NCR and FPA should also be studied, especially with respect to rationality. FPA uses terms such as bounded rationality and satisficing. NCR conforms to the rationality assumption but it is qualified and contingent and referred as confined rationality (Juneau, 2010).

Neoclassical realism and postclassical realism

This variant of NCR shares a common ground with postclassical realism coined by Stephen Brooks (1997). According to Brooks, neorealism and postclassical realism have important similarities. A major difference between neorealism and postclassical realism is that while the former is a systemic and structural theory, the latter is only a systemic theory, i.e. it is not concerned with polarity. Moreover, neorealism is concerned with the possibility of conflict but postclassical realism is concerned with the probability of conflict. Due to growing disenchantment with neorealism, realists like Robert Jervis, Barry Buzan, Charles Glaser, Stephen Van Evera, Stephen Walt, Stephen Krasner, Robert Gilpin and William Wohlforth have pointed out the importance of technology, geography and international economic pressures to elucidate the divergences between neorealism and postclassical realism.[1]

Like postclassical realism, NCR also uses the systemic variable as the independent variable. Apart from works by some neoclassical realists discussed in Chapter 1, much of the focus of NCR is to use the systemic variable to explain foreign policy outcomes. Moreover, the manner in which political economy is incorporated in NCR in this study does not explain a structural outcome like polarity. Additionally, with respect to India and China in West Africa, economic imperatives are driving FP and diplomacy. Thus, this variant of NCR also utilises international political economy, i.e. there is fusion of IPE into NCR. It illustrates how SOEs become instruments of foreign policy or how diplomacy is conducted to achieve economic ends which are related to regime survival and/or augmenting absolute and/or relative power and/or security. Thus, further research should be undertaken to integrate material factors like technology, geography and international economic pressures pointed out by scholars above as the intervening variable into NCR.

Note

1 See Brooks (1997) for a detailed analysis of the differences and similarities between classical realism, neorealism and postclassical realism.

References

Brooks, Stephen (1997). Duelling Realisms. *International Organization*, 51 (3), pp. 445–477.

Juneau, Thomas (2010). Neoclassical Realist Strategic Analysis. In: Graduate Student Conference, European Consortium of Political Research. Online. Dublin, Ireland, 30 August–1 September 2010, pp. 1–28. Available at: www.ecprnet.eu/databases/conferences/papers/308.pdf (accessed 29 October 2011).

Lobell, Steven E., Ripsman, Norrin M. and Taliaferro, Jeffrey W. (eds) (2009). *Neoclassical Realism, the State, and Foreign Policy*. Cambridge: Cambridge University Press.

Mastanduno, Michael, Lake, David A. and Ikenberry, John G. (1989). Towards a Realist Theory of State Action. *International Studies Quarterly*, 33 (4), pp. 457–474.

Rose, Gideon (1998). Neoclassical Realism and Theories of Foreign Policy. *World Politics*, 51 (1), pp. 144–172.

Singh, Sushant K. (2007). Peacekeeping in Africa: A Global Strategy. *South African Journal of International Affairs*, 14 (2), pp. 71–85.

Epilogue

India and China are two of the oldest civilisations steeped in history, culture, traditions and values dating back more than 3000 years. They share numerous similarities and differences. The re-emerging Asian giants have an extremely important role to play in global affairs in the coming decades. They share similar concerns and have co-operated with each other in climate change, in their quest for a multipolar global order, fight against terrorism and provision of global public goods among others. They have also co-operated with each other in the oil industry in Iran, Sudan and Russia. They will also compete with each other in the energy realm as evidenced in Africa, Central Asia and other parts of the world. However, most significantly, competition between the two will be for influence and strategic space not only in Asia but also globally. This will give rise to tense rivalry. Due to Tibet and the border dispute, there exists a possibility of conflict between the two countries.

Since there is no guarantee that even a limited land war would not escalate, the naval, air and missile balance is always pertinent in how a clash might play out. This does not augur well not only for India and China but also for the Asia-Pacific and the entire world. The crucial lesson for India and China is that, like in all bilateral relations on the world stage, the main glue in India–China relations is trust and mutual respect to each other's concerns. How the Sino-Indian relationship pans out in the future will depend on a number of internal, bilateral, regional and global factors. The relations will continue to be marred by rivalry, distrust, conflict, insecurity, estrangement and containment. Both countries want to avoid conflict because their development programme will be affected and may derail their quest for superpower status.

Africa, long known as the 'Dark Continent', is the future engine of growth. It is in Africa that close to a billion people will become part of the middle class in the next 20–30 years, where millions of jobs will be created. Africa is the continent of hope. India and China ventured into Africa in the twenty-first century for new markets for goods and services, natural resources, especially oil, timber, metals and minerals, and for political and economic influence. African countries, especially those rich in natural resources such as oil and gas, timber, mineral and metals, experienced high levels of economic growth due to the rapid surge in demand for their natural resources from rapidly growing China and less so due to India.

Chinese SOEs, especially NOCs, have made deep and substantial inroads in various sectors of Africa due to China's economic, political and diplomatic influence. India has had to take a back seat in Africa despite its historical relations with the continent. The asymmetry in all facets of power tremendously favours China. In this context, it may be difficult for Indian corporations and oil companies to compete with China in direct competitive bidding. However, China and China's economy are evolving. There is a concerted attempt by the Chinese government to reform the SOEs (including NOCs), to make them more efficient and competitive globally. There is movement towards making the SOEs operate on market principles. The three powerful Chinese NOCs have learnt from their mistakes in Angola and other countries. The deals in Angola and other countries have not resulted in good return on investment. There is a realisation in the government and the NOCs that the policies and actions need to change. After 2014, the NOCs are more concerned about the rate of return and not only about the size of the asset. The SASAC, CIC, CDB and EXIM Bank are no longer closely related to NOCs. The banks are becoming commercial and driven by market principles. They are no longer development banks. CDB is a development bank and now it also runs on market principles. Thus, there is movement towards being driven by market principles although the SOEs will still be bailed out by the government if they incur losses. Additionally, in the first decade of the twenty-first century, the Chinese government was able to provide a package deal and co-ordinate the functions of SOEs. However, in recent years, the government's influence has decreased. China has also learnt from its policy of acquiring equity oil.

The question that arises is will Indian oil companies be able to acquire oil blocks in Angola and Nigeria and other parts of Africa? It is too early to say whether there will be a change in China's strategy in Angola, Nigeria and other parts of Africa and the world. It is not easy for China to change its policy due to vested interests in the SOEs, especially the powerful and influential NOCs. The fact that China does not have an oil and gas or energy ministry bears testimony to the power and influence of the three NOCs. If China continues with its previous policy, it would be highly unlikely that Indian oil companies will be able to compete with Chinese NOCs in acquiring oil blocks.

It might be argued that the slowing down of China's economy may offer a silver lining to India in the oil sector in Angola and Nigeria, especially Angola. According to the Chinese government, the 'new normal' in China is going to be 6.5 per cent. However, some economists aver that even 5.5–6.0 per cent growth is also acceptable in very near future. This implies that China's thirst for oil may decline in the near future. On the other hand, the Indian economy is expected to keep growing at a minimum of 7 per cent per annum for at least a decade. This implies an increase in demand for oil imports given that oil production is not increasing at a commensurate rate to match demand. Additionally, oil reserves are also declining in India due to the lack of good quality or high yield oilfields. This provides India with an opportunity to increase imports from Angola and Nigeria and invest in the oil industry of the two countries. However, it will still be difficult for India to replace China in Angola. Amidst a weak global economy, India is the fastest growing major economy in the world. Growth will become stronger in India. Eventually India will become the size China is today. Then India will have the ability to replace Chinese growth. But India cannot be an engine of growth now. India can be an engine of growth in the future. India is one-fourth to one-fifth China's size. So even if India overtakes China in terms of GDP growth rates, the magnitude of the effect will be far smaller for a long time to come. Additionally, India's demand for oil is way lower as compared to China. It will take another decade for India to become a major player and driver of the global price of oil and it will take at least 10–15 years before India will be able to match China's import of oil. Thus, *ceteris paribus*, it is difficult to foresee a change in the oil equation between India and China in Africa and other parts of the world before 2025 or even 2030.

In light of the above, a second edition of the book is highly unlikely in the near future. As the Indian economy grows, its thirst for natural resources, especially oil and gas, will increase at a rapid rate. India's engagement with Africa and the oil industry in Africa will also keep increasing. A meta-comparative analysis of India and China in the upstream oil industry in all the countries in Africa – now and in future – is a task I leave for others.

The book employs NCR as the theoretical construct. Despite gaining steam since the beginning of the new millennium, NCR is still developing. A debate existed between scholars whether NCR is a natural extension of neorealism or it explains foreign policy muddles or is a framework or a theory of foreign policy or theories of foreign policy. The debate on whether it explains foreign policy muddles or is a natural extension of neorealism is more or less settled. The debate now is whether NCR is a framework or a theory of foreign policy or theories of foreign policy. NCR is a realist theory or theories of foreign policy or a realist framework to explain foreign policy outcomes. I believe that NCR is theories of foreign policy and this approach is used in the book. However, after 15–20 years, if and when a meta-analysis is done, then maybe we will have a better idea about NCR. FPA is much broader compared to NCR. FPA incorporates not only the realist school but also other schools from IR. This study has made an attempt to incorporate elements of FPA into NCR. I hope more research is undertaken to bridge the gap between NCR and FPA and to highlight the commonalities and differences between the two. Scholars from both fields have a lot to learn from and share with each other. I hope the twain do meet. The book has also made an attempt to fuse international political economy and NCR, and postclassical realism and NCR. Thus I have planted some seeds for future research with respect to IR in general and especially NCR. I also hope more research is undertaken on NCR and political economy, and NCR and postclassical realism.

Appendix A
List of interviews

Appendix A

	Name	Designation/job title	Institution	Date
1	Dr Keun-Wook Paik	Associate Fellow; Senior Research Fellow and Consultant to CNPC	Chatham House; Oxford Institute of Energy Services	29 August 2012
2	Dr Anupama Sen	Research Fellow	Oxford Institute of Energy Services	30 August 2012
3	Professor Srikanth Kondapalli	Centre for East Asian Studies, School of International Studies	Jawaharlal Nehru University	19 September 2012
4	Professor Ajay Dubey	Centre for African Studies, School of International Studies	Jawaharlal Nehru University	18 September 2012
5	Professor Madhu Bhalla	East Asian Studies	Delhi University	22 September 2012
6	Dr A.S. Yaruingam	Head, Department of African Studies	Delhi University	19 September 2012
7	Ambassador M.K. Rasgotra	Former Foreign Secretary, GoI and President, Centre for International Relations	ORF	18 September 2012
8	Ambassador H.H.S. Viswanathan	Distinguished Fellow	ORF	18 October 2012; 19 February 2013
9	Mr Ashok Dhar	Distinguished Fellow	ORF	3 October 2012
10	Mr Sunjoy Joshi	Director	ORF	26 March 2013
11	Mr Samir Saran	Senior Fellow and Vice President	ORF	22 February 2013
12	Ms Lydia Powell	Head, Centre for Resources Management	ORF	18 September 2012
13	Mr Nanda Unnikrishnan	Vice President, Centre for International Relations	ORF	18 September 2012
14	Mr Umashankar Sharma	Former Joint Secretary, Ministry of Petroleum and Natural Gas, GoI and General Manager	ORF	24 September 2012

continued

Appendix A Continued

	Name	Designation/job title	Institution	Date
15	Dr P.K. Ghosh	Senior Fellow	ORF	17 September 2012
16	Dr Satish Mishra	Senior Fellow	ORF	17 September 2012
17	Ambassador Kishan Rana	Honorary Fellow	Institute of Chinese Studies	22 September 2012
18	Dr Jabin T. Jacob	Assistant Director and Fellow	Institute of Chinese Studies	24 September 2012
19	Ambassador Rajiv Bhatia	Director General	Indian Council on World Affairs	25 September 2012
20	Dr G. Balachandran	Consulting Fellow	IDSA	28 September 2012
21	Dr Kalyan Raman	Research Fellow	IDSA	28 September 2012
22	Ms Ruchita Beri	Senior Research Associate	IDSA	5 October 2012
23	Ms Shebonti Ray Dadwal	Research Fellow	IDSA	26 September 2012
24	Major General (retired) Dipanakar Banerjee	Founding Director and Mentor	Institute for Peace and Conflict Studies	22 September 2012
26	Anonymous	–	OVL[a]	5 October 2012
27	Anonymous	–	OVL[b]	25 February 2013
28	Anonymous	–	IOCL[a]	26 September 2012
29	Anonymous	–	IOCL[b]	1 October 2012
30	Anonymous	–	OIL	1 October 2012
31	Anonymous	–	Essar Oil	25 October 2012
32	Anonymous	–	US IOC	28 December 2012
33	James Byrne	Reporter	Interfax	19 December 2012
34	Dr Bonnie Ayodele	Associate Prof, Department of Political Science	University of Ado Ekiti	28 January 2013
35	Dr Lu Bo	Deputy Director and Research Fellow, Department of World economy and Trade, Chinese Academy of International Trade and Economic Cooperation	Ministry of Commerce, PRC	9 March 2013
36	Professor Pang Zhongying	School of International Studies	Renmin University	28 January 2013
37	Professor He Maochun	Department of International Relations, and Director of the Research Centre for Economic Diplomacy Studies, Tsinghua University Institute of International Studies	Tsinghua University	8 March 2013

	Name	Position	Institution	Date
38	Professor Li Anshan	Director of Centre for African Studies, School of International Studies	Peking University	5 March 2013
39	Professor Zha Daojiong	Centre for International and Strategic Studies, School of International Studies	Peking University	13 March 2013
40	Professor Wang Li	Department of World History	Nankai University	7 March 2013
41	Professor Xiao Tang	Department of Political Science, and Director of African Studies Centre	China Foreign Affairs University	8 March 2013
42	Professor Xia Liping	Department of Diplomacy, and Deputy Dean	China Foreign Affairs University	5 March 2013
43	Dr Zhang Cuizhen	Associate Professor, School of International Economics	China Foreign Affairs University	8 March 2013
44	Dr Guo	Associate Professor, School of International Economics	China Foreign Affairs University	8 March 2013
45	Dr Liu Feitao	Deputy Director for the Division for American Studies and Associate Research Fellow	CIIS	5 March 2013
46	Dr Li Qingyan	Assistant Researcher, Department for International Strategic Studies	CIIS	5 March 2013
47	Dr Zhang Chun	Senior Fellow and Deputy Director Centre for West Asian and African Studies	SIIS	11 March 2013
48	Mr Zhu Ming	Institute for Global Governance Studies and Centre for West Asian and African Studies	SIIS	11 March 2013
49	Dr Li Wengang	Assistant Professor, Institute of West Asian and African Studies	Chinese Academy of Social Sciences	12 March 2013
50	Ambassador Shu Zhan	Senior Research Fellow Centres for African Studies	Zhejiang Normal University	6 August 2015
51	Annonymous	–	CNOOC	8 September 2015
52	Ambassador A.R. Ghanshyam	Former Ambassador to Angola and High Commissioner to Nigeria	–	8 March 2016
53	Mani Shankar Aiyar	Member Rajya Sabha and former Minister Oil and Gas, GoI	–	8 February 2016
54	Ambassdor Debnath Shaw	Fromer High Commissioner to Tanzania	–	4 March 2016

Bibliography

African Energy (2015). Equatorial Guinea: Block S Discovery for CNOOC. Online. 17 April. Available at: http://archive.crossborderinformation.com/Article/Equatorial+Guin ea+Block+S+discovery+for+CNOOC.aspx?date=20150417 (accessed 21 April 2016).

Aguilar, R. and Goldstein, A. (2009). The Chinisation of Africa: The Case of Angola. *World Economy*, 32 (11), pp. 1543–1562.

Alao, Abiodun (2010). Chinese Business Interests and Banking in Nigeria. Online. Policy Briefing 20 South African Institute of International Affairs. Available at: www.saiia. org.za/policy-briefings/chinese-business-interest-and-banking-in-nigeria.html (accessed 20 June 2015).

Alao, Abiodun (2011a). Nigeria and the BRICs: Diplomatic, Trade, Cultural and Military Relations. Online. Occasional Paper No 101 South African Institute of International Affairs. Available at: www.saiia.org.za/occasional-papers/nigeria.html (accessed 10 January 2013).

Alao, Abiodun (2011b). Nigeria and the Global Powers: Continuity and Change in Policy and Perceptions. Online. Occasional Paper No 96 South African Institute of International Affairs. Available at: www.saaia.org.za/occasional-papers/nigeria-and-the-global-powers-continuity-and-change-in-policy-and-perceptions (accessed 10 January 2013).

Alden, Chris (1997). Solving South Africa's Chinese Puzzle: Democratic Foreign Policy Making and the "Two Chinas" Question. *South African Journal of International Affairs*, 5 (2), pp. 80–95.

Alden, Chris (2007). *China in Africa*. London and New York: Zed Books.

Alden, Chris (2011). China in Africa: Challenges and Opportunities for Angola. Online. South African Institute of International Affairs, 21 February. Available at: www.saiia. org.za/events/china-in-africa-challenges-and-opportunities-for-angola (accessed 1 May 2016).

Alden, Chris and Hughes, Chris (2009). Harmony and Discord in China's Africa Strategy: Some Implications for Foreign Policy. *The China Quarterly*, 199, pp. 563–584.

Alden, Chris and Vieira, Marco (2005). The New Diplomacy of the South: South Africa, Brazil, India and Trilateralism. *Third World Quarterly*, 26 (7), pp. 1077–1095.

Alden, Chris, Large, Daniel and de Oliveira, Ricardo Soares (2008). *China Returns to Africa: A Rising Power and a Continent Embrace*. New York: Columbia University Press.

Alessi, Christopher and Hanson, Stephanie (2012). Expanding China-Africa Oil Ties. Online. Backgrounder, Council on Foreign Relations, 8 February. Available at: www. cfr.org/china/expanding-china-africa-oil-ties/p9557 (accessed 15 June 2015).

Aljazeera (2013). Nigerian Leader Secures $1.1bn on China Trip. Online. 11 July. Available at: www.aljazeera.com/news/africa/2013/07/2013710171651692540.html (accessed 30 April 2016).

Allison, G. (1971). *Essence of Decision: Explaining the Cuban Missile Crisis*. Boston: Little, Brown.

Alves, Ana Christina (2010). The Oil Factor in Sino-Angolan Relations at the Start of the 21st Century. Online. Occasional Paper No 55 South African Institute of International Affairs, February. Available at: www.saiia.org.za/occasional-papers/the-oil-factor-in-sino%E2%80%93angolan-relations-at-the-start-of-the-21st-century (accessed 15 November 2015).

Alves, Ana Cristina (2008). China and Gabon: A Growing Resource Partnership. Online. China in Africa Project Report No 4, Johannesburg: South African Institiute for International Affairs. Available at: www.saiia.org.za/research-reports/267-china-africa-policy-report-no-4-2008/file (accessed 15 June 2015).

Amanor, Samuel (2013). Chinese Money for Ghana's Natural Resources: The Real Cost. Online. *Modern Ghana*, 12 August. Available at: www.modernghana.com/news/484254/chinese-money-for-ghanas-natural-resources-the-real-cost.html (accessed 21 April 2016).

Ampiah, Kweku and Naidu, Sanusha (eds) (2008). *Crouching Tiger, Hidden Dragon? Africa and China*. Scottsville: University of KwaZulu-Natal Press.

ANGOP (Agencia Angola Press) (2015). Angola/India Cooperation Agreement in Pipeline – Foreign Minister. Online. 30 October Available at: www.portalangop.co.ao/angola/en_us/noticias/politica/2015/9/44/Angola-India-cooperation-agreement-pipeline-Foreign-minister,4f05f547-fe3a-4cb7-a525-25d61429391c.html (accessed 1 May 2016).

AP (2013). Operations: Gabon. Online. Available at: www.addaxpetroleum.com/operations/cameroon (accessed 11 January 2013).

AP (2016a). Nigeria: Operations. Online. Available at: www.addaxpetroleum.com/operations/nigeria (accessed 1 May 2016).

AP (2016b). Operations: Gabon. Online. Available at: www.addaxpetroleum.com/operations/gabon (accessed 20 April 2016).

AP (2016c). Operations: Cameroon. Online. Available at: www.addaxpetroleum.com/operations/cameroon (accessed 20 April 2016).

Ashley, Richard K. (1986). The Poverty of Neorealism. In: Robert O. Keohane, ed. *Neorealism and its Critics*. New York: Columbia University Press, pp. 255–300.

Barth, Aharon (2005). American Military Commitments in Europe: Power, Perceptions and Neoclassical Realism. PhD thesis. Georgetown University.

Basrur, Rajesh M. (2009). Theory for a Strategy: Emerging India in a Changing World. *South Asian Survey*, 16 (1), pp. 5–21.

BBC (2005). India Blocks West Africa Oil Deal. Online. 16 December. Available at: http://news.bbc.co.uk/1/hi/business/4534412.stm (accessed 1 May 2016).

BBC (2010). Chinese PM Wen Jiabao Begins Bumper Indian Trade Trip. Online. 15 December. Available at: www.bbc.co.uk/news/world-south-asia-11997221 (accessed 30 December 2012).

BBC (2012). UN Security Council – Profile. Online. 21 February. Available at: www.bbc.co.uk/news/world-11712448 (accessed 30 December 2012).

BBC (2015a). Angola Profile-Timeline. Online. 4 June. Available at: www.bbc.com/news/world-africa-13037271 (accessed 1 May 2016).

BBC (2015b). Gabon Country Profile. Online. Available at: www.bbc.com/news/world-africa-13376333 (accessed 3 May 2016).

BBC (2015c). Equatorial Guinea Country Profile. Online. Available at: www.bbc.com/news/world-africa-13317175 (accessed 3 May 2016).

BBC (2015d). Mauritania Country Profile. Online. Available at: www.bbc.com/news/world-africa-13881985 (accessed 3 May 2016).

BBC (2015e). Niger Country Profile. Online. Available at: www.bbc.com/news/world-africa-13943663 (accessed 3 May 2016).

BBC (2016a). India Outpaces China in 2015 Economic Growth. Online. 8 February. Available at: www.bbc.com/news/business-35519671 (accessed 1 May 2016)

BBC (2016b). Country Profile Nigeria. Online. Available at: www.bbc.com/news/world-africa-13949550 (accessed 1 May 2016).

BBC (2016c). Angola Country Profile. Online. 11 January. Available at: www.bbc.com/news/world-africa-13036732 (accessed 1 May 2016).

BBC (2016d). Cameroon Country Profile. Online. Available at: www.bbc.com/news/world-africa-13146029 (accessed 3 May 2016).

BBC (2016e). Liberia Country Profile. Online. Available at: www.bbc.com/news/world-africa-13729504 (accessed 3 May 2016).

Benazeraf, David and Alves, Ana (2014). Oil for Housing: Chinese-Built New Towns in Angola. Online. Policy Briefing 88, April South African Institute of International Affairs. Available at: www.saiia.org.za/policy-briefings/507-oil-for-housing-chinese-built-new-towns-in-angola/file (accessed 1 May 2016).

Beri, Ruchita (2003). India's Africa Policy in the Post-Cold War Era: An Assessment. *Strategic Analysis*, 27 (2), pp. 216–232.

Beri, Ruchita (2007). China's Rising Profile in Africa. *China Report*, 43 (3), pp. 297–308.

Beri, Ruchita (2008). India's Role in Keeping Peace in Africa. *Strategic Analysis*, 32 (2), pp. 197–221.

Beri, Ruchita (2010). Prospects of India's Energy Quest in Africa: Insights from Sudan and Nigeria. *Strategic Analysis*, 34 (6), pp. 897–911.

Beri, Ruchita and Sinha, Uttam Kumar (eds) (2009). *Africa and Energy Security: Global Issues, Local Responses*. New Delhi: Academic Foundation in association with Institute of Defence Studies and Analyses.

Berto, Massimiliano, Appolloni, Omar, Izquierdo, Juana Bustamante, De Angelis, Francesco, Lelli, Edoardo and Vesenjak, Slavko (2009). China and the Different Regional Approaches in Africa. *Transition Studies Review*, 16 (2), pp. 404–420.

Bhattacharya, Abanti (2005). Revisiting China's "Peaceful Rise": Implications for India. *East Asia*, 22 (4), pp. 59–80.

Bhattacharya, Abanti (2010). China's Discourse on Regionalism: What it Means for India. *Asia-Pacific Review*, 17 (1), pp. 97–123.

Bhattacharya, Sanjukta Banerji (2010). Engaging Africa: India's Interest in the African Continent, Past and Present. In: Fantu Cheru and Cyril Obi, eds. *The Rise of China and India in Africa*. London and Uppsala: Zed Books and Nordiska Afrikainstitutet, pp. 63–76.

Blumental, David, Chua, Tju Liang and Au, Ashleigh (2009). Upstream Oil and Gas in China. Industry Sector Reports, Doing Business in China. Online. Available at: http://chinanationalrefinerycorporation.com/upload/1.pdf (accessed 2 August 2012).

BMI (Business Monitor International) (2012a). India: Oil and Gas Report Q3 2012. Online. Part of BMI's Industry Report & Forecasts Series. Available at: www.businessmonitor.com (accessed 18 April 2016).

BMI (2012b). India: Oil and Gas Report Q3 2012. Online. Part of BMI's Industry Report & Forecasts Series. Available at: www.businessmonitor.com (accessed 18 April 2016).

BMI (2016a). India: Oil and Gas Report Q2 2016. Online. Part of BMI's Industry Report & Forecasts Series. Available at: www.businessmonitor.com (accessed 18 April 2016).

BMI (2016b). China: Oil and Gas Report Q2 2016. Online. Part of BMI's Industry Report & Forecasts Series. Available at: www.businessmonitor.com (accessed 18 April 2016).

BP (British Petroleum) (2012). Statistical Review of World Energy 2012. Online. June 2012. Available at: www.laohamutuk.org/DVD/docs/BPWER2012report.pdf (accessed 2 January 2013).

BP (2015). Statistical Review of World Energy 2015. Online. June 2015. Available at: www.bp.com/content/dam/bp/pdf/energy-economics/statistical-review-2015/bp-statistical-review-of-world-energy-2015-full-report.pdf (accessed 2 January 2016).

Bräutigam, Deborah A. (2009a). *The Dragon's Gift: The Real Story of China in Africa*. Oxford and New York: Oxford University Press.

Bräutigam, Deborah A. (2009b). China's Challenge to the International Aid Architecture. *World Politics Review*, 1 (4), pp. 1–10.

Bräutigam, Deborah A. and Tang, Xiaoyang (2009). China's Engagement in African Agriculture: Down to the Countryside. *The China Quarterly*, 199, pp. 686–706.

Bräutigam, Deborah A. and Tang, Xiaoyang (2011). African Shenzhen: China's Special Economic Zones in Africa. *Journal of Modern African Studies*, 49 (1), pp. 27–54.

Brawley, Mark R. (2009). Neoclassical Realism and Strategic Calculations: Explaining Divergent British, French and Soviet Strategies toward Germany between the World Wars (1919–1939). In: Steven E. Lobell, Norrin M. Ripsman and Jeffrey W. Taliaferro, eds. *Neoclassical Realism, the State, and Foreign Policy*. Cambridge: Cambridge University Press, pp. 75–98.

Brawley, Mark R. (2010). *Political Economy and Grand Strategy: A Neoclassical Realist View*. London: Routledge.

Broadman, Harry G. (2008). China and India Go to Africa: New Deals in the Developing World. *Foreign Affairs*, 87 (2), pp. 95–109.

Broadman, Harry G. and Isik, Gozdel (2007). *Africa's Silk Road: China and India's New Economic Frontier*. Washington, DC: World Bank.

Brookes, Peter (2007). Into Africa: China's Grab for Influence and Oil. Online. Heritage Lecture 1006, The Heritage Foundation, 26 March. Available at: www.heritage.org/Research/Africa/hl1006.cfm (accessed 18 April 2012).

Brooks, Stephen (1997). Duelling Realisms. *International Organization*, 51 (3), pp. 445–477.

Brooks, Stephen and Wohlforth, William C. (2000/1). Power Globalisation and the End of the Cold War: Re-Evaluating a Landmark Case for Ideas. *International Security*, 25 (3), pp. 5–53.

Brown, Michael E., Lynn-Jones, Sean M. and Miller, Steven E. (eds) (1995). *The Perils of Anarchy: Contemporary Realism and International Security*. Cambridge, MA: MIT Press.

Bull, Hedley (1977). *The Anarchical Society*. London: Macmillan.

Burgis, Tom (2010). China to Expand Niger Operations. Online. *Financial Times*, 20 May. Available at: www.ft.com/intl/cms/s/0/3eac7388-5d17-11df-8373-00144feab49a.html (accessed 23 April 2016).

Business Standard (2010). Enterprise India, 21st Century's First Decade Growth Driven by Private Sector. Online. 30 June. Available at: www.business-standard.com/india/news/enterprise-india/399818/ (accessed 24 July 2012).

Buzan, Barry (1993). Rethinking System and Structure. In: Barry Buzan, Charles Jones and Richard Little, eds. *The Logic of Anarchy: Neorealism to Structural Realism*. New York: Columbia University Press, pp. 72–80.

Buzan, Barry (2003). Security Architecture in Asia: The Interplay of Regional and Global Levels. *Pacific Review*, 16 (2), pp. 143–173.

Buzan, Barry (2004). *The United States and the Great Powers: World Politics in the Twenty-First Century*. Oxford: Polity.

Byman, Daniel L. and Pollack, Kenneth M. (2001). Let Us Now Praise Great Men: Bringing the Statesman Back In. *International Security*, 25 (4), pp. 107–146.

Cabestan, Jean-Pierre (2014). Gabon-China Relations: Towards a More Cautious Partnership. *African East-Asian Affairs*, 2, pp. 6–37.

Campbell, Horace (2008). China in Africa: Challenging US Global Hegemony. In: Firoze M. Manji and Stephen Marks, eds. *African Perspectives on China in Africa*. Oxford: Fahamu, pp. 119–137.

Campos, Indira and Vines, Alex (2008). Angola and China: A Pragmatic Partnership. In: Jennifer G. Cooke, ed. *U.S. and Chinese Engagement in Africa: Prospects for Improving U.S.–China–Africa Cooperation*. Washington, DC: CSIS Press, pp. 33–48.

Carmody, Padraig (2011). India and the "Asian Drivers" in Africa. In: Emma Mawdsley and Gerrad McCann, eds. *India in Africa: Changing Geographies of Power*. Cape Town: Pambazuka Press, pp. 30–48.

Caverley, Jonathan D. (2010). Power and Democratic Weakness: Neo-Conservatism and Neoclassical Realism. *Millennium: Journal of International Studies*, 38 (3), pp. 593–614.

Cha, Victor (2001). Abandonment, Entrapment and Neoclassical Realism in Asia: The United States, Japan and Korea. *International Studies Quarterly*, 44 (2), pp. 261–291.

Cha, Victor (2002). Hawk Engagement and Preventive Defence on the Korean Peninsula. *International Security*, 27 (1), pp. 40–78.

Chai, Joseph C.H. (2003). Privatisation in China. In: David Parker and David Saal, eds. *International Handbook on Privatization*. Cheltenham: Edward Elgar, pp. 235–261.

Chan-Fischel, Michelle (2007). Environmental Impact: More of the Same? In: Firoze M. Manji and Stephen Marks, eds. *African Perspectives on China in Africa*. Oxford: Fahamu, pp. 139–152.

Chandran, Bipin (2006). China Wants Indian Firms to Take Part in its Privatisation Process. Online. *Business Standard*, 21 April. Available at: www.business-standard.com/india/news/china-wants-indian-firms-to-take-part-in-its-privatisation-process/242711/ (accessed 28 July 2012).

Channel News Asia (2016). With Gambia Move, China Ends Diplomatic Truce with Taiwan. Online. 17 March. Available at: www.channelnewsasia.com/news/asiapacific/with-gambia-move-china-e/2612146.html (accessed 20 May 2016).

Chao, Chien-min and Hsu, Chih-chia (2006). China Isolates Taiwan. In: Edward Friedman, ed. *China's Rise, Taiwan's Dilemmas and International Peace*. London and New York: Routledge, pp. 41–67.

Chapnick, Adam (1999). The Middle Power. *Canadian Foreign Policy*, 7 (2), pp. 73–82.

Chen, Aimin and Li, Peng (2007). Corporate Governance and the Development of Private Enterprise in China. In: Shuanglin Lin and Shunfeng Song, eds. *The Revival of Private Enterprise in China*. Aldershot and Burlington: Ashgate, pp. 237–255.

Chen, Aizhu (2008). CNOOC in Surprise Exit of Nigeria Oil Block-Source. Online. Reuters, 18 August. Available at: http://uk.reuters.com/article/2008/08/18/cnooc-nigeria-idUKPEK25462220080818 (accessed 19 January 2013).

Cheng, Joseph Y.S. and Shi, Huangao (2009). China's Africa Policy in the Post-Cold War Era. *Journal of Contemporary Asia*, 39 (1), pp. 87–115.

Cheru, Fantu and Obi, Cyril (eds) (2010a). *The Rise of China and India in Africa: Challenges,*

Opportunities and Critical Interventions. London and Uppsala: Zed Books and Nordiska Afrikainstitutet.

Cheru, Fantu and Obi, Cyril (2010b). Introduction – Africa in the Twenty-First Century: Strategic and Development Challenges. In Fantu Cheru and Cyril Obi, eds. *The Rise of China and India in Africa*. London and Uppsala: Zed Books and Nordiska Afrikainstitutet, pp. 1–9.

Cheru, Fantu and Obi, Cyril (2011). India-Africa Relations in the 21st Century: Genuine Partnership or a Marriage of Convenience. In: Emma Mawdsley and Gerrad McCann, eds. *India in Africa: Changing Geographies of Power*. Cape Town: Pambazuka Press, pp. 12–29.

China Daily (2014). Nigeria, China Trade Volume Hits $13b in 2013. Online. 20 January. Available at: www.chinadaily.com.cn/business/2014-01/20/content_17244697.htm (accessed 30 April 2016).

China.org.cn (2016). Xi Jinping Meets Nigerian President Buhari in Beijing. Online. 13 April. Available at: www.china.org.cn/video/2016-04/13/content_38232661.htm (accessed 1 May 2016).

Chow, Edward C. (2009). China's Soft Power in Developing Regions: New Major Player in the International Oil Patch. In: Carola McGiffert, ed. *Chinese Soft Power and its Implications for the United States: Competition and Cooperation in the Developing World, A Report of the CSIS Smart Power Initiative*. Washington, DC: CSIS Press, pp. 91–96.

Christensen, Thomas J. (1996). *Useful Adversaries: Grand Strategy, Domestic Mobilisation, and Sino-American Conflict, 1947–1958*. Princeton: Princeton University Press.

CIA (Central Intelligence Agency) (n.d.). The World Factbook: Cameroon. Online. Available at: www.cia.gov/library/publications/the-world-factbook/geos/cm.html (accessed 12 January 2016).

CNOOC (n.d.a). About Us. Online. Available at: www.cnoocltd.com/col/col7261/index.html (accessed 1 May 2016).

CNOOC (n.d.b). Key Operating Areas. Online. Available at: www.cnoocltd.com/col/col7321/index.html (accessed 1 May 2016).

CNOOC (n.d.c). Nigeria. Online. Available at: www.cnoocltd.com/col/col7321/index.html (accessed 1 May 2016).

CNPC (n.d.a). CNPC at a Glance. Online. Available at: www.cnpc.com.cn/en/cnpcataglance/cnpcataglance.shtml (accessed 30 April 2016).

CNPC (n.d.b). CNPC Worldwide. Online. Available at: www.cnpc.com.cn/en/cnpcworldwide/cnpcworldwide.shtml (accessed April 30 2016).

CNPC (n.d.c). CNPC in Chad. Online. Available at: www.cnpc.com.cn/en/Chad/country_index.shtml (accessed 22 April 2016).

CNPC (n.d.d). CNPC in Equatorial Guinea. Online. Available at: www.cnpc.com.cn/en/Chad/country_index.shtml (accessed 22 April 2016).

CNPC (n.d.e). CNPC in Mauritania. Online. Available at: www.cnpc.com.cn/en/cnpcworldwide/mauritania/ (accessed 12 January 2016).

CNPC (n.d.f). CNPC in Niger. Online. Available at: www.cnpc.com.cn/en/Niger/country_index.shtml (accessed 22 April 2016).

CNPC (2016). CNPC in Nigeria. (online) Available at: www.cnpc.com.cn/en/Nigeria/country_index.shtml (accessed 17 April 2016).

Comarmond, Cecile de (2011). China Lends Angola $15bn, But Few Jobs Are Created. Online. *Mail and Guardian*, 6 March. Available at: http://mg.co.za/article/2011-03-06-china-lends-angola-15bn-but-few-jobs-are-created (accessed 1 May 2016).

Consulate General of PRC in Johannesburg (2016). Yu Zhengsheng Pays Official Goodwill Visit to Ghana. Online. 19 April Available at: http://johannesburg.chineseconsu-
late.org/eng/xwdt/zgyw/t1357309.htm (accessed 3 May 2016).

Cooke, Jennifer G. (ed.) (2008). U.S. and Chinese Engagement in Africa: Prospects for
Improving U.S.-China-Africa Cooperation. Washington, DC: CSIS Press.

Cooke, Jennifer G. (2009). China's Soft Power in Africa. In: Carola McGiffert, ed.
*Chinese Soft Power and Its Implications for the United States: Competition and
Cooperation in the Developing World, A Report of the CSIS Smart Power Initiative.*
Washington, DC: CSIS Press, pp. 27–44.

Cooper, Andrew F., Higgott, Richard A. and Nossal, Richard Kim (1993). *Relocating
Middle Powers: Australia and Canada in a Changing World Order*. Canada: UBC
Press.

Corkin, Lucy (2011). Uneasy Allies: China's Evolving Relations with Angola. *Journal of
Contemporary African Studies*, 29 (2), pp. 169–180.

Coroado, Herculno and Brock, Joe (2015). Angolans Resentful as China Tightens its
Grip. Online. Reuters, 9 July. Available at: www.reuters.com/article/us-angola-china-
insight-idUSKCN0PJ1LT20150709 (accessed 1 May 2016).

Costalli, Stefano (2009). Power over the Sea: The Relevance of Neoclassical Realism to
Euro-Mediterranean Relations. *Mediterranean Politics*, 14 (3), pp. 323–342.

Cox, Robert (1989). Middlepowermanship, Japan and Future World Order. *International
Journal*, 44 (4), pp. 823–862.

Cropley, Ed (2009). China Shunts U.S. into Second Place in Scramble for Africa. Online.
Reuters, 7 August. Available at: http://blogs.reuters.com/africanews/2009/08/07/china-
shunts-us-into-second-place-in-scramble-for-africa/ (accessed 20 April 2012).

Dadwal, Shebonti Ray (2011). India and Africa: Towards a Sustainable Energy Partnership.
Online. Occasional Paper No 75, South African Institute of International Affairs. Avail-
able at: dspace.cigilibrary.org/jspui/.../saia_sop_75_dadwal_20110222.pdf (accessed 10
January 2013).

Daily Post (2016). Buhari's Visit to China Yielded Billions in Investments for Nigeria –
Presidency. Online. 15 April. Available at: http://dailypost.ng/2016/04/15/buharis-visit-to-
china-yielded-billions-in-investments-for-nigeria-presidency/ (accessed 30 April 2016).

Daly, John K.C. (2014). China's Bold $10 Billion Investment in Nigerian Hydrocarbons.
Online. *The Diplomat*, 17 January. Available at: http://thediplomat.com/2014/01/
chinas-bold-10-billion-investment-in-nigerian-hydrocarbons/ (accessed 30 April 2016).

Danilovic, Vesna (2002). *When the Stakes are High: Deterrence and Conflict among
Major Powers*. Ann Arbor: University of Michigan Press.

Davidson, Jason W. (2002). The Roots of Revisionism: Fascist Italy, 1992–39. *Security
Studies*, 11 (4), pp. 125–159.

Davidson, Jason W. (2006). *The Origin of Revisionist and Status Quo States*. New York:
Palgrave Macmillan.

Davies, Martyn (2008). China's Developmental Model Comes to Africa. *Review of
African Political Economy*, 35 (115), pp. 134–137.

Deepak, B.R. (2006). Sino-Pak "Entente Cordiale" and India: A Look into the Past and
Future. *China Report*, 42 (129), pp. 129–151.

Dent, Christopher M. (ed.) (2011). *China and Africa Development Relations*. Abingdon:
Routledge.

Department of Petroleum Resources, Government of Nigeria (2014). Oil and Gas Industry Annual Report. Online. Available at: https://dpr.gov.ng/index/wp-content/
uploads/2016/01/2014-Oil-Gas-Industry-Annual-Report-1.pdf (accessed 2 May 2016).

Desai, Ashok V. (1999). *Transition to an Open Market Economy: India's Policy Experience of Controls over Industry*. New Delhi: Sage.

Diao, Ying (2007). Steelmaker Forges Ahead. Online. *China Daily*, 8 September. Available at: www.chinadaily.com.cn/cndy/2007-09/08/content_6090789.htm (accessed 28 July 2012).

Dittgen, Romain (2011). To Bélinga or not to Bélinga? China's Evolving Engagement in Gabon's Mining Sector. Online. Occasional Paper No 98 South African Institute of International Affairs. Available at: www.org.za/occasional-papers/to-belinga-or-not-to-belinga-china-s-evolving-engagement-in-gabon-s-mining-sector.html (accessed 30 December 2012).

Dittgen, Romain and Large, Daniel (2012). China's Growing Involvement in Chad: Escaping Enclosure? Online. Occasional Paper 116 South African Institute for Internatonal Affairs. Available at: www.saiia.org.za/occasional-papers/chinas-growing-involvement-in-chad-escaping-enclosure (accessed 15 April 2016).

Dowding, Keith (2012). Why Should We Care About the Definition of Power. *Journal of Political Power*, 5 (1), pp. 119–135.

Downs, Erica S. (2007). The Fact and Fiction of Sino-African Energy Relations. *China Security*, 3 (3), pp. 42–68.

Downs, Erica S. (2008). Business Interest Groups in Chinese Politics: The Case of the Oil Companies. In Cheng Li, ed. *China's Changing Political Landscape: Prospects for Democracy*. Washington, DC: Brookings Institution, pp. 121–141.

Downs, Erica S. (2011). China Development Bank's Oil Loans: Pursuing Policy and Profit. *China Economic Quarterly*, December, pp. 43–47.

Downs, Erics S. and Meidan, Michal (2011). Business and Politics in China: The Oil Executive Reshuffle of 2011. *China Security*, 19, pp. 3–21.

Dueck, Colin (2005). Realism, Culture and Grand Strategy: Explaining America's Peculiar Path to World Power. *Security Studies*, 14 (2), pp. 195–231.

Dueck, Colin (2006). *Reluctant Crusaders: Power, Culture, and Change in American Grand Strategy*. Princeton: Princeton University Press.

Dutta, Sujit (2008). Revisiting China's Territorial Claims on Arunachal. *Strategic Analysis*, 32 (4), pp. 549–581.

Ebel, Robert E. (2005). *China's Energy Future: The Middle Kingdom Seeks its Place in the Sun*. Washington, DC: The CSIS Press Center for Strategic and International Studies.

Economic Times (2012). India-China Trade Expected to Touch $100 Billion by 2015. Online. Available at: http://articles.economictimes.indiatimes.com/2012-10-26/news/34750100_1_india-china-trade-china-international-auto-parts-bilateral-trade (accessed 30 December 2012).

Economic Times (2013). ONGC-Lakhsmi Mittal JV Give Up Nigerian Oil Block. Online. 29 January. Available at: http://articles.economictimes.indiatimes.com/2013-01-29/news/36616167_1_signature-bonus-omel-opl-285 (accessed 2 May 2016).

Economist, The (2012). China's State Capitalism: Not Just Tilting at Windmills. 6 October.

Edelstein, David M. (2002). Managing Uncertainty: Beliefs about Intentions and the Rise of Great Powers. *Security Studies*, 12 (1), pp. 1–40.

Ejiofor, Clement (2015). Inside Story Of Buhari's Trip to India-Adesina. Online. Available at: hwww.naij.com/623642-interesting-inside-story-president-buharis-trip-india.html (accessed 1 May 2016).

Embassy of India, Beijing (n.d.a). Economic and Trade Relations. Online. Available at:

www.indianembassy.org.cn/DynamicContent.aspx?MenuId=97&SubMenuId=0 (accessed 5 May 2016).

Embassy of India, Beijing (n.d.b). Political Relations. Online. Available at: www.indianembassy.org.cn/DynamicContent.aspx?MenuId=97&SubMenuId=0 (accessed 5 May 2016).

Embassy of the PRC in Ghana (n.d.). Introduction of China–Ghana Relations. Online. Available at: http://gh.chineseembassy.org/eng/zjgx/zzwl/t177920.htm (accessed 22 April 2016).

Energy-pedia News (2004). Nigeria: Sinopec Signs Oil Development Agreement. Online. 20 December. Available at: www.energy-pedia.com/news/nigeria/inopec-signs-oil-development-agreement- (accessed 1 May 2016).

Energy-pedia News (2008). Nigeria: CNOOC Sends Shockwaves Over Licence Exit. Online. 20 August. Available at: www.energy-pedia.com/news/nigeria/cnooc-sends-shockwaves-over-licence-exit- (accessed 1 May 2016).

Energy-pedia News (2010). Nigeria: Nexen Updates Operations Offshore Nigeria. Online. 21 February Available at: www.energy-pedia.com/news/nigeria/nexen-updates-operations-offshore-nigeria (accessed 1 May 2016).

Energy Business Review (2012). African Petroleum Enters Investment Deal with PetroChina. Online. Exploration and Development News. 18 July. Available at: http://explorationanddevelopment.energy-business-review.com/news/african-petroleum-enters-investment-deal-with-petrochina-180712 (accessed 15 August 2012).

Engardio, P. (ed.) (2007). *Chindia: How China and India are Revolutionizing Global Business*. New York: McGraw-Hill.

ESRC (2002). Privatisation, Chinese Style: Can China's State Owned Enterprises Compete in International Markets. Science Blog. Available at: http://scienceblog.com/community/older/2002/F/20022414.html (accessed 29 July 2012).

Essar (n.d.a). Corporate Profile. Online. Available at: www.essar.com/section_level1.aspx?cont_id=SD7sjPUVBkw= (accessed August 2012).

Essar (n.d.b). Essar Energy Business. Online. Available at: www.essarenergy.com/about-us/essar-business.aspx#business1 (accessed 1 May 2016).

Evans, Gareth and Grant, Bruce (1991). *Australia's Foreign Relations in the World of the 1990s*. Australia: Melbourne University Press.

ExpoGroup (2014). Total Resumes $2.5bn Usan Deepwater Oil Block Sale. Online. 17 September. Available at: www.expogr.com/kenyaoil/detail_news.php?newsid=353&pageid=2&t=Total%20resumes%20$2.5bn%20Usan%20Deepwater%20oil%20block%20sale (accessed 1 May 2016).

Farooki, Masuma (2011). China's Structural Demand and Commodity Prices: Implications for Africa. In: Christopher M. Dent, ed. *China and Africa Development Relations*. Abingdon: Routledge, pp. 121–142.

Ferguson, Chaka (2011). Soft Power as the New Form: How the Chinese-Russian Strategic Partnership (Soft) Balances American Hegemony in the Era of Unipolarity. PhD thesis. Florida International University.

Ferreira, Manuel Ennes (2008). China in Angola: Just a Passion for Oil? In: Chris Alden, Daniel Large and Ricardo Soares de Oliveira, eds. *China Returns to Africa: A Rising Power and a Continent Embrace*. New York: Columbia University Press, pp. 295–317.

FICCI (2010). Oil and Natural Gas. Online. Available at: www.ficci-b2b.com/sector...pdf/OIL_AND_NATURAL_GAS.pdf (accessed 2 August 2012).

FOCAC (Forum on China-Africa Cooperation) (2004a). Nigerian President, China's Top Legislator Hold Talks on Bilateral Ties. Online. 9 November. Available at: www.focac.org/eng/zt/sbfw/t169441.htm (accessed 30 April 2016).

FOCAC (2004b). China's Top Legislator Meets Nigerian Parliamentarian Leaders. Online. 8 November. Available at: www.focac.org/eng/zt/sbfw/t169182.htm (accessed 30 April 2016).

FOCAC (2005a). Top Legislator Meets Nigerian President. Online. 21 April. Available at: www.focac.org/eng/zt/sbfw/t192563.htm (accessed 30 April 2016).

FOCAC (2005b). Wen Jiabao Meets Nigerian President. Online. 21 April. Available at: www.focac.org/eng/zt/sbfw/t192561.htm (accessed 30 April 2016).

FOCAC (2005c). Foreign Minister Li Zhaoxing Meets Nigerian National Security Adviser. Online. 20 July. Available at: www.focac.org/eng/zt/sbfw/t204273.htm (accessed 30 April 2016).

Fontevecchia, Agustino (2012). The End Of Exxon's Reign? PetroChina Now The Biggest Oil Producer. Online. 29 March. Available at: www.forbes.com/sites/afontevecchia/2012/03/29/the-end-of-exxons-rein-petrochina-now-the-biggest-oil-producer/ (accessed 6 August 2012).

Foot, Rosemary (2006). Chinese Strategies in a US-Hegemonic Global Order: Accommodating and Hedging. *International Affairs*, 82 (1), pp. 77–94.

Fortune (n.d.). Global 500. Online. Available at: http://fortune.com/global500/ (accessed 19 April 2016).

Foster, Vivien, Butterfield, William, Chen, Chuan and Pushak, Nataliya (2009). *Building Bridges: China's Growing Role as Infrastructure Financier for Sub-Saharan Africa.* Washington, DC: World Bank/Public-Private Infrastructure Advisory Facility.

Frynas, Jedrzej G. and Manuel, Paulo (2007). A New Scramble for African Oil? Historical, Political, and Business Perspectives. *African Affairs*, 106 (422), pp. 229–251.

Gabon Embassy, India (n.d.). India-Gabon Ties: Warm and Friendly. Online. Available at: www.gabonembassynewdelhi.com/index.php?option=com_content&view=article&id=26&lang=en (accessed 15 January 2016).

Gaddis, John L. (1987). *The Long Peace: Inquiries into the History of the Cold War.* New York: Oxford University Press.

Gandel, Stephen (2016). The Biggest American Companies Now Owned by the Chinese. Online. *Fortune*. Available at: http://fortune.com/2016/03/18/the-biggest-american-companies-now-owned-by-the-chinese/ (accessed 10 May 2016).

Garst, Daniel (1989). Thucydides and Neorealism. *International Studies Quarterly*, 33, pp. 3–27.

Gaye, Adama (2008). China in Africa: After the Gun and the Bible: A West African Perspective. In: Chris Alden, Daniel Large and Ricardo Soares de Oliveira, eds. *China Returns to Africa: A Rising Power and a Continent Embrace.* New York: Columbia University Press, pp. 129–141.

Gill, Bates and Reilly, James (2007). The Tenuous Hold of China Inc. in Africa. *The Washington Quarterly*, 30 (3), pp. 37–52.

Gill, Bates, Huang, Chin-hao and Morrison, J. Stephen (2006). China's Expanding Role in Africa: Implications for the United States. A Report of the CSIS delegation to China on China–Africa–U.S. Relations, November 28–December 1. Washington, DC: CSIS Press. Available at: www.comw.org/cmp/fulltext/0701gill.pdf (accessed 12 November 2012).

Gilpin, Robert G. (1981). *War and Change in World Politics.* Cambridge: Cambridge University Press.

Gilpin, Robert G. (1986). The Richness of the Tradition of Political Realism. In: Robert O. Keohane, ed. *Neorealism and its Critics.* New York: Columbia University Press, pp. 301–321.

Glaser, Charles L. (2003). The Necessary and Natural Evolution of Structural Realism. In: John A. Vasquez and Colin Elman, eds. *Realism and the Balancing of Power: A New Debate*. Upper Saddle River: Prentice Hall, pp. 266–279.

Glenn, John (2009). Realism versus Strategic Culture: Competition and Collaboration? *International Studies Review*, 11 (3), pp. 523–551.

Global Edge (n.d.). Nigeria: Trade Statistics. Online. Available at: http://globaledge.msu.edu/countries/nigeria/tradestats (accessed 30 April 2016).

Goldstein, Andrea E., Pinaud, Nicolas, Reisen, Helmut and Chen, Xiaobao (eds) (2006). *The Rise of China and India: What's in it for Africa?* Paris: Organization for Economic Co-operation and Development.

Goldstein, Avery (1997–8). Great Expectations: Interpreting China's Arrival. *International Security*, 22 (3), pp. 36–73.

Goldwyn, David L. (2009). Pursuing U.S. Energy Security Interest in Africa. In: Jennifer G. Cooke and Stephen J. Morrison, eds. *U.S. Africa Policy Beyond the Bush Years: Critical Challenges for the Obama Administration*. Washington, DC: CSIS Press, pp. 62–90.

Goldwyn, David L. and Morrison, Stephen J. (2004). Promoting Transparency in the African Oil sector: Recommendations for US Foreign Policy. A Report of the CSIS Task Force on Rising US Energy Stakes in Africa. Washington, DC: CSIS Press.

Goldwyn, David L. and Morrison, Stephen J. (2005). A Strategic U.S. Approach to Governance and Security in the Gulf of Guinea. A Report of the CSIS Task Force on Gulf of Guinea Security. Washington, DC: CSIS Press.

Gourevitch, P. (1978). The Second Image Reversed: The International Sources of Domestic Politics. *International Organization*, 32 (4), pp. 881–912.

Government of Ghana (n.d.). Ghana-China Trade is More Than $5 Billion. Online. Available at: www.ghana.gov.gh/index.php/media-center/news/1579-ghana-china-trade-is-more-than-5-billion (accessed 21 April 2016).

Greenfield, Gerard (1997). Concerning Privatisation in China. Online. 20 November. Available at: www.hartford-hwp.com/archives/55/214.html (accessed 29 July 2012).

Gregory, Paul R. and Stuart, Robert C. (1999). *Comparative Economic Systems*, 3rd edn. Boston: Houghton Mifflin.

Guerrero, Dorothy-Grace and Manji, Firoze (eds) (2008). *China's New Role in Africa and the South: A Search for a New Perspective*. Oxford: Fahamu.

Gupta, Amit (2006). US.India.China: Assessing Tripolarity. *China Report*, 42 (69), pp. 69–83.

Gupta, Sanjeev, Carey, Kevin Joseph and Jacoby, Ulrich (2007). *Sub-Saharan Africa: Forging New Trade Links with Asia*. Washington, DC: International Monetary Fund.

Gyamerah, Emmanuel Adu (2014). China's Investments in Ghana Increase. *Business News*, 22 March. Available at: http://business.peacefmonline.com/pages/news/201403/193742.php (accessed 21 April 2016).

Gyasi Jnr, Stephen (2014). Ghana and China, Friends for Life? (Part 1). Online. *New African*, 14 April. Available at: http://newafricanmagazine.com/ghana-and-china-friends-for-life-2/ (accessed 21 April 2016).

Haggard, Stephen and Huang, Yasheng (2008). The Political Economy of Private Sector Development in China. In: Loren Brandt and Thomas Rawski, eds. *China's Great Economic Transformation*. New York and Cambridge: Cambridge University Press, pp. 337–374.

Haglund, David G. and Onea, Tudor (2008). Sympathy for the Devil: Myths of Neoclassical Realism in Canadian Foreign Policy. *Canadian Foreign Policy*, 14 (2), pp. 53–66.

Hanson, Stephanie (2008). China, Africa and Oil. Online. Council on Foreign Relations, Backgrounder, 9 June. Available at: www.washingtonpost.com/wp-dyn/content/article/2008/06/09/AR2008060900714.html (accessed 12 April 2012).

Hao, Yufan and Hou, Ying (2009). Chinese Foreign Policy Making: A Comparative Perspective. *Public Administration Review*, 69, pp. s136–s141.

Harneit-Sievers, Axel, Marks, Stephen and Naidu, Sanusha (2010). *Chinese and African Perspectives on China in Africa*. Oxford: Pambazuka.

Hicks, Celeste (2015). Is Chad Managing to Beat the "Oil Curse"? Online. *Guardian*, 14 April. Available at: www.theguardian.com/global-development/2015/apr/14/chad-oil-curse-africa-challenge-negative-impact (accessed 22 April 2016).

High Commission of India, Nigeria (n.d.). India-China Bilateral Relations. Online. Available at: http://hcindia-abuja.org/display_content.php?id=28 (accessed 1 May 2016).

Holbraad, Carsten (1984). *Middle Powers in International Politics*. UK: Macmillan Press.

Holmes, John (1976). *Canada: A Middle-Aged Power*. Canada: McClelland and Stewart.

Holslag, Jonathan (2011). China and the Coups: Coping with Political Instability in Africa. *African Affairs*, 110 (440), pp. 367–386.

Houser, T. (2008). The Roots of Chinese Oil Investment Abroad. *Asia Policy*, 5, pp. 141–166.

Huang, Chin-Hao (2008). China's Renewed Partnership with Africa: Implication for the United States. In: Robert I. Rotberg, ed. *China into Africa: Trade, Aid, and Influence*. Washington, DC: Brookings Institution Press, pp. 296–312.

Huang Kaixi, Wang Xiaobing and Yu Ning (2015). Auditors Probe Sinopec, Savvy Broker in Angola. Online. Caixin Online, 4 August. Available at: http://english.caixin.com/2015-08-04/100836237.html (accessed 1 May 2016).

Huang, Yasheng (2003). *Selling China: Foreign Direct Investment During the Reform Era*. Cambridge: Cambridge University Press.

Iaccino, Ludovica (2015). Nigeria's President Muhammadu Buhari Arrives in New Delhi for India-Africa Forum. Online. Available at: www.ibtimes.co.uk/nigerias-president-muhammadu-buhari-arrives-new-delhi-india-africa-forum-1526036 (accessed 30 April 2016).

IBEF (India Brand Equity Foundation) (2016). Indian Pharmaceutical Industry. Online. September. Available at: www.ibef.org/industry/pharmaceutical-india.aspx (accessed 5 May 2016).

Idun-Arkhurst, Isaac (2008). Ghana's Relations with China. Online. Report No. 3 South African Institute of International Affairs. Available at: www.saiia.org.za/research-reports/china-in-africa-policy-reports.html (accessed 11 January 2016).

IMF (2014). Angola: Selected Issues Paper. Online. IMF Country Report No. 14/275. Available at: www.imf.org/external/pubs/ft/scr/2014/cr14275.pdf (accessed 1 May 2016).

IMF (2016). Statement by IMF Deputy Managing Director Min Zhu on Angola. Online. 6 April. Available at: www.imf.org/external/np/sec/pr/2016/pr16155.htm (accessed 1 May 2016).

India Today (2016). India Rejects China Claim of PLA Not Crossing Border, Says Transgression Has Increased. Online. 15 March. Available at: http://indiatoday.intoday.in/story/india-rejects-china-claim-of-pla-not-crossing-border-says-transgression-has-increased/1/620757.html (accessed 10 May 2016).

Infield Rigs (2006). Obo-1 Discovery in Block 1 of the Nigeria Sao Tome and Principe Joint Development Zone Confirmed. Online. 30 May. Available at: www.infield.com/rigs/news/obo-1-discovery-in-block-1-of-the-nigeria-sao-tome-and-principe-joint-development-zone-confirmed/288 (accessed 1 May 2016).

IOCL (n.d.). Forays into E&P. Online. Available at: www.iocl.com/Aboutus/e_and_p. aspx (accessed 1 May 2016).

Jain, Bharti (2010). India "Succumbs" to Chinese Pressure on Arunachal at WB Meet. Online. *The Times of India*, 6 March. Available at: http://articles.timesofindia.india-times.com/2010-03-06/india/28121047_1_arunachal-pradesh-world-bank-ed-china-shaolin-yang (accessed 30 December 2012).

Jakobson, Linda (2009). China's Diplomacy toward Africa Drivers and Constraints. *International Relations of the Asia-Pacific*, 9 (3), pp. 403–433.

Jervis, Robert (1978). Cooperation Under the Security Dilemma. *World Politics*, 30 (2), pp. 183–186.

Jiang, Wenran (2009). Fuelling the Dragon: China's Rise and Its Energy and Resources Extraction in Africa. *The China Quarterly*, 199, pp. 585–609.

Johnson, Paul M. (2005). Political Economy. Online. A Glossary of Political Economy Terms. Available at: www.auburn.edu/~johnspm/gloss/political_economy (accessed 29 October 2011).

Joshi, Shashank (2011). Why India Is Becoming Warier of China. *Current History*, 110 (735), pp. 156–161.

Juan, Du (2011). Sinopec Agrees Nigerian Oil Deal. Online. *China Daily*, 21 November. Available at: http://usa.chinadaily.com.cn/business/2012-11/21/content_15947643.htm (accessed 1 May 2016).

Juneau, Thomas (2010). Neoclassical Realist Strategic Analysis. In: Graduate Student Conference, European Consortium of Political Research. Online. Dublin, Ireland, 30 August–1 September 2010, pp. 1–28. Available at: www.ecprnet.eu/databases/confer-ences/papers/308.pdf (accessed 29 October 2011).

Kambara, Tatsu (1974). The Petroleum Industry in China. *The China Quarterly*, 60, pp. 699–719.

Kambara, Tatsu and Howe, Christopher (2007). *China and the Global Energy Crisis: Development and Prospects for China's Oil and Natural Gas*. Cheltenham and North-ampton, MA: Edward Elgar.

Katzenstein, P. (1978). *Between Power and Plenty: The Foreign Economic Policies of Advanced Industrial States*. Madison: University of Wisconsin Press.

Keenan, Jeremy (2008). US Militarization in Africa: What Anthropologists Should Know About AFRICOM. *Anthropology Today*, 24 (55), pp. 16–20.

Kennedy, Charles (2015). India Becomes the 3rd Largest Oil Importer. Oilprice.com. Online. Available at: http://oilprice.com/Energy/Crude-Oil/India-Becomes-3rd-Largest-Oil-Importer.html (accessed 10 January 2016).

Keohane, Robert O. (1969). Lilliputians Dilemmas: Small States in International Politics. *International Organization*, 23 (2), pp. 291–310.

Kiala, Carine (2010). China–Angola Aid Relations: Strategic Cooperation for Develop-ment? *South African Journal of International Affairs*, 17 (3), pp. 313–331.

King, K. (2010). China's Cooperation in Education and Training with Kenya: A Different Model? *International Journal of Educational Development*, 30 (5), pp. 488–496.

Kitchen, Nicholas (2010). Systemic Pressures and Domestic Ideas: A Neoclassical Realist Model of Grand Strategy Formation. *Review of International Studies*, 36 (1), pp. 117–143.

Kitissou, Marcel (ed.) (2007). *Africa in China's Global Strategy*. London: Adonis & Abbey.

Klare, Michael and Volman, Daniel (2006). The African "Oil Rush" and US National Security. *Third World Quarterly*, 27 (4), pp. 609–628.

Kong, Bo (2010). *China's International Petroleum Policy*. Santa Barbara: ABC-CLIO.

Kosmos Energy (n.d.). Operations: Jubilee Field. Online. Available at: www.kosmosenergy.com/operations-ghana-jubilee-field.php (accessed 22 April 2016).

KPMG (2009). China's Energy Sector: A Clearer View. Online. Industrial Markets. Available at: www.kpmg.de/14427.htm (accessed 4 August 2012).

Krasner, Stephen (1978). *Defending the National Interest: Raw Materials Investments and U.S. Foreign Policy*. Princeton: Princeton University Press.

Krasner, Stephen D. (1985). *Structural Conflict: The Third World against Global Liberalism*. Berkeley: University of California Press.

Kumar, N. (2012). Preface. In: Suseela Yesudian, ed. *India: Acquiring its Way to a Global Footprint*. Basingstoke and New York: Palgrave Macmillan.

Kumar, N., Mohapatra, P. and Chandrasekhar, S. (2009). *India's Global Powerhouses: How they are Taking on the World*. Boston, MA: Harvard Business Press.

Lake, Anthony, Whitman, Christine Todd, Lyman, Princeton N. and Morrison, Stephen J. (2006). More Than Humanitarianism: A Strategic US Approach Towards Africa. Independent Task Report No. 56. Council on Foreign Relations. Available at: file:///C:/Documents%20and%20Settings/Administrator/My%20Documents/Downloads/Africa_Task_Force_Web.pdf (accessed 20 November 2012).

Larcon, Jean-Paul (2009). Conclusion: China's Unique Advantage. In: Jean-Paul Larcon, ed. *Chinese Multinationals*. Singapore and Hackensack: World Scientific, pp. 229–230.

Lardy, Nicholas R. (2003). Trade Liberalization and Its Role in Chinese Economic Growth, Prepared for an International Monetary Fund and National Council of Applied Economic Research Conference, A Tale of Two Giants: India's and China's Experience with Reform and Growth New Delhi, 14–16 November. Online. NR Lardy – Institute of International Economics. Available at: perjacobsson.org (accessed 27 July 2012).

Lardy, Nicholas R. (2014). *Markets over Mao: The Rise of Private Business in China*. Washington: Peterson Institute for International Economics.

Larry, Dasmani (2015). Ghana-China Trade Surpasses $5 Billion. Online. 3 July. The Africa Report. Available at: www.theafricareport.com/West-Africa/ghanas-china-trade-surpasses-5-billion.html (accessed 21 April 2016).

Layne, Christopher (2006). *The Peace of Illusions: American Grand Strategy from 1940 to the Present*. Ithaca: Cornell University Press.

Le Pere, Gareth (ed.) (2007). *China in Africa: Mercantilist Predator, or Partner in Development?* Midrand: Institute for Global Dialogue.

Lee, H. and Shalmon, D. (2008). Searching for Oil: China's Oil Strategies in Africa. In: Robert I. Rotberg, ed. *China into Africa: Trade, Aid and Influence*. Washington, DC: Brookings Institution Press, pp. 109–135.

Levkowitz, Lee, Ross, Marta McLellan and Warner, J.R. (2009). The 88 Queensway Group, A Case Study in Chinese Investors' Operations in Angola and Beyond. Online. Report US-China Economic & Security Review Commission, 10 July Available at: www.uscc.gov/Research/88-queensway-group-case-study-chinese-investors%E2%80%99-operations-angola-and-beyond (accessed 1 May 2016).

Levy, Roy (2009). China's Peacekeeping Deployments in Africa. In Carola McGiffert, ed. *Chinese Soft Power and Its Implications for the United States: Competition and Cooperation in the Developing World, A Report of the CSIS Smart Power Initiative*. Washington, DC: CSIS Press, pp. 37–38.

Li, Xiaokun (2013). New Deals for Prosperity. Online. *China Daily*, 19 July. Available at: http://africa.chinadaily.com.cn/weekly/2013-07/19/content_16799228.htm (accessed 30 April 2016).

Li, Yining (2007). *On the Private Economy*. Peking: Peking University Press.

Li, Zhaoxi (2009). China's Outward Foreign Direct Investment. In: Jean-Paul Larcon, ed. *Chinese Multinationals*. Singapore and Hackensack: World Scientific, pp. 49–75.

Lin, Shuanglin (2007). Resource Allocation and Economic Growth in China. In: Shuanglin Lin and Shunfeng Song, eds. *The Revival of Private Enterprise in China*. Aldershot and Burlington: Ashgate, pp. 33–50.

Lin, Shuanglin and Song, Shunfeng (2007). Introduction. In: Shuanglin Lin and Shunfeng Song, eds. *The Revival of Private Enterprise in China*. Aldershot and Burlington: Ashgate, pp. 1–8.

Lobell, Steven E. (2003). *The Challenge of Hegemony: Grand Strategy, Trade and Domestic Politics*. Ann Arbor: University of Michigan Press.

Lyman, Princeton (2005). China and the US in Africa: A Strategic Competition or an Opportunity for Cooperation. Online. Council on Foreign Relations. Available at: www.cfr.org/content/thinktank/ChinaandUS_Africa.pdf (accessed 18 April 2012).

Malik, J. Mohan (2001). South Asia in China's Foreign Relations. *Pacific Review*, 13 (1), pp. 73–90.

McAllister, James (2002). *No Exit: America and the German Problem, 1943–1954*. Ithaca: Cornell University.

McCarthy, Tom (2011). Assessing China and India's New Role in Africa. Online. e-International Relations. Available at: www.e-ir.info/2011/07/26/assessing-china-and-india%E2%80%99s-new-role-in-africa/ (accessed 2 April 2012).

McFate, Sean (2008). US Africa Command: Next Step or Next Stumble. *African Affairs*, 107 (426), pp. 111–120.

McGroarty, Patrick (2015). Angola's Boom, Fueled by China, Goes Bust. Online. *Wall Street Journal*, 28 October. Available at: www.wsj.com/articles/angolas-boom-fueled-by-china-goes-bust-1446072930 (accessed 1 May 2016).

McLellan, Amy (2015). African Petroleum Lands Funding as it Advances Farm-Out Talks for its "Big Company Portfolio". Online. 24 February. Available at: http://masterinvestor.co.uk/uncategorized/african-petroleum-lands-funding-as-it-advances-farm-out-talks-for-its-big-company-portfolio/ (accessed 23 April 2016).

Manji, Firoze M. and Marks, Stephen (eds) (2007). *African Perspectives on China in Africa*. Oxford: Fahamu.

Mantzopoulos, V. and Shen, R. (2011). *The Political Economy of China's Systemic Transformation: 1979 to the Present*. New York: Palgrave Macmillan.

Marathe, Sharad S. (1986). *Regulation and Development: India's Policy Experience of Controls over Industry*. Sage: New Delhi.

Marathon Oil Corporation (2013). Marathon Oil Announces $1.5 Billion Sale of Interest in Angola Block 31. Online. 25 June. Available at: http://ir.marathonoil.com/releasedetail.cfm?ReleaseID=773689 (accessed 1 May 2016).

Marks, Stephen (2007). Introduction. In: Firoze M. Manji and Stephen Marks, eds. *African Perspectives on China in Africa*. Oxford: Fahamu, pp. 1–14.

Mastanduno, Michael, Lake, David A. and Ikenberry, G. John (1989). Towards a Realist Theory of State Action. *International Studies Quarterly*, 33 (4), pp. 457–474.

Mawdsley, Emma and McCann, Gerrad (eds) (2011). *India in Africa: Changing Geographies of Power*. Cape Town: Pambazuka Press.

MEA (Ministry of External Affairs), GoI (2013). India–Republic of Gabon Relations. Online. May. Available at: http://mea.gov.in/Portal/ForeignRelation/Republic_of_Gabon.pdf (accessed 15 April 2016).

MEA, GoI (2014a). India–Angola Relations. Online. August. Available at: www.mea. gov.in/Portal/ForeignRelation/Angola_August_2014.pdf (accessed 2 May 2016).

MEA, GoI (2014b) India–Nigeria Relations. Online. August. Available at: www.mea. gov.in/Portal/ForeignRelation/Nigeria_Aug_2014.pdf (accessed 30 April 2016).

MEA, GoI (2015). India–Ghana Relations. Online. June. Available at: www.iafs.in/down-loads/Ghana.pdf (accessed 15 April 2016).

Melber, Henning, Lee, Margaret Carol, Naidu, Samusha and Taylor, Ian (2007). *China in Africa.* Uppsala: Nordiska Afrikainstitutet, Crrent African Issues, Issue 35.

Men, Jing and Barton, Benjamin (2011). *China and the European Union in Africa: Partners or Competitors.* Farnham and Burlington: Ashgate.

Michel, Serge, Beuret, Michel and Woods, Paolo (2009). *China Safari: On the Trail of Beijing's Expansion in Africa.* New York: Nation Books.

Military Balance (2012). London: International Institiute for Strategic Studies.

Military Balance (2016). London: International Institiute for Strategic Studies.

Ministry of Foreign Affairs, PRC (n.d.) China and Gabon. Online. Available at: www.fmprc. gov.cn/mfa_eng/wjb_663304/zzjg_663340/fzs_663828/gjlb_663832/2989_663994/ (accessed 1 May 2016).

Ministry of Foreign Affairs, PRC (2016). Yu Zhengsheng Pays Official Goodwill Visit to Gabon. Online. Available at: www.fmprc.gov.cn/mfa_eng/zxxx_662805/t1355715. shtml (accessed 1 May 2016).

Ministry of Mines, Industry and Energy, Republic of Equatorial Guinea (n.d.). Exploration History. Online. Available at: www.equatorialoil.com/Petroleum_Exploration_history.html (accessed 22 April 2016).

Modi, Renu (2010). The Role of India's Private Sector in the Health and Agricultural Sectors of Africa. In: Fantu Cheru and Cyril Obi, eds. *The Rise of China and India in Africa.* London and Uppsala: Zed Books and Nordiska Afrikainstitutet, pp. 120–131.

Mohan, T.T. Ram (2005). *Privatization in India: Challenging Economic Orthodoxy.* Abingdon and New York: RoutledgeCurzon.

Mol, Arthur P.J. (2011). China's Ascent and Africa's Environment. *Global Environmental Change,* 21 (3), pp. 785–794.

Morgenthau, Hans J. (1948). *Politics Among Nations: The Struggle for Power and Peace,* 1st edn. New York: Alfred A. Knopf.

Morrissey, Oliver and Zgovu, Evious (2011). *The Impact of China and India on Sub-Saharan Africa: Opportunities, Challenges and Policies.* London: Commonwealth Secretariat.

Mthembu-Salter, Gregory (2009). Elephants, Ants and Superpowers: Nigeria's Relations with China. Online. Occasional Paper No 42 South African Institute of International Affairs. Available at: www.org.za/occasional-papers/elephants-ants-and-superpowers-nigeria-s-relations-with-china.html (accessed 30 December 2012).

Naidu, Sanusha (2010). India's African Relations: In the Shadow of China. In: Fantu Cheru and Cyril Obi, eds. *The Rise of China and India in Africa.* London and Uppsala: Zed Books and Nordiska Afrikainstitutet, pp. 34–49.

Naidu, Sanusha (2011). Upping the Ante in Africa: India's Increasing Footprint across the Continent. In: Emma Mawdsley and Gerrad McCann, eds. *India in Africa: Changing Geographies of Power.* Cape Town: Pambazuka Press, pp. 48–67.

Naidu, Sanusha and Davies, Martyn (2006). China Fuels its Future with Africa's Riches. *South African Journal of International Affairs,* 13 (2), pp. 69–83.

Nation, The (2008). $2b Block Sold at $5m in Oil Bazaar. Online. 31 July. Available at: www.thenationonlineng.net/archive2/tblnews_Detail.php?id=57584 (accessed 1 May 2016).

Natural Resource Governance Institute (2015). An Analysis of Ghana's 2005 Oil Revenue Performance: Testing the Model. Online. 17 December. Available at: www.resource-governance.org/blog/analysis-ghanas-2015-oil-revenue-performance-testing-model (accessed 20 April 2016).

Nayak, Amar J.K.R. (2011). *Indian Multinationals: The Dynamics of Explosive Growth in a Developing Country Context.* Basingstoke and New York: Palgrave Macmillan.

Nexen (2015). About Nexen: In West Africa. Online. June. Available at: file:///C:/Documents%20and%20Settings/Administrator/My%20Documents/Downloads/Nexen-WestAfricaFactSheet.pdf (accessed 1 May 2016).

NNPC (2015). NNPC Discovers More Crude Oil. Online. 6 August. Available at: www.nnpcgroup.com/PublicRelations/NNPCinthenews/tabid/92/articleType/ArticleView/articleId/152/NNPC-DISCOVERS-MORE-CRUDE-OIL.aspx (accessed 1 May 2016).

Noble, Josh (2015). Doubts Rise Over China's Official GDP Growth Rate. Online. *Financial Times*, 16 September. Available at: www.ft.com/cms/s/0/723a8d8e-5c53-11e5-9846-de406ccb37f2.html#axzz46WvqAahP (accessed 10 April 2016).

Nordtveit, Bjørn H. (2011). An Emerging Donor in Education and Development: A Case Study of China in Cameroon. *International Journal of Educational Development*, 31 (2), pp. 99–108.

North, Douglass C. (1990). *Institutions, Institutional Change and Economic Performance.* Cambridge: Cambridge University Press.

North, Douglass C. (1994). Economic Performance through Time. *American Economic Review*, 84 (3), pp. 359–368.

Nye Jr., Joseph S. (2008). Public Diplomacy and Soft Power. *The ANNALS of the American Academy of Political and Social Science*, 616 (1), pp. 94–109.

Obi, Cyril (2010). African Oil in the Energy Security Calculations on India and China. In: Fantu Cheru and Cyril Obi, eds. *The Rise of China and India in Africa: Challenges, Opportunities and Critical Interventions*. London and Uppsala: Zed Books and Nordiska Afrikainstitutet, pp. 181–192.

OEC (Observatory of Economic Complexity) (n.d.). Angola. Online. Available at: http://atlas.media.mit.edu/en/profile/country/ago/ (accessed 1 May 2016).

OIL (n.d.a). Profile. Online. Available at: www.oil-india.com/Profile.aspx (accessed 20 August 2012).

OIL (n.d.b). Exploration. Online. Available at: www.oil-india.com/Exploration.aspx (accessed 20 August 2012).

OIL (n.d.c). JVs/PSCs/Alliances: Nigeria. Online. Available at: www.oil-india.com/JVs.aspx (accessed 2 May 2016).

OIL (n.d.d). JVs/PSCs/Alliances: Gabon. Online. Available at: www.oil-india.com/JVs.aspx (accessed 20 April 2016).

OIL (2015). Chairman's Address. Online. Available at: www.oil-india.com/CAddress.aspx (accessed 20 April 2016).

Oil and Gas Journal (2014). Total, Partners Reach FID for Kaombo Project Off Angola. Online. 14 April. Available at: www.ogj.com/articles/2014/04/total-partners-reach-fid-for-kaombo-project-off-angola.html (accessed 1 May 2016).

Ojiabor and Oluwasegun, Victor (2008). Eight Oil Blocks "Sold Illegally" at N14b. Online. *The Nation*, 11 September. Available at: www.thenationonlineng.net/archive2/tblnews_Detail.php?id=62306 (accessed 1 May 2016).

Ojonugwa, Ugboja Felix (2015). Nigeria Economy: How China and US Battle for Relevance. Online. *Leadership*, 20 May. Available at: http://leadership.ng/features/434584/nigeria-economy-how-china-and-usa-battle-for-relevance (accessed 30 April 2016).

Oladunjoye, Phillip (2015). Nigeria: Seven Energy Begins Crude Oil Production From Stubb Creek. Online. *Daily Independent*, 1 May. Available at: http://allafrica.com/ stories/201505010555.html (accessed 1 May 2016).

de Oliviera, Ricardo Soares (2008). Making Sense of Chinese Oil Investment in Africa. In: Chris Alden, Daniel Large and Ricardo Soares de Oliveira, eds. *China Returns to Africa: A Rising Power and a Continent Embrace*. New York: Columbia University Press, pp. 83–109.

Out-Law.com (2014). China Issues First Oil Import Licence to Private Company. Online. 29 August. Available at: www.out-law.com/en/articles/2014/august/china-issues-first-oil-import-licence-to-private-company/ (accessed 1 May 2016).

OVL (n.d.a). About ONGC Videsh. Online. Available at: www.ongcvidesh.com/ company/about-ovl/ (accessed 1 May 2016).

OVL (n.d.b). Assets. Online. Available at: www.ongcvidesh.com/assets/ (accessed 1 May 2016).

OVL (2012). Africa: Assets. Online. Available at: www.ongcvidesh.com/Assets. aspx?tab=0 (accessed 4 December 2012).

Owen, Charlotte (2012). China to Encourage Local Private Investment in Energy Projects. Business Strategy, Oil and Gas Technology. Online. 19 June. Available at: www. oilandgastechnology.net/business-strategy/china-encourage-local-private-investment-energy-projects (accessed 4 August 2012).

Patey, Luke (2014). *The New Kings of Crude: China, India and the Global Stuggle for Oil in Sudan and South Sudan*. London: Hurst & Company.

Pathak, Kalpana (2010). Essar May Farm Out 37 Per Cent in Nigerian Block. Online. *Business Standard*, 9 September Available at: www.business-standard.com/article/ companies/essar-may-farm-out-37-in-nigerian-block-110090900093_1.html (accessed 3 May 2016).

Patra, Debesh C. (2004). *Oil Industry in India: Problems and Prospects in Post-APM Era*. New Delhi: Mittal Publications.

Petlane, Tsoeu (2009). Gabonese Election Aftermath Confirms Worrying Trends in African Politics. Online. Diplomatic Pouch: South African Institute of International Affairs. 10 December. Available at: www.saiia.org/za/diplomatic-pouch/gabonese-election-aftermath-confirms-worrying-trends-in-african-politics.html (accessed 15 January 2013).

PetroChina (n.d.). About PetroChina. Online. Available at: www.petrochina.com.cn/ptr/ gsjj/gsjs_common.shtml (accessed 1 May 2016).

Petroleum Africa (2012). PetroChina's MoU for Liberia Stake Expires. Online. 4 September. Available at: www.petroleumafrica.com/en/newsarticle.php?NewsID=14175 (accessed 12 January 2016).

Petzet, Alan (2012). Gabon: CNOOC Joins Shell on Two Offshore Blocks. Online. *Oil and Gas Journal*, 25 July. Available at: www.ogj.com/articles/2012/07/gabon-cnooc-joins-shell-on-two-offshore-blocks.html (accessed 20 April 2016).

Pfeifer, Sylvia (2013). Sinopec Pays $1.52bn for Stake in Angolan Field. Online. *Financial Times*, 24 June. Available at: www.ft.com/intl/cms/s/0/2425aa52-dcee-11e2-9700-00144feab7de.html (accessed 1 May 2016).

Pham, Peter J. (2011). AFRICOM from Bush to Obama. *South African Journal of International Affairs*, 18 (1), pp. 107–124.

Posen, Barry R. and Ross, Andrew L. (1996/7). Competing Visions for US Grand Strategy. *International Security*, 21 (3), pp. 5–53.

Pradhan, Jay Prakash (2008). *Indian Multinationals in the World Economy: Implications for Development*. New Delhi: Bookwell.

Putnam, Robert (1988). Diplomacy and Domestic Politics: The Logic of Two-Level Games. *International Organization*, 42 (3), pp. 427–460.

PwC (PricewaterhouseCoopers) (2012). Emerging Opportunities and Challenges: Oil and Gas. Online. WEC-IMC. 23 January. Available at: www.pwc.in/assets/pdfs/publications-2011/wec-pwc-report.pdf (accessed 2 August 2012).

PwC (2014). Nigeria Sao Tome and Principe, Joint Development Zone First EITI Report 2003–2013. Online. November. Available at: https://eiti.org/files/First%20Report%20 %202003-2013%20(Nigeria-Sao%20Tome%20and%20Principe).pdf (accessed 1 May 2016).

Quanyu, Shang (2005). Sino-Indian Friendship in the Nehru Era: A Chinese Perspective. *China Report*, 41 (237), pp. 237–252.

Rathbun, Brian (2008). A Rose by Any Other Name: Neoclassical Realism as the Logical and Necessary Extension of Structural Realism. *Security Studies*, 17 (2), pp. 294–321.

Reed, John and Ward, Andrew (2010). Geely Buys Volvo for $1.8bn. Online. *Financial Times*, 29 March. Available at: www.ft.com/cms/s/0/e6874a70-3a93-11df-b6d5-00144feabdc0.html#axzz21vW2tsTP (accessed 28 July 2012).

Rehman, Iskander (2009). Keeping the Dragon at Bay: India's Counter-Containment of China. *Asian Security*, 5 (2), pp. 114–143.

Reuters (2008). China Offers Nigeria Export Credit Guarantees-FT. Online. 2 April. Available at: http://uk.reuters.com/article/china-nigeria-idUKPEK9950620080402 (accessed 30 April 2016).

Rigzone (2004). Sinopec Henan Oilfield in Study of Nigeria Oil Prospects. Online. 29 April. Available at: www.rigzone.com/news/oil_gas/a/12758/Sinopec_Henan_Oilfield_ in_Study_of_Nigeria_Oil_Prospects www.rigzone.com (accessed 1 May 2016).

Rigzone (2006). CNOOC Inks Deal for Block S in Equatorial Guinea. Online. 17 February. Available at: www.rigzone.com/news/oil_gas/a/29548/CNOOC_Inks_Deal_for_ Block_S_in_Equatorial_Guinea (accessed 21 April 2016).

Rigzone (2009). Sinopec Acquires 100% of Addax Petroleum's Shares. Online. 6 October. Available at: www.rigzone.com/news/oil_gas/a/81087/Sinopec_Acquires_100_of_Addax_ Petroleums_Shares (accessed 1 May 2016).

RIL (n.d.a). About Us. Online. Available at: www.ril.com/html/aboutus/aboutus.html (accessed 2 August 2012).

RIL (n.d.b). Exploration and Production. Online. Available at: www.ril.com/html/business/exploration_production.html (accessed 2 August 2012).

RIL (n.d.c). Exploration and Production. Available at: www.ril.com/OurBusinesses/ Exploration.aspx (accessed 1 May 2016).

Ripsman, Norrin M. (2001). The Curious Case of German Rearmament: Democracy and Foreign Security Policy. *Security Studies*, 10 (2), pp. 1–47.

Ripsman, Norrin M. (2002). *Peacemaking by Democracies: The Effect of State Autonomy on the Post-World War Settlements*. University Park: Pennsylvania State University Press.

Ripsman, Norrin M., Taliaferro, Jeffrey W. and Lobell, Steven E. (2009). Conclusion: The State of Neoclassical Realism. In: Steven E. Lobell, Norrin M. Ripsman and Jeffrey W. Taliaferro, eds. *Neoclassical Realism, the State, and Foreign Policy*. Cambridge: Cambridge University Press, pp. 282–287.

Rocha, John (2007). A New Frontier in the Exploration of Africa's Natural Resources: The Emergence of China. In: Firoze M. Manji and Stephen Marks, eds. *African Perspectives on China in Africa*. Oxford: Fahamu, pp. 15–34.

Roehrig, Terrence (2009). An Asian Triangle: India's Relationship with China and Japan. *Asian Politics & Policy*, 1 (2), pp. 163–185.

Rogowski, R. (1987). Political Cleavages and Changing Exposure to Trade. *American Political Science Review*, 81 (4), pp. 1121–1137.

Rooyen, Frank van (2010). Blue Helmets for Africa: India's Peacekeeping in Africa. Online. Paper No 60 South African Institute of International Affairs Occasional, pp. 3–26. Available at: www.org.za/occasional-papers/blue-helmets-for-africa-india-s-peacekeeping-in-africa.html (accessed 2 April 2012).

Rose, Gideon (1998). Neoclassical Realism and Theories of Foreign Policy. *World Politics*, 51 (1), pp. 144–172.

Rosenstein-Rodan, P. (1943). The Problem of Industrialization of Eastern and South-Eastern Europe. *Economic Journal*, 53 (210/211), pp. 202–211.

Rosser, Jr. J. Barkley and Rosser, Marina V. (2004). *Comparative Economics in a Transforming World Economy*, 2nd edn. Cambridge, MA: MIT Press.

Rotberg, Robert I. (ed.) (2008). *China into Africa: Trade, Aid, and Influence*. Washington, DC: Brookings Institution Press.

Roy, Subhajit (2014). Day After, China Daily Says Modi Remarks for Media Hype. Online. *The Indian Express*, 3 September. Available at: http://indianexpress.com/article/india/india-others/day-after-china-daily-says-modi-remarks-for-media-hype/ (accessed 10 May 2016).

Samy, Yiagadeesen (2010). China's Aid Policies in Africa: Opportunities and Challenges. *The Round Table*, 99 (406), pp. 75–90.

Sautman, Barry and Yang, Hairong (2007). Friends and Interests: China's Distinctive Links with Africa. *African Studies Review*, 50 (3), pp. 75–114.

Schmidt, Brian C. (2004). Realism as Tragedy. *Review of International Studies*, 30 (3), pp. 427–441.

Schweller, Randall R. (1994). Bandwagoning for Profit: Bringing the Revisionist State Back In. *International Security*, 19 (1), pp. 72–107.

Schweller, Randall R. (1997). New Realist Research on Alliances: Refining, Not Refuting Waltz's Balancing Proposition. *American Political Science Review*, 91 (4), pp. 927–930.

Schweller, Randall R. (1998). *Deadly Imbalances: Tripolarity and Hitler's Strategy of World Conquest*. New York: Columbia University Press.

Schweller, Randall R. (2001). The Twenty Years' Crisis, 1919–39: Why a Concert Didn't Arise. In: Colin Elman and Mirium Fendius Elman, eds. *Bridges and Boundaries: Historians, Political Scientists and the Study of International Relations*. Cambridge, MA: MIT Press, pp. 181–212.

Schweller, Randall L. (2003). The Progressiveness of Neoclassical Realism. In: Colin Elman and Mirium Fendius Elman, eds. *Progress in International Relations Theory: Appraising the Field*. Cambridge, MA: MIT Press, pp. 311–347.

Schweller, Randall L. (2004). Unanswered Threats: A Neoclassical Realist Theory of Underbalancing. *International Security*, 29 (2), pp. 159–201.

Schweller, Randall L. (2006). *Unanswered Threats: Political Constraints on the Balance of Power*. Princeton: Princeton University Press.

Segal, Gerald (1999). Does China Matter. *Foreign Affairs*, 75 (5), pp. 24–36.

Seven Energy (n.d.). Upstream: South East Niger Delta. Online. Available at: www.sevenenergy.com/operations/upstream/south-east-niger-delta (accessed 2 May 2016).

Sharma, Devika and Ganeshan, Swati (2011). Before and Beyond Energy: Contextualising the India–Africa Partnership. Online. Occasional Paper No 77 South African Institute of International Affairs. Available at: www.org.za/occasional-papers/before-and-beyond-energy-contextualising-the-india-africa-partnership.html (accessed 5 January 2013).

Sharma, Devika and Mahajan, Deepti (2007). Energising Ties: The Politics of Oil. *South African Journal of International Affairs*, 14 (2), pp. 37–52.

Sharma, Rakesh and Ordonez, Isabel (2010). Bid for Ghana Oil Field Rebuffed: Kosmos Energy of U.S. Rejects $5 Billion Offer From CNOOC and GNPC. Online. 2 November. Available at: http://online.wsj.com/article/SB10001424052748704141104575588111375730330.html (accessed 6 January 2016).

Sharma, Shalendra D. (2010). The Uncertain Fate of "Chindia". *Current History*, 109 (728), pp. 252–257.

Shell (2014). Shell Announces Gabon Deep-Water Gas Discovery. Online. 22 October. Available at: www.shell.com/media/news-and-media-releases/2014/shell-announces-gabon-deep-water-gas-discovery.html (accessed 20 April 2016).

Sheth, V.S. (2008). India–Africa Relations: Emerging Policy and Development Perspective. Papers presented at the International Seminar on India Africa Relations: Emerging Policy and Development Perspectives, held at Mumbai during 23–25 July 2006. Delhi, India: Academic Excellence.

Shrinate, Supriya (2009). Ghana Blocks in ONGC Crosshairs: OVL in Talks with GNPC to Bid for Kosmos Energy's Stake in Giant Offshore Jubilee Field. Online. *The Economic Times*, 9 November. Available at: http://epaper.timesofindia.com/Default/Layout/Includes/ET/ArtWin.asp?From=Archive&Source=Page&Skin=ET&BaseHref=ETD%2F2009%2F11%2F19&ViewMode=HTML&PageLabel=16&EntityId=Ar01601&AppName=1 (accessed 25 April 2016).

Singh, Sushant K. (2007a). India and West Africa: A Burgeoning Relationship. Online. Africa Programme/Asia programme briefing paper Chatham House. London: Royal Institute of International Affairs, pp. 1–16. Available at: www.chathamhouse.org/publications/papers/view/108471 (acessed 2 April 2012).

Singh, Sushant K. (2007b). Peacekeeping in Africa: A Global Strategy. *South African Journal of International Affairs*, 14 (2), pp. 71–85.

Sinha, Pranay Kumar (2010). Indian Development Cooperation with Africa. In: Fantu Cheru and Cyril Obi, eds. *The Rise of China and India in Africa*. London and Uppsala: Zed Books and Nordiska Afrikainstitutet, pp. 77–93.

Sinopec (n.d.a). About Sinopec: Our Company. Online. Available at: http://english.sinopec.com/about_sinopec/our_company/20100328/8532.shtml (accessed 1 May 2016).

Sinopec (n.d.b). Exploration and Oil Production. Online. Available at: http://english.sinopec.com/about_sinopec/our_business/exploration_oil_production/ (accessed 1 May 2016).

SIPC (n.d.). About SIPC. Online. Available at: http://sipc.sinopec.com/sipc/en/about_us/erp_profile/ (accessed 1 May 2016).

Snyder, Jack L. (1991). *Myths of Empire: Domestic Politics and International Ambition*. Ithaca: Cornell University Press.

Soni, Sharad K. and Marwah, Reena (2011). Tibet as a Factor Impacting China Studies in India. *Asian Ethnicity*, 12 (3), pp. 285–299.

Srinivasan, T.N. (1996). Liberalisation and Economic Development in India. *Journal of Asian Economics*, 7 (2), pp. 203–216.

Srinivasan, T.N. and Tendulkar, S.D. (2003). *Reintegrating India with World Economy*. Washington, DC: Institute for International Economics; New Delhi: Oxford University Press.

Sterling-Folker, Jennifer (1997). Realist Environment, Liberal Process, and Domestic-Level Variables. *International Studies Quarterly*, 41 (1), pp. 1–26.

Sterling-Folker, Jennifer (2002a). *Theories of International Cooperation and the Primacy of Anarchy: Explaining US International Monetary Policy Making after Bretton Woods*. New York: State University of New York Press.

Sterling-Folker, Jennifer (2002b). Realism and the Constructivist Challenge: Rejecting, Reconstructing or Rereading. *International Studies Review*, 4 (1), pp. 73–97.

Sterling-Folker, Jennifer (2004). Realist-Constructivism and Morality. *International Studies Review*, 6 (2), pp. 341–343.

Stiglitz, Joseph E., Ocampo, José Antonio, Spiegel, Shar, Ricardo, Ffrench-Davis and Nayyar, Deepak (2006). *Stability with Growth: Macroeconomics, Liberalization, and Development*. Oxford: Oxford University Press.

Strauss, Julia C. and Saavedra, Martha Eileen (2009). *China and Africa: Emerging Patterns in Globalization and Development*. Cambridge: Cambridge University Press.

Sun Group (n.d.). Energy. Online. Available at: www.sungroup-global.com/english/sectors/suntera1.asp (accessed 2 May 2016).

SWFI (Sovereign Wealth Fund Rankings) (n.d.). Largest Sovereign Wealth Funds by Assets Under Management. Online. Available at: www.swfinstitute.org/sovereign-wealth-fund-rankings/ (accessed 1 May 2016).

Taliaferro, Jeffrey W. (2004). *Balancing Risks: Great Power Intervention in the Periphery*. Ithaca: Cornell University Press.

Taliaferro, Jeffrey W. (2006). State Building for Future Wars: Neoclassical Realism and the Resource Extractive State. *Security Studies*, 15 (3), pp. 464–495.

Taliaferro, Jeffrey W., Lobell, Steven E. and Ripsman, Norrin M. (2009). Introduction: Neoclassical Realism, the State, and Foreign Policy. In: Steven E. Lobell, Norrin M. Ripsman and Jeffrey W. Taliaferro, eds. *Neoclassical Realism, the State, and Foreign Policy*. Cambridge: Cambridge University Press, pp. 1–41.

Taylor, Ian (2002). Taiwan's Foreign Policy and Africa: The Limitations of Dollar Diplomacy. *Journal of Contemporary China*, 11 (30), pp. 125–140.

Taylor, Ian (2006a). *China and Africa: Engagement and Compromise*. London and New York: Routledge.

Taylor, Ian (2006b). China's Oil Diplomacy in Africa. *International Affairs*, 82 (5), pp. 937–959.

Taylor, Ian (2009). China's Africa Policy in Context. In: Ian Taylor, ed. *China's New Role in Africa*. Boulder: Lynne Rienner Publishers, pp. 1–36.

Taylor, Ian (2012). India's Rise in Africa. *International Affairs*, 88 (4), pp. 779–798.

Taylor, Ian and Xiao, Yuhua (2009). A Case of Mistaken Identity: "China Inc." and its "Imperialism" in Sub-Saharan Africa. *Asian Politics & Policy*, 1 (4), pp. 709–725.

Tegler, Eric (2015). Are China's GDP Numbers Believable? Online. *The Diplomat*, 24 August. Available at: http://thediplomat.com/2015/08/are-chinas-gdp-numbers-believable/ (accessed 1 May 2016).

Tendulkar, Suresh D. and Bhavani, T.A. (2007). *Understanding Reforms: Post 1991 India*. New Delhi and New York: Oxford University Press.

The High Commission of Ghana in India (n.d.). Trade and Investment. Online. Available at: www.ghana-mission.co.in/hcg.php?id=trade1 (accessed 16 April 2016).

The Hindu (2012a). Oil India Starts Drilling Operation in Gabon, Africa. Online. 1 November. Available at: www.thehindubusinessline.com/companies/oil-india-ltd-commences-drilling-operation-in-gabon-africa/article4054855.ece?ref=wl_opinion (accessed 20 April 2016).

The Hindu (2012b). Only Pvt Sector Investment Can Give Leg-Up to Economy: Crisil. Online. 17 July. Available at: www.thehindu.com/business/Economy/only-pvt-sector-investment-can-give-legup-to-economy-crisil/article3649282.ece (accessed 6 November 2012).

Tian, Xiaowen (2007). The Prospect of Private Economy in China. In: Shuanglin Lin and Shunfeng Song, eds. *The Revival of Private Enterprise in China.* Aldershot and Burlington: Ashgate, pp. 271–283.

Trading Economics (2016). China Foreign Exchange Reserves. Available at: www.tradingeconomics.com/china/foreign-exchange-reserves (accessed 12 January 2016).

Tull, Dennis M. (2008). The Political Consequences of China's Return to Africa. In: Chris Alden, Daniel Large and Ricardo Soares de Oliveira, eds. *China Returns to Africa: A Rising Power and a Continent Embrace.* New York: Columbia University Press, pp. 111–128.

Ugwuanyi, Emeka (2008). DPR Clarify Deal on OML 65. Online. *The Nation,* 6 August. Available at: www.thenationonlineng.net/archive2/tblnews_Detail.php?id=62306 (accessed 30 April 2016).

UNDP (2015). *Human Development Report 2015: Work for Human Development.* UNDP: New York.

US EIA (2012). Gabon: Country Analysis Brief. Online. Available at: www.eia.gov/beta/international/analysis.cfm?iso=GAB (accessed 15 January 2013).

US EIA (2013). Chad: Country Analysis Brief. Online. Available at: www.eia.gov/beta/international/analysis.cfm?iso=TCD (accessed 21 April 2016).

US EIA (2014). Gabon: Country Analysis Brief. Online. Available at: www.eia.gov/beta/international/analysis.cfm?iso=GAB (accesesd 3 May 2016).

US EIA (2015a). China Country Analysis Brief. Online. Available at: www.eia.gov/beta/international/analysis.cfm?iso=CHN (accessed 1 May 2016).

US EIA (2015b). Ghana: Country Analysis Brief. Online. Available at: www.eia.gov/beta/international/analysis.cfm?iso=GHA (accessed 21 April 2016).

US EIA (2015c). Equatorial Guinea: Country Analysis Brief. Online. Available at: www.eia.gov/beta/international/analysis.cfm?iso=GNQ (accessed 21 April 2016).

US EIA (2016a). Angola: Country Analysis Brief. Online. 1 May. Available at: www.eia.gov/beta/international/analysis.cfm?iso=AGO (accessed 20 April 2016).

US EIA (2016b). Nigeria: Country Analysis Brief. Online. Available at: www.eia.gov/beta/international/analysis.cfm?iso=NGA (accessed 1 May 2016).

Utomi, Pat (2008). China and Nigeria. In: Jennifer G. Cooke, ed. *U.S. and Chinese Engagement in Africa: Prospects for Improving U.S.-China-Africa Cooperation.* Washington, DC: CSIS Press, pp. 49–58.

Van Dijk, Meine Pieter (ed.) (2009). *The New Presence of China in Africa.* Amsterdam: Amsterdam University Press.

Van Evera, Stephen (1990–1). Primed for Peace: Europe After the Cold War. *International Security,* 15 (3), pp. 14–16.

Van Evera, Stephen (1997). *Guide to Methods for Students of Political Science.* Ithaca and London: Cornell University Press.

Vanguard (2009). Sinopec Acquires Addax for $7.2bn. Online. 25 June. Available at: www.vanguardngr.com/2009/06/sinopec-acquires-addax-for-72bn/ (accessed 1 April 2016).

Vasquez, John (1997). The Realist Paradigm and Degenerative versus Progressive Research Programs. *American Political Science Review,* 91 (4), pp. 899–912.

Vasudevan, Parvathi (2010). The Changing Nature of Nigeria–India Relations. Online. Programme Paper: AFP 2010/02, Chatham House. Available at: www.chathamhouse.org/publications/papers/view/109543 (accessed 3 April 2012).

Verma, Raj (2012a). Can Africa Become the New Persian Gulf? (LSE Africa blog). 19 December. Available at: http://blogs.lse.ac.uk/africaatlse/2012/12/19/can-africa-become-the-new-persian-gulf/ (accessed 24 December 2012).

Verma, Raj (2012b). India and Africa: Towards Greater Cooperation and Growth (LSE Africa blog). 11 April. Available at: http://blogs.lse.ac.uk/africaatlse/2012/04/11/india-and-africa-towards-greater-cooperation-and-growth/ (accessed 24 December 2012).

Vines, Alex (2011). India's Security Concerns in the Western Indian Ocean. In: Emma Mawdsley and Gerrad McCann, eds. *India in Africa: Changing Geographies of Power*. Cape Town: Pambazuka Press, pp. 187–202.

Vines, Alex and Campos, Indira (2010). China and India in Angola. In: Fantu Cheru and Cyril Obi, eds. *The Rise of China and India in Africa: Challenges, Opportunities and Critical Interventions*. London and Uppsala: Zed Books and Nordiska Afrikainstitutet, pp. 193–207.

Vines, Alex and Oruitemeka, Bereni (2007). Engagement with the African Indian Ocean Rim States. *South African Journal of International Affairs*, 14 (2), pp. 111–123.

Vines, Alex and Oruitemeka, Bereni (2008). India's Engagement with the African Indian Ocean Rim States. Online. Africa Programme Paper AFP P 1/08. Chatham House, London, UK. Available at: www.chathamhouse.org/publications/papers/view/108782 (accessed 2 April 2012).

Vines, A., Weimer, M. and Campos, I. (2009). Asian National Oil Companies in Angola. In: Alex Vines, Lillian Wong, Markus Weimer and Indira Campos, eds. Thirst for African Oil: Asian National Oil Companies in Nigeria and Angola. Online). Chatham House Report, London: Royal Institute of International Affairs, pp. 29–60. Available at: www. chathamhouse.org/sites/files/chathamhouse/r0809_africanoil.pdf (accessed 18 May 2016).

Vines, A., Wong, L., Weimer, M. and Campos, I. (2009). Thirst for African Oil: Asian National Oil Companies in Nigeria and Angola. Online. Chatham House Report, London: Royal Institute of International Affairs, pp. 1–74. Available at: www.chatham-house.org/sites/files/chathamhouse/r0809_africanoil.pdf (accessed 18 May 2016).

Vittorini, Simona and Harris, David (2011). India Goes Over to the Other Side: Indo West-African Relations in the 21st Century. In: Emma Mawdsley and Gerrad McCann, eds. *India in Africa: Changing Geographies of Power*. Cape Town: Pambazuka Press, pp. 203–217.

Volman, Daniel (2009). China, India, Russia and the United States: The Scramble for African Oil and the Militarization of the Continent. Online. Current Africa Issues 43, Nordiska Afrikainststitutet. Available at: http://nai.diva-portal.org/smash/record.jsf?pid=diva2:272960 (accessed 12 April 2012).

Wagle, Dileep M., Gregory, Niel and Teney, Stoyan (2000). *China's Emerging Private Enterprises: Prospects for the New Century*. Washington, DC: International Finance Corporation.

Walker, Andrew (2016). Angola Seeks IMF Help in Wake of Oil Price Falls. Online. BBC, 6 April Available at: www.bbc.com/news/business-35981850 (accessed 2 May 2016).

Walt, Stephen M. (1987). *The Origins of Alliances*. Ithaca: Cornell University Press.

Waltz, Kenneth N. (1959). *Man, the State, and War: A Theoretical Analysis*. New York: Columbia University Press.

Waltz, Kenneth N. (1979). *Theory of International Politics*, 1st edn. Boston, MA: McGraw-Hill.

Waltz, Kenneth N. (2003). Evaluating Theories. In: John A. Vasquez and Colin Elman, eds. *Realism and the Balance of Power: A New Debate*. Upper Saddle River: Prentice Hall, pp. 49–57.

Wang, Jian-Ye (2007). What Drives China's Growing Role in Africa. Washington, DC: International Monetary Fund, IMF Working Paper (WP/07/211).

Wang, Ying (2011). Pertamina Edges Out Sinopec for Stake in Angolan Oil. Online. 5 November. Available at: www.chinadaily.com.cn/business/2011-05/11/content_12489760. htm (accessed 25 April 2016).

Wax, Emily and Lakshmi, Rama (2010). Obama Supports Adding India as a Permanent Member of U.N. Security Council. Online. Washington Post Foreign Service, 8 November. Available at: www.washingtonpost.com/wp-dyn/content/article/2010/11/08/AR2010110800495.html?hpid=topnews&sid=ST2010110402773 (accessed 30 December 2012).

Weimer, Markus (2012). The Peace Dividend: Analysis of a Decade of Angolan Indicators, 2002–2012. Online. Chatham House, London: Royal Institute of International Affairs, pp. 1–19. Available at: www.chathamhouse.org/sites/files/chathamhouse/public/Research/Africa/0312pp_weimer.pdf (accessed 1 May 2016).

Weingast, Barry R. and Wittman, Donald A. (2006). *The Oxford Handbook of Political Economy*. Oxford: Oxford University Press.

Weiss, Moritz (2009). Power and Signals: Explaining the German Approach to European Security. *Journal of International Relations and Development*, 12 (3), pp. 317–348.

Wild, Leni and Mepham, David (eds) (2006). *The New Sinosphere: China in Africa*. London: IIPR.

Winsor, Morgan (2015). Angola Economic Woes: Chinese Slowdown, Global Crude Glut Hit Angola's Oil-Dependent Economy. Online. 1 September. Available at: www. ibtimes.com/angola-economic-woes-chinese-slowdown-global-crude-glut-hit-angolas-oil-dependent-2077944 (accessed 2 May 2016).

Woetzel, Jonathan R. (2008). Reassessing China's State-Owned Enterprises. Online. McKinsey Quarterly. Available at: www.forbes.com/2008/07/08/china-enterprises-state-lead-cx_jrw_0708mckinsey.html (accessed 27 July 2011).

Wohlforth, William C. (1993). *The Elusive Balance: Power and Perceptions during the Cold War*. Ithaca: Cornell University Press.

Wohlforth, William C. (1994–5). Realism and the End of the Cold War. *International Security*, 19 (3), pp. 91–129.

Wohlforth, William C. (2003). Measuring Power—and the Power of Theories. In: John A. Vasquez and Colin Elman, eds. *Realism and the Balancing of Power: A New Debate*. Upper Saddle River: Prentice Hall, pp. 250–279.

Wong, Lillian (2009). Asian National Oil Companies in Nigeria. In: Alex Vines, Lillian Wong, Markus Weimer and Indira Campos, eds. Thirst for African Oil: Asian National Oil Companies in Nigeria and Angola. Online. Chatham House Report, Royal Institiute of International Affairs, pp. 29–60. Available at: www.chathamhouse.org/sites/files/chathamhouse/r0809_africanoil.pdf (accessed 18 May 2016).

World Data Bank (n.d.). World Bank. Available at: http://data.worldbank.org/indicator (accessed 20 April 2016).

Xinhua (2012). MOC Encourages Private Oil Companies. Online. *China Daily*, 28 June. Available at: www.chinadaily.com.cn/bizchina/2012-06/28/content_15530126.htm (accessed 4 August 2012).

Xinhua (2016). China's Private Sector Put on Equal Footing. Online. 12 March. Available at: http://news.xinhuanet.com/english/2016-03/12/c_135181860.htm (accessed 1 May 2016).

Xu, Lixin C., Zhu, Tian and Lin, Yi-min (2007). Political Control, Agency Problems and Ownership Reforms: Evidence from China. In: Shuanglin Lin and Shunfeng Song, eds. *The Revival of Private Enterprise in China*. Aldershot and Burlington: Ashgate, pp. 199–221.

Xu, Yi-Chong (2008). China and the United States in Africa: Coming Conflict or Commercial Coexistence? *Australian Journal of International Affairs*, 62 (1), pp. 16–37.

Yang, Yao (2004). Government Commitment and the Outcome of Privatisation in China. In: T. Ito and A.O. Krueger, eds.*Governance, Regulation and Privatisation in the Asia Pacific Region*. NBER–EASE Volume 12. Chicago: University of Chicago Press, pp. 251–275.

Yesudian, S. (ed.) (2012). *India: Acquiring its Way to a Global Footprint*. Basingstoke and New York: Palgrave Macmillan.

Yin, Robert K. (2009). *Case Study Research: Design and Methods. Applied Social Research Method Series*. Volume 5, 4th edn. Los Angeles: Sage Publications.

Yu, George T. (2010). China's Africa Policy: South-South Unity and Cooperation. In: Lowell Dittmer and George T. Yu, eds. *China, the Developing World, and the New Global Dynamic*. Boulder: Lynne Rienner Publishers, pp. 129–155.

Yue, Jianyong (2012). What Does Globalization Mean for China's Economic Development? Online. *Global Policy*, 24 May. Available at: www.globalpolicyjournal.com/blog/24/05/2012/what-does-globalization-mean-china%E2%80%99s-economic-development (accessed 1 April 2013).

Yusuf, Omotayo (n.d.). China to Import More Crude Oil from Angola. Online. NAIJ.com. Available at: www.naij.com/762937-good-news-china-shows-interest-nigerian-oil.html (accessed 1 May 2016).

Zakaria, Fareed (1992). Realism and Domestic Politics: A Review Essay. *International Security*, 17 (1), pp. 177–198.

Zakaria, Fareed (1998). *From Wealth to Power: The Unusual Origins of America's World Role*. Princeton: Princeton University Press.

Zee News (2009). Essar Regains Oil Block in Nigeria. Online. 19 March Available at: http://zeenews.india.com/home/essar-regains-oil-block-in-nigeria_516209.html (accessed 1 May 2016).

Zhang, Baohui (2011). Taiwan's New Grand Strategy. *Journal of Contemporary China*, 20 (69), pp. 269–285.

Zheng, Hongliang and Yang, Yang (2009). Chinese Private Sector Development in the Past 30 Years: Retrospect and Prospect, Discussion Paper 45. Online. China Policy Institute, the University of Nottingham. Available at: www.nottingham.ac.uk/cpi/documents/events/2008/ifccs/hongliang-zheng.pdf (accessed 25 July 2012).

Zhu, Zhiqun (2010). *China's New Diplomacy: Rationale, Strategies and Significance*. Farnham: Ashgate.

Index

Page numbers in *italics* denote tables, those in **bold** denote figures.

Taylor & Francis eBooks

Helping you to choose the right eBooks for your Library

Add Routledge titles to your library's digital collection today. Taylor and Francis ebooks contains over 50,000 titles in the Humanities, Social Sciences, Behavioural Sciences, Built Environment and Law.

Choose from a range of subject packages or create your own!

Benefits for you

» Free MARC records
» COUNTER-compliant usage statistics
» Flexible purchase and pricing options
» All titles DRM-free.

Benefits for your user

» Off-site, anytime access via Athens or referring URL
» Print or copy pages or chapters
» Full content search
» Bookmark, highlight and annotate text
» Access to thousands of pages of quality research at the click of a button.

REQUEST YOUR FREE INSTITUTIONAL TRIAL TODAY

Free Trials Available
We offer free trials to qualifying academic, corporate and government customers.

eCollections – Choose from over 30 subject eCollections, including:

Archaeology	Language Learning
Architecture	Law
Asian Studies	Literature
Business & Management	Media & Communication
Classical Studies	Middle East Studies
Construction	Music
Creative & Media Arts	Philosophy
Criminology & Criminal Justice	Planning
Economics	Politics
Education	Psychology & Mental Health
Energy	Religion
Engineering	Security
English Language & Linguistics	Social Work
Environment & Sustainability	Sociology
Geography	Sport
Health Studies	Theatre & Performance
History	Tourism, Hospitality & Events

For more information, pricing enquiries or to order a free trial, please contact your local sales team: www.tandfebooks.com/page/sales

Routledge
Taylor & Francis Group

The home of
Routledge books

www.tandfebooks.com

For Product Safety Concerns and Information please contact our EU
representative GPSR@taylorandfrancis.com
Taylor & Francis Verlag GmbH, Kaufingerstraße 24, 80331 München, Germany

www.ingramcontent.com/pod-product-compliance
Ingram Content Group UK Ltd.
Pitfield, Milton Keynes, MK11 3LW, UK
UKHW021619240425
457818UK00018B/650